THE TRUTH
SHALL
MAKE YOU FREE

The Compasrose, the symbol of the Anglican Communion, was dedicated by the Archbishop of Canterbury during the Sung Eucharist in Canterbury Cathedral at the conclusion of the Lambeth Conference 1988.

The original design was by Canon Edward West of St John's Cathedral, New York. The Canterbury Cathedral Compasrose was designed by Giles Bloomfield and is in brass, placed in the stone floor before the Nave altar of the Cathedral.

The Greek inscription reads, 'The truth shall make you free': this is an appropriate title for this report and relates to a quotation from the Archbishop of Canterbury's closing Plenary Address: 'Truth is to be trusted'.

The Compasrose is reproduced by courtesy of the Dean and Chapter of Canterbury.

The drawings by Giles Harcourt, London.

Cover design by Justin Swarbrick, London.

THE TRUTH SHALL MAKE YOU FREE

THE
LAMBETH CONFERENCE 1988

The Reports, Resolutions

& Pastoral Letters from the Bishops

PUBLISHED FOR
THE ANGLICAN CONSULTATIVE COUNCIL

This edition by
Church House Publishing,
Church House, Great Smith Street,
London SW1P 3NZ

ISBN 0 7151 4772 2

Printed by The Print Business Ltd.

CONTENTS

Opening Prayer

Eternal God, your greatness is beyond our understanding and your generosity beyond our deserving. Give to your Church and all who are called to minister in your name the knowledge of your truth; where we serve you faithfully, build us up and keep us loyal; where our weakness and folly hinder our witness to your love, reprove and change us; but above all continue to grant us the assurance of your forgiveness, so that the world may come to see that all we do we do only by relying on your saving power given in your Son Jesus Christ our Lord. Amen.

Jesus said, 'You will know the truth, and the truth will make you free' (John 8.32).

The Fellowship of the Spirit : Being with one another at Lambeth 1988

The twelfth Lambeth Conference was not only the largest ever held (518 bishops compared to the 76 at the first), it was also perhaps the best prepared. The Archbishop of Canterbury had first mooted the idea of another Lambeth Conference to the Primates of the Anglican Communion at their meeting in Limuru, Kenya in 1983. After that consultations and preparations began in earnest.

PREPARATION FOR THE CONFERENCE

At an early stage, Canon Samuel Van Culin and Mr David Long were appointed Secretary and Deputy Secretary respectively to the Conference. Canon Van Culin's office rapidly became a focal point for Conference preparations. Both the sixth and seventh meetings of the Anglican Consultative Council devoted a great deal of their time and attention to a consideration of the four themes for the Conference which had been agreed upon by the Primates. Regional meetings were held in Africa, North and South America, Asia, Europe and in other parts of the world to prepare the bishops and their churches for the Conference. A programme of preparatory studies was established with the Archbishop of Canterbury's theological adviser, Bishop Michael Nazir-Ali, as its Co-ordinator. Bishops were mailed material on some of the outstanding issues which the Communion has to face and resolve. Matters addressed in these preparatory studies ranged from questions of inter-faith dialogue and theological method in a plural world to ways in which the Churches of the Communion were responding to contemporary pressures on family life. The bishops were invited to study this material along with clergy and lay people in their dioceses and provinces and then to make their response. In this way a very large number of clergy and lay people were involved in the process of preparation for the Conference. It is well known that the Archbishop of Canterbury had invited the bishops to 'bring their diocese' with them to the Conference. The overwhelming response to the mailing, from a wide cross-section of the Communion, showed how seriously his invitation had been taken.

In July 1987, some forty-five bishops, consultants and staff, drawn from different parts of the Communion, assembled together at the Church Army's Wilson Carlile College of Evangelism at Blackheath, London. The purpose of the gathering was to reflect on how best to present to the Lambeth Conference the issues raised by the preparatory studies, by the diocesan and provincial responses to these studies, and by ACC-6 and ACC-7. In the event, the gathering produced a collection of *Working Papers for the*

Lambeth Conference 1988. These papers were dispatched to all the bishops and others invited to participate in the Conference. They provided a further stage in the preparations for the Conference. Each of the four Sections of the Conference was assigned a theme, and the working paper on their theme became the basic documentation for the work of that Section. The working papers, moreover, were divided into material on particular subjects. These subjects were assigned to small groups of ten or twelve within each Section.

THE WORK OF THE CONFERENCE

These small working groups, which were coterminous with the Bible Study groups which met daily, proved to be the basic building blocks of the Conference. Meeting together every day for a study of the Scriptures, with the help of the excellent outline *Briefing for Apostles* provided by Bishop John V. Taylor, created an atmosphere of trust and mutual caring which became crucial when it came to tackling controversial and potentially divisive issues. The material produced by a working group was eventually presented to the Section of which the group was a part. It was then debated and amended by the whole Section before it was approved for inclusion in the Section Report. The Section Reports themselves were not further debated in plenary and so, strictly speaking, carry only the authority of the Sections which produced them. The editors met frequently with the Section Secretaries and Staff to review the progress being made in the writing of the Reports and to ensure consonance between the work of the different Sections. Out of the work of the Sections emerged certain matters which needed to be brought to the attention of the whole Conference. These were brought to a *Resolutions Committee* in the form of motions to be debated in plenary sessions. The Resolutions Committee was ably chaired by Bishop David Gitari of Mt Kenya East.[1]

Four participants from each Section, usually bishops, but in one case a woman member of the Anglican Consultative Council, were appointed to assist the officers of their Section and the editors in identifying significant issues which could become the subjects of pastoral letters from the Lambeth Conference to members of the Churches of the Anglican Communion, Christians of other Churches and other men and women of goodwill. Outlines of seven such letters (two each from the Sections on Mission and Ministry, Dogmatic and Pastoral Concerns and Christianity and the Social Order and one from the Ecumenical Section) were approved by the whole Conference in plenary session. The letters have now been edited and published under the title *Trustworthy and True.*[2] A video presentation, highlighting the themes of the Conference, has also been prepared and will be available by the end of the year. The Pastoral Letters, the Report of the Conference and the video presentation will help the bishops in 'taking Lambeth back to their dioceses'.

2

Towards the end of the Conference, Canon Vincent Strudwick outlined an 'audit' which he had prepared for the bishops' use at the final session of the Conference. During this final session, bishops, once again in their small Bible Study and working groups, reflected on the expectations which they and their people had had of the Conference, whether these had been fulfilled or not and how the Conference was going to affect their plans for the future. In their reflection on the relevance of the Conference to their work, they were asked to give particular attention to the work of policy-making groups such as diocesan officers, councils and synods. They were asked also to consider how the work of the Conference could inspire and inform clergy and lay people (particularly young people) in their various ministries. During this period of reflection, suggestions were made in several quarters that there ought to be a study-guide to help people in their evaluation of the work of Lambeth 1988.

In addition to the official post-Lambeth programme, several books are also being written by accredited authors present at the Conference. The first of these, *Church at the Crossroads* by Bishop Michael Marshall, has already been published by Collins. SPCK is publishing a book by Vinay Samuel and Christopher Sugden which will focus on the relevance of the Conference to the Church in the two-thirds world, and Forward Movement of Cincinnati, USA, is publishing Bishop John Krumm's *Letters from Lambeth*.

PLENARY ADDRESSES AND PRESENTATIONS

While much of the work of the Conference was done in the working groups or in Sections, there was considerable input in the form of plenary addresses and presentations. The first of these, the Archbishop of Canterbury's keynote address *The Nature of the Unity We Seek,* along with the four responses from ecumenical partners, is to be found within the pages of this Report. The Archbishop's address was very wide-ranging and in it he sought to set the task of achieving unity among Christians within a wider vision of the unity of the whole *oikoumene,* of the whole human family living at peace with all of God's creation. The address was very warmly received and influenced a great deal of the Conference's work. Archbishop Keith Rayner's address on *Authority,* and the responses to it by Professor Rowan Williams and Dr Stanley Samartha, became crucial for those working on the sources and the exercise of authority in the Anglican Communion. The addresses on *Evangelisation and Culture* by Bishops David Jenkins, Bashir Jiwan and David Gitari alerted the Conference to the very diverse contexts in which the Churches fulfil their mission. There was a special hearing on the matter of *the ordination of women to the priesthood and the episcopate.* Again, a very wide range of views were presented. Speakers included Bishop Graham Leonard of London, Bishop Samir Kafity of Jerusalem, Archbishop Michael Peers of Canada and the Revd Nan Peete, a woman priest from the

USA and a consultant to the Conference. There was another plenary session devoted almost wholly to a presentation by women on how they related to the themes of the Conference. This presentation was organised by Dr Mary Tanner of the Church of England's Board for Mission and Unity. There was strong criticism during the presentation of the discrimination experienced by women throughout the history of the Christian Church. There was also powerful advocacy for the ministry of women. Appropriately enough, the presentation was followed by a fireworks display! From Fr Gustavo Gutierrez the Conference heard not only of commitment to the poor but of friendship with them. This friendship with the poor, being with them, is a necessary aspect of following Jesus. It provides a touchstone by which we must test our theological thinking. *Liberation Theology* is a way of expressing the necessary relation between our affirmation of faith and our practice.

Anglicans of African descent from Africa, the Caribbean, North and South America and Europe had gathered together at Cambridge just before the Conference began. The gathering had produced the *Cambridge Declaration* which set out the priorities of this group of Anglicans. There was a special plenary hearing on African affairs when these priorities were set out before the Conference. The East Asians and the Pacific 'rim' also got their chance to explain to their brother bishops the problems and opportunities which they encountered in that part of the world. It was a particular joy to hear from Bishop K.H. Ting of the progress being made by the China Christian Council in the formation of a united Church.

Where Africa is concerned, Bishop David Gitari had raised the question of polygamy in his address on *Evangelisation and Culture* early in the second week of the Conference. While acknowledging the right of African bishops to deal with the matter 'on African soil', the Conference passed a resolution recommending that a polygamist desiring baptism should not be refused but may be baptised along with his believing wives and children, provided that he undertakes not to marry again as long as any of his wives at the time of conversion are alive (see Resolution 26).

Professor Owen Chadwick provided the Conference with a most informative (and also entertaining) account of how the Lambeth Conference had come into existence and how it had developed into its present form. He pointed out that councils of bishops were 'built into the structure of the universal church' from the very beginning. When bishops, in apostolic succession and in communion with the See of Canterbury, came to a consciousness of their world-wide distribution, something like a Lambeth Conference had to emerge. It is necessary, furthermore, for an episcopal Communion, to maintain and to strengthen such a Conference. As a matter of fact, all the speculation about the future of Lambeth Conferences was put to rest by the manifest desire of the bishops to continue to meet together. As Professor Chadwick reminded us, the first Lambeth Conference had been convened at the request of the 'overseas' bishops. There were some English bishops at

4

the time who had participated only reluctantly and, in a few cases, not at all! In 1988 too some English bishops had come with only moderate expectations but these were often the ones who returned greatly renewed and refreshed as a result of the fellowship which they experienced during the course of the Conference.

FELLOWSHIP, COMMUNION AND KOINONIA

The New Testament uses the term *Koinonia* to describe both our fellowship with God (1 John 1.3 and 2 Pet. 1.4) and our fellowship with each other (Acts 2 .42, 1 Cor. 10.16, 17, 1 John 1.3). The term has become very important in recent discussion as a way of speaking about the Church, its unity and the role of the ministry, particularly of the episcopate, in maintaining and nurturing this unity. In this Report, it has been used as a way of describing the relation that exists between the Churches of the Anglican Communion. It has also been used in the ecumenical context, both in the sense of a present reality between Christians of different Churches by virtue of their common baptism and as a goal towards which we must press. Communion together at the Eucharist is an important stage in our common search for unity. The discussion at the Conference was always, however, in the context of our 'union with God in Christ' and also in the context of a real experience of fellowship common to all the participants. These included bishops of the Anglican Communion, bishops of Churches in full communion with the Anglican Communion, clerical and lay members of the Anglican Consultative Council, consultants, observers from other Churches and staff. It is not perhaps an exaggeration to say that fellowship characterised the life of the Conference and also became the paradigm for its theological reflection.

EMBODIMENTS, AGENTS OR INSTRUMENTS OF COMMUNION

In its consideration of the fellowship that exists between the Churches of the Anglican Communion, the Conference once again examined the place of the See and the Archbishop of Canterbury, of the Conference itself, of the Primates' Meeting and of the Anglican Consultative Council in maintaining and nurturing this fellowship. In the event, the Conference, while affirming all these embodiments of unity, particularly wished that the Primates' Meeting, under the presidency of the Archbishop of Canterbury, should have an 'enhanced role' in caring for 'the universal coherence of the Communion'. The Conference also gave consideration to a possible fifth agent of unity, when it asked that the Theological and Doctrinal Commission should study the *Draft Common Declaration* set out in the discussion paper *Instruments of Communion and Decision-Making: The Development of the Consultative Process in the Anglican Communion*[3] which had been circulated to all the participants and should then report its findings to the Primates.

5

THE COMMUNION AND CHRISTIAN UNITY

In the discussion on the development of these agents or instruments of communion, concern was repeatedly expressed that they should not develop in a way which would jeopardise the Anglican Communion's commitment to Christian unity. The Conference reiterated the position taken by previous Lambeth Conferences that the Anglican Communion is provisional and that none of its structures should impede the movement towards greater unity between Christians. The presence of bishops from Churches where Anglicans have united with Christians of other traditions as full members of the Conference was a sign of the capacity of Anglican structures to develop in an ecumenical direction. Bishop Alexander Malik of Lahore, in his response to the paper on *Instruments of Communion and Decision-Making* and also in his speech as the mover of a resolution on united Churches, expressed the satisfaction of these Churches in being invited to Anglican gatherings as full members. He pointed out, however, that these Churches valued their autonomy quite as much as Anglican Provinces and also that they wished to maintain their close relations with other families of Churches with which they had historic connections.

THE APPOINTMENT OF INTER-ANGLICAN BODIES

The Conference resolved that the Archbishop of Canterbury, in consultation with the Primates, should appoint a *Commission on the Ordination of Women to the Episcopate and on the implications of such ordinations for relations between the Churches of the Anglican Communion.*

The Conference asked that an Inter-Anglican Commission be established to undertake an exploration of the meaning and nature of *communion,* with particular reference to the doctrine of the Trinity, the unity and order of the Church, and the unity and community of humanity. Such a Commission was also asked to consider the *Draft Common Declaration* and to report to the Primates' Meeting. The Conference also requested the Archbishop of Canterbury, with all the other Primates, to appoint an *Advisory Body on Prayer Book Revision.* Such a body would ensure mutual consultation between the Provinces on matters related to liturgical revision and development. The Conference recommended that the Anglican Consultative Council should give consideration to the setting up of an *Inter-Faith Committee* which would offer guidelines towards establishing a common approach to people of other faiths on a Communion-wide basis. The Conference expressed its desire that the ACC should enter into consultation with the relevant Oriental Orthodox authorities with a view to the establishment of a *Commission on Anglican – Oriental Orthodox relations.* The ACC was also asked to initiate conversations with the *World Methodist Council* and with the *Baptist World Alliance* with a view to the beginning of international dialogues with these two traditions.

COMMUNICATIONS

One of the features of Lambeth 1988 was the unprecedented interest of the media in the personalities and the work of the Conference. The enormous amount of work which this created was managed extremely well by the Episcopal Co-ordinator for Communication, Bishop Ronald Bowlby, and by the Director of Communication, Mr Robert Byers. There was a team of 46 professional church communicators drawn from different parts of the Anglican Communion and from partner Churches who managed the task of relating Conference participants to the world-wide media. They were responsible also for looking after the 220 accredited media representatives who were present at the Conference and for the dissemination of information to Conference participants. The main way in which this latter task was carried out was by the publication of *The Lambeth Daily,* a four-page tabloid which gave news and information of interest to Conference participants. The Conference, recognising the importance of quick communication in the contemporary world, directed the ACC to explore the establishment of a telecommunication network linked to every Province of the Anglican Communion. Such a network would improve significantly the communication and consultation process throughout the Communion and would ensure that accurate information became available quickly to the Churches.

WORSHIP

The work of the Conference was carried out in an atmosphere of prayer and worship. Plenary sessions began, and often ended, with prayer, at midday there was a pause for silent meditation, there was Morning Prayer and the Eucharist each morning and Evensong just before dinner. Towards the end of the day, there were informal meetings for prayer and praise. The Conference *Worship Book* was designed to give 'space', within a supportive framework, for self-expression to the rich diversity of cultures, languages and traditions represented at the Conference. The Chaplain, Bishop Alastair Haggart, and his assistant, Mother Janet OHP, were ubiquitous and always willing to give advice on the many problems which arose in organising worship for such a large number of people. The great services of the Conference were the opening and closing Eucharists at Canterbury Cathedral and the Eucharist at St Paul's Cathedral, London , midway through the Conference. The Archbishop of Canterbury presided and preached at the Opening Service, with the Primates of Japan and Kenya assisting. At St Paul's, the president was the Primate of Australia, as the service also marked the Australian bicentennial, and the preacher was the Primate of Central Africa. The Archbishop of Canterbury presided at the Closing Eucharist, assisted by the Primate of Southern Africa and the Moderator-Bishop of the Church of South India. The Presiding Bishop of the Episcopal Church,

USA, was the preacher. While much of the style of the worship was, perhaps necessarily, characterised by a British love of order and beauty in worship, attempts were made to accommodate aspects of worship from other parts of the Anglican Communion. At the Opening Service, for example, the Canterbury Cathedral choir valiantly attempted to sing a Tanzanian and a Jamaican anthem! The choir at St Paul's sang the translation of a Swahili hymn, and in the Worship Book there were a couple of choruses from Africa. During the Closing Service, the intercessions were led by five Primates from different parts of the Communion, in their own languages. A particular feature of this service was the dedication of the Compasrose, the symbol of the Communion, which has been set into the floor of the nave in Canterbury Catherdal. Just before the Conference began, Lambeth Palace Chapel, which has been renovated, was rededicated. The Chapel now has a special stall for each of the Primates of the Anglican Communion. Some other occasions deserve notice too; one was a Service of Light led by Archbishop Desmond Tutu in preparation for an all-night vigil to pray for those who live in areas of conflict. The other was a celebration of the Feast of the Transfiguration which was followed by a tree-planting ceremony by the Primate of Japan to mark Hiroshima Day. Orthodox Vespers, in celebration of the millennium of Christianity in Russia, were sung at Canterbury Cathedral and were a notable ecumenical occasion.

RECREATION

Apart from worship and work, there was a great deal of recreation too. The highlights of the *London Day* were lunch at Lambeth Palace and a Garden Party at Buckingham Palace. At lunch the guests were entertained by Mrs Rosalind Runcie and several of her colleagues who presented a musical composition called *A Lambeth Garland*. The piece was especially composed as an encomium to Mrs Runcie for her creative use of the Palace Gardens. Her Majesty The Queen had been away in Canada during the last Lambeth Conference and was said to be particularly looking forward to her 'purple Garden Party' on this occasion. The Royal Party consisted of HRH Prince Philip, the Duke of Edinburgh, the Prince and Princess of Wales and HRH The Princess Margaret, Countess of Snowdon. The Royal Party mixed easily with Conference participants, their spouses and special guests. Not even a fairly heavy downpour could dampen the spirits of those at the Garden Party and the band continued to play right through the rain! The Party had begun in brilliant sunshine and towards the end, the sun shone brightly again!

The Lord Mayor of Canterbury (whose office has recently been elevated by Her Majesty The Queen) held a reception for the Conference participants on the first day of the Conference and also invited several of them to lunch in his tent during the Canterbury Cricket Week. Cricket, in fact, was in high profile throughout the Conference! The former England captain,

Colin Cowdrey, had invited a number of bishops to witness a match at Lords. Not only was the hospitality marvellous and the cricket good but they were also shown around the Long Room and even the Committee Room by members of the MCC. On a rather damp afternoon, the Archbishop of Canterbury's XI met an eleven from the Diocese of Canterbury for the traditional cricket match. The Archbishop's XI had elected to field and had made a good start when, with only fifteen overs bowled, the rain came down very heavily and the match had to be abandoned!

The Gulbenkian Theatre, on the University Campus, was the venue for several programmes put on for the benefit of the Conference. These included films such as Sir Richard Attenborough's *Cry Freedom,* which is a story of the life and death of Steve Biko, and other items such as Paul Alexander's reading of *The Gospel According to St John.* Performances of T.S. Eliot's *Murder in the Cathedral* were staged in Canterbury Cathedral. The Cathedral also held an Open Evening for Conference participants. There were excursions to several places of interest and opportunity for participants to explore the ancient city of Canterbury itself.

As in the past, a leading characteristic of this Lambeth Conference was the fellowship experienced by the bishops and the other participants who all came from very different backgrounds and cultures. Given the tremendous centrifugal pressures on the Anglican Communion at this time, this experience was nothing short of the miraculous. There was a manifest desire to stay together, to consult with each other, to meet as often as possible, to pray for each other and to receive from each other. The fellowship of the Holy Spirit was truly experienced in being together at Lambeth 1988. Some of the lines from Psalm 122, which was sung at the Closing Eucharist, are entirely appropriate as a prayer for the Anglican Communion:

Jerusalem is built as a city : that is at unity in itself...

O pray for the peace of Jerusalem : they shall prosper that love thee.

Peace be within thy walls : and security within thy towers.

For my brethren and companions' sake : I will wish thee prosperity.

Yea, because of the house of the Lord our God : I will seek to do thee good.

Advent 1988   The CO-EDITORS

NOTES

[1] It is well known, of course, that Resolutions passed by a Lambeth Conference do not have legislative authority in any Province, until they have been approved by the provincial synod of the Province.

[2] ACC, London, 1988.

[3] See Appendix 5 p.293.

President of the Conference: The Most Revd and Rt Hon. Robert A. K. Runcie, Archbishop of Canterbury

The Archbishop of Canterbury's Opening Address 'The Nature of the Unity We Seek'

INTRODUCTION

Let me begin with a homely illustration. My mother read detective stories – mystery stories, where the secret is revealed on the last page. But she had a habit of reading the last chapter first, thus seeing how it all fitted together. I follow her in turning your attention to the last chapters of the last book of the Bible.

In the Book of Revelation we are given a vision: a new heaven and a new earth, and the holy city, New Jerusalem, coming down from God out of heaven. Here is God's disclosure of the unity of the whole human family. The Lord God Almighty and the Lamb are the central focus of the holy City. All the nations shall walk in the light of the glory of God and of the Lamb. The Kings of the earth shall bring with them the glory and honour of the nations. *And the gates of the City shall not be shut* (Rev. 21.22-27). Exclusiveness is not a characteristic of the City of God.

In this vision there is ultimately no difference between the quest for the Church's unity and the quest for human healing in the widest sense. The Church is the model towards which the whole human family will look for its healing and reconciliation. To the degree that the Church is effectively gathered in unity in the assembly of worship around God and the Lamb, it is the sign of hope and the bearer of good news to the whole world.

Neither the Church nor the world 'sets the agenda': God has *his* agenda of shalom, unity and communion. *We* must seek to be loyal to it. So the question of Christian unity always needs to be considered in the light of what it is *for*. What would be the value of unanimity without purpose? Human unity is the goal of God's mission to his creation – though in relation to the Lamb on the throne. Christian unity is part of our share in that mission, the sending of God's Son and his Gospel and his Church to the ends of the world.

But here is another picture. During the sunset years of European colonialism, a young British District Officer wrote to his fiancée in England describing the home in East Africa that he looked forward to sharing with her. 'From the hillside,' he wrote, 'I see the smoke rising from the cooking fires in a dozen villages scattered along the valley – part of the forty thousand subsistence farmers who live all around. My nearest neighbours are three hours' drive away, but we usually meet for tennis once a fortnight.' Nor is this limited definition of the neighbour peculiar to Europeans. I have been told a Ghanaian proverb which runs: 'The stranger who came says he saw no-one in the town and those he met said they saw no-one come.'

All talk of human unity without the vision of the heavenly city wherein the

11

nations walk becomes an arrogant attempt to rebuild the Tower of Babel. Is this not the lesson of the rise and fall of empires both ancient and modern? And are we not seeing this re-enacted in the contemporary resurgence of nationalism and tribalism?

As I look around this plenary assembly of the Lambeth Conference I see in so many of you the personal embodiment of God's mission to a broken and divided world. As Anglican bishops, bishops in full communion, and as ecumenical observers, you come with wounds humanity cannot by itself heal: the wounds of Southern Africa and Uganda, Sudan and Ethiopia; the wounds of the Philippines, Korea and Sri Lanka; of Nicaragua, of South America; of Jerusalem and the Middle East; the wounds of Ireland; the great global wounds of distrust between East and West, and the increasing disparity between North and South. Look at each other as human beings bearing the marks of human brokenness. But look at each other also as fellow citizens of the heavenly city, as those who worship the Lamb and who are thus constituted within Christ's Church as a sign of hope for the whole human race, the bearers of the Gospel of reconciliation.

It is within this broad agenda – God's agenda for the unity of all creation – that we must set the no less divine agenda of Christian unity and the unity of the Anglican Communion. An ecumenical observer put this strongly at the meeting of the Anglican Consultative Council in Singapore last year. All discussion of ecumenical matters, he argued, should constantly have in mind the *purpose* of the Church as sign and sacrament of the Kingdom. 'It is', he said, 'only where people actually bleed and weep that their wounds can be bound up and their tears wiped away.' How can we see the heavenly vision and at the same time tolerate women and men, God's masterpieces, belittled by reason of their colour, sex, or social class?

It has been one of the great strengths of the World Council of Churches – whose fortieth anniversary falls this year – that it has always set the search for Christian unity in this wider context. From the days of a divided and shattered Europe after the Second World War till the present time, this has never been forgotten.

The structure of my address is dictated by this fundamental agenda. But we have to begin somewhere specific and concrete. Only when the burning glass is focused is fire kindled. What story would Our Lord have told to that young District Officer in East Africa? Surely the parable of the Good Samaritan, with its fundamental interrogation: *Who is my neighbour?* At this Lambeth Conference we may well ask the same question ourselves. And the answer must be the fellow bishop who differs from us theologically, politically, or culturally, as radically as the Jew from the Samaritan. For a while bishops with deeply opposing convictions must live and debate and pray together as neighbours.

We shall do this in the company of representatives of the world-wide Church through the presence of bishops in communion and the ecumenical observers. We shall be taking important decisions about our relations with other Churches and looking with some rigour at the goal of Christian unity.

So we begin where we are. I shall speak in what follows of unity within the Anglican Communion, of ecumenical unity among the Christian Churches, and finally of the unity of all creation.

UNITY WITHIN THE ANGLICAN COMMUNION

I want to begin what I say about unity within the Anglican Communion with a strong affirmation of gratitude. Our mood is eucharistic, in spite of the conflict and debate we must realistically anticipate. We give thanks to God for our communion with him and with each other as Anglican Christians. As I travel round the Anglican Communion I am filled with enthusiasm for what I see and hear, and especially for the people I meet at the local level.

I think of a hispanic 'street' celebration of the eucharist on the West Coast of the USA; of the consecration of four new churches on one boiling hot day in the outback of Australia; of the indomitable enthusiasm and valour of the Church in South Africa at Archbishop Desmond's enthronement; of the beauty and reverence of worship in Japan; and of the fresh idealism of young Anglicans at their meeting in Northern Ireland. Many of you could tell similar stories, especially from Partnership in Mission consultations and the regional preparatory meetings for this Lambeth Conference.

So I have had to say with some vigour to the British press of late that the Anglican Communion is not about to dissolve. And to the Church of England Synod that it is a little early to be taking the covers off the lifeboats and abandoning ship.

So let us maintain the note of joy and thanksgiving with which we began the Conference at the eucharist yesterday and with which we begin each day. The ecumenical presence among us is also a sign of mutual confidence and trust. Our partners in the Gospel may have their problems with us, though they also say to us 'There are good things in the Anglican Communion'.

But I want to say too that we must never make the survival of the Anglican Communion an end in itself. The Churches of the Anglican Communion have never claimed to be more than a part of the One Holy Catholic and Apostolic Church. Anglicanism has a radically provisional character which we must never allow to be obscured.

One of the characteristic features of Anglicanism is our Reformation inheritance of national or provincial autonomy. The Anglican tradition is thus opposed to centralism and encourages the thriving of variety. This is a great good. There is an important principle to be borne witness to here: that nothing should be done at a higher level than is absolutely necessary.

So Anglicans have become accustomed to speak of a dispersed authority. And we are traditionally suspicious of the Lambeth Conference becoming anything other than a Conference. We may indeed wish to discuss the development of more solid structures of unity and coherence. But I for one would want their provisional character made absolutely clear; like tents in the desert, they should be capable of being easily dismantled when it is time for the Pilgrim People to move on. We have no intention of developing an alternative Papacy. We would rather continue to deal with the structures of the existing Petrine Ministry, and hopefully help in its continuing development and reform as a ministry of unity for all Christians.

But Anglican unity itself is most characteristically expressed in terms of worship. Here we have much in common with the Eastern Churches, whose very name implies a unity through right worship – *Orthodoxy*. This is a proper corrective to an over-institutional view of Christian unity and to an over-intellectual understanding of unity through assent to confessional formulae.

In liturgical worship the Scriptures are proclaimed, the Creed is confessed, the Sacraments are celebrated, and all is given order through an authorised episcopal ministry. You will recognize here the elements of the Chicago-Lambeth Quadrilateral, first formulated one hundred years ago. It is a description of the cohesive ingredients of the worshipping community, the glue which binds us together.

Nevertheless, I do not wish to sound complacent. There are real and serious threats to our unity and communion and I do not underestimate them. Some of them are the result of Gospel insights; for example the proper dignity of women in a Christian society. We need to recognise that our unity is threatened over the ordination of women to the priesthood and episcopate in *whatever we ultimately decide to do*. There are dangers to our communion in this Lambeth Conference endorsing or failing to endorse such developments. And there are equal dangers to communion by trying to avoid the issue altogether.

Such conflict is particularly painful, because the glue which binds us together is not so much juridical, but personal, informal and expressed in worship. An impairment of communion for Anglicans is not essentially about canon law but at the much deeper personal level of sharing in the eucharistic worship of the Holy Trinity. So we tend to shy away from a conflict which has such destructive potential. This is of course a serious mistake.

We need to recognize the persistence and place of conflict in Christian history. There has never been sharper conflict among Christ's people than the great debate over the admission of the Gentiles to the Church without the ceremonial law. Think of Paul withstanding Peter to the face (Gal. 2.10). Nor were the early Ecumenical Councils of the Church any easier. Tempers blazed on the doctrines of the person of Christ and the Holy Trinity, charges and counter-changes were levelled, coalitions were formed. At the Council of Ephesus the monk Shenouda hurled a copy of the Gospels at Nestorius. A gesture at once orthodox and effective, for it struck him on the chest and bowled him over! Mind you, I'm not advocating this as a procedural device here.

And yet in and through such unholy conflict the Church eventually, and never without difficulty, came to a common mind. Through the initiatives of prophets and primates, the deliberations of synods, and the active response of the whole Church, the Holy Spirit has been at work. Conflict can be destructive. It can also be creative. We are not here to avoid conflict but to redeem it. At the heart of our faith is a cross and not, as in some religions, an eternal calm.

The creative use of conflict is part of the process of discerning the truth. As the Rabbinic scriptures put it, 'controversies for the sake of heaven'. This is not to propagate polemics but to explore truth. There is a constant dialogue here between revelation and culture in every age. Tradition is not archaeology but the contemporary expression of 'the faith which was once delivered unto the saints' (Jude 3). Consistency with Scripture and continuity with the past there must be. But this does not entail the mere duplication of the past.

So the Church has a living tradition which develops and grows in the tension between that which has been given and the present experience of the community. At the Lambeth Conference the Anglican Communion tries to discern what is of the Spirit, and what is not, and to express this in a living voice. Conflict, then, far from being an unmitigated evil, is, if handled creatively, an essential part of our understanding of the processes whereby the Church speaks with a living voice today.

In any case the problem that confronts us as Anglicans arises not from conflict over the ordination of women as such, but from the relationship of independent provinces with each other. Although we have machinery for dealing with problems within a diocese and within a Province, we have few for those which exist within the Communion as a whole.

Another reason for looking critically at the notion of the absolute independence of Provinces arises from our ecumenical dialogues with worldwide communions. These require decision and action at more than provincial level. And our own experience as a world Communion also teaches us the importance of a global perspective at a time when political concerns for 'national security' often militate against international co-operation and diminish the significance of world organisations such as the United Nations.

The New Testament surely speaks more in terms of *interdependence* than *independence*. The relationship of Jesus with the Father in the bond of the Holy Spirit as witnessed in St John's Gospel surely gives us the pattern of Christian relationship. Life together in communion implies basic trust and mutuality. Think of Paul speaking of life in the Body in his first letter to the Corinthians: 'The eye cannot say to the hand, I have no need for you, nor again the head to the feet, I have no need of you'. (1 Cor. 12.21). The good of the Body requires mutual recognition and deference in Christ. Or think of Paul's collection for the saints in Jerusalem, a practical expression of communion on the theological ground of unity in Christ.

The idea of interdependence is not new to Anglicanism. The Toronto Conference of 1963 which gave us the slogan 'mutual responsibility and interdependence in the Body of Christ' also gave birth to the whole Partners in Mission process. But the full consequences of such mutual responsibility and interdependence have hardly yet been realised. It has taken the conflict over the ordination of women to point up the implications for the Communion. Here is powerful illustration of the fact that conflict has creative potential.

It can be put this way: are we being called through events and their theological interpretation to move from independence to interdependence? If we answer yes, then we cannot dodge the question of how this is to be given 'flesh': how is our interdependence articulated and made effective; how is it to be structured? Without losing a proper – but perhaps modified – provincial autonomy this will probably mean a critical examination of the notion of 'dispersed authority'. We need to have confidence that authority is not dispersed to the point of dissolution and ineffectiveness.

Should our answer be 'yes' to a minimum structuring of our mutual interdependence – that which is actually *required* for the maintenance of communion and no more – we would in fact be challenging the alarming isolationism and impatience I detect on both sides of the debate about the ordination of women. We would challenge not only the 'go it alone' attitudes of enterprising independence but also the 'I and only I am left' attitudes of those who believe they are the sole repositories of 'true' Anglicanism.

Let me put it in starkly simple terms: do we really *want* unity within the Anglican Communion? Is our worldwide family of Christians worth bonding together? *Or* is our paramount concern the preservation or promotion of that particular expression of Anglicanism which has developed within the culture of our own province? Wouldn't it be easier and more realistic to work towards exclusively European, or North American, or African, or Pacific forms of Anglicanism? Yes, it might. Cultural adaptation would be easier. Mission would be easier. Local ecumenism would be easier. Do we actually need a worldwide Communion?

I believe we do because Anglicans believe in the One Holy Catholic and Apostolic Church of the Creed. I believe we do because we live in one world created and redeemed by God. I believe we do because it is only by being in communion *together* that diversity and difference have value. Without relationship difference divides.

This is why I have called the present Lambeth Conference. This is why I have visited many of the Provinces of the Anglican Communion in solidarity with both your joys and your sufferings. I have tried to be a personal and visible presence of the whole Anglican family in places like the Province of Southern Africa where solidarity between the worldwide Church and particular Christians is a Gospel imperative if ever there was one.

So I believe we still need the Anglican Communion. But we have reached

16

the stage in the growth of the Communion when we must begin to make radical choices, or growth will imperceptibly turn to decay. I believe the choice between independence and interdependence, already set before us as a Communion in embryo twenty-five years ago, is quite simply the choice between unity or gradual fragmentation. It would be a gentle, even genteel, fragmentation. That much of Englishness still remains. Nor would it be instant. As I have said, the Communion is not about to disappear tomorrow. But decisive choice is before us. Do we want the Anglican Communion? And if we do, what are we going to do about it?

ECUMENICAL UNITY AMONG THE CHRISTIAN CHURCHES

When we turn to unity among the Churches we have a similar hard question to ask. For there is a feeling that the ecumenical movement has run into the sand and there is a lassitude and scarcely veiled apathy about unity discussions. A prominent English spiritual writer has called ecumenism 'the last refuge of the ecclesiastical bore'.

Certainly there have been ecumenical failures to account for the evaporation of the enthusiasm of a generation ago. And Anglican Churches have been prominent in all parts of the world – except the Indian sub-continent – for failing to endorse national unity schemes.

But my answer to ecumenical apathy is to say look at the *local* scene. The most encouraging sign of ecumenism in the last few years in many parts of the world has been the startling growth of local covenants and areas of ecumenical experiment. There is the Interim Eucharistic Sharing agreement between Anglicans and Lutherans in North America. Perhaps I can also be allowed to give a British example of local ecumenical initiatives as we are in the middle of a process called *Not Strangers But Pilgrims*. For the first time, Christians of almost all the Churches are working together to find ways of expressing their unity more visibly. This includes black-led Churches, the Roman Catholic Church and Orthodox Churches, as well as Anglicans, Methodists, and other Reformed Churches.

Couple this local activity to the achievements of the various theological conversations between the Churches – you have the *Emmaus Report* as part of your preparatory material – and it is hard to sustain objectively the view that ecumenism is in the doldrums.

But as well as apathy there is also some *hostility* to the idea of Christian unity. The very process of ecumenical discussion raises the question of what each partner believes. The issues of the *identity* of separate Churches is sharpened. I like to tell the story of the old Scotsman who became more and more agitated at the time of the Anglican-Presbyterian unity discussions some years ago. He would not have bishops in the Scots Kirk. His family could not understand this. 'But, father,' they said, 'you're an atheist.' 'Aye,' he replied, 'but I'm a Presbyterian atheist.'

17

My answer to this is to agree that ecumenism is a risk. We risk the loss of *denominational* identity in the search for *Christian* identity – what C.S. Lewis meant by 'Mere Christianity'. Ecumenism is not in fact a threat to our identity but its enlargement.

An additional consequence of this anxiety about identity is that we may be tempted to rest content with *denominational federalism* rather than the catholic diversity of the coming Great Church. Agreement in faith, it is argued, is impossible to achieve, nor does the New Testament give warrant for it. For communion in faith we must substitute the co-existence of radically different styles of faith and ecclesial life. Instead of visible organic unity grounded in agreement in faith it would be better to lower our sights and work for the lesser goal of a federal ecumenism.

But does New Testament diversity license us to settle for coexistence? I would want to argue that this is a curiously 'fundamentalist' view. It fails to take account of the development of 'catholic' structures within the New Testament itself. The Pastoral Epistles witness to a recognition of the need for bonds of unity to hold the diverse Christian communities together. Such a view fails to take account of the significance of the Canon of Scripture, which declines to parcel out diversity in separate containers and insists that 'all things are yours'. Thus we are not called to choose between Johannine and Pauline Christianity, but are called to be confronted and enriched by both.

There is need here to attend carefully to the evangelical contribution to ecumenism. For, despite the doubts of evangelicals about structures and ministries for unity, I look forward to a major contribution from them because of their unwavering and biblically grounded conviction that there is One Lord and One Faith. This is itself a wholly constructive critique of the position of those who simply want to rest content with pluriformity. And from the conviction of One Lord and One Faith we shall all then be able to advance to the consequences of the recognition of One Baptism; the visible unity of the One Church.

Another important evangelical insight – derived from the Reformation – is that the Church is in constant need of renewal. The Church exists for the Gospel and not for itself. We would all want to acknowledge the achievements and growth of contemporary renewal movements. Before this Conference I attended SOMA – Sharing of Ministries Abroad – which is powerful in charismatic enthusiasm and remains eager to be loyally Anglican. I applaud their loyalty to our Communion and their longing for the renewal of the whole Church in the freshness of faith. There are many groups like them, in all the Churches, who are in revolt against cerebral, institutional religion – and, to be frank, some of the ingredients of this lecture and my recipe for unity. They feel themselves already one in the Holy Spirit.

My hesitations are that such movements can tend to sit in judgement on the institutional Church. It's safer – it is said – to stick with 'real' Christians! But it was Luther himself who said that you needed the Church to preach the

Gospel in the first place. Furthermore, such attitudes leave little room for the seeking pilgrim. The student who said, when asked to give his whole life to Christ, 'I still know so little of my own life and need to know so much more of the Christ to whom I am to be committed', should not be lost to the Church. We need commitment: yes. But expressed in a variety of styles: some enthusiastic and emotional; others questioning and intellectual; yet others through traditional rite and ceremony. This brings me to the question of diversity.

In my strong reaffirmation of the vision of *one* Church I hope it is no longer necessary to stress that unity is not a synonym for uniformity. Though we would be naive to suppose that we are the only comprehensive Church, it has been a particular characteristic of Anglicanism to stress diversity. Without diversity the body cannot flourish, grow or develop. If diversity is not fostered, schism ferments. The presence among us of representatives of the Eastern and Oriental Orthodox Churches reminds all Western Christians that the fullness of Christian unity can never be bland homogeneity. The body of Christ is an organism of many cells and of different kinds.

Fundamental to the unity of the Body of Christ is our common confession of Jesus as Lord. Subordinate to this are a number of visible signs of the existing communion between the Christian Churches which institutional schism has impaired but not altogether taken away: the confession of one apostolic faith revealed in the Scriptures and set forth in the Catholic Creeds; the practice of one baptism with water in the name of the Trinity; a common concern for the poor and powerless, manifesting itself in a community of resources; an acknowledgement of shared goals and values, derived from the belief that humanity is created in the image of God; and a common commitment to the apostolic mission Christ has entrusted to his Church.

All these are largely and widely shared by the ecumenical community. They point to an *existing* communion between the Churches. But for full ecclesial communion, for the fullness of the unity we seek, this existing unity requires development and embodiment. This brings us inevitably to the *structures* which will serve both the unity and diversity of the Church.

One such instrument of unity is the *historic episcopate*. But here Anglicans have to be very careful to commend episcopacy without the negative overtones, which Christians of 'non-episcopal' Churches have so often heard. I hope our discussion of Anglican-Lutheran relations and the Lima text can be the context for a new affirmation of the value of episcopacy as a sign of the apostolicity of the whole Church, the continuity of the Christian community in time and space. 'No "unchurching" and no denials of the experience of any Christians need accompany the firmest insistence on Episcopacy',wrote Michael Ramsey.

This will become clearer if we Anglicans could learn from the Lutheran rediscovery that apostolic succession is in *faith* before it is in *order*. The trad-

19

itional ceremonial for episcopal ordination includes the holding of the gospels over the head of the episcopal ordinand. Had that ceremony been reflected in reality in the sixteenth century, the Lutheran and Reformed Churches would not have been put in the agonising predicament of having to choose between bishops and gospel. None the less, the episcopate is for Anglicans one of the instruments of unity.

Another is the *council* or *synod*. From the beginning of the Church it has been necessary to come together for conference, debate and decision. Here I am particularly anxious that we listen to the voice of the Orthodox Churches, for whom Synods and councils have such an important place. I was present at the recent Synod of the Russian Orthodox Church and I was humbled by the reminder that their first modern Synod (of bishops, clergy and laity) took place in 1917, rather before my own Church of England – though not of course before many of the Churches of the Communion.

It would be good if there could be some conversation between our Orthodox observers and the bishops from Africa, because I am struck by some similarities in the way in which decisions are reached. In an Orthodox Synod much emphasis is given to the achievement of moral consensus. In the African tradition this is also the case. The Synod will debate an issue until there is a common mind and the decision will only then be taken. In other parts of the Communion we have developed a more legalistic attitude to councils. In the Church of England, when a decision is about to be taken in Synod, the Registrar calls 'divide': the very word for schism and the exact opposite of the true meaning of Synod – to come together.

If we still have some things to learn about synodical government, I also believe we have something to give to the Church of Rome. For me the major criticism of ARCIC must be its lack of emphasis on the role of the laity in the decision-making of the Church.

As *Anglicans* we are trying to learn how conciliar bodies such as this Conference, the Primates' Meeting and the Anglican Consultative Council all relate together. We should be particularly glad to welcome the ACC's full presence among us as we explore how we maintain our unity together. As bishops we bring our diocese with us. But we also need the special interest groups the ACC can represent.

An urgent task for our *ecumenical* conversations, especially in Faith and Order, will be the elaboration of wider conciliar models of *common* decision-making at local, national and global level.

To bishops and councils I would also want to add primacy. ARCIC puts before Anglicans the question of an episcopal primacy in the Universal Church: an instrument of unity we have been lacking since Henry VIII's juridical break with Rome in the sixteenth Century. Not all Anglicans view the restoration of such an office with equanimity. ARCIC, it must be remembered, is not proposing *restoration* but a *reform* of primacy as a ministry of unity.

In October 1986 I visited Assisi to pray for peace at the invitation of Pope John Paul with Christians ranging over the whole Christian spectrum. And alongside Christian leaders were representatives of all the great world religions. That Day of Prayer for Peace was something I had wanted to see since Pope John Paul made his ecumenical pilgrimage to Canterbury Cathedral. We spoke of the idea then and I gave it all the encouragement I could. Whether we like it or not there is only one Church, and one bishop, who could have effectively convoked such an ecumenical gathering. At Assisi I saw the vision of a new style of Petrine ministry – an ARCIC primacy rather than a papal monarchy. Pope John Paul welcomed us – including other Anglican primates present here at this Conference – but then he became, in his own words, 'a brother among brothers'. And at the end we all bundled into the same bus and the Pope had to look for a seat!

Our own Anglican experience of belonging to a world communion also points to the need of a personal focus of unity and affection. Of course a Canterbury primacy is very different from the kind of sovereignty which has been exercised by the popes for many years. But could not all Christians come to reconsider the kind of primacy exercised within the Early Church, a 'presiding in love' for the sake of the unity of the Churches?

In serving the Gospel and thus the unity of the Church, *bishops, synods* and *primacy* are structures in radical need of reform and renewal. But we must beware of an ecumenical idealism which prefers to wait around until episcopacy, synods or popes are exactly as we would have them. Renewal then would become an excuse for inaction, a retreat from committing ourselves to each other as we are. It would be like a perpetual engagement in which marriage was for ever being postponed until the partners were perfect. No, the way to perfect your partner is to enter a new and more intimate relationship so that mutual change comes by intrinsic desire rather than extrinsic demand.

As with the Anglican Communion, so ecumenically: we must move from independence to interdependence. And the same question necessarily arises: 'Do we want unity'? I do, because our Lord prayed for it on the eve of his passion. I do, because our Lord prayed for it in the context of mission – 'That they all may be one ... that the world may believe'. I do, because neither conflicting Churches, nor competitive Churches, nor co-existing Churches, will be able to embody effectively the Gospel of reconciliation while the Churches themselves remain unreconciled. Do we Anglicans *really* want unity? We must do if we are to be instruments of unity and communion to a divided world.

THE UNITY OF ALL CREATION

This leads me to that wider ecumenism which is the original meaning of *oikoumene* with which we began. I have not ventured into inter-faith dialogue, because I am conscious that this address is directed to those who can respond tomorrow. But a comprehensive coverage of my title would certainly demand from me something of the encounter with world religions. It will be an important part of the Conference agenda. For me all people of faith, all those with spiritual awareness, possess potential for greater unity through dialogue, through fellowship, and the service of the wider community. That is why I went to Assisi.

I make no apologies, however, for spending time on unity among Anglicans and with fellow Christians. It would be hypocritical to avoid our particular domestic problems for the sake of a rhetorical concern for global unity, about which this conference can itself *do* very little. Indeed, the penitential recognition of the fragmented nature of the Christian family may usefully prevent us from glib talk about human unity which only too easily slides into secular optimism and the discredited liberal notion of inevitable progress. To speak (in the language of our conversations with Reformed Christians) of the Church as the sign, instrument and foretaste of the Kingdom is *not* to be equated with Utopianism.

I was reminded of this vividly in Moscow recently. There is an obelisk in the Kremlin near the Tomb of the Unknown Warrior commemorating the forerunners of the Revolution. It includes the name of Thomas More, the author of *Utopia*. The trouble with earthly Utopias is that by leaving out God they take short cuts: 'All men are brothers except those who in the name of brotherhood need to be eliminated.' It is a remarkable fact that when men leave out the heavenly city they cannot build a tolerable city on earth.

Yet though the Kingdom is not susceptible of political arrangement, the Christian leader cannot escape specific political questions. If bishops keep to the safe paths of moral generalities, they are dismissed as impractical idealists. If they chance their arm and venture social comment, they are accused of technical incompetence and political interference. We cannot win. Here I believe the Churches need to listen to each other's experience. The older Churches can learn much by sharing in the debate of the younger Churches about 'liberation theology'. Not that Kingdom imperatives will mean the same solutions in each place, but that we must all bring a gospel critique to our respective societies.

Christians have particular insights. Because their ultimate vision is of the kingdom of God, of men and women caught up in the divine interdependence of the Holy Trinity, they are unlikely to rest content with any existing political arrangements. The *Christian* vocation is to live in society, in communion. And so the search for communion among Christians gives us a pattern for the wider communion of all humanity.

I have glimpsed this among Christians in many different parts of the world. I think of a Lutheran eucharist in Dresden, East Germany, totally destroyed by Allied bombing in the Second World War. There were hundreds of young people in the congregation. I was invited to assist in the distribution of the Sacrament, and as the people received Communion some whispered 'thank you for coming', or the like, after their Amen to the Blood of Christ. Here was the Church of Jesus Christ transcending the man-made political divide between East and West.

In India I was able to meet Mother Teresa of Calcutta. In her home for the dying she was washing out the ward. She put down her bucket, took my hand, and looked deeply into my eyes. As someone said, she makes you feel big and small at the same time. But what I had not realised was that the home for the dying is built on temple ground. The temple is dedicated to the godness Kali, from whom the city of Calcutta derives its name. Here is the Church giving Easter hope, peace and dignity to the dying next door to a temple of a goddess associated with death and destruction.

Again, an AIDS clinic in San Francisco supported by the Episcopal and Catholic Churches, embodying the same Gospel message of love, pastoral care and hope. You, too, will have stories from your own Churches: the Church as a model of what it is to be human.

But the unity God intends does not fall short of the *whole* creation. Someone said recently, 'preoccupation with the *human* is beginning to sound distinctly parochial.' Kiev, which I visited recently, the cradle of the Russian Church, is not far from Chernobyl. Perhaps because of this, one of the Metropolitans stressed the urgency of a serious Christian discussion of environmental and ecological issues. Scientists today would also wish to stress the 'interdependence' and balance of nature, rather than a misunderstood, competitive, evolutionary theory. So I would want to urge strong Anglican support for the World Conference on *Peace, Justice and the Integrity of Creation*. As the late Barbara Ward said at our last Conference, 'We have only one earth. Is it not worth our love?'

Earlier in the year I was in Australia for the Bicentennial Celebrations. But I visited the Aboriginal people as well as those who had arrived more recently. I went to the Northern Territory and worshipped with Aboriginal Anglicans. We shared a fellowship meal in the open air: a kind of communion with God, each other and the earth. I also saw a remarkable relationship between a progressive mining company, the Church, and the Aborigine community. Whereas in the past the Aboriginal people and the environment had been exploited, *now* there is co-operation and partnership: a living example of that interdependence between humanity and creation which is the Creator's plan.

I am reminded of a prayer of the Ojibway people of Canada:
'Great Father,
Look on our brokenness.
We know that in all creation
Only the human family
Has strayed from the Sacred Way.

23

> Great Father,
> Holy one,
> Teach us love, compassion and honour,
> That we may heal the earth
> And heal each other.

I began with the Heavenly City. If you go on to the final chapter of Revelation you will remember that the River of the Water of Life flows through the city and on either side there is the Tree of Life. *A Garden City* – an echo of that original paradise of the first book of the Bible in which, under God, Man and Woman are the gardeners of creation.

It is our conviction as Christians that in Jesus Christ (himself once mistaken for a gardener) we come to share in the New Man, the Second Adam, the renewed humanity. It is the task of the *one* Church of Jesus Christ to embody more visibly this new humanity as Good News for all people and all creation. Let me end with two verses from the Epistle to the Ephesians, the Epistle of Unity, which brings all this together:

> For (God) has made known to us in all wisdom and insight the mystery of his will, according to his purpose which he set forth in Christ as a plan for the fullness of time, to unite all things in him, things in heaven and things on earth. (Eph. 1.9-10)

This is the unity Christians seek.

SECTION REPORTS

Mission and Ministry

Chairman	The Rt Revd James Ottley (Panama, ECUSA)
Vice-Chairman	The Rt Revd David Sheppard (Liverpool, England)
Secretary	The Rt Revd Patrick Harris (Partnership for World Mission, Bishop-elect of Southwell, England)
Staff	The Revd Mano Rumalshah
Communicator	Mr Jerry Hames

Secretary to the Conference: The Revd Canon Samuel Van Culin

THE NATURE AND MEANING OF MISSION

MISSION TODAY
1   'God so loved the world.' God still loves his world, and as Jesus was sent by the Father so the Church is sent by Jesus, in the name of the Father and in the power of the Holy Spirit (John 20.21). The mission of the Church is:

1   to proclaim the good news of the kingdom;
2   to teach, baptise and nurture new believers;
3   to respond to human need by loving service;
4   to seek to transform unjust structures of society.[1]

A sense of immediacy sprang from Jesus as he stood up in the synagogue to announce, 'Today, this scripture has been fulfilled in your hearing' (Luke 4.21). The scripture he claimed as his own referred to deliverance for the poor, for those without sight, for prisoners and for the oppressed (cf. Isaiah 61.1-2). He had been sent by the Father to convert yesterday's vision into today's mission.

2   We embrace this mission with all its urgency. The time is short for those who do not know Christ and for those who are suffering as refugees, as the homeless, as victims of disease, or as addicts. People lost in a world of hopelessness need to hear that 'the Kingdom of God is at hand' and discover the community where its power is operative. We recognise also the poverty of the wealthy, sinfulness in followers of all religions, and the cruelty of nations. We turn, therefore, in penitence to God, trusting in his mercy and grace, while at the same time proclaiming his presence in and purposes for the whole world.

Our Churches are always in danger of diverting the energies and focus of their members from their essential task of mission, to an introverted pre-occupation with ecclesiastical concerns. We call our Churches and all Christians back to mission and we urge them to respond with all their heart to our Lord's commission to go out into the world in his name.

THE ARENA OF MISSION
3   The arena of mission is the whole world – a hungry world, an unjust world, an angry world, a fearful world. A world that has been polluted and is in danger of irreparable damage. A world that is governed by many false gods and pays little heed to the God and Father of our Lord Jesus Christ. It is also a world of beauty and hope in which goodness and love abound. A world which struggles for justice, integrity and peace. A world which belongs to God.

4   Modern technology has brought us closer together into one 'global village'. As Christians we rejoice in the developments in medicine, in industry, in communications and in travel, that have benefited millions. Education

and mobility have made it possible for some individuals and communities to make fresh choices. Ease of instant communication and rapid travel have strengthened our sense of interdependence, whether as individuals, nations or churches.

5 Mission involves proclamation. Proclamation must proceed from a Church and a people who reflect the love and goodness of God. We are called to proclaim God's love and forgiveness by word and by deed. We must use every means available to spread the message of salvation. Our proclamation must be sensitive to the culture and beliefs of others. Nevertheless, Christ calls all people to turn from evil and all that hurts or enslaves and to receive the fullness of life which he alone can give.

6 The salvation we proclaim is concerned with both the wholeness of individuals and the wholeness of society. Any understanding which focuses on the individual and ignores society as a whole, or vice versa, is not true to the Gospel. Abuse or exploitation of others is contrary to God's purpose. Part of our mission is to challenge that in society or in us which is life-denying. It is also to bring hope, love and trust, so that all are raised to the full dignity and stature of their humanity.

7 We are deeply concerned at the growing gap between wealth and poverty among the nations and within nations. 'There is also the tragic coincidence that most of the world's poor have not heard the Good News of the Gospel of Jesus Christ; or they could not receive it, because it was not recognised as Good News in the way in which it was brought. This is a double injustice: they are victims of the oppression of an unjust economic order or an unjust political distribution of power, and at the same time they are deprived of the knowledge of God's special care for them.'[2] The comfortable as well need to be liberated. It is indeed good news that one can live simply and does not have to make the pursuit of wealth and security the prime purpose of life. God's good purpose is for all people in one whole world. It is God's concern, and therefore ours, to heal the wounds of poverty and to break down the barriers which divide people. If we are to respond effectively to that call, we need to act as the whole people of God, in ecumenical partnership and with all people of good will. Then we begin to be a sign to one whole world.

A BIBLICAL BASIS FOR MISSION
8 What is the imperative for mission?

(a) *We are inspired* by God's deep love for the world as demonstrated in the sending of the Son to live and die for and among us. 'For the love of Christ controls us, because we are convinced that one has died for all ... therefore, we regard no one from a human point of view' (2 Cor. 5.14,16).

(b) *We are compelled* by our understanding that God is a calling and sending God. Abraham is called and sent. Moses and the prophets are called and sent. The Father sends the Son. The Holy Spirit is sent at Pentecost. Jesus sends the disciples.

(c) *We are challenged* by the example of Jesus' mission as inaugurating the Kingdom of God – 'The Kingdom of God is at hand; repent and believe in the gospel' (Mark 1.15). Jesus calls all people into this Kingdom by their acceptance of his lordship over all creation and by their experience of salvation in following his way. Yet this is only a foretaste of a reality that is not fully achieved in this life. Here 'the aim of Jesus' ministry was not to build or create the Kingdom by carrying out some sort of plan or programme. Rather, his mission was to announce and signify it – to open people's eyes to the fact that God was with them in a new way for grace and for judgement'[3] This aim Jesus accomplished primarily through preaching, teaching and healing, and through his life, death and resurrection. These become the Church's model for mission.

(d) *We are empowered* by the Holy Spirit for mission. In the exuberance of the joy we have experienced in being healed, restored, forgiven and freed from bondage, we seek to proclaim and demonstrate the good news of the Kingdom. In mission the Church often appears as 'a rag-tag army' – not resplendent with medals of victory but rather bearing on its body the marks of the passion of Jesus. We believe, nevertheless, that in this weakness the Church carries the life and the power of Jesus (2 Cor. 4.7-12).

(e) We see signs of the Kingdom's presence, as Jesus promised:

> when men and women, being justified by faith, become a new creation in Christ;
>
> when women and men are being healed at their deepest spiritual, physical and emotional levels;
>
> when the poor are no longer hungry and are treated justly as God's beloved;
>
> when the Church takes seriously the formation of women and men into the likeness of Christ through the work of the Holy Spirit;
>
> when unjust structures of society are changed into structures of grace.[4]

THE CONCLUDING CHALLENGE

9   Christian history shows that men and women have been enabled by the Holy Spirit to respond to the Gospel out of infinitely different situations and contexts. For example, the same Gospel which invites the affluent and powerful to share wealth more generously as part of their joyful response, can enable the poor to find blessedness even in their poverty as well as promising hope of deliverance from it. (Mother Teresa's work in Calcutta is a sign of blessedness in the midst of poverty as well as being good work in the field of development and social reform.) What the Spirit therefore says to the Churches today is precisely what Jesus said to the disciples he first called.

'Repent and believe in the Gospel' (Mark 1.15). In every diocese of our Communion we are called urgently – today – to renewed faith in him who sends us to proclaim the message of God's love.

MISSION TO WHOM?

10   Jesus commanded his Church to 'go into all the world'. The whole inhabited earth provides the context for mission. The world provides a great variety of social settings, cultures and sub-cultures. Every local church, in order to be faithful to the mission of Christ, needs to understand and be responsive to the particular context into which it is sent in Christ's name.

11   'Though there are notable exceptions, the dominant model of the Church within the Anglican Communion is a pastoral one. Emphasis in all aspects of the Church's life tends to be placed on care and nurture, rather than proclamation and service.'[5]

12   The pressing needs of today's world demand that there be a massive shift to a 'mission' orientation throughout the Communion. The bishop would then become more than ever a leader in mission, and the structure of dioceses, local churches, theological training, etc. would be so reshaped that they would become instruments that generate missionary movement as well as pastoral care. At the heart of this would be a revolution in the attitude to the role of the laity. Such a revolution would enable us to see every Christian as an agent of mission. This will never be simply a matter of technique or programmes, important as these are, but the result of openness to the same Holy Spirit who sent the New Testament Church to turn the world upside down (Acts 17.6).

13   This is beginning to happen in many parts of Africa, Asia and Latin America where pioneers such as Roland Allen have been a creative influence. We still need to learn from a wide variety of models across the Communion – the wide use of paid lay evangelists and catechists in Africa and Asia, 'Living our Baptismal Covenant' training and the rediscovery of the catechumenate in the USA, programmes for growth in ministry in South America, etc. Such models have at their centre a dynamic through which the whole People of God can experience transformation; they energise them, as in the continuing Revival Movement in East Africa, with the fire of personal faith and a passion to serve Christ through his people. It is the fruit of that 'contemplation allied to commitment' (G. Gutierrez) or of 'contemplation alongside struggle' (Brother Roger, Taizé). There are whole armies of lay people in our churches to be revitalised.

The Unevangelised

14   By 'unevangelised' we mean not only those who have not been baptised, but also those who have never even been touched by the Gospel. 'We acknowledge afresh our responsibility to share the Gospel with people of

other faiths and none, always remembering the need for sensitive listening to and dialogue with them.[6]

15   There are still large areas of the world where there has been no Christian presence or proclamation; there is a pressing need for primary evangelism in such places. Even where the Church has been present for many years, there is still a need for primary evangelism among significant sections of the population. A renewed mood of confidence is growing as modernisation gives access to hitherto unreached population groups. A whole new evangelistic approach to nomadic tribes such as the Masai and the Fulani (in East and West Africa respectively) has developed.[7] Clergy and laity attach themselves to the clan on the move and traverse the terrain with them. In other regions people are moving out of the traditional religions, such as the 'Maguzawa' ('the ones who ran away', i.e. from Islam) in North Nigeria, a group which had long resisted the attempts of Islam to win their allegiance. Tribal peoples in India respond to local church teams of women and young people spreading the Gospel from village to village. Even in the more Christianised areas of Uganda and parts of Kenya, the unbaptised are coming to faith in response to a fresh approach. In West and East Africa alike, even some Muslim groups have yielded to a love that is prepared to seek them where they are.

16   In all these movements, like Peter with Cornelius, both evangelists and the evangelised are transformed by a fresh apprehension of the Good News (Acts 10.1f). Structures are rethought in the face of new situations and Christ is continually disclosed afresh in a world which is increasingly a melting-pot of faiths and cultures.

17   It is said that in Latin America the majority may not be Christians but are certainly Roman Catholics. During the last two generations, however, vast numbers have become alienated from the faith, while parallel to the official Church there are expressions of 'popular religiosity', stemming often from pre-Columbian Indian and even African religions, and appearing as 'pagan festivals' (e.g. La Tirana in Chile), the cult of the spirits of departed legendary figures (e.g. Difunta Correa in Argentina), and Voodoo (in Brazil). All of these cults claim massive adherence. It is this that has led Roman Catholic writers to describe South America as a continent that has been 'baptised but not evangelised'. Alongside other Churches, and spurred by Lambeth 1958, Anglicans have sought to minister both to Indian communities and to unchurched Spanish-speaking peoples, many of whom are open to a dynamic presentation of the Christ, and in so doing have been able to employ new approaches (such as house churches, base communities, every-member ministry and training by extension). In middle and upper class sectors, families are sometimes brought to faith through a Marriage Encounter Ministry (in close collaboration with the Roman Catholic Church).

18   Within the great melting-pot of the ancient religions of Asia, and especially the whole world of Islam, small ingrown Churches can often feel threatened, struggling for survival, not unlike some of their counterparts in the secularised West or communist East. It is here that across the Communion a movement of the Holy Spirit has begun to bring to some a fresh confidence in their resources as groups of ordinary Christian people and in the message of Christ which can suddenly become refreshingly attractive and relevant to their neighbours. We need to encourage this new trust in the Spirit within them, so that they become more and more open to the inspiration of life from within and less dependent on human and financial resources from outside.

19   People of all faiths seem to be reaching out and feeling for a God who suffers with them and meets them in their inner need. In the midst of such a search the story of Christ has a natural appeal, freshly told and strongly lived out in 'long-term loving' (a term used by Max Warren in one of his CMS Newsletters). This is surely the main approach left to those in the West as they encounter the unevangelised, those of the ethnic minorities who belong to other faiths as well as members of a largely alienated working class culture. Many of the ethnic minorities have suffered at the host community's hands and will only respond as they are befriended in love by Christians flexible enough to enter their world and prepared to stand with them, cost what it may. The negative associations Christianity has had for them have first to be exorcised.

20   But equally there are large groups of people in traditionally 'Christian' countries who belong to the dominant majority community, yet know nothing of Christ. In some countries the old pattern of Sunday school has changed and religious education in schools has born scant fruit, so that whole generations have grown up without knowledge of the Bible. As societies increasingly become secularised and technology focuses on the material realm, new generations drift into a world where Christianity has limited influence. Many today are unbaptised. This situation calls for fresh approaches and for a willingness to enter the worlds of others through costly friendships.

21   There is an imperative laid upon the Church today to move out again into the unknown, 'outside the gate', where the hard questions are asked, on the frontier, where other gods hold sway. We must help every member to realise that they have a message and a capacity to communicate it that they never imagined and to enjoy the surprise of finding that God can use them.

22   'The tasks of mission include proclamation of salvation through faith in Christ with a view to making new Christians. Another task is serving Christ in relieving human need, whether of hunger, homelessness, sickness or

injustice. There is also working for change of social structures that oppress.[8]

23   With this in mind, in the closing years of this millennium, we want to commend the vision of a 'Decade of Evangelism' already under consideration, in one form or another, by other Christian groupings. We can see few better ways by which the quality and diversity of the ministry of the whole of our Church could be enhanced than by a new determination to evangelise. We believe that upon this foundation, other aspects of Mission, as for example in the relief of need, the revision of unjust structures of society, or the transforming of the levels of human existence, must no less painstakingly be built. (See Resolution 43.)

The Lapsed

24   By 'lapsed' we mean those who have been baptised but have fallen away from their commitment to Christ and his Church.

25   Across the world, societies are all at different places in the process of technological and social transformation. This inevitably brings with it, through urbanisation, a new individualism and self-sufficiency along with fragmentation and loneliness, new freedoms of choice as well as disorientation. All societies are entering into this experience.

26   In the West this has meant a new mobility, a division between work and leisure, between a neutral public world and a private leisure world of many choices, like the different and increasingly numerous channels available on a television receiver. This brings with it a sense of rootlessness and makes it seem that the controlling forces of life and society are not under divine direction. It is here that the Churches are dissolving. The old social pressure to belong to a church is eroded in a variety of ways so that it becomes rare, even eccentric, to attend worship. The Church has not been able to handle this, not knowing even how to recapture the commitment of its nominal members. Some have lapsed due to hostility. Some feel rejected by a demanding or misapplied church discipline. Others are reacting to liturgical change or social activism. People find as many reasons as there are members for drifting away – irrelevant, boring worship, unhelpful styles of leadership, an absence of a living fellowship, professionalism. In some cases, of course, people are simply unwilling to face up to the challenges of Christian commitment, while others find that their love grows cold and their resolve to follow Christ is weakened. Today's world offers so much to distract; tolerance deteriorates into indifference and passivity, and a vague faith in science becomes fashionable. On top of all this are the pressures of competition at work and a godless working environment. To counteract these features of the modern world the Church has to create a strong interdependent community and an attractive atmosphere that nourishes people, reaching out into the world of work.

27   In Africa there are whole groups even within the Church that have been torn by conflict between their new-found faith and traditional religions (e.g. in situations of fear of witchcraft, sickness, joblessness, marital problems, polygamy). Some turn away because the moral demands of the Christian way of life are too great for them. Others, especially those who have spent time in the West, are affected by secularism, while others again who go to communist countries return immersed in ideas and a lifestyle also at loggerheads with their culture of origin. A growing need is appearing for those who are equipped intellectually and spiritually to help such people in their pilgrimage back to their culture as well as to the Church.

28   Many of the same forces are at work in the Indian sub-continent, where lapses occur due to the strenuous demands of commitment, or the problems of marriage to non-Christians, or because rural Christians are not being welcomed into an urban church. If rural Christians do become affluent in their new setting, they experience the same disintegrating forces on their faith as the West has suffered and with which urban Indian Christians are all too familiar.

29   It is here that the Churches in the Western world can give help to forewarn and forearm, as they have learnt hard lessons from their own experience of the onslaught of the forces that have swept their countries. Modern science and technology bring a new culture to the developing nations that sweeps over the scene possibly even more rapidly than in the countries where it was born. It will certainly affect the Churches in Asia, Africa and Latin America.

30   But the Western Churches also need both the ancient and the newer non-western Churches to help bring about a deep re-conversion of the soul of the West. Above all it is these Churches that can help to rekindle a passionate concern for sinners, sufferers, victims of injustice, the confused and the lost.

31   The world is needing a Church that is deeply rooted in the life of Christ, yet open and loving. When this grips our imagination once again, we may be able to begin to penetrate and permeate our world with a new sense of the presence and love of 'God with us'. Across the world, partner Churches can help each other to discover insights into the ways the Good News is lived and spread.

Unreached Young People

32   In the face of increasing secularism and pluralism in many countries, the influence of any one faith, or of religion generally, is deliberately excluded from education as potentially divisive. We must, however, emphasise that for public education to have integrity, it must be concerned with teaching human and religious values, and those subjects and concerns that benefit

particular culture as well as society at large. The Church must play a significant role in enabling this to happen and in challenging the educational systems of our communities.

33   We have an urgent and essential mission to young people; but they, in
turn, can assist the Church greatly in its mission to the rest of society. Present
structures do not readily invite or encourage youth to participate meaning-
fully in the life and work of the Church. Those who remain in the Church
often do so by being silent and obedient, without voice or participation.
Meanwhile, they are often the sacrificial victims of war, unemployment,
military regimes and other prejudice.[9]

34   Christians need to study and understand the new international youth
culture of our day, by reading its literature, being familiar with its art, and
listening to its lyrics and music.

All of these often express the shared hopes, fears and desperation of
today's youth. In many ways, the youth of today's world share a lifestyle that
has strikingly similar elements, often marked by the signs of death and
despair. If the Spirit is to liberate and transform them, we need to know what
separates young people from their elders, what causes them to despair. In
our mission to them, we need to speak much more sensitively and attentively
to the questions they are asking, and in a language that relates to their needs.
Above all, we need to train and mobilise Christian young people to be witnesses and agents of mission to their contemporaries.

35   As we seek to develop our own way of reaching out to young people, we
need to recognise and affirm the significant experience and ministries of ecumenical, interchurch and para-church agencies which already have effective
youth ministries. (See Resolution 48.)

The Rural Poor

36   Poverty has economic aspects but it is more than that. Poverty brings
cultural death; it brings destruction of individuals, of cultures, of nations.
Women most frequently bear the heavier burdens of poverty. As Christians,
we are called to enter the world of the poor; and if we think we have nothing
to receive from them, we do not love. 'God is the ultimate reason why we
should love the poor: not because the poor are good but because God is
good' (G. Gutierrez).

37   The forces which marginalise the rapidly growing numbers of urban
dwellers, likewise make victims among rural people. Although each group
presents different needs and makes different demands of our mission, urban
and rural are in many instances inextricably inter-related by virtue of political and economic systems; to pursue mission to the one without due concern
for the other is unrealistic and incomplete.

37

38   Rural areas are frequently perceived as being places where unimportant things happen, as if tilling the land and tending the herds are not vital and honourable occupations. Thus, countless numbers of rural folk drift to the cities every year, only to find squalor and deprivation of the harshest sort. In its mission to the rural poor, the Church needs to affirm by every means possible the inherent goodness of the countryside, and to teach that all of life and creation is important and potentially viable. Yet some of our sisters and brothers in the developing nations are too hurt to hear the Gospel, and too hungry to concentrate on its message. In such cases, the *deeds* of mission need to accompany the *words* of the evangel.

39   We recognise the long-standing deprivation of millions of people in rural areas. The isolation of many of the rural communities heightens their sense of being excluded from the main-line life of the community. They are especially vulnerable to economic disasters. The fact that no one visits them adds to their feeling of hopelessness and to the lack of a sense of their own value. The Church must not turn from their cry for material and spiritual food.

Refugees
40   Among those marginalised by societies and government, and for whom the compassionate mission of Jesus Christ needs special focusing, are refugees and immigrants. The former generally suffer from loss of identity, respect, community and hope, while the latter too frequently are forced to leave culture, country and native language behind.

41   This Lambeth Conference commends the *1988 Report of the Anglican Refugee Ministry Network,* which describes the situation and needs of refugees throughout the world.

The Urban Poor and the Marginalised
42   In Europe and North America, the 'mainline' Churches have persistently failed to root themselves among the urban poor. As the self-confident succeed in moving away to better jobs and better housing, huge one-class quarters have developed both in the inner city and in more modern public housing developments around the edges of many cities. People there face interlocking deprivations, experiencing the greatest unemployment, the poorest housing, least access to health care, transport and schools. Their poverty is not absolute, as in some 'Third World' countries; but relative poverty hurts in the middle of affluent societies, in which advertising proclaims that all can expect to enjoy life in its fullness through material possessions. Relative poverty brings the sense of being marginalised and excluded from the normal life of affluent nations. As long as the majority of members of the Church seem bound up with the comfortable and the successful, expecting to find leadership only from those who achieve successfully in school, people who are excluded and powerless feel the Church has nothing to say to them.

43 The ranks of those left behind among the urban poor are swelled by migrant groups or minority ethnic groups who may have lived, as Black Americans have, for generations in those cities or who may be recent arrivals. Black people, Asians and Hispanic people frequently find themselves trapped in the poorest quarters of such cities which had seemed to beckon with opportunities. In particular, racial disadvantage makes it twice as unlikely, for example in Britain, for black young persons to obtain jobs, as compared with white.

44 Research has been carried out in this area of concern in several Provinces; a recent example has been *Faith in the City,* the 1985 report of the Archbishop of Canterbury's Commission on Urban Priority Areas. This challenged the Church of England to make space for black Christians, many of whom still cling to their membership and faith in the Church's leadership and decision-making. Many who had been churchgoers, for example in the West Indies, moved away from the mainline Churches within a few years of coming to British cities. Perhaps they were tolerated up to certain numbers and certain levels, but they felt they were not given any say in the making of decisions of a white-led Church. Some have turned to black-led Churches: some have given up any connection with the Christian Church. *Faith in the City* pressed the Church of England to recognise God-given gifts by more appropriate training for black or white people whose self-confidence had been damaged. The report also said there should be a major shift in resources, to pay for clergy in the poorest areas and to help lift the burden of the maintenance of old church buildings which so dominates the life of some small congregations.

45 In the developing nations, it is rural poverty which drives people into the cities to search for jobs and survival. Around great cities like Mexico City, Sao Paulo, Rio de Janeiro, Lima, Ibadan, Nairobi, Johannesburg and Calcutta, vast shanty towns or townships grow uncontrollably. Barbed wire and security devices protect factories and gracious homes from the poor. Fear leads the better-off to believe that the only answer lies in tougher policies of law and order.

46 There is a great challenge to national Churches in such countries to avoid repeating the failures of European and North American Churches. Do they give to churches in poor districts similar resources as to those in well-off suburbs where there are strong congregations? Do they believe that God can plant strongly-rooted churches within the most hurt parts of the cities, or do they expect only to recruit individuals whose ambition is to move out of such communities? Do they work for justice and better opportunities for the urban poor? These questions apply also in Europe, North America, Australia and New Zealand.[10]

47   'Hopelessness, isolation, lack of vision and destruction of the spirit are the faith issues that underlie the worldly dilemmas of helplessness, hunger, unemployment, inadequate housing, lack of education, and crime...[11]

48   Renewal is God's gift to the Church through the Holy Spirit. Christians individually and corporately receive it by being open to the Holy Spirit and being sensitive at the same time to realities of the context in which they live. Among both clergy and laity there may be unwillingness for the changes that renewal will entail, involving new ideas, concepts and attitudes. It is important to remember that in renewal there is both divine initiative and human response.

49   While renewal covers all aspects of the Church's life, it is renewal in mission with which we are particularly concerned here. If mission in any or all of its aspects is not being fulfilled it may be because of lack of motivation and concern to share the faith with others or to serve the purpose of God's Kingdom in the world. There may be a lack of vision of what God intends or of how the Gospel may be effectively proclaimed in particular situations. There is need, therefore, for all God's people to be prepared to wait upon him in prayer, open to him to show how they are to fulfil his mission where they are. They are to be ready to receive his enabling with whatever gifts and new experiences of his grace he wills to give them.

RENEWAL OF THE CHURCH IN MISSION

CHARISMATIC RENEWAL

50   We rejoice and give thanks for all God has done within Anglican and other Churches through charismatic renewal. The benefits both to congregations and individuals are enriching the whole Body of Christ. Exclusive claims on behalf of the charismatic renewal, however, lead to damaging divisions within the Church. For any person or group to make their own experience of God's renewal the standard for all is to ignore the comprehensive nature of God's dealings with men and women in different generations and a diversity of cultural situations.

51   The words 'renewal' and 'charismatic' can cause confusion. 'Renewal' can apply to every aspect of the Church's life. 'Charismatic' can be used to identify a particular experience of the Holy Spirit, and thus a movement within the Church of those who had that experience.

52   The word is also taken to mean inspirational, gifted, outstanding in characteristics. Here it touches the original idea of Spirit-given gifts. And indeed the *charismata* of the Spirit are for the use and sharing of the whole Church. In welcoming the gifts, however, we emphasise the need for their exercise to be subject to the discipline of the Body of Christ within the Church where they are used.

53   Baptism, as well as being the seal of the Spirit, is the sacramental pledge and promise of the gifts of the Spirit. Each baptised person is called to enter increasingly into and to know in experience those gifts God has for him or her. An active seeking with open mind of all the Spirit wills to give is essential. For some, particularly those in the charismatic movement, the realisation in experience of the Spirit's gifts may happen suddenly and even dramatically. For others, it may be a gradual process through life. Again, there may be a combination of both, with many new stages of development in the renewing of the Spirit.

54   All renewal is essentially the Spirit's work, though an openness to his working is required of his people. All true gifts and authentic experience of the Spirit's renewing grace are for sharing with the whole Church in a spirit of love, the highest gift. While recognising the importance of a living experience of God's renewal, emphasis is laid, nevertheless, on the need to test the authenticity of any claimed experience by Scripture. Such testing cannot be by individual judgement alone, but must be carried out communally, within the shared life of the Church, where the accumulated wisdom of past and present insights may be applied.

55   In paying particular attention to charismatic renewal, we do not wish to deny that Anglicanism has nurtured many different traditions of spirituality. We rejoice in the different ways God leads his people into deeper fellowship with himself in holiness and service. The book *Open to the Spirit* identifies among these traditions the Catholic, Evangelical, Liberal, Monastic, as well as the Charismatic, which itself has influenced the others. The book also illustrates how spiritualities like that of the Orthodox tradition may enrich our relationship with God. All in their own way need constant renewal by openness to the Spirit.[12]

56   It is important that all renewal be firmly set within a Trinitarian theology. The communion of the people of God is life with the Father through the Son in the Spirit. Here we recognise the particular responsibility of Christian leaders in teaching, especially that of a bishop, lest unbalanced expressions of spirituality prevail.

57   The effects of renewal on churches and individuals can be revolutionary, leading to revitalised worship, new attention to the Scriptures, especially in joint study, deepened mutual care, an upsurge in lay ministry, greater commitment in witness and stewardship, enlarged involvement in ecumenical relationships and activity, and heightened expectation of signs of God's presence. In some such situations clergy may feel threatened. They need encouragement to be alert to genuine signs of the Spirit's work and to exercise a teaching and guiding role.

58   One of the gifts evident in the charismatic renewal, *glossolalia,* speaking in tongues, deserves particular comment. By its very nature it exists as a salutary reminder of the sovereign freedom of the Spirit, but like all other spiritual gifts it must take its place under the discipline of the Body of Christ, the Church, as one and only one of all the diverse manifestations of the Spirit given to nurture its members (1 Cor. 12–14).

RENEWAL OF THE CHURCH IN LITURGY
59   The renewal of the Church for its mission is intimately bound up with its worship. Our worship should in fact, by the power of the Spirit, bring renewal to the Church. But we are also aware that more specific guidance on the subject of liturgy might, for all our purpose of mission, appear somewhat inward-looking and over-concerned with detail if set out in full here. We therefore provide a fuller discussion of worship as the last section of the Report (paras. 177-209), and recommend that it be both studied there and taken into account in the developing argument of our statement here.

RENEWAL IN THEOLOGY
60   We are concerned with the renewal of the Church for mission because we want the Church to do what God wants. The commandment to love the Lord our God is clear, doing so with all our *mind* as well as heart, soul and strength. We are no less aware that we are to love our neighbour as ourselves. 'Doing theology' is an important aspect of that loving, both of God and of our fellow human beings.

61   It is the theologians' responsibility to ensure that any longing for renewal is not the sort that bypasses the task of wrestling with the Word of God.

62   So much of our talking is to ourselves. We need to affirm the gift or the ability to do theology and apply it to the encounter of the Church with the secular world where knowledge of God has been excluded. Another area of encounter is with other faiths, where there may be a sense of the supernatural but where God as revealed uniquely in Jesus Christ is not known. Those who are particularly gifted in doing theology should, through the consecration of their gift for theological reflection, enable believing men and women to conduct their mission in the world and help them to speak a 'language' that can be understood.

63   It is clear that we do not think of theologians as being separate from the common life of either the Church or the wider community in which the Church is placed and where it is to witness to God's love. Talking about God cannot be separated from talking to God. Theological reflection is not separate from Bible study, prayer and the life of worship and commitment of the community of believers. Gustavo Gutierrez, for example, is a theologian

whose doing of theology happens in the environment of a parish ministry near the university where he is a teacher of theology. His name is associated with Liberation Theology but this title does not restrict the 'doing' to any particular mode nor is it applicable to only one kind of social order. 'This way of doing theology which begins where we find ourselves (in a specific political, social or economic environment) and beginning to ask questions from there, has been found useful in many "developing" countries and might very well serve even in some "developed" countries, where the Church also needs to proclaim and to live out the "Good News".'[13] Since people's questions are different in different parts of the world we would stress the importance of a dialogue within the Anglican Communion, which would prevent us from growing apart because of the theological work we have to do.

EVANGELISM AND TRANSFORMATION
64   Renewal is a mystery, for the Spirit, like the blowing of the wind, renews wherever he wills. However we can discern that a renewed people will

(1) seek to deepen their relationship with God and with each other in prayer, love and truth

(2) seek to share the message and their experience of the Gospel

(3) seek to be agents in the formation of communities which accept the values of the Kingdom of God.

65   Evangelism is the communication of the good news of Christ's Kingdom and his accompanying command to people to repent, believe and be baptised into his Body, the Church.

66   Transformation is the positive action of establishing conditions where wholeness in human life may be enjoyed. Transformation is to be preferred to the word 'development', which can give the impression that some countries have arrived at a particular stage of development and therefore do not need any further change. Transformation is equally applicable to the developed and the so-called developing countries. Transformation of structures will often involve political action. Transformation will mean that all that demeans human dignity (e.g. discrimination on grounds of race, sex or class), or prevents proper access to basic community resources (e.g. medical and educational facilities), or pollutes the environment or allows natural resources to be plundered (e.g. the removal of fish by some powers in the Pacific Ocean or the removal of indigenous people from their land) is to be resisted.

67   Both evangelism and the transformation of society are responsibilities to be fulfilled by the whole people of God. In some cases, they will go hand in hand; the efforts for transformation will be visible expressions of the

Church's concern for the total person as the evangelistic message is proclaimed and shared. On other occasions, transformation will follow as people turn to God, are incorporated into the Church, and seek, as they are taught, to witness in the world by their lifestyle as they serve their fellows, conscious of their weakness but also of the power of God. Transformation is often a radical process in danger of being identified with a political programme or being manipulated by political powers. Thus it must have a clear Christian and biblical base. We have noted the critical problems which arise in a culture when it encounters the Gospel of Christ. It requires wisdom to know how and what to preserve and to liberate in the culture itself. The vision is before us of the new Kingdom where 'the glory and the honour of the nations will be brought into it' (Rev. 21.26). This gives us encouragement to transform culture so that it is free from all that restricts human wholeness. We also observe the special difficulties in penetrating a truly secular culture with the Good News of Jesus. We need to discover new entry points into a world view which has excluded the knowledge of God.

68   We must repent of our failure to be deeply committed to the proclamation by word and deed of the Good News of Jesus. Our preoccupation with the maintenance of church structures has often absorbed our time and energies and it is here that we need to be renewed, for the Gospel has been entrusted to us to share. Likewise we must repent of our failure to be deeply committed to the questions of justice and the stewardship of our resources. It has been easy to fit in with the world's standards. Here too we must be renewed.

69   A key to renewal will be the renewal of the teaching and prophetic ministry in our Communion. Not only in ancient times did people perish because of a lack of vision. We need actively to encourage serious, thoughtful preaching and teaching in its many forms, so that God's people can engage in both evangelism and transforming service in love and hope.

THE MINISTRY OF THE WHOLE CHURCH

70   To the many baptised members of the one Body of Christ, the Lord of the Church gives a variety of spiritual gifts. Yet the primary ministry of the great majority of Christians is their service of humanity in the everyday work of the world. The Church needs to own and value such a ministry of service in the name of Christ. We need not suppose that the various New Testament summaries of gifts for ministry are complete or exhaustive: the stress is on the variety of such gifts, their God-given nature, and their widespread distribution. No one member, however 'gifted', can meet the needs of the Body (let alone the world) from his or her gifts alone.

71   The fact that the ministry belongs to every baptised member of the

Body of Christ has important consequences for the selection and training of clergy. They must primarily be those 'apt to teach' (1 Tim. 3.2), and 'able to teach others also' (2 Tim. 2.2) – not in any theoretical or academic sense alone, but in 'the equipping of the saints for the work of ministry' (Eph. 4.11). If all Christian people, ordained and lay, are to be able with confidence to become involved in the Church's mission, they need help in learning how to give a reason for the hope that is in them (1 Pet. 3.15). Many appear increasingly ill-instructed in the Scriptures, confused about their faith, and lacking in courage and confidence in witness. This underlines the Church's need for a new concern about its teaching ministries. The effects are seen not only in the weakness of our mission, but in the Church's failure to take seriously the world of work in which most of her members spend most of their lives.

72   We see a need for Christian teaching related to issues in the workaday world, as well as Christian professional support-groups. But, more generally, we look for an increased seriousness in the whole task of building mature and informed disciples. The ordained ministry must be a primary resource here, with its preaching and teaching, and skills in pastoral care and formation. But often lay-led groups, or groups in which ministerial teams of lay and ordained work together, have much to offer. We instance the all-age Sunday school programme of many local churches in America; and the account from Nigeria of how a regular Day of Fasting and Prayer, held weekly in every church, gave freedom for informal worship, spiritual fellowship and sharing, and serious study of the Scriptures in company with fellow-Christians.

73   By such means the Church, as well as the individual Christian, will be built up in the faith, and the whole People of God, in community, be equipped 'to carry the whole Gospel to the whole world ... to young and old, sick and poor, male and female – to all races in all places and in every conceivable circumstance' (including, we would add, the rich and healthy, some of whom are also to be numbered among the lost).[14]

74   We were reminded of the example of John Wesley, and of the need to meet people with the Gospel where they are – to go out to them in villages and market-places (and their urban equivalents) and not remain confined 'within the four corners of a sacred building'. Part of the reason why in some Western Churches evangelisation today seems stifled must lie in the dominant clerical emphasis on ministry that has so often prevailed: whereas it is in truth the lay Christian who lives 'on the frontier', who mixes most readily with non-Christian workmates, neighbours and friends, and who is able to extend the 'fringe contacts' of the Church, who may under God be next year's enquirers and converts.

45

THE MINISTRY OF YOUNG PEOPLE

75 We affirm particularly the calling of young people within this ministry, not as future servants of the Church, but as present ministers, called within the whole body of Christ. The Belfast '88 Report, *Love in any Language,* issued:

(1) a call for the priority of mission both in prayer and action;

(2) a call for education in mission, liturgy and Scripture to be made more available to lay people;

(3) a call for increased participation by young people in Church life and decision-making;

(4) a call for 'a planned and co-ordinated effort towards renewal within the Churches', supported by a programme of training (and re-training) and mission audit and analysis.[15]

INCLUSIVE LANGUAGE

76 An all-male group is not best equipped to speak on the issue of inclusive language. Nevertheless we believe that it affords an important indication of the Church's resolve to take seriously the full range of ministries of all its members. We look for its adoption, as confirming the common humanity of men and women, in all appropriate statements and liturgies which bear upon ministry and mission. We believe the Church should be sensitive to this issue in all languages and particularly in current and contemporary writing and drafting. Respect must, however, be shown to the linguistic integrity of older and traditional texts. Changes, where possible, should be sensitive and unobtrusive; also not every ancient text may in fact lend itself to verbal changes even of this kind and still remain suitable for liturgical use. We take it as axiomatic that any version of the Holy Scriptures must remain a faithful translation; and we cannot countenance variations which do violence to the original, whether in the interests of inclusive language or for any other reason.

77 Perhaps of more profound significance are issues raised by a call for inclusive language regarding the Deity. In our understanding, Almighty God is without gender, and the image of God given to humanity in our creation is reflected equally in male and female. It is true that the revelation of God is to be seen at its fullest in Jesus Christ, the Incarnate Son; yet this 'scandal of particularity' must be seen in the light of Christ's significance for all as well as the inclusiveness of the Risen and Ascended Lord. The Bible – including the New Testament – pictures God in 'female' a well as 'male' roles. The issue of inclusive language is not simply a psychological or sociological concern of our day, but a reminder to us all of aspects in our image of God not officially denied, but perhaps little considered.

78   The fact that the Bible uses male imagery (Lord, King, Father, etc.) and male pronouns to speak about God, does not excuse us from using such language with awareness and sensitivity: inclusive language issues are more than mere semantics. They invite us to be attentive to the whole of God's self-revelation, to rejoice in the redemption given to all people in the Person of Jesus, and to proclaim the ultimate unity of all the People of God, gathered into one in the eternal Godhead.

THE MINISTRY OF HEALING

79   In the widest sense of the words, healing and salvation are two ways of describing the work of Jesus Christ. Within the work of Christ's salvation the healing of the sick holds a significant place because by it he both demonstrated the love of God and proclaimed that the Kingdom had come in his person (Luke 7.21-22). Jesus did not intend the Good News to be proclaimed by word alone, but also by the mighty works of God. (See, for example, the use of words 'seen' and 'heard' in Luke 7.22 and in Acts 8.6; also the prayer in Acts 4.29-30.)

80   Jesus commanded his disciples to heal the sick and cast out demons as well as to preach the Kingdom of God (Luke 9.1-2,6; 10.9,17; Mark 6.12-13; Matt 10.7-8). This they continued to do after his Ascension, as Acts and various references in the Epistles evidence. This ministry did not cease with the Apostles but throughout the history of the Church, God has not left himself without witness in any generation to his power to heal. In most parts of the Anglican Communion today the healing ministry is pursued, along with the preaching of the Gospel, in obedience to Christ's command, and is seen as a normal part of the ministry of the Church to its members, and as a sign of the power and truth of the Gospel in evangelism.

81   The Lambeth Conference of 1920 called for a report on the subject, which urged the whole Communion to be involved in the ministry of healing by teaching about it, co-operating with the medical profession, and developing intercessory prayer groups in every parish. These same three words – teaching, co-operation and prayer – were taken up in 1944 by Archbishop William Temple when he set up in England the Churches' Council for Health and Healing.

82   'The Church is called to exercise a ministry of healing to the sick whatever their condition of mind and body. Such a ministry of love aims:

   (1) to restore the sense of relationship with God and the community;

   (2) to affirm the body's natural powers of healing;

   (3) to use all medical knowledge and skills to assist restoration or relieve pain;

47

(4) to establish peace as we acknowledge that we are mortal and yet are born for eternity.'[16]

83   This ministry is part of a total ministry which includes:

(a) medical research, the prevention of disease and the promotion of healthy lifestyles;

(b) the work of the medical and caring professions;

(c) ministries of prayer and sacrament;

(d) the counselling and support of the troubled, the sick and the dying.

84   All the baptised and not only the clergy can be involved in the Church's ministry of healing (James 5.13f), but there are those to whom the Holy Spirit gives special gifts of healings (1 Cor. 12.9); both words are plural in Greek).

85   Both in his earthly life and now through his Body the Church, Jesus' healing work is concerned with the wholeness of the person in body, mind and spirit. In obedience to his command and with the guidance of and strength of the Spirit, we offer the prayer of faith for the sick (James 5.15) with humility and love, but we leave to his wisdom the way in which he acts. There remains a mystery why one person recovers and one does not when there has been equally faithful prayer for both, but acknowledging God's sovereignty in all things we continue to offer this ministry. Even physical impairment can be used to God's glory and, for the Christian, death itself is swallowed up in victory.

86   We urge all Bishops to encourage, to oversee and to be themselves involved in the ministry of healing in their dioceses. The following are some ways of being obedient to our Lord's commission:

(1) to declare that the ministry of healing should be a regular part of the ministry in every congregation;

(2) to encourage intercessory prayer by members of every congregation, remembering our Lord's promise about agreeing together in prayer (Matt. 18.19);

(3) to foster the use of the laying on of hands with prayer by the clergy and members of the congregation;

(4) to bless and provide oil for the anointing of the sick and to encourage priests to make this anointing a regular part of their ministry;

(5) to develop counselling ministries, concerned with inner healing and the healing of relationships, and to provide for the ministry of absolution and the assurance of forgiveness;

(6) to provide and oversee ministries of deliverance from demonic

oppression where this is needed, and, where appropriate, with medical consultation;

(7) to establish in each Province and/or diocese centres for the ministry of healing, both for ministry to the sick and for the teaching and support of those engaged in this ministry at the local level;

(8) to work in partnership with doctors, nurses and all involved in the care of the sick, and to encourage medical research and the study of related ethical issues;

(9) to ask for a fair distribution of resources and personnel so that all nations and all sections of the community may receive adequate health care;

(10) to embrace the sick and impaired, for example, drug addicts and sufferers from AIDS, as part of the fellowship of the whole Church;

(11) to support the Church's medical mission work throughout the world as a vital arm of its ministry and outreach;

(12) to work for the establishment of hospices for the terminally ill and to provide appropriate ministry for the dying and their families; this will need to include counselling regarding the continuance or otherwise of life-support systems.

THE MINISTRY OF THE LAITY IN THE WORLD AND IN THE CHURCH

87   There is one mission and one ministry which comes from Christ. This is expressed in various ways in different cultures. Despite the fact that we come from a variety of backgrounds, we have come to a common concern that both the mission and maintenance of the Church in the future depend upon a radical commitment to the central role of the laity.

88   We understand by 'laity' every baptised member of the Church – men and women, old and young. This definition also includes the threefold order of ordained ministry, called out by God to serve the Church principally by enabling others to exercise that ministry which is given to them by God, as well as existing as a sign to the local church of its membership of the wider Christian family.

89   We are convinced that the process of mission and ministry begins with the local community. For this to become a reality the Church as a whole needs to reverse many of its habitual ways of thought. The local congregation determines the agenda for the Church at other levels, whose principal vocation is to respond to and support the mission of the local Church.

90   This local mission is discerned through prayer, the study of God's Word, and reflection upon the situation in which the Church is set. 'What do we believe to be the will of God for this community?' must be a primary

question. An immediate further question involves the identification of the resources necessary to carry out his will. Faithfulness to this search leads always to new commitment and specific action in worship, fellowship, evangelism and service. Through this the laity will find their ministry. It cannot be sufficiently emphasised that this conviction calls for a radical change of attitude on behalf of most clergy and laity, who must come now to a new understanding of their role and of their dependence on each other.

EMPOWERING THE WHOLE PEOPLE OF GOD FOR HIS MISSION AND MINISTRY

91 The risen Christ says,
As the Father has sent me, even so I send you.
... Receive the Holy Spirit. (John 20.21,22).

God's initiative in Jesus Christ is the source of all mission and ministry of the whole people of God (*laos*). God graciously calls us to share in his mission and ministry. *All* are called; the *laos* includes men and women, young and old, the ordained and those called 'laity'.

92 We had the thrill of meeting with some of the young people who had attended the International Conference of Young Anglicans in Belfast, and we want to endorse their conviction that mission and ministry arise from a strong personal relationship with God and through personal and corporate renewal by the Spirit of God. In our working group we had collaborating testimony to add to theirs: that people spontaneously offer their lives to be used by God in his Church and world when this happens. The young people pleaded with the bishops 'to provide strong spiritual leadership' in this regard. We would urge all bishops to take back to their dioceses what the young people are saying to us, especially on pages 5 to 10 of their report.

93 'All over the Anglican Communion, lay people are asking for more training for ministry. It is evident that wherever there is renewal in the Church they are in the middle of it ... The need is not confined only to equipping Christians for tasks in the life of the Church, but for serving God as thoughtful human beings in a rapidly changing world where lay people are in the vanguard of the Church's Mission.'[17] We note that in some places in our Communion such training is already developing and we recommend that a listing of models, training programmes and available resources be made and shared widely. Clergy and lay leaders will need to be helped to become 'enablers' of this process, and effective methods and appropriate materials need to be developed.

94 All this will take an investment of people, time and money. We noted further that those dioceses which were willing to set people aside for this work and spend a significant portion of their budget on training were already experiencing a growth and spread of ministry. In particular the youth were

asking for such an investment in them as 'today's Church'. This point is related to the issue of stewardship and tithing.

A THEOLOGY OF LAY MINISTRY

BAPTISM AND MINISTRY

95 'If you are a baptized Christian, you are already a minister. Whether you are ordained or not is immaterial. No matter how you react, the statement remains true. You may be surprised, alarmed, pleased, antagonized, suspicious, acquiescent, scornful or enraged. Nevertheless, you are a minister of Christ.'[18]

96 The Anglican Communion is caught up in an intense and far-reaching revolution through which we are discovering that the old and traditional distinctions between lay and ordained ministry are dissolving and new concepts of total ministry are evolving. (See Resolution 45.)

97 Where shall we look for the theology of this modern revolution? If it has no sound theology then it will soon pass away. We believe that our baptism, resting as it does on the work of the risen Christ, is both the call and the empowering of all ministry in the Church: and that the theological expression of that ministry is seen in the liturgical rites of initiation contained in the various Prayer Books of the Anglican Communion.

98 We must go further back. Our own baptism becomes significant for us only when we become conscious of being a part of the saving life and work of Jesus Christ, our Lord. It is his work, in his Incarnation, Passion, Resurrection and Ascension, which gives new life to us. (See Rom. 6.3-11.)

THE AUTHENTICATION OF MINISTRY

99 This gift of new life received at our baptism carries with it the implied gift of authority for ministry. That graceful authority grows and develops within us throughout our lives by the presence and operation of the Holy Spirit.

THE MINISTRY OF THE LAITY AND THE ORDAINED MINISTRY

100 It is a particular test of ordained ministers to lead and to enable the laity in ministry within the Church and to the world.

THE PRIESTLY TASK

101 There are many biblical models and figures for this ministry, each of which gives a particular insight. We offer a reflection on just one of these, but would urge that other biblical models be also pursued, in order that a richer theological understanding of the laity's ministry be developed.

102   The biblical model we have chosen is that of the 'priesthood of all believers'. In the New Testament Jesus is seen as our great High Priest (Heb. 3.1; 7.26; 8.1,2) in whom his followers become *as an entirety* a holy nation, a royal priesthood (1 Pet. 2.9), whose calling is *together* to declare 'the wonderful deeds' of their Lord. It is therefore within this people who together are a priesthood that the ordained are called to their particular task and the lay to theirs.

103   What is implied by this description of the Church as a 'priesthood of believers'? Priestly tasks may involve prophecy and pastoring, liturgy and teaching, but it can be said that traditionally, in expressing divine dealings with humanity, priesthood has always done three things: it blesses, it absolves and it sacrifices. This holds true for all sorts and conditions of priests in all times and in all places. We believe it is possible to expand our more narrow understanding of blessing, absolving, and sacrifices, to include the work of all believers who are ministering in the world rather than at the altar.

104   So the ministry of the laity must also, but *in its own way,* be to bless in God's name, to absolve in God's name, and to celebrate the sacrifice of the Lord Jesus. The characteristic arena of such ministry is the world which the Church exists to save. What therefore does it mean to say that the laity must bless, absolve and sacrifice within it?

105   It is the particular vocation of the Christian laity to declare by word and silence, by action and suffering, that the world is *God's,* created by him and redeemed by him. *This* is the nature of the 'blessing' lay Christians bestow in the context of their secular callings. Similarly their 'priestly absolution' is in the quality of costly forgiving they live out in their encounter with the world in the name of Jesus and the power of the Spirit. Their celebration of the sacrifice of Jesus occurs whenever in sharing the tragedy and suffering of the society around them they draw it in to the costly forgiving they live out in their encounters in the world in the name of Jesus and the power of the Spirit. Their celebration of the sacrifice of Jesus also occurs whenever in sharing the tragedy and suffering of the society around them they draw it in to the costly gift of Christ himself and rest it there in the confidence of the Resurrection.

THE RESPONSIBILITY OF THE CHURCH

106   This means that lay people must take hold of their ministerial responsibility for doing their Christian living out in the world. And *only when their Church requires of them* that they see their sharing of the life of the streets and shops, of wrestling with the land, of feeding, housing and transportation, of business and unemployment, *as their Christian vocation of ministry,* will they begin to be effective. For then through the Holy Spirit they will bring blessing, forgiveness and the sacrifice of the Lord Jesus for the world.

107   The ministry of the lay Christian in the midst of the everyday affairs of this world is often the point at which the world and the Church meet in person to person encounter. It is through such encounter that the grace of Christ is often experienced. The buildings, bureaucracy and other resources of the Church are not ends in themselves but must be seen to support such ministry.

THE MINISTRY OF THE LAITY IN THE CONGREGATION

108   Though the special calling of the laity is a Christian vocation to the world, sustaining this requires that there be a 'gathered Church' to support, solace and upbuild. This is the particular (though not the only) function of the ordained to serve, both by formal liturgical service and by pastoring and teaching. But there will be laity whose special calling is to work with the ordained in maintaining the worship, servicing fabric and buildings, sharing in the teaching and the building up of the Church community.

109   We affirm the *mutuality* of lay and ordained ministry *within* the gathered church: (a) in sharing responsibility for decision-making; (b) in laity nurturing clergy even as clergy nurture laity; (c) in relating to ordained and lay in the wider Church; (d) in sharing together in the work of the formal liturgy of worship.

THE MISSION OF THE LAITY

110   The basic point we would make is that our work as ministers is rooted and grounded in the work of the Risen Christ. It is at our baptism that we are made children of God with both power and authority to go out and to 'turn the world upside down' (Acts 17.6). (See Resolution 42.)

PHYSICAL STRUCTURES

111   Delegates to the 1988 International Conference of Young Anglicans gave us evidence of the alienation young people can experience on account of church buildings. They find it hard to achieve a sense of belonging when facilities for meeting are limited and the shape of buildings inhibits variety in worship. Some of the difficulties arise from the resistance of established believers, who sense that reordering and redeveloping is based on passing fashion, and are not convinced of any theological grounding for it.

112   In this aspect, as in many others, there is a need for *theological exploration of the relationship between past inheritance and present renewal*. Without it, convictions are likely to remain polarised between loyalty to Gospel inheritance and obedience to the leading of the Spirit. This is particularly so in countries where the Church has been planted for many centuries.
   We urge:
   (a) that new church buildings should be in a local style rather than that

of an unfamiliar culture, and that full provision should be made for every section of the believing community;

(b) that in adaptation of church buildings for uses additional to that of worship, the needs of different age-groups be taken into account.

THE ORDAINED MINISTRY

113   We acknowledge that the foundation of all ministry is that royal priesthood of all God's people within which, by virtue of his or her baptism, every Christian is called to exercise a ministry of witness, love and service. So we welcome unreservedly that broad variety of lay and ordained ministries which now witness to the vitality of the Church in many parts of the Anglican Communion.

114   Indeed we have come to see that the need is now for greater clarification and sharper delineation of the ordained ministries of bishop, priest and deacon within the life of the Church.

115   We do not feel it necessary to set out again that understanding of the ordained ministry, firmly placed in the context of the ministry of the whole Church and existing for the service of all the faithful, that is illuminated in ARCIC I and *Baptism, Eucharist and Ministry* (WCC). We hope that these documents together with the ACC reports will continue to be studied to help the Church to a richer understanding of her ordained ministry.

116   We believe in the soundness of the perception of many Christians that the marks of a minister they respect and love are a mysterious amalgam of personal witness, faithful preaching, competent teaching, liturgical presence and courageous leadership.

117   We ask that in our search for a deeper understanding of the role of the ordained ministries in the Church of God special attention should be given to:

(a) The significance of vocation. Some feel called by God to give their lives back to him in a special way. The Church recognises, tests and accepts these offerings;

(b) The quality of the ministerial life. The Christian tradition recognises that the minister, if not a person of prayer, is nothing. We affirm that the minister's chosen path of close discipleship of Jesus Christ should show itself in holiness of life;

(c) The reality of authority. Those accepting ordination should willingly place themselves under the authority of the bishop and the Church;

(d) The meaning of apostolicity. Jesus chose, empowered and sent out the twelve. The anointing and commissioning for the ordained ministry comes from the Lord, who constantly calls the Church to go out in obedience to his sending.

We wish to commend the following passage.

118   *Guiding Principles for the Exercise of the Ordained Ministry in the Church (BEM, para 26)*

Three considerations are important in this respect. The ordained ministry should be exercised in a *personal, collegial* and *communal* way. It should be *personal* because the presence of Christ among his people can most effectively be pointed to by the person ordained to proclaim the Gospel and to serve the Lord in unity of life and witness. It should also be *collegial,* for there is need for a college of ordained ministers sharing in the common task of representing the concerns of the community. Finally, the intimate relationship between the ordained ministry and the community should find expression in a *communal* dimension where the exercise of the ordained ministry is rooted in the life of the community and requires the community's effective participation in the discovery of God's will and the guidance of the Spirit.[19]

MINISTERIAL PRIESTHOOD

119   While noting the work done in particular Provinces on the ministerial priesthood, we ask for further work to be done on a Communion-wide basis. In the meanwhile we commend the following passage from the Lambeth Conference Report of 1968, page 101, 'The Work of a Priest'.

Ministry means *service.* A priest is called to be the servant of God and of God's people, to be conformed to the life of Christ who took upon himself the form of a servant. As *priest* he serves by faithful obedience in prayer and worship, in ministering the sacraments and in absolving sinners. As *pastor* he serves in gladly accepting the discipline imposed upon his time, his energy, and his compassion ... As *prophet* he serves in proclaiming God's word, not only in preaching but in pronouncing God's judgement on sin and his mercy in forgiveness, and in equipping and renewing God's people for mission ... A priest, himself a sinful man, is set apart by Christ in ordination to minister to Christians living within the tension between nature and grace – a tension which he shares – in order that he and they may be transformed into Christ's likeness.[20]

THE DISTINCTIVE DIACONATE

120   'A deacon is to focus or be a sign of the ministry of servanthood in the Church and in the world. As the New Zealand Ordinal indicates, the diaconate is to remind the whole Church that the essence of ministry is service. The ministry of servanthood is particularly directed to those in need. This is evident from Acts 6. So service to the poor and troubled, the outcasts and voiceless ones, the sick and destitute within the Church and in the world, is especially signified in the deacon's ministry. But the ministry is not only directed outwards. As Ordinals in Brazil, Canada and ECUSA show, the functions of the deacon include the interpretation of the needs, concerns and hopes of the world to the Church, thus informing the Church's intercession,

helping its understanding of the world in the light of the Gospel and making more effective its participation in God's transforming work in the world.'[21]

121 In response to this sort of understanding of the office and work of a deacon there is a growing demand in several parts of the Anglican Communion for the revival of a permanent and distinctive diaconate. For example, recent experience in the Episcopal Church in the United States, a recent report to the House of Bishops of the Church of England, and the considered advice of ACC-6 all point in this direction. We are confident that there is a need for a more credible expression of the diaconate. We need to rediscover the diaconate as an order complementary to the order of priesthood rather than as a merely transitional order which it is at present. We should ensure that such a diaconate does not threaten the ministry of the laity but seeks to equip and further it. Such a diaconate, furthermore, would serve to renew the *diakonia* of the whole Church; laity, deacons, priests and bishops.

122 We feel it right to draw attention to some difficulties.

(a) In some Provinces, particularly those in which women are not ordained to the priesthood but *are* ordained to the diaconate, the deacon's ministry is rarely distinctively diaconal. These deacons are given training identical to that of priests for a ministry that closely parallels that of their colleagues. It is difficult to see a permanent diaconate with an entirely distinctive diaconal ministry coming into existence in such circumstances.

(b) Similarly the long-standing tradition that the diaconate is an 'inferior' order (cf, the old ordinals) through which you pass on the way to the priesthood is also an obstacle to the emergence of a distinctive diaconate.

(c) There are difficulties too over stipend, status, distinctive dress, title and relationship to the parish and bishop.

123 These difficulties together with our enthusiasm for this ministry encourage us to commend to the Provinces the need:

(a) to review and if necessary to revise ordinals and canons to recognise the distinctive and permanent diaconate;

(b) to share our experiences of this ministry.[22]

THE VARIETY OF ORDAINED MINISTRIES

124 For many there is an unchanged belief that the normal pattern of ministry is still the multi-purpose and full-time stipendiary priest. Recent developments have shown, however, that this is only one of a number of possible patterns of ministry. We welcome the many new varieties of ministry and believe that they should be encouraged. Especially notable has been the increase in non-stipendiary ministry, which in some dioceses is becoming the norm. In welcoming this development we recognise that no term is entirely

satisfactory, but of the names before us we like best 'self-supporting ministry'. A clear and generally used name would be an important step forward.

125   There are recognisable differences between:

(i)   a diocese (or parish) whose ministers are paid through secular employment because there is no other source of finance;

(ii) a diocese (or parish) which on theological grounds is committed to a self-supporting ministry;

(iii) a diocese (or parish) with widespread growth which is best met by a mixture of Church-supported and self-supporting ministry;

(iv) a diocese (or parish) which, conscious of the alienation of many people and institutions from the life of the Church, welcomes the ordination of people for the exercise of ministry within the context of their daily work;

(v)   a Christian community in which, by reason of size, widely scattered churches, isolation, or distinctive culture, there is a home-bred local ministry closely related to the needs of that community.

We are convinced that the need of the world for the Gospel cannot be met without a massive expansion of all forms of both lay and ordained ministry. We believe that such an increase in ordained 'self-supporting' ministries can take place without threatening existing lay ministries.

TRAINING FOR THE ORDAINED MINISTRY

126   ACC-5 reported in 1981 that 'local situations and needs have given rise to a wide variety of patterns of training throughout the Anglican Communion – including traditional seminary education, theological education by extension, and a number of practical and pastoral field training schemes'.[23] Because of the varying forms of the ordained ministry the Church needs to be open to the varying benefits that come from different methods of training. These should include residential training, non-residential training, local training and post-ordination training.

127   Something of this wider experience would be achieved if there could be a greater sharing of expertise in training and personnel throughout the Anglican Communion.

128   Within this wide variety of training it should not be thought that non-residential training is appropriate only for self-supporting ministers, because this could encourage the idea that there is a 'second class training for a second class ministry'. At the same time, at least some of the Church's ministers should be trained in a way that gives them a wider experience than that of their own church and community.

129   In the training of ordinands attention should not merely be focused on

academic excellence, but ordinands should be persons of Christian integrity with a strong devotional life. They must show proven leadership in the community and be people who are able to share and communicate the faith in the language and idiom of their people. It is important that programmes of training are evaluated on a regular basis with a view to ensuring that the training is forming an effective servant-ministry. Those who seek to speak in the name of the 'Son of Man who came not to be served but to serve' should be able to work as servants of a servant Church (Mark 10.35-45).

130   We call attention to the growing recognition that selection for ordained ministry should be preceded by a careful process of discernment of gifts for ministry and leadership. This can be done when a candidate is actually tested in a supervised experience of ministry. Only those who demonstrate genuine fitness should be encouraged to go into further training.

131   In the business world, continuing education is regarded as essential for the maintenance of standards. In the same way, it is also desirable that all ordained ministers should take sabbaticals for rest, refreshment and study, and that seminary training courses, clergy schools and regular clergy meetings be made obligatory for clergy in each diocese.

WOMEN AND ORDINATION

132   As this Lambeth Conference has considered the issues of the ordination of women as priests and their possible ordination to the episcopate, we have been acutely aware of the pain experienced both by women who sense God's call to Holy Orders and by those who believe that women cannot be called to these Orders. In our discussions, we have also been aware that different Provinces of our Communion have different understandings of God's will for his Church in this matter.

133   We have reviewed the resolutions of previous Lambeth Conferences, as well as of meetings of the Anglican Consultative Council. We believe that in these gatherings of our Communion the concept of reception has affected the consideration of the ordination of women to the presbyterate and episcopate. The following points have been noted and acknowledged:

the integrity of each Province to pursue this matter in its own time and in its own way as its response to God's call in mission;

the recognition that, in determining its practice on this issue, any diocese or Province must have the substantial support of its people;

that in the process of reception the issue continues to be tested until it is clearly accepted or not accepted by the whole Church;

it is important that Provinces should respect each other's processes in this matter and also that they should communicate fully their decisions to each other.

134   We have concentrated in our discussions on how we might best respect and honour differences in understanding and continue to maintain communion with one another. This report, with the resolutions which accompany it, sets forth a possible basis for remaining in communion (albeit impaired communion) if and when one of our Provinces elects to consecrate a woman to the episcopate. (See Resolution 1).

135   The Church is the body of Christ. We are cleansed and called into mission by baptism, empowered for mission and commissioned by the Holy Spirit. Our mission is to be a sign of the Kingdom of God to the world, and to 'go forth into the world, making disciples of all nations'. This mission is universal (catholic) and belongs to the Church at all times and in all places. It is in our acceptance of this mission that we discover and enjoy our unity.

136   Our ministry is given to us by Christ for the fulfilment of the Church's mission. The ordained ministry enables the whole body to pursue that mission, and that ministry is experienced in a variety of ways at different times and places.

137   While we acknowledge that the threefold order of ministry is instituted and established by Holy Writ and Sacred Tradition, it is also maintained by some that the expressions of the threefold ministry can vary from time to time and from place to place in the light of particular circumstances. The Lambeth Conference in 1888, in the formulation of the fourth point of the Quadrilateral, suggested that local adaptation was applicable to the Episcopate ('The Historic Episcopate, locally adapted in the methods of its administration to the varying needs of the nations and peoples called of God, into the unity of His Church').

138   A century later, the implied flexibility in the phrase 'locally adapted' is understood in various ways.

(a) In some Provinces, this may involve the ordination of women to each order within the threefold order of ministry. For these Provinces, this is understood as a faithful response of the Church, on a compelling theological basis, to the demands of mission in its context.

(b) For some other Provinces, there may be need for a significant further discussion regarding the ordination of women to the presbyterate and the episcopate for reasons of consensus both within the Communion and ecumenically.

(c) In others again, the ordination of women to the presbyterate and episcopate would be regarded as a change in the essential nature of the threefold ministry and would not be an instance of local adaptation, as envisaged in the Quadrilateral.

It is clear that it may be many years before the Anglican Communion can be said to be of a single mind regarding the ordination of women.

139 When a Province believes that its call to mission signals the inclusion of women in the threefold order, that Province must consider the following questions, as identified by the Anglican Consultative Council, before any decision is taken.

140 For such a Province, is the ordination of women to the threefold order of ministry a legitimate development of the theology and the practice of ministry, as understood by this Communion? What are the criteria by which this decision shall be made?

141 How will the ordination of women to the episcopate affect the episcopal ministry and its relationship to the communion or fellowship of the Church? The episcopate has long been seen as the focus of unity in the Church. Can unity be sustained when a woman is ordained to the episcopate? And, if so, what is the nature of that unity?

142 What will be the effect of the ordination of women to the episcopate on the process of consultation and decision-making in the fellowship of the Anglican Communion? Will a woman ordained to the episcopate enjoy communion with bishops from those Provinces which have elected not to ordain women to that office?

143 What will be the effect of the ordination of women to the episcopate on the process of consultation and decision-making when there is division in the universal Church? Also, how long and how far-reaching a process of reception should be anticipated among the Provinces?

144 What will be the effect of the ordination of women to the episcopate on the nature of the Church and of the unity we seek as a credible sign of the Kingdom in a divided world? Unity is traditionally seen as a mark of truth. How will lack of unity affect the Church as a credible sign of the Kingdom?[24] To these we would add yet one other.

145 Does the ordination of women to the episcopate at this time and in this place enhance the mission of the Church?

146 As these decisions are being made throughout the Communion by Provinces at different stages in their respective understandings of both mission and ministry, attention must be given now to a continuing process of communication on this matter among the Primates, and through them among the various Provinces.

147 There must be diverse means of expression of mission and ministry in the Anglican Communion for the foreseeable future. A proper doctrine of reception will go a long way in the maintenance of unity.

148　To some the episcopate, as a sign of unity in the Anglican Communion, will be impaired by the inclusion of women. To others, the episcopate, as a sign of unity in the Anglican Communion, is already impaired by its being, in fact, exclusively male.

149　It is clear that many, on both sides of the ordination issue, will experience the pain of feeling that their conscience has been offended. We acknowledge that pain, and indeed enter into it with them.

150　We acknowledge that we already experience impaired communion, and have known that state in times past over various issues and for considerable lengths of time. This issue too may continue to be unsettled for a considerable period. We are committed, however, each Province to the other, to continue in dialogue and to remain one in the Body of Christ.

THE MINISTRY OF BISHOPS

151　Within the wider context of the mission and ministry of the whole Church, the diocese is often seen as basic to the life and unity of the local Church. This unity is personified and symbolised in the office of the bishop. Under God, the bishop leads the local church in its mission to the world.
　Among other things, the bishop is:

(a)　a symbol of the Unity of the Church in its mission;

(b)　a teacher and defender of the faith;

(c)　a pastor of the pastors and of the laity;

(d)　an enabler in the preaching of the Word, and in the administration of the Sacraments;

(e)　a leader in mission and an initiator of outreach to the world surrounding the community of the faithful;

(f)　a shepherd who nurtures and cares for the flock of God;

(g)　a physician to whom are brought the wounds of society;

(h)　a voice of conscience within the society in which the local Church is placed;

(i)　a prophet who proclaims the justice of God in the context of the Gospel of loving redemption;

(j)　a head of the family in its wholeness, its misery and its joy. The bishop is the family's centre of life and love.

COLLEGIALITY AND ACCOUNTABILITY

152　The Church by biblical definition is a body and within it all members are mutually inter-dependent, accountable to God and to one another. The holder of the office of bishop needs to work corporately within the total Church in a number of ways:

with the laity, deacons, priests and other bishops (if applicable) of the diocese;

with the bishops of other dioceses with whom the bishop is 'in communion';

with other Christian Churches with whom some degree of communion exists.

153 An important element within the Church, as the Anglican Communion understands it, is the diocese, in which all kinds of ministry exist – lay, diaconal, presbyteral and episcopal. Within the diocese the bishop is called to work in full collaboration with the clergy and laity. This can be expressed through consultation or through a synodical form of church government.

154 To express the principle of accountability, there are varieties of canonical and semi-official structures within the dioceses and Provinces of the Anglican Communion, such as Standing Committees, Boards, Councils and Synods, which express the mutual accountability of bishops, clergy and laity. The method of electing or appointing bishops varies considerably from Province to Province. All systems, however, now seem to include the involvement of clergy and laity at some level in the process. Other bishops in the Province also tend to have a place in the process.

155 Through its bishop each diocese expresses its relationship with other dioceses. Within a Province, bishops act corporately as a 'House of Bishops' to express their collegiality.

(1) We note the need for the bishop and the diocese to be encouraged to see themselves as mutually accountable to each other for their ministries as well as to the Provinces to which they belong.

(2) We recommend that, to emphasise the Communion-wide relationship and the catholicity of the Church, whenever possible, a bishop from another Province or from a Church in communion be included at each episcopal ordination.

(3) We recommend that the Primates be asked to exchange with each other (and they with the bishops of their Provinces) the lists of those they ordain to the episcopate, along with the names of dioceses.

(4) We recommend that, whenever possible, isolated dioceses be related to other nearby and/or culturally compatible dioceses in order to share in the collegiality which such relationships afford.

156 Along with other Churches, the Anglican Communion has allowed the ordination of bishops who will not be bishops of dioceses. These are called assistant or suffragan bishops. Their method of election and their place in decision-making is sometimes different from that of diocesan bishops.

157   We believe that all bishops by virtue of their ordination share in the fullness of episcopacy.

Accordingly, we recommend that each Province re-examines

(a) the position and work of all bishops active in full-time diocesan work, including those known in the various Provinces as suffragans, assistants, assisting, area, or regional bishops to ensure that all bishops have a true *episcope* of jurisdiction and pastoral care and are seen as belonging fully to the local college of bishops;

(b) the principle that all bishops active in full-time diocesan work be made full members, with seat, voice and vote, of all provincial, national and international gatherings of Anglican bishops. (Resolutions 46 and 46A.)

FUNDING OF THE EPISCOPATE

158   The method by which a bishopric is funded may have consequences for the bishop as he seeks to make decisions in the diocese and to contribute to the *collegium* on a wider basis.

The effect of the method of funding on accountability was considered particularly where:

the diocese is short of funds and has to contribute all the costs of the bishops out of current income, which may be very small;

the diocese is dependent on external grants to support the bishop;

the diocese is about to be divided into two or more dioceses;

the diocese lacks proper provision for the retirement of the bishops, particularly in the areas of housing and pensions;

the diocese lacks proper provision for widows and dependents of deceased bishops.

159   Having listened to a Province, and recognising the experience of lack of funds and other pastoral concerns, the Conference recommends to the Anglican Consultative Council that

(a) in the planning of the Partners-in-Mission Consultation with the dioceses of the Francophone Province of Burundi, Rwanda and Zaire, to be held in 1989, adequate time be given to a consideration of Primatial appointment, matters of financial and manpower needs, provision of theological and teacher training staff, development and leadership structures and programmes.

(b) the procedure recommended for the Francophone Province be a model followed in *such other province* where the need exists. (See Resolution 49.)

INITIAL PREPARATION AND CONTINUING SUPPORT FOR THE EPISCOPATE

160   The Lambeth Conference in 1968 and more fully in 1978 highlighted

the need for the training of and support for the bishops of the Anglican Communion. The 1978 Report requested:

> That written guidelines be prepared for episcopal training ... (and) that member churches prepare their own versions of these guidelines in order to cover the training requirements of bishops functioning in their particular circumstances.[25]

161   In 1985 a small group met with the Secretary for the 1988 Lambeth Conference to survey the progress on this request, and they subsequently circulated a report to each of the Primates in 1986 entitled *Reflections on the Theology of, and the Practice of, the Episcopate*. This report went beyond the question of initial training for bishops, to deal with the theology and practice of the episcopate and the particular ways in which to give bishops continuing support and training. As a result, a number of Provinces have joined those who had acted earlier in establishing schemes for initial training and continuing support for bishops, and also in many cases their spouses.

162   The diverse contexts in which bishops exercise their episcopate makes a standard pattern of training impossible, but the need for help and training at the point of entry into the episcopate is now well established. It is accepted in Canada, USA, England, the Council of the Churches of East Asia, New Zealand, Australia and many of the Provinces in Africa. Other Provinces have the matter under review.

163   We recommend such programmes as are outlined below, and ask each Province to implement programmes relevant to the particular needs of the Province, the bishop, and the bishop's spouse and the bishop's family where appropriate. Such programmes should encompass the significant change in understanding and role that occurs during the transition from being a parish priest, or the holder of some other office, to being a bishop. They should also include such practical issues as financial and management skills required for the organisation and funding of a diocese. All such training needs, ideally, to be in the language and the culture of the bishop concerned.

Initial Preparation

164   The change from one ministry to another should always be an opportunity for establishing priorities, taking stock and setting new directions. Because the bishop's office has a high public profile, this change of ministry should be marked by ample time for preparation. One month should be the minimum preparation period *after* the completion of the bishop's previous work. Each Province should be ready to provide suitable programmes and locations for the pre-ordination preparation. The receiving diocese should see that the preparation costs are adequately funded, either from its own funds or from other sources as appropriate.

165   Each Province or Area Council should set out clearly the known tasks

and functions of a bishop, both in mission as well as in administration and corporate duties, and have these available for study by the bishop-elect.

166   Time should also be allowed for spiritual refreshment and family preparation.

In-Service Support
167   The work of a bishop is draining both in terms of energy and in terms of spiritual resources. In-service support is therefore essential if the Church is to gain most benefit from its bishops. This should take the form of programmes of mutual support for the bishops of a Province and also more personal support at a diocesan level.

168   It should be possible for the Primate or Dean of each Province to arrange for all bishops to have group meetings on a regular basis throughout the year.

169   Spiritual refreshment should be part of the pattern of life of every bishop. We encourage all bishops to seek the support and guidance of a spiritual director/counsellor.

170   It is very clear that the office and work of a bishop can create personal, physical and mental stress resulting in ill-health. For this reason we recommend that all bishops should present themselves for medical examination at least once a year.

Study/Refreshment/Sabbatical Leave
171   The need for such leave for clergy has been established in many parts of the Anglican Communion. In the past, such leave was rare for bishops except perhaps in relation to major church gatherings such as the Lambeth Conference or a World Assembly of the WCC.

172   We would recommend that bishops be granted leave after approximately six years in office to attend to theological, pastoral and personal concerns. Without such opportunities, a bishop is unlikely to be able to fulfil the tasks of teaching, of being an example, and of witnessing for mission.

173   We encourage Provinces and dioceses to provide financial assistance so that the bishops can participate in such opportunities. Occasional sabbaticals, study leave or 'in-service' growth opportunities throughout the period of episcopacy are recommended.

Family Support
174   We recommend that where a bishop is married the spouse, and as far as possible other family members, should also be offered opportunities for support, preparation for a changed role and continuing opportunities for fellowship with others in similar positions. (See further Resolution 41.)

65

Liturgies of Ordination

175   The 1958 Study Group highlighted the need for the Lambeth Conference to consider the theology of the episcopate, its relationshop to the mission of the church, and to compare the services for the ordination of a bishop that are in use in various Provinces. Such a study would allow each Province to ensure that it shared, with the rest of the Communion, a common understanding of the role of the bishop as it consecrated a new bishop.

176   We endorse the need for such a study and recommend that this should be pursued, with a full interchange of information between the various Provinces.

THE RENEWAL OF THE CHURCH IN LITURGY

177   Although the Anglican Consultative Council has given *some* consideration to liturgical matters at various meetings, it is 30 years since a Lambeth Conference gave any extensive guidance on liturgical matters. Since 1958 there has been great liturgical change. Texts have been revised and modernised all over the world. Vatican II has touched us all. The Liturgical Movement has reshaped Sunday, the eucharist, and even church interiors. Also it has significantly reshaped the mentalities and expectations of the worshippers as well. Around us the world to which we are sent has changed astonishingly also, as other parts of this statement reflect. It is time to consider the worship of the Church afresh.

THE HEART OF WORSHIP

178   Christian worship has its own self-authenticating character as the prime duty of the Church of God. It should be offered to God by the Church for his glory and without any conscious eye to some other ulterior purpose. The mystery of worship is that the Church is caught up into the heavens, so as to be forgetful of herself and simply to gaze on the vision of God.

WORSHIP AND MISSION

179   Yet it is also true that in worship the Church should so rediscover both herself and God's purposes for her, every member should so meet God and the people of God, that through the rhythm of the Church's worshipping life all are richly equipped for service in the world. The Church's liturgy, thus, is bound up with her mission, and the renewal of her liturgy is bound up with the renewal of her mission.

THE UNIVERSALITY OF WORSHIP

180   The catholicity of the visible Church must be expressed in some common forms and rituals. The people of God are joined together in one Body by baptism and faith. By the power of the Holy Spirit they continue in the

Body through sharing the eucharist, through dependence upon God's word, through fellowship in prayer, service, and suffering. In our Communion we expect that proper regard to these catholic features of worship will be paid in a responsible way by all our Provinces. In principle, we commend all means of communication and co-ordination in respect of liturgy between our Provinces, while not wishing to compromise their proper constitutional autonomy.

In this respect we note the ACC-7 Resolution concerning the creation of an International Anglican Liturgical Commission. We request that the Standing Committee of the ACC, when it next meets, considers carefully how such a Commission could actually fulfil the hopes being placed upon it.[26]

LOCAL EXPRESSION OF THE LITURGY

181   The liturgy of the Church must ever draw upon the past and conserve the best of the tradition. In particular it must enshrine and hand on the work of God, in the written liturgical texts, in the lectionary provision, and in a vigorous pattern of preaching and teaching. These provide much of the spiritual resources by which the Church lives in the world. Yet the liturgy must at the same time give authentic expression to the common life in Christ of the people of God present at each particular gathering, in whatever generation and in whatever country and culture (cf. Article 34 of the Thirty-nine Articles).

182   Thus, for instance, the hymnody of each place and time will both express the timeless and universal Word of God and express it in a poetic and musical form appropriate to the worshippers. Hymnody and Christian singing generally are an instance of a marvellous means of worship, a great channel of the truths of God, an expression of faith and joy which springs from the heart of the worshippers – and yet one open to the possibility of fossilisation if the times move on and the music and singing slowly become that of a cultural ghetto. The Church has to worship incarnationally, separated from the world by the offence of the Cross, but not by any alien character of its culture. We affirm expressions of true local creativity within the life of the worshipping local community which well up from within the people in response to the stirrings of the Spirit. Thus we commend and encourage authentic local inculturation of the liturgy, and fear lest in some parts of the Anglican Communion we have been all too hesitant about it.

LITURGY COMES ALIVE

183   Authorised liturgical forms embody doctrine, and the stance of faith of each Province is in part discerned from its liturgical forms. Such forms, nevertheless, provide but a part of the actual event of the liturgy, and the totality will usually include scripture reading, hymnody, locally devised forms of intercession, preaching or other communication, movement (e.g.

at the Peace or during the administration of communion), and silence. In addition to these, the actual 'ethos' of worship is determined also by the number and disposition of the participants, by the buildings, furnishings, art, ornamentation, vesture, musical resources and ceremonial associated with a particular liturgical event. A welcome trend is towards much fuller active participation by the congregation, and this helps us conceive of liturgy as a function of living people actually participating in an *event*. Worship involves the people of the Spirit worshipping in spirit and in truth and we must not equate it solely with texts, however scriptural and commendable, on the pages of a book.

1662 AND OTHER PRAYER BOOKS

184   The 1662 Book of Common Prayer of the Church of England, and along with it the other Prayer Books of the Anglican Communion, have been hugely influential in shaping the identity of the Communion as a seriously liturgical fellowship of Churches. The 1662 Prayer Book, in particular, has been influential not only in England but in many other parts of the world as well. In some Provinces, especially where it is used in a local vernacular tongue, it still feeds people with a secure spirituality; and in these and other Provinces it often remains as a standard of doctrine. But if we do not dwell on its *strengths* today it is because we judge its era is slipping irretrievably into the past. Cranmer's liturgical language is that of another age – though we recognise this is not always the case in translation into other languages.

185   The presuppositions of the 1662 Book itself were of a static 'Christendom' England, so that little awareness of mission touches its pages; its requirements of the laity were of largely passive participation; and, for all its ancient beauties, its liturgical structuring has been called heavily into question in Province after Province by scholars, pastors, and worshippers alike. There is inevitable pain for those who for perhaps half a century have found the approach to God through a well-loved pattern of language, and who then find it removed from them almost literally within a single night. But once a general direction of change is set, the transition, however painful, is better undertaken than evaded. Changes to modern idiom are not in fact confined in our Communion to liturgical English, but there are parallels, with a parallel transition, in at least one or two other languages.

FLEXIBILITY IN RITES

186   Another traditional feature of Anglican rites is their fixedness and even rigidity. We seek now a far greater freedom, which has its own marks of the Spirit. Whilst a set liturgy properly provides a ground-plan structure and the text of central prayers, yet nowadays it can and should often provide for material written for the occasion, for extemporary contributions, and for singing of items (whether time-honoured hymns or more instant choruses)

chosen spontaneously. Provinces should be ready to have basic authorised forms for the central parts of certain rites such as the Eucharist, and for those forms to give an appropriate part to the congregation. But they should also provide outline structure into which a choice of materials, already existent or written for the occasion, can be fitted. And we look for further openness still which will encourage the truly spontaneous contributions of spiritually alive congregations. (See Resolution 47.)

MODERN LITURGICAL ENGLISH

187   A modern liturgical English is emerging. For somewhat more than twenty years worshippers have used texts which have abandoned 'thou' and address God as 'you'. A simpler more contemporary English has inevitably accompanied the change. We commend this, and welcome the efforts first by the International Consultation on English Texts (ICET) and more recently by the English Language Liturgical Consultation (ELLC) to find modern texts for 'common forms' which can be shared by all English-speaking countries across all the denominations. We recognise that ambiguous generic terms such as 'man', 'men', and 'mankind', which arise through accidents of the English language rather than through anything ultimate or divine, have caused hurt to many, as they touch deep emotions. We welcome the coming of 'inclusive' language.

LANGUAGE ABOUT GOD

188   The question of using masculine terminology for God is treated more fully in paragraphs 77 and 78. Questions have been raised in some parts of the Communion as to whether such terminology has not been too dominant in our liturgical formulations. Some modern texts have found ways of softening it without eliminating it or raising doubts over it. However, even to raise the question would be inappropriate in other cultural contexts, and in the face of some other faiths. Even where it is raised, it provokes fundamental questions about the nature of the scriptural revelation, its particularity as well as its universality.

SIMPLICITY OF LANGUAGE

189   We are also aware of a need emerging in some parts of our Communion for a simpler style of liturgical language, language which, nevertheless, retains the essentially poetic and memorable character of all good liturgical writing, and in its content still conveys the word of God. It need not always have great marks of permanence upon it, nor seek the weightiest provincial authorisation. It may be sufficient that its provisionality and trial character enables it to be used for a period. What is true of spoken texts is the more so of hymnody, songs, and choruses.

Contemporary materials will often enable worshippers to learn and maintain their faith through the character of what they say and sing, rather than through their ability to follow the printed page.

NON-VERBAL SHARING IN LITURGY
190   If we are not to be in captivity to a wholly 'word' and wholly 'book' liturgical culture, then we need to encourage communication by the visual and other senses, and to provide for congregational participation by action, gesture, movement and ceremonial. This should be such as to underline and reinforce the Word of God rather than to indicate a departure from it. A more uninhibited style of participation would be needed than has been usual amongst many Anglicans.

SILENCE
191   Our commendation of new styles of writing and of full congregational participation is not intended to subvert the role of silence in liturgy. Quite the reverse – the very liturgies which encourage active congregational responsiveness depend in their character upon silence structured alongside the activity. Anglicans generally should be ready for more of this arising from the very nature of the liturgy, and to be profitably used by the worshippers.

BAPTISM
192   Baptism by water is the scriptural sacrament of once-for-all initiation into Christ and into his Body. The New Testament imagery displays a great spectrum of significance, from union with Christ in his death and resurrection to incorporation by the Spirit into the one Body. The Church has always marked this life-changing step with vows expressing repentance and faith, the basic constituents of a response to the Gospel. The actual demands of repentance, and the Church's assessment of whether profession of it is genuine or not, will depend upon the specific needs and character of the social and religious context. All that is involved in being Christian is signified in baptism – God through baptism calls upon those who receive it to walk in his paths by the power of the Holy Spirit all the days of their lives.

The Baptism of Infants
193   We reaffirm the baptism of infants as scriptural, deriving in principle from the missionary baptism of households, (e.g. Acts 16.15,33), a practice exemplified today in parts of our Communion. The baptism of infants shares as fully in the character of the one baptism as the baptism of adults, but we accept the Lima Judgement that indiscriminate infant baptism should not be practised. It obscures the purpose of such baptism, not only from those who request it, but also from those many others who are doubtful about its propriety. Whilst we are aware of the vastly differing contexts in which baptism is sought, we encourage the development of standards and guidelines for the preparation of parents and sponsors, with a view to a common discipline.

Admission to Communion

194   The argument that baptism should in principle lead into sharing in communion has been strongly expressed in the call of the Boston Statement (1985).[27] The statement asks Provinces to cease to require confirmation, or any given standard of educational or other attainment, as a post-baptismal prerequisite for admission to communion. ACC-7 in May 1987 recorded in *Many Gifts, One Spirit* the situation in various Provinces.[28] This may indicate the likely future directions which are emerging in the Communion. The report also encouraged study of both the Lima Text and the Boston Statement (published as a separate eight-page pamphlet or contained within *Nurturing Children in Communion: Essays from the Boston Consultation)*[29], whilst raising its own questions over the latter. These questions range from concern about 'unworthy reception' (1 Cor. 11.27f) and the need for repentance, to questions about the relation of baptism, as a complete rite of initiation, to a public profession of faith in the presence of the bishop, representing the wider Church. We recommend that the text of the Boston Statement and the ACC questions put to it should be widely circulated throughout our Communion and a careful study made by Provinces which have not so far considered it. We judge that Provinces should be free to provide their own rules for the admission of the baptised to communion. Where two Provinces (or smaller units) have differing patterns, great sensitivity is needed when young children admitted to Holy Communion under one discipline then present themselves as communicants where a different discipline obtains.

Worship for All Ages

195   A corollary of infant baptism is that the main worship events of the Church should in principle be open to children. We should value their presence, treat their participation as natural, and ensure that the contents and ethos of the rite do not proclaim a spoken or silent message of rejection to them.

Confirmation of those Baptised in Infancy

196   The confirmation of those baptised as infants is by the laying on of the bishop's hands with prayer. In some cases it comes after admission to communion. The rite should include the first and major reaffirmation by the candidate of his or her baptismal covenant, prayer by the Church for a renewal of the baptismal life in the Spirit, and recognition by the Church of the candidate's adult participation in the mission of the Church.

Baptism of Adults

197   We judge that there is a growing proportion of adult candidates for baptism in our Communion, as compared with infants. We also note a slowly rising interest in some Provinces in the use of total immersion for such baptisms.[30] We also detect a widespread (though far from universal) expectation that the bishop will preside in person over the baptismal liturgy for adults

(and for infants also where possible). The confirmation of those baptised in infancy (and the renewal of the baptismal vows of others) fits well with the ritual for baptism itself. We welcome these trends.

The Laying on of Hands After the Baptism of Adults

198   The baptism of adults has since 1662 generally been followed by the laying on of hands by the bishop. Whilst questions have been raised recently about this, two clear patterns are to be found thus far in our Communion:

(i) The 1662 Prayer Book tradition is that an adult is baptised by the local pastor, perhaps at an early stage after professing faith, or sometimes on the eve of the bishop's visit to administer confirmation. This practice continues in many places.

(ii) A more recent development has been to combine adult baptism with confirmation in a single rite over which the bishop presides. This is found in many new rites of the last two decades.

Preparation

199   Just as we urge thorough preparation of parents for the baptism of an infant, so all the more we recommend thorough preparation of both candidate and sponsors at the baptism of an adult. Because it is entry into the missionary Body of Christ, baptism should lead, through the supportive fellowship of the Church, to a maturing process in the Spirit and to a sharing of Christ's ministry of service to the world. We note and commend a widespread interest in the revival of an adult catechumenate, and invite Provinces to consider the provision of guidelines for this.

Testimony

200   We also recommend in a baptism and confirmation context, what Lambeth 1978 said in an evangelistic tone, that there is great effectiveness in 'a personal word of testimony',[31] and we suggest provision for this in the rites of our Communion.

Reaffirmation of Baptismal Vows

201   Because baptism is once-for-all and for life, it cannot be repeated and, once given, must not be denied. We commend experiments with the reaffirmation of the baptismal covenant over and above confirmation, and, provided that the givenness of earlier baptism itself is not obscured or threatened, we recognise the possibilities of such reaffirmation being accompanied by appropriate meaningful ceremonies. One such possible ceremony is the laying on of hands, which is provided in at least two recent Worship Books in a way which is clearly distinguished from traditional confirmation.[32]

RITES OF RECONCILIATION

202   Whilst rites of reconciliation of a penitent may be regularly used for

Christians in all patterns of life, we also see a case, closely allied to the rite of reaffirmation of the baptismal covenant, as set out in paragraph 199 above, for a special and public restoration of those who, once baptised (and indeed also confirmed), are now returning from being 'lapsed' and are best welcomed in this public way.

EUCHARIST: MEETING AND MISSION

203 We do not attempt here to discuss textual technicalities of the eucharistic rites. Instead we note that in the eucharist the Church unites in the praises of God, receives God's holy word, expresses her life in the Spirit, sustains the mutual fellowship of her members, recommits herself to Almighty God, and, from this holy feast, returns to the world to fulfil God's mission. The eucharist is a locus for mutual sharing and ministry for the 'building up' of the Church (1 Cor. 14). The eucharist may include: various teaching methods to minister the word, drama, dance, extemporary prayer, groups for study or intercession, healing ministries, weddings, and other public activities of the local Christian community. Christian mission itself is vitiated if the Church's eucharistic practice does not in fact build up the people of God.

THE AGAPE

204 We note signs of the re-emergence of the *agape* or love feast. It appears in two forms; eucharistic, in the sense of having the sacrament of the Lord's Supper at its heart, or non-eucharistic, though still with elements of Christian worship within it. It is interesting to note that, in its non-eucharistic form, it is often used by local groups of Christians in the absence of a duly ordained minister.[33]

PRESIDENCY AT THE EUCHARIST

205 We note the received tradition that the president at the eucharist should be a bishop or presbyter. We also note that in dioceses which are geographically large, or offer grave hindrances to easy travel, the ready availability of an ordained presbyter may not match the proper sacramental hopes or expectations of some or all of the congregations. Two practices have found acceptance in some parts of the Communion:

(i) The ordination of local persons – who are acknowledged leaders in the congregation or congregations, but who may lack some of the traditional requirements for ordination. Such people can then provide the presidency required at the eucharist, in addition to their other roles in the Church.

(ii) the 'extending' of communion through space and time by the hands of specially authorised lay persons (or deacons) who take the elements from a normal celebration (with a presbyter or bishop presiding) to needy individuals and congregations.

DISTRIBUTION OF COMMUNION

206 No important principles are breached if authorised lay persons of either sex minister either element to the communicants. In some situations, indeed, it is more appropriate to pass the elements along rows of worshippers than to administer to each individually.

NON-EUCHARISTIC WORSHIP

207 We look for the emergence of richer forms of non-eucharistic worship throughout the Communion. We note particularly the need for the development of offices, particularly where a simple daily lay office is desired; family services, particularly for those on the fringe of church life and commitment; liturgies for informal groups, such as bible study groups or adult enquirers' classes, and material for ecumenical worship particularly for use with those with whom we cannot share communion. The principles of such worship need to be articulated afresh and specific models need to be worked out.

A COMMON LECTIONARY

208 We note the call of Lambeth 1978 for a 'common lectionary' both as a unifying factor within the Communion and for use ecumenically.[34] We urge, once again, that everything possible should be done to reach an agreement on such a lectionary.

ORDINATION

209 The 1958 Lambeth Conference Report, while drawing attention to certain features in the 1662 Ordinal, particularly emphasised the centrality of *prayer* as the 'form' of the ordination rite. Most revisions of the last thirty years, stemming from valuable work in the Church of South India, are based on this insight. We believe that they should be acceptable to the worldwide Communion and to our ecumenical partners. We know of no doubtful revisions. It is perhaps an area where very careful co-ordination of provincial revisions is vital. We recommend that all Provinces should study the character of these revised rites with a view to the emergence of a common mind in this matter. (See Resolution 18.6c.)

NOTES

[1] *Bonds of Affection: Proceedings of ACC-6, Badagry, Nigeria,* ACC, London, 1984, p.49.

[2] *Progress in Partnership: Report of the Mission Agencies Conference, Brisbane, Australia,* ACC, London, 1987, pp.64f.

[3] * *For the Sake of the Kingdom: A Report of the Inter-Anglican Theological and Doctrinal Commission,* ACC, London, 1986, p.20.

[4] For a further discussion on mission see the ACC-6 Report, pp.46f.

[5] *Giving Mission its Proper Place: Report of the Mission Issues and Strategy Advisory Group,* ACC, London, 1985, p.9.

[6] *Progress in Partnership,* p.9.

[7] See Vincent Donovan, *Christianity Rediscovered: An Epistle from the Masai,* SCM Press, London, 1978.

[8] Michael Nazir-Ali and W.D. Pattinson (eds), *Working Papers for the Lambeth Conference 1988,* 1987, Mission and Ministry, para. 75.

[9] *Love in Any Language: The Report of the First International Conference of Young Anglicans, Belfast, Northern Ireland, 1988,* p.32.

[10] Vinay Samuel and C.M.N. Sugden, *Evangelism and the Poor: A Third World Study Guide,* Bangalore, 1982; Lourdino Yuzon (ed.), *Mission in the Context of Endemic Poverty,* CCA, Singapore, 1983.

[11] A. Theodore Eastman, 'The Mission of Christ in Urban America', in *Crossroads Are For Meeting* (Philip Turner and Frank Sugeno (eds.), SPCK USA, Sewanee, 1986, p.229.

[12] Colin Craston (ed.), * *Open to the Spirit,* ACC, London, 1987.

[13] *Working Papers for the Lambeth Conference 1988,* Mission and Ministry, para. 74.

[14] *Working Papers,* Mission and Ministry, para. 13.

[15] *Love in Any Language,* pp. 6, 7 and 10.

[16] *Working Papers,* Mission and Ministry, para. 153.

[17] *Working Papers,* Mission and Ministry, paras. 95, 96.

[18] Francis Ayres, *The Ministry of the Laity,* Westminster Press, Philadelphia, 1962.

[19] *Baptism, Eucharist and Ministry,* Ministry, para. 26, WCC, Geneva.

[20] *The Lambeth Conference 1968,* SPCK/Seabury, 1968, p.101.

[21] *Working Papers,* Mission and Ministry, para. 103.

[22] An organ that encourages the sharing of such experiences is *Distinctive Diaconate,* edited by Sr Teresa of the Community of St Andrew in London.

[23] ACC-5, London, 1981, p.52.

[24] * *Many Gifts, One Spirit: Report of ACC-7,* London 1987, pp.42f; see also *Women and the Episcopate: A Report of the Primates' Working Party,* 1987, p.25.

* indicates a title published through the Inter-Anglican Publishing Network.

[25] *Report of the Lambeth Conference 1978,* CIO Publishing, London, 1978, p.78.

[26] *Many Gifts, One Spirit,* pp.74-76.

[27] This statement emerged from an international consultation of a number of Anglican liturgists, the first of a series of such consultations, which was held in Boston, Mass., USA 29-31 July 1985.

[28] *Many Gifts, One Spirit,* pp.68f

[29] C. Buchanan (ed.), Grove Books, Nottingham, 1985.

[30] Such a practice is also known as baptism by *submersion.*

[31] *Report of the Lambeth Conference 1978,* p.94.

[32] e.g. *The Book of Common Prayer* of the Episcopal Church, USA (Church Hymnal Corp., New York, 1979) and *The Book of Alternative Services* of the Anglican Church in Canada (Anglican Book Centre, Toronto, 1985).

[33] Leonardo Boff, *Ecclesio-Genesis,* Collins, London, 1986, pp.61f.

[34] *Report of the Lambeth Conference 1978,* p.47.

RESOLUTIONS

Resolutions 1, 41-51, 65, 67, 69 and 72 fall within the purview of the Section on Mission and Ministry.

BIBLIOGRAPHY

ACC-5: Newcastle-upon-Tyne, ACC, London, 1981.

Bonds of Affection: Proceedings of ACC-6, Badagry, Nigeria, ACC, London, 1984.

*Many Gifts, One Spirit: Report of ACC-7, ACC, London, 1987.

The Lambeth Conference 1958: Resolutions and Reports, SPCK/Seabury, 1958.

The Lambeth Conference 1968: Resolutions and Reports, SPCK/Seabury 1968.

The Report of the Lambeth Conference, 1978, CIO Publishing, London, 1978.

Progress in Partnership: Report of the Mission Agencies Conference, Brisbane, Australia, ACC, London, 1987.

* For the Sake of the Kingdom: A Report of the Inter-Anglican Theological and Doctrinal Commission, ACC, London, 1986.

Giving Mission its Proper Place: Report of the Mission Issues and Strategy Advisory Group, ACC, London, 1988.

Vincent Donovan, Christianity Rediscovered: An Epistle from the Masai, SCM, London, 1978.

Michael Nazir-Ali and W.D. Pattinson (eds.), *Working Papers for the Lambeth Conference 1988,* ACC, London, 1987.

Love in any Language: The Report of the First International Conference of Young Anglicans, Belfast, Northern Ireland, 1988. Church of England National Youth Work Office, London, 1988.

Faith in the City: The Report of the Archbishop of Canterbury's Commission on Urban Priority Areas, Church House Publishing, 1985.

Vinay Samuel and C.M.N. Sugden, *Evangelism and the Poor: A Third World Study Guide,* Bangalore, 1982.

Lourdino Yuzon (ed.), *Mission in the Context of Endemic Poverty,* CCA, Singapore, 1983.

Philip Turner and Frank Sugeno (eds.), *Crossroads Are For Meeting,* SPCK USA, Sewanee, 1986.

Colin Craston (ed.), **Open to the Spirit,* ACC, London, 1987.

Francis Ayres, *The Ministry of the Laity,* Westminster Press, Philadelphia, 1962.

Baptism, Eucharist and Ministry: The Lima Report, WCC, Geneva, 1982.

The Priesthood of the Ordained Ministry, Church House Publishing, 1986.

Women and the Episcopate: A Report of the Primates' Working Party ACC, London, 1987.

Colin Buchanan (ed.), *Nurturing Children in Communion: Essays from the Boston Consultation ,* Grove Books, Nottingham, 1985.

Leonardo Boff, *Ecclesio-Genesis,* Collins, London, 1986.

Gustavo Gutierrez, *The Power of the Poor in History,* SCM Press, London, 1983.

Carroll Stuhlmueller (ed.), *Women and Priesthood,* Collegeville, Minnesota, 1978.

* indicates a title published through the Inter-Anglican Publishing Network.

The Chaplain: The Rt Revd Alastair Haggart

Dogmatic and Pastoral Concerns

Chairman   The Most Revd Keith Rayner (Adelaide, Australia)
Vice-Chairman   The Rt Revd Mark Dyer (Bethlehem, USA)
Secretary   Dr John Pobee
Staff   The Revd Dr Bert Breiner
Communicator   Mr Stephen Webb

OUTLINE OF THE ARGUMENT

1   The starting-point is the affirmation that we are caught up into a 'great pattern of relation' in the Christian Trinitarian revelation. According to this God's own life is 'being with' us, and ours a way of learning to 'be with' God and at the same time to 'be with' one another in the communion of the Spirit. The Church is a community with its own language and culture, a way of being human which can never be fully assimilated into any society in which it finds itself.

2   This raises the problem of Christ and culture, which is in large part the question of how to communicate the Gospel faithfully and effectively in a context already shaped by historical forces. We identify a continuous process of proclamation and reflection with a number of stages and facets, from which we can learn much by listening to the Christian experience of others.

3   Part of this process is necessarily the encounter with other faiths and ideologies. Here too we start with God's self-revelation in Jesus Christ and his longing to 'be with' all men and women. By listening to others we can learn what dialogue there may have been between God and persons of other faiths. Such listening and learning is not in competition with proclamation, but is characterised by certain features. Relations with other faiths are briefly reviewed and practical issues considered.

4   The view of the Church as a society with its own culture and language informs also our approach to authority. The Lambeth Quadrilateral formulated a pattern of things done, highlighting the use of the Scriptures, the Creeds, the dominical sacraments and the apostolic ministry of pastoral *episcope*. These are dynamically related to each other and manifest the fundamental nature of authority as nurture. The Church itself is a community of interpretation, understanding and applying the mind of Christ using reliable sources and reliable agencies. This involves the co-ordinated use of scripture, tradition and reason, guided by ordained office holders, prophets and sages and the whole body of believers.

5   All that has gone before helps us to understand what it means for Anglicans to be 'in communion' and how central to Christian living is growth in deeper communion. The Church has to make provision for decision-making, so that the transcendent gospel may be really communicated in particular cultures. This is why Anglicans have encouraged decision-making at Provincial level, but at the same time are obliged to give expression to interdependence, a duty discharged by four embodiments and agencies of unity at universal level. These are reviewed, and a description of the enhancement of the role of Primates is given. There is an account of decision-making on two questions (answers to ecumenical documents and the ordination of

women). 'Reception' and 'discovering the mind of the Church' are seen to be dynamic processes in which bishops have a continuing theological and pastoral responsibility.

COMMUNION WITH GOD AND THE LIFE OF THE CHRIST

6 'Have I been all this time with you, Philip, and you still do not know me? He who has seen me has seen the Father' (John 14.9,10). So Jesus replies to Philip's plea on behalf of the disciples that the Father be revealed to them. It declares not only that God is revealed in Jesus, but that it is this God's will to be *with* us and *for* us. The good news of the Christian Gospel is that Jesus' life among us is God's life – God breaking down the barriers of our bondage and our sinfulness. In Jesus, God is with us in all our human helplessness, with us in our life and in our death, with us 'even to death on a cross'. In Jesus God is faithful to us even at our worst, faithful to us when our fear and sin bring Jesus to the cross. In the risen Jesus, God is with us to transfigure and set free all those who are bound by fear and sin. Jesus is God with us, and to know God is to be *with* Jesus. God has shared our human world with us, and through the great events of cross and resurrection we are empowered and invited to share God's world – to show God's glory and freedom, to proclaim God's holiness and mercy in word and act. As we read the Bible and celebrate the sacraments, we continually seek to be with the God who wants to be with us. We invite Jesus to be the foundation of hope in our lives, the point of reference by which we orient our lives, the question that disturbs us and the friendship that gives us courage to trust God, ourselves, and one another.

7 We know God as we live with Jesus: so that we can and must say that Jesus' life is the act and expression of God. The God *shown* here is a God whose very life is a 'being with'. God is no individual to be 'known' from a distance, an object to walk around and collect information about. God's life is itself mission, address, communication: God's life is a life reaching out in and to what is other than God. God is not only the mysterious source and cause of all, but also an outpouring of divine life rejoicing in itself and seeking to share itself. God is not only Father but Word or Son, so that Jesus embodies in his life the divine act of sharing, communicating and rejoicing. His life is given its shape and destiny by *being with* the Father, fully fleshing out God's own joy in and awareness of the depth and generosity of the divine life in its primary character as *source* of all and *giver* of all. And we only know that primal generosity through Jesus' wholeness of response: we know the Father as the God who is *with* the Son, sustaining and forming this life of response, the power that draws out the radical, self-forgetful love and prayer of Jesus.

8   The radical love of Jesus is *creative*. It creates new life through healing and forgiveness, it sets captives free. Above all, in the resurrection it creates a community, a new pattern of human relations in which this creative healing, forgiveness and liberation are continued, and the *authority* of Jesus over everything that cripples and enslaves people goes on being effective.[1] Jesus' life with the Father is now lived *with* and *in* us: God witnesses to the divine life lived in Jesus' being with the Father; he does so by acting to bring us into the full measure of Jesus' humanity and by making us partakers of the divine nature – by bringing us to life 'in Christ', as St Paul says. God is with the community of Jesus as counsellor, advocate, challenge and guide, continuing Jesus' work of new creation. God is with us as 'Spirit'.

9   So it is that the God of Christians cannot be imagined or talked about except in this great Trinitarian pattern of relation. God's life is in the sending and sharing of God's very being. Our redeemed life is a matter of learning Jesus' way of *being with* God, so that we too may call God 'Abba'; and we shall only learn that by *being with* Jesus. How are we to do this? By being together in his name, under his authority, as we experience his life through Word and Sacrament – in other words, by *being with* each other in the 'communion' of the Spirit, which is the Body of Christ.

10   There is no way of being a Christian that does not involve being with other human beings. Christianity, no less than Judaism or Islam, is a *social* reality, even though it is not based, like the other two, on a detailed legal system.

11   Like all social realities, then, Christianity needs a common means of communication. No society can survive if people do not have ways of learning what other people *mean:* a society must agree about its 'symbols', about what words, gestures, pictures and sounds stand for. To grow up and become a real member of a society is to acquire the skill of recognising what such things stand for and being able to express oneself by their means. If I think a certain word or a certain gesture is a sign of friendship when everyone else sees it as a sign of insult or hostility, I have not yet learned how to belong in my society – and I am at some real risk! It is because such systems of symbols and patterns of communication are always, in our world, shifting and changing as time goes on that no society is free from the risk of misunderstanding and conflict.

12   But we go on working at the idea that we must try to make sense of and with each other; and so we assume that societies need regular patterns and limits for what can be said or done. It must be possible – if a community is to have any coherence – to say that such-and-such a way of saying or doing things does not make sense in the terms of *this* group. Social realities, in other words, have some structure or grammar in the language they use together. If Christianity is a social reality, it is bound to have distinctive fea-

tures, points of reference that can tell you what sort of thing it is to be a Christian and what sort of thing it would not make sense for a Christian to say or do. So when Christians identify themselves, they point not simply to shared feelings but to the things they *do* together. They proclaim what Jesus has done. They baptise, give thanks and share bread and wine. In the context of these activities, they read a particular collection of books and (in the case of the majority of believers) recite particular summaries of their faith to renew their promised loyalty to the God who has called them together. They point, in short, to sacramental worship, to the Bible and to the Creeds. They should also have a concern to listen carefully to the voices of the past and to attend to exemplary and significant lives, because their 'society' involves them in *being with* those who have walked the paths of faith before. We shall be looking later at how these things are given particular expression in the Anglican tradition.

13   If the Christian community is a society, though, its existence poses some problems. The Church itself has a language and a 'culture', a way of making sense of things, a way of being human; and so it can never fully be assimilated to any society in which it finds itself.

14   The Christian way of being human – being with others, with Jesus, with the one Jesus called Father – is not the same as any of the various ways of being human that evolve in the 'natural' communities of ethnic and language groups, tribes and nations. The Christian way claims to have something for human beings *as such,* whatever their cultural or ethnic starting-point. It claims to be beyond nationalism; and however much that claim may have become hollow in the past, however much the Church has identified itself with particular cultures and languages (and particular aspirations for conquest and dominance in these cultures), it is still true that what makes people Christian, the things Christians characteristically do together, is not something bound to any one context. The Church exists in an extraordinary variety of settings. It is *free* from cultural constraint, at least in principle, and capable of challenging its cultural context.

15   The Christian way of being human is simply not compatible with any and every way of being human: it will at certain points be in conflict with aspects of the Indian or Melanesian or Irish or American way of being human. Being with Jesus by being with each other means that Christians are not going to be *uncritically* with, or on the side of, any one 'natural' culture for good and all. The Church is, by its nature, an uncomfortable presence anywhere. Because it has its own standards of human relations, it will not let itself be just the religious department of a nation-state – however often, as with the English Establishment, it has been lured into something dangerously like that role.

84

16   All this is part of what it means to say that the Church is the sign and presence of a new *humanity,* a pattern of relationships which is in principle unconfined in its appeal and relevance. But at the same time the Church is not a *total* environment; it makes claims on our whole existence, but does not set out to constitute our whole existence. It is the key to our identity before God, but it does not define the whole of that identity in its own terms. Although who I am is defined for me above all by my being the object of God's creative love and acceptance, it is also defined by language and family, nation, history, and so on. This is the material, so to speak, upon which God works the work of redemption. The ministry of Jesus did not occur in a vacuum, and he did not deal with 'abstract' persons. So being with Jesus does not annihilate who and what I am, reducing to a lowest common denominator of 'humanity' the actual rich and complex life I inherit from my context. Christianity does not offer to *replace* cultures, but to *change* them through the pervasive challenge of another way of being human, God's way in Jesus.

17   And if this is true, what exactly being a Christian will mean and look like will be different in different settings. Christianity and culture will be talking to each other, questioning each other, disagreeing with each other, at different levels, different points. This feature or that feature of Christian language will come into focus in a specific situation and need to be explored and expressed in new ways. In an important sense, then, we discover what Christian belief can *concretely* be only in this encounter. To try and conserve a timeless and comprehensive system for living the Christian way is to deny those gifts and pressures from our environment that make us the people we actually are – and, in the long run, it is to deny God's creative presence in our *nature.* So within the general limits of what it is that Christians do and what they believe they are answerable to, there will be a widely varying sense of what matters and what needs attention here and now – a variation through time and a variation in different places at the same time. The next section of our report will discuss some of the concrete problems in this area of belief and culture.

18   So we learn the Christian way of being human *in* our being with the context where we find ourselves. We shall inevitably identify ourselves in these terms, and we are often bound to take sides in the human conflicts of our environment. The Christian dimension is given by the conviction that beyond our present local identities and local struggles is the call to be with all God's human children, the possibility of a universal network of relations in which all have a full part and full freedom to learn and realise who they may be by being with Jesus. Loyalty to that call and that possibility gives a critical edge to all other loyalties.

19   This means too that being with others in the Christian community is being with those who are genuinely different, in ways that may even hurt and disturb us. The *catholicity* of the Church is not just an abiding fact about its faith and order: it is also the reality of active exchange between diverse Christian enterprises.

20   I discover a great deal about what I am called to preach, and how, in the pressures of my particular situation; and what I discover I must offer to and share with other believers. But then, also, I must discover something about the gospel through what they share with me – not in terms of models or policies I must follow, but in terms of going deeper into the strange resource-fulness of the gospel in diverse settings, its freedom to engage with cultures and its freedom from them. Whether or not I endorse or even fully understand what another Christian community does, it will be potentially a gift for me and mine, as my policies and reflections may be for it. What is done in Christ's name, within a common declared faithfulness to the marks that identify an action as Christian, can always offer me the chance of growing further myself, in my context with my agenda and my people, towards Christ's fullness. Shared experience is also shared spirituality, shared discovery of a life in Christ.

21   For the Church to be 'catholic' is for it to be actively committed to a twofold encounter: the discovery of itself and its resources in attending to the needs of its context, and the discovery of what is at the heart of its worldwide common life in the sharing of reflection and experience within the Church across cultural and historical boundaries. Thus the *catholic* nature of the Church is inseparable from its *mission* (its *apostolic* character, its being sent into all the world) and its *unity* – which is not a monolithic sameness but a unity in relation. Such a unity *depends* on the willingness to be true to our calling in the specific context we stand in, to share what that means, and to be ready to hear what others have to share with us. Through this manifold quest to be faithful to each other and to be christianly responsible in our context, the Church is maintained in *holiness;* for this commitment to *being with* one another, in Church and society, is the means of being with Jesus. To share his life, to be where he is, to be in him, is the only way for the Christian to be holy – not by achievement, not by spiritual mastery, but by trustful fidelity.

22   Thus the kind of God we believe in, the God shown to us in Jesus, determines the kind of Church we have. Our God is a God whose nature it is to communicate, to share the divine life. God *is* a life of communication, response and rejoicing, before the world is made. God comes to us in the form of Jesus' invitation to be with him in his ministry of healing, exorcism and absolution, in his suffering, in his risen life. We learn how to be with him in ministry to the world and each other, in vulnerability and identification

with pain and oppression, in the communication of the creative freedom of the risen life, both in the celebration of the breaking of bread with the risen Lord, and in the struggle and exchange of our shared life. The structures of the Church must serve two functions above all: to keep before us the liberating history of Jesus crucified and risen; and to enable us to give thanks to God for one another by holding us in communion, in active unity and communication. They must help us to be free to enter the conversation with our culture and with one another; they must remind us of the structure, the 'grammar' of Christian talk which we possess together. They must equip us for realistic engagement with the present, but they must also speak of that future when the 'catholic' work of God in Jesus is finished and all peoples walk with each other and with Jesus in the light of the city of God.

CHRIST AND CULTURE

23   It should be clear from what has been said in the introduction that there is no form of Christian life and language that is quite free from the influence of the culture in which it exists. This is only a problem or a weakness where the fact is not recognised. It is right and proper that the one faith and discipline of the Church should be 'incarnate' in varied cultural forms; as was said earlier, the Gospel of Jesus does not come to people in the abstract, but to specific men and women. It is as persons *already* created in the image of God that we meet Jesus and learn to live with him; God the Redeemer is the same as God the Creator. The work of Jesus does not destroy but fulfils the work of the God of creation, the God already with us in the natural forms of our lives together and in our relation with our whole environment.

24   But if we imagine that we have discovered a way of being Christian quite independent of culture, or if we fail to notice that what we think is distinctly Christian is actually cultural, we are liable to put serious obstacles in the way of preaching the Gospel. We may encourage our hearers to think that the Gospel depends on things quite foreign to them, so that in rejecting the cultural forms they reject the Gospel too.

25   So the problem of 'Christ and Culture' is in large part a problem of how to communicate the Gospel effectively. There is, however, a further issue that must be mentioned here, though it cannot be fully resolved. If God is embodied in a human being of a particular culture – first-century Palestine – how far can we conclude that God affirms as part of divine revelation various features of that culture? If the Bible generally belongs, as it does, in specific cultural settings, how much in it can we safely assume to be *only* the result of cultural conditioning? These matters arise with special force in debates about marriage and sexuality and about the status and role of women.

26 Two observations may be made here. First, it is possible to recognise that the Christian Gospel cannot be made intelligible without some reference to the historical context in which it first appeared while at the same time recognising that Jesus and the New Testament writers are also already in conflict with aspects of that context which *restrict* the Gospel. Second, the judgement as to which of these aspects do restrict the Gospel, which are matters of indifference, and which are lastingly bound to the heart of the Gospel is a complex and long drawn out process, in aspects of which there may be legitimate disagreement. Only as we *now* seek to make the Gospel liberating and intelligible, in the light of our whole heritage, can we begin to discern where the distinctive heart of the Gospel lies. We are taught in and by our endeavours in mission.

27 The Gospel, then, is always being communicated in a framework shaped by the historical and social situations of believers. It acquires a kind of 'sediment' of local idiom and tradition. It is both the glory and the deadly danger of Christianity that it can enter deeply into a people's soul, so that it carries the most profound hopes and values of a nation or civilisation. The Russian Christianity whose millennium we celebrate this year is still one of the most important identifying symbols of the Russian-speaking people. The Roman Catholicism of France and Spain or the Lutheranism of Denmark are still – for good or ill – part of the identity and mythology of these nations. In the same way pre-Chalcedonian orthodoxy is very closely related to Armenian, Coptic or Ethiopian culture. All such distinctive styles have enormous richness and resource. But when the Gospel is communicated from these nations to other settings, that very richness becomes a source of difficulty, preventing newer Churches from accumulating riches and resources of their own, 'drinking from their own wells'.[2]

28 Especially difficult is the situation in which Christianity has come in harness with a colonial power. Here the communication of a Gospel embedded in one culture is bound up with some of the most problematic features of cultural life – the realities of a foreign system of economic power and political and legal control. Such a transmission of Christianity has happened more than once in history and has occurred in many different cultural settings. Thus when Anglicanism was exported to other continents, it came not only with the 'Englishness' of certain styles of clothing, music and worship, but with certain assumptions about who made decisions, who had authority in social life, who had ultimate control in economic affairs, markets, production, land ownership. The dominance of English styles – neo-Gothic churches, English church music, a concern with European church history, western clerical dress, and so on – could be seen as a reflection of the plain facts of political and economic dominance.

29 It is appropriate that the 'sending churches' of the last great missionary

era look back on all this with a critical and penitent eye. Yet many African Christians, for example, would still want also to express their gratitude for the gift of the Gospel, their appreciation of good intentions, and their indebtedness for some of the incidental effects of mission during the colonial period – advanced medical care, for instance, or the campaign against slave-trading. For some, to become a Christian might have been to become deeply estranged from an indigenous culture; but it might also be to find a new freedom from the oppressions of an indigenous culture.

30 In time, however, the cultural forms of colonial churchmanship revealed their own oppressiveness. All too often, especially in styles of worship, they offered little more than blanket condemnations of the 'old' culture. Their own cultural forms ceased to be effective carriers of good news. Newer Churches found that they had learned a lesson that could be applied against those who had first taught it. If the Gospel can free you from cultural oppression, it can also free you from the cultural oppression of a Church that does not know how culturally conditioned it is. The process of finding an authentically *local* Christian identity may begin. It is worth adding that the same process happens within Churches in what has been thought to be a single culture, when disadvantaged or powerless people in England or North America – working-class people, Black people, women – begin to discover how to be Christian in their own style and their own voice. It is a process that still has far to go in the Churches of the northern hemisphere, bound as many of them are to a 'suburban' culture. But it is a process – whether in the northern hemisphere or in the countries of the developing world – which we wish to encourage as strongly as possible and for which we, as pastors in the Churches, are profoundly thankful.

31 We must also recognise, however, that the process we are talking about is multi-faceted. At least four stages can be distinguished.

32 There is the period of primary evangelistic activity. At this stage, the distinction between the 'culture' of the Gospel itself – the values and priorities of the human and divine vision that are involved in being with Jesus – and the culture of the *preachers* of the Gospel has yet to be discerned.

33 There follows the period in which this has begun to be recognised. The Church seeks to contextualise, to draw on and affirm the resources of the culture in which it has taken root. This has involved the adoption of indigenous styles of music and dance, the attempt to employ locally meaningful language and imagery in liturgy, and, more tentatively, to work through local methods of decision-making and local models of authority.

34 This is not the end of the process. The Indian experience, both ancient and modern, in particular, has pointed up the possible ambiguities of the inculturation of Christianity. It can suggest the endorsement of some of the

social forms or mythologies from which people actually seek to be free. It can take for granted that a particular culture is more static and more monolithic than in fact it is. It can run counter to the social processes, even the religious ideals, within the overall context, which make for creativity and change. It can appear as patronising, romantic and unreal, especially when industrialisation, urbanisation and secularisation are proceeding at a rapid pace. An uncritical approach to traditional social forms has little to say to those caught up in the poverty traps of the exploding cities in the developing world, where new social patterns and educational needs appear.

35   But the Church, then, also has the further and difficult task of assisting a *critique* of industrialisation, urbanisation and secularisation. It must not become once again the ally of a narrow and oppressive definition of what cultural (including political and economic) development means. For this to be possible, the Church needs, first of all, the kind of identification with and awareness of the realities of its situation which gives it some genuine authority to resist the pressures of a new cultural imperialism. The Church needs to be *alongside* the people it seeks to serve, rather than assuming glibly and hastily that it has the right to speak for them whether or not it shows practical solidarity. Secondly, the Church, both in the industrialised nations and in the developing world, needs constantly to reflect on and to deepen its understanding of its *distinctive* models of human *relation,* so that it has the moral and theological resources to evaluate the processes of political and economic development. Christians must be free to assess how these processes do or do not fit with what the Gospel sets before us as the proper patterns of human growth and human relation.

36   Thus the business of freeing the Church from the 'Babylonish capivity' of colonial culture is multi-faceted and long-term; and it requires more than a merely guilty or sentimental politeness to what is thought to be 'indigenous' culture. It involves an imaginative sensitivity to the concrete social processes at work in specific contexts – to how nations and peoples are *actually* becoming themselves – and a serious listening to how people themselves perceive their hopes for fuller liberation from alien systems of domination. The question is that of how these hopes may be 'at home' with the freedom promised by the Gospel. How can the Gospel help to shape the struggle against the deadening conformity (at one level) and the dehumanising poverty (at another level) which are produced by the present international economic order?

37   All this also gives some further insight into how the Church learns from its cultural context something about its own Gospel – how, indeed, the Church may even hear its *judgement* from this context. It may be shown how restricted its vision of humanity, and of the future and hopes of humanity, has been. A local church that has begun to learn this has a great gift to offer to other Christian communities.

38   In this way the younger Churches of Asia, Africa and Latin America have often become evangelists to the Churches of the northern hemisphere. What were, during the last three hundred years or so, the 'sending Churches' have had many of their comfortable assumptions shaken. New kinds of theology (not only liberation theology but the Minjung theology or 'water buffalo theology' of East Asia) have questioned the rather parochial methods and interests of western academic theology and ministerial training. The ancient Christian Churches of Asia and Africa are experiencing renewal. The pressures of grassroots evangelism and the renewing power of charismatic movements are a reminder that western rationalism is also in many respects a 'local culture' that programmes out those things with which it is uncomfortable. The privatised or individualist character of much religion in the industrialised countries is put in question by the centrality of community and social involvement for many Churches, which do not make the fatal split between sacred and secular realms and between individual and communal well-being. The suffering of Churches, both ancient and newer, confronting a militant and exclusivist vision of Islam (a problem much in the mind and in the prayers of this Conference) disturbs some western hopes for a calm and conflictless dialogue between religions. More positively, western Churches have received a new sense of the freshness of Christ, the witness, tragic and compelling, of martyrs, and a new impetus towards celebration.

39   These are things which press the western Churches to re-examine what is and is not essentially part of the Gospel in their own witness and mission, and to free them further for mission in their own context. Not that western Churches any more than others can possibly look for a Christianity absolutely free of cultural trappings; all we have said here assumes that this would be a false goal. But we may learn better what in our culture serves preaching and what subtly and imperceptibly gets in its way. By listening to the Christian experience of others, we can become more, not less, aware of our own situation.

40   What are the limits of this catholic pluralism? Does all this imply that we should also be listening to the experience of people in other religious traditions as well as other Christian contexts? We have already said that the Church can learn from those outside it, and even be 'judged' by them. But we have also noted the difficulties in making glib and generalised statements about dialogue. In Great Britain, for example, the Churches are rightly eager to give a voice to disadvantaged people belonging to other religious traditions, who often live at the most vulnerable level of society and are victims of persistent and outrageous racism. But elsewhere, *Christians* are a disadvantaged minority in an overwhelmingly hostile non-Christian environment, and those of the majority religion, in such contexts, who in the western world may be marginal and vulnerable, are in a position to put great pressure on the Churches. The worldwide Church includes people per-

secuted for their faith by members of other faiths – the very faiths with which many Christians wish to develop a dialogue. The problem is to know how such a dialogue can be carried forward while being faithful to Jesus Christ and those who suffer for his sake. In our next section we shall turn to examine this complex of questions. (See further Resolution 22.)

CHRIST AND PEOPLE OF OTHER FAITHS

41 When speaking about the relationship between Christ and people of other faiths, it is important not to lose sight of the basic affirmations about God in Christ from earlier sections of this report. The God and Father of our Lord Jesus has been revealed as one whose very life is a 'being with'. The Son or Word, incarnate in Jesus Christ, is himself an outpouring of divine life rejoicing in itself and seeking to share itself. God is now with the community of Jesus as counsellor, advocate, challenge and guide, continuing Jesus' work of new creation. On this basis we have affirmed that the Christian way of being human is simply not compatible with any and every way of being human: it will conflict at certain points with aspects of particular cultures and, indeed, religions. It is against the background of these affirmations that we must raise the question of God's relationship to people of other faiths in the light of his self-disclosure in Jesus Christ.

42 The very life of God is a 'being with'. This was true in the beginning, is true today, and will be the source of the greatest joy at the end of time. Creation itself is an act of 'being with'; there was never a time nor a place when this fundamental affirmation about God was not true. There is not a single person whose very being is not a manifestation of this truth that God is, by nature, a 'being with'. The Son or Word, the longing of God to share the divine life with others, was the one through whom all things were made. The Word who became incarnate in Jesus *is* the unquenchable desire of God to be with us (Emmanuel). The incarnation is itself the definitive expression of this longing on the part of God. How do we express in our own day the relationship between the universal longing on the part of God to be with all men and women, and Jesus who is the very incarnation of this divine reality?

43 The intimate relationship between God and humanity which we know in the person of Jesus *is* the fundamental paradigm of God's relationship with the world. It is for that reason that the Bible proclaims that God's purpose since before creation has been to sum up all things in Christ, so that Christ might in the end present them to the Father, that God might be all in all (Eph. 1.10, 1 Cor. 15.24-28).

44 To read in this statement the doctrine of 'universal salvation' is to miss the point. Its ultimate significance is Christological. It is a statement about who this Lord Jesus truly is. It is, however, intended as a corrective to an

uncritical reading of certain 'exclusivist' passages in the Bible. Anything which is 'exclusively' true of the incarnate Lord is true of one who is precisely the most 'inclusive' reality, the divine life rejoicing in itself and seeking to share itself. All of creation is caught up in this movement, for all of creation has been called into existence by this movement of divine love.

45   On the other hand, we must not underestimate the reality of our estrangement from God. We recognise that throughout much of history human beings have often said 'No' to God. Many Christians believe that this is not a final word; and in any case the sole final word is God's Word in Christ, whose full meaning will become apparent only in the day when 'the secrets of all hearts shall be revealed'. Nevertheless this human 'No' is a real word which marks the need for repentance on the part of believers and non-believers alike.

46   That does not mean, however, that every human way which has not yet said 'Yes' to the incarnate Lord has said 'No' to the ultimate reality of his divine being. There are those who said 'Yes' to God before his gift of his Son. We believe, with the author of the Letter to the Hebrews, that their positive response to God could receive its full reward only in the reality of the incarnate Lord; but their fidelity was acceptable and accepted. This is not strange if, as we confess, all things have by God's will been appointed their fulfilment in Christ since before the foundation of the world. There are important Christological issues at stake here. We wish to continue to affirm, with the Creeds of the early Church, that the Lord assumed the fullness of our humanity. The 'scandal of particularity' is bound up with the universal significance of the particular person we confess as saviour. It involves us in proclaiming that the God whose Word of love became fully incarnate in Jesus is the God of all creation. There is much in him which we shall see to be his only in the fullness of time.

47   The same is true of the counsel, challenge and guidance of the Holy Spirit. Jesus warned that the Spirit was wont to blow where it willed. The gift of the Spirit to the Church at Pentecost is again remarkable precisely because the Spirit who is given is the universal Spirit of God. Any interpret-ation of the person of Christ or of the Spirit which diminishes the universality of their presence or of their work ultimately diminishes the significance of the reality of the Church. To deny that the Lord of the Church is the one who is universally the Lord of creation, in presence, in sharing, in communica-tion as well as in power and judgement, runs the risk of turning the God and Father of our Lord into a tribal God.

48   We look and listen, therefore, when we encounter men and women of other faiths, indeed of other kinds of deep commitment as well. We listen in order to overhear what dialogue there may be between God and these people – between the God who calls all into being by a process of sharing and

communication, and other people in their religious cultures. This is difficult. We may not know the language and culture in which the faith of the other person is expressed. But without learning this we cannot understand either what they are hearing or what they are saying back. We listen not only, or even primarily, to judge but also in order to learn. We have already spoken of the need to correct our particular expression of Christian faith in the light of other Christian experience. We may also have to correct it in the light of the commitment of non-Christians. We may not yet have even heard the questions which, in their context, they are struggling to answer. There may be new questions for us to explore, questions which have not been our questions before. There may be new aspects of the human condition which we have not experienced. Our understanding of Christ, the only fully human person, can only be enriched by such exploration. But we may entirely miss the challenge unless we can be open to the searchings of others. God is surely there. It is God who calls our brothers and sisters into being and who stands over against them in the reality of their partial, human lives. How much of the fullness of Christ there is to learn in the experience of all those he loves! But this will be the case only if we care, truly care, to learn their words, their means of expression; and only if we dare to believe that we will see there something of the presence of the God who called them, no less than us, into being who and what they are.

49   Because of this, it does not surprise us to find echoes of the Gospel in the deep convictions of our non-Christian brothers and sisters. It would be surprising if we did not. Neither is it strange that the Church has constantly deepened its faith in its struggle with questions, concepts and experiences which ultimately derived from philosophies, religions and patterns of thought to which the Gospel of Christ was as yet unknown. We are the richer for the struggle of the Church to understand the implications of the Gospel in the light of the religious and philosophical experience of the Jewish and Hellenistic worlds of the first few centuries of our era. We shall be poorer when Christians stop exploring the full meaning of Christ in the light of the experiences and languages of the many cultures and religions in which human life is lived to the full.[3]

50   There seems to be no reason, therefore, to break the long tradition of the majority of Christian apologists in affirming what we can in the deep commitments of our non-Christian neighbours. Christian faith throughout the ages has been able, in its encounters with other traditions, to deepen its understanding of and its faith in the nature and work of God as presented to us in the Scriptures. The general approach of early Christian apologists was that all truth is the truth of Christ. Not only did they affirm what was true, wherever they may have found it, they actually appropriated it and claimed that ultimately it was 'Christian truth'.[4] It is to be hoped that Anglicans will continue to be open to the search for an ever-deeper understanding of the

things of God, calling upon the insights of the many traditions, cultures and languages in which the Churches of the Communion are to be found.

51   People sometimes fear that to affirm the presence of any encounter with God outside of Christianity is to imply that any truth to be found there may, in its own right, be 'saving truth'. We wish to affirm that the only 'truth' which has saving power is *God*. The incarnate Lord said, 'I am the truth'. It is this truth alone which saves. Since the only truth to which we are prepared to ascribe saving power is God, there is a sense in which no human know-ledge has saving power at all. This means that such questions about the ulti-mate salvation of non-Christians are perhaps not possible of a definitive ans-wer on the part of the Church. A number of contemporary theologians, among them leading Anglican Evangelicals like John Stott and Sir Norman Anderson, have professed a certain 'agnosticism' on this particular ques-tion. It is undoubtedly healthier to be 'agnostic' here than to claim for our-selves a judgement which is finally God's alone. Sir Norman, indeed, seems to move beyond agnosticism to a more positive evaluation of those followers of other religions who, in repentance and brokenness, are seeking God.[5]

52   Men and women today live by a number of rival views of reality which claim their allegiance and to which they struggle to be faithful with varying degrees of commitment. Some of these systems of life and thought have traditionally been called 'religious', such as Judaism, Christianity, Islam, Sikhism, Buddhism, Hinduism, African traditional religions, among others. Some have not traditionally been called religious, such as secular humanism, existentialism, Marxism among others. All of them, however, have shown themselves capable of claiming the allegiance of large numbers of men and women. Christians can and should explore together with all such committed individuals and groups the fullness of humanity which, for them, is summed up in Christ.

53   Such common exploration of the ultimate significance of the human condition has recently been called 'dialogue'. The word is not new, but its use in a phrase like 'inter-faith dialogue' has been the cause of some confu-sion and controversy. To some, dialogue, because it implies the need to lis-ten seriously and openly to the other person, seems to suggest that procla-mation of the Good News of what God has done in Christ is not necessary. There seems to be some fear that the use of the word 'dialogue' is intended to preclude such a proclamation. In the light of what has been said here, dialogue is a common and mutual exploration of the ultimate significance of the human condition. Understood in this way, it can not preclude the procla-mation of the Gospel. On the contrary, such open and honest discussion necessitates proclamation, for we come to 'dialogue' already enriched by a particular understanding of the significance of our common humanity, an understanding which is both grounded in and defined by the reality of Christ.

54 It is true that there will be a stage in this process when we do not yet understand our partners' language, culture and commitment well enough to make our own viewpoint accessible and intelligible to them. We should not look for short cuts here that would relieve us of the hard work of listening. Human history is full of tragic episodes due largely to the failure of groups or individuals to communicate with each other. It can be disheartening to struggle with learning a foreign language. In the case of dialogue we may be struggling with two foreign languages at once. Our partner may literally speak a different language from our own as well as having a *religious* language which requires patient learning in order for us to understand. At this stage we may be tempted to take a short cut and start speaking before we have mastered either language, or having mastered only one. If the dialogue is to progress, someone must take the trouble to be sure that there is a common area of discourse.

55 This common exploration of the ultimate significance of the human condition which we have called 'dialogue' is not only the realm of specialists. To be sure, they are needed. The Church must especially prepare some who are given the time and training necessary to go deeply into the languages and scholarly disciplines involved in the rich and varied traditions which hold the allegiance of our brothers and sisters. But it must never be restricted to specialists. There is a real sense in which *dialogue may begin whenever people meet each other.* We know that this is true even when Christians meet each other. It is also true when we meet people of other faiths and ideologies. If we are seriously open to their experience, we share together much of what it means to be human and, perhaps, share new insights with each other.

56 For such an encounter to take place, however, *there must be mutual understanding and mutual trust.* This may take a long time to establish. It does not mean that there can be no dialogue until there is *perfect* understanding and trust. To whatever extent there is mutual trust and understanding, we can honestly explore together the common implications of our humanity and of our individual hopes, fears and commitments. Such a sharing can become the basis for a deeper trust and understanding. Even if only one partner is truly interested in understanding the experience of the other partner, there can be the beginning of dialogue.

57 Such mutual exploration of the implications of our life together *makes it easier to share in service to the community.* When we realise how much we have in common with other human beings, when we allow ourselves to feel their pains and their joys, to fear their fears and sing their songs, to see them as they see themselves (and perhaps ourselves as they see us), then we find much on which we can co-operate. This is also a way of dialogue. To work together on a common problem, to pursue a common goal, means learning

to communicate. If co-operation requires some ability to communicate as a prerequisite, it also develops and trains that ability to an even higher level.

58   The experience of meeting, understanding and co-operating with others becomes *an effective medium of authentic witness to the Gospel of Christ.* When we reach the point where we can actually work together with men and women of other commitments, then we are in a position actually to demonstrate how our understanding of the ultimate significance of the human condition in Christ affects the life we live. (Paras. 55-58; cf. Resolution 20.)

59   In the course of this we shall have had the privilege of being near to the presence of God in one whom he loved into existence. In time, we will learn to hear something of the hidden conversation between God and another human being. We shall be richer for that; our understanding of God will be richer for that. Perhaps, our partner will also be richer for that.[6]

60   For some Churches of the Anglican Communion, there is much opportunity for dialogue with secular humanism, which is historically derived from the Renaissance in Western Europe. As Western culture has become secularised, humanism has cut itself off from its Christian roots, and is now a rival religion in that it commands ultimate allegiance in the place of a faith relationship with Jesus Christ. But it also hold values, attitudes and cultural goals in common with those of Christians. This common ground opens up tremendous possibilities for dialogue in terms of the understanding of dialogue set forth in this report.

61   In addition to secular humanism, there is the need to be in dialogue with other forms of secular ideology which have grown up beside it. In particular, there is an urgent need to speak with men and women who are committed to various forms of Communist ideology. In many parts of the Christian world such a dialogue is already a reality. Our deeply committed Christian brothers and sisters tell us that their faith has been deepened even as it has been challenged by the deep commitment of Communists in their struggle for human liberation and for a just society. Their experience is calling many of us in the Church to a renewed struggle for human rights, justice and peace. It is a good example of a dialogue which has a profound influence on our Christian awareness, even among Christians who are not themselves directly involved in it.

62   Many Christians have felt that their faith has been deepened and their understanding of the human condition broadened through dialogue with Buddhism, Hinduism and Sikhism.[7] Unfortunately, we have not had the opportunity to review much of this work at this Conference. We urge those of our Communion who live in contact with men and women committed to those faiths to explore with them their experiences and to reflect together on

the problems and also on the rich tradition of Asian countries and civilisations. We hope that they will share with all of us what new insights are gained into the reality of the fullness of humanity which is ours in Christ.

63　However, it is the 'Abrahamic' faiths, as they are often called, of Judaism and Islam with which dialogue is both most immediate and most difficult. Where Judaism is concerned, Christians in the West must not be allowed to forget how centuries of antisemitism led up to the unparalleled atrocity of the Holocaust in our century. It is only by showing some authentic repentance and identification with the victims of antisemitism that western Christians can earn the right to challenge the violent reactions of an insecure and threatened Jewish state, and to do so not only on behalf of Christian and Muslim Arabs, especially in Palestine, but in the name of the Jewish heritage itself. We note with interest and sympathy the emergence of a 'Jewish Theology of Liberation' which we may expect to take up the cause of the oppressed from within the international Jewish community.[8]

64　Islam has long been seen – especially in the Middle Ages – as a negative counter-force to Christianity. The rich legacy of Islamic art and literature, theology and mysticism, to which oriental Christians have made a significant contribution, and the profound Muslim concern for true social *equity* under God are things for which we give thanks. We remember too that there have been Muslim states whose religious tolerance puts Christians of the same era to shame (as in early mediaeval Spain). Today, as sometimes in the past, many of our Christian brothers and sisters face an aggressive and exclusivist Islam, threatening the very life of the Church in many lands. They have our prayers and support. If there is to be dialogue with Islam, it must be on the basis that modern 'Islamic fundamentalism' is no more the whole story of Islam than the Crusades are of Christianity. We can be enriched by the Muslim way of being human in its historical fullness. A truly informed Christian dialogue may be one factor which helps Muslims themselves to recognise that fullness and resist the pressures towards a violent and narrow response to Christians and others.[9]

65　From a commitment to inter-faith dialogue, there arise a number of practical issues concerning which brief comments can be made here.

66　Can persons of differing religious traditions worship together? Such persons share a common belief in 'that which is other' and through common concern for the unity and well-being of the human race have sometimes felt it right to pray together for justice and peace. The Assisi event in October 1986 was one such occasion. The form of this event itself, however, suggests that we cannot share anything like a common liturgy, the specific act of a specific community, but can only pray alongside each other.

67　Is there a Christian obligation of hospitality to persons of other faiths?

In many Provinces, Christians have shown a desire to welcome and help immigrant and refugee communities. Part of this help has sometimes consisted in sharing and selling church property so that persons of other faiths may have places to meet and worship. At times such hospitality has embarrassed Christians in countries where the Church is a beleaguered minority, and where such hospitality has been used as an opportunity for religious and political propaganda. Despite this, we wish to reaffirm our commitment to *proper* hospitality for those who are strangers and disadvantaged. In this we believe we are following the example of our father Abraham.

68 We believe that freedom for religious communities to gather for their characteristic activities and liturgies is a fundamental human right, and that it should be granted and protected by all governments. We regret that in some Islamic states such freedoms are not granted or protected. (See Resolution 23.)

69 The problem as to whether shared worship is legitimate brings us back to the kind of thing Christianity actually is. It is an active response to God's atoning and reconciling work in Christ, which takes shape primarily as a pattern of things done, and not primarily as a system of ideas. So we turn next to the question of how the 'pattern of things done' makes a coherent whole and what the Anglican Communion in particular understands to be the authoritative points of reference for its life and teaching.

THE CHRISTIAN INHERITANCE: ELEMENTS OF AUTHORITY

70 In any human society, of whatever sort, authority has its basis in the shared life of the community, and in the practices, rituals, and language which embody that shared life and convey the attitudes, values, and beliefs it entails. The task of authority is to transmit, safeguard, and diffuse a way of life that is embodied in this fashion.

71 In the case of the Christian community and fellowship, the life which its members share does not derive from itself but is rooted in that of the crucified and risen Christ and is conferred by God through the working of the Holy Spirit. God sends 'the Spirit of his Son into our hearts, crying, "Abba", "Father",' (Gal. 4.6) and the relationship that is thus established founds the Church and constitutes the shared life of the whole people of God. For this reason, the practices, liturgies, and language of the Church have as their primary function the mediation of this relationship to God in Christ with which the Church is gifted. In prayer, praise, and thanksgiving the Church offers itself to God, and that very action becomes the vehicle through which God is with us. Accordingly we say that the primary task of authority in the Church is to enable 'every member of the same' to enter into this relationship and to live it out. As disciples, believers begin here and now to live, and to share and bear witness to the life of the coming reign of God.

72   When earlier Lambeth Conferences formulated the *Chicago-Lambeth Quadrilateral,* they defined, in effect if not by intent, what Anglicans mean by the most universal and fundamental practices, liturgies, and language of the Church. The Church expounds the Scriptures and uses the ecumenical Creeds both as confessions of faith and as schemes of instruction. Further- more, it does this in its characteristic liturgies, focused as these are in bap- tism and eucharist, and under the presidency of a pastoral ministry of over- sight that binds the Church together in time and in space. Taken together, these institutions constitute an interlocking, interdependent set of activities and practices that both sustain the Church and identify it as the people of God in Christ. They are a necessary condition of the Church's unity, holi- ness, catholicity, and apostolicity: they mark essential points in its life where the grace and truth which are in the Word made flesh are conveyed and mediated to believers.

73   The first thing to be said, then, about authority as Christians under- stand it, is that its source is the divine Trinity. God has given the risen Christ authority over all creation (Matt. 28.18). The Church, of which Christ is the head because it lives by his life, is that portion of humanity which recognises Christ's authority.

74   In the world, Christ's authority is exercised in a multitude of ways, but it only becomes explicit in the life of the Church which is his Body. That is: Christ exercises authority in the world through the lives and deeds of those who by baptism are united with him in the likeness of his death. Through their mortal bodies, he continues to vanquish the powers of darkness, to heal the sick in body and spirit, and to draw all people to himself. The authority of Christ in and over the world is thus significantly but not exclusively exer- cised in the witness of the Church, through which his work of redemption is being brought to fulfilment in all the world, until God shall be all in all.

75   Within the community of believers, Christ exercises authority for a par- ticular purpose. His authority calls and holds the Church together in order that it may be his Body – the visible sign of his presence for the world, and the priestly people that offer spiritual sacrifices to God. The Church's mem- bers, then, have a calling to be children of God, disciples and co-workers of God's Word; and his vocation is opened to them and conferred on them in quite concrete ways: namely, through the organically related, humanly con- ducted set of practices and liturgies by which the Holy Spirit binds the Church in with Christ and enables it to share his calling and destiny.

76   Human beings, however, are intelligent, self-conscious creatures who discern meaning in their experience, and communicate that meaning, by means of language, i.e. by the use of sign and symbol. For this reason, the question of Christ's exercise of authority in the Church has tended, for prac- tical purposes, to centre around the issue of his communicable teaching: that

is, the issue of how believers are to understand and communicate, in doctrine and in deed, what Christ through the Spirit shows them about God and themselves. No sooner is this question raised, however, than one matter becomes clear. The Church is, not by accident but of necessity, an ongoing *community of interpretation*. Its search for understanding of the teaching – or the 'mind' – of Christ takes the form of a process in which it ever and again interprets and applies the language of the sources from which it learns of Christ and through which it hears him. This in turn, requires that it identify both reliable ways of understanding those sources and reliable agencies for their interpretation.

77   Regarding the identity of what we have called 'the sources' of the Church's knowledge of Christ there can be little doubt, whether for Anglicans or for their fellow Christians of other traditions. All affirm the sovereign authority of the holy Scriptures as the medium through which God by the Spirit communicates his word in the Church and thus enables people to respond with understanding and faith. This medium of God's Word is, of course, a collection of human writings, a whole literature that records – in historical narrative, legend, prophecy, poem, parable, and letter – the story of God's way with a continuing series of human communities and their response to his judgements and his salvific acts. These Scriptures the Church receives as 'the uniquely inspired witness to divine revelation', and 'the primary norm for Christian faith and life'. It turns to them for its understanding of God, of Christ in whom God is 'with us', and hence of its own salvation and calling.

78   The Scriptures, however, must be translated, read, and understood, and thus their meaning is to be grasped only through a continuing process of interpretation. Their essential message is not veiled or ambiguous but plain and intelligible. Nevertheless, that message must be, and in fact is, declared and explained in ever-changing circumstances, cultural settings, and languages. Hence the question arises, what principles shall govern the Church's exposition of the Scriptures and what guides shall be accepted for their interpretation. To this question Anglicanism has, since the seventeenth century, returned a straightforward, if broad and general, answer. Scripture is to be understood and read in the light afforded by the contexts of 'tradition' and 'reason'.

79   Take the word 'tradition'. In one sense that term can denote the Scriptures themselves, in that they embody 'the tradition', 'the message', 'the faith once delivered to the saints'. But tradition can also, in another and wider sense, denote not the 'deposit of faith' itself, but the ongoing, Spirit-guided life of the Church which receives, and in receiving interprets, God's message. The Scriptures themselves are a product of tradition so understood. They are the literature which the Church gradually received and

defined as the authoritative interpretation and embodiment of the word by which it lives. Once acknowledged as 'the Church's books' in this special sense, however, they themselves become the subject of an ongoing process of interpretation that assumes myriad forms. In preaching and teaching, in patterns of common and individual prayer, in learned exegesis, in habits of behaviour and action, and in dogmatic definition, the Church appropriates the Scriptures and expresses its understanding of them. This living tradition of ongoing interpretation gives rise to weighty, influential and authoritative formulae: classical eucharistic prayers, for example, and popular hymns, not to mention the ecumenical Creeds, which stand alongside the Scriptures themselves as summaries of their essential message.[10]

80   Nevertheless, tradition in this sense is not to be equated simply with the classical formulae or formularies it produces. Rather, it is the living and growing 'mind' of the Church that has from generation to generation been formed and challenged by the scriptural Word in the process of appropriating that Word in liturgy, life and teaching. The appeal to tradition is the appeal to this 'mind' – the mind carried and articulated by the very language that the Church speaks in worship and preaching – as a receiver better attuned than most to the frequency of God's Word.

81   What, then, are we to make of 'reason'? Properly speaking, 'reason' means simply the human being's capacity to symbolise, and so to order, share, and communicate, experience. It is the divine gift in virtue of which human persons respond and act with awareness in relation to their world and to God. Understood in this way, reason cannot be divorced either from Scripture or from tradition, since neither is even conceivable apart from the working of reason.

82   Considered in another perspective, however, 'reason' means not so much the *capacity* to make sense of things as it does 'that which makes sense', or 'that which is reasonable'. The appeal to reason then becomes an appeal to what people – and that means people in a given time and place – take as good sense or 'common' sense. It refers, in short, to what we can call the 'mind' of a particular culture, with its characteristic ways of seeing things, asking about them, and explaining them. If, then, tradition is the mind that Christians share as believers and members of the Church, reason is the mind that they share as participants in a particular culture. It is the distillation, in language and outlook, of the experience that constitutes a certain way of life. There have been times and places in history when the 'mind' of a culture and the 'mind' represented by the Church's tradition have virtually coincided: the Latin Europe of the Middle Ages and the culture of the Armenians might be cited as examples. For the most part, however, this is not and has not been the case – and particularly not in modern times, which have been called modern precisely because they challenged Christian tradition in the name of reason.

83   This circumstance has occasioned, among Christians, a certain distrust of 'reason', and perhaps understandably. Deprecation of reason – of what 'makes sense' to the world – has become almost habitual in the Churches. Nevertheless, Anglicanism sees 'reason', in the sense of the 'mind' of the culture in which the Church lives and the Gospel is proclaimed, as a legitimate, and indeed necessary, instrument for the interpretation of God's message in the Scriptures. The Word of God, embodying as it does 'God with us', is not addressed to the Church in and of itself, but to the Church as it is part of its world. Hence the Gospel borne by the Scriptures must be heard and interpreted in the language that bears the 'mind' and distils the experience of the world which God is calling to be transformed and renewed in the Kingdom that Jesus announced.[11]

84   Tradition and reason, then, are two distinct contexts in which the Scriptures speak and out of which they are interpreted. It is in the interplay and the conflict between them – between the common mind of the Church and the common mind of a culture – that the meaning of the Gospel for a particular time and place is to be discerned. Indeed it could be argued that tradition – what we have called the 'mind' of the Church – is the repository of just such discernments, discernments stimulated by the tradition and the language of a particular culture. To be involved in this dialogical situation is always uncomfortable. It becomes dangerous, perhaps, only when what is properly a dialogue becomes a monologue delivered at length by only one of its parties. Tradition and reason need each other if God's Word is to be shared.

85   The process of interpretation, however, through which God calls, teaches, and nurtures people as disciples of the Word requires that Scripture, reason and tradition speak through the voices of living human persons. They can often remain dead and silent apart from the activity of human agents, individual and collective teachers who bear witness to the fruit of study, prayer and experience by declaring, explaining and clarifying God's message.

86   Here we think in the first instance of the 'official ministry', the pastors and teachers whom Christ calls in the Church to 'testify to the Gospel of the grace of God' (Acts 20.24) and to 'guard the truth entrusted to them' (2 Tim. 1.14). Such persons as ministers of Word and Sacrament are the primary agents through whom the nurturing authority of Christ is represented in the Church. They above all are responsible for the interpretation of the Scriptures in proclamation, teaching, and counsel and have a special calling to speak out of the tradition and mind of the Church.

87   But the teachers of the Church are not confined to the ranks of the ordained holders of office. God raises up in the Church prophets and sages, wise and holy men and women, who, whether ordained or not, incarnate in their lives and their words the grace and demands of the Gospel. To such

persons the Church inevitably and gladly listens, weighing their words and appropriating their guidance as it can. Such persons may be scholars and thinkers, or unlearned followers of the Way. They may speak and work in the public arena or within individual relationships. They may voice their personal experience or that of groups of persons within the Church and the world. In any case, their ministry is a significant part of the economy of authority in the Church.

88   Finally, there is an essential authority that belongs to the body of believers as a whole. It is the task of the community's pastors and teachers to teach the whole faith of the Church and nothing more. The community for its part exercises a critical judgement upon the teaching and leadership it receives. This is not principally or even primarily a matter of votes in synods or conventions. The faithful exercise their judgement for the most part quietly and without much notice by recognising or not recognising their own Christian identity in the teaching, leadership, and nurture of their pastors and sages. 'Authority stems not only from the office but also from what is said. Authority is undermined when its teaching does not reflect the experiences of those subject to it'.[12] In the end doctrine, however proposed or defined, must be *received* by the body of believers to whom it is addressed as consonant with Scripture and tradition.

89   The operation of authority in the Church is complex. Its primary function is to nurture the faithful in the way of discipleship for the sake of God's kingdom. This nurturing, however, takes place through a continuing process of interpretation, at the centre of which is the exposition of the Scriptures in the setting of the liturgy itself. This process involves appeal to the settled mind of the Church as well as to the standard of what is 'reasonable' in the culture in which the Church is set. Inevitably the relationship between these different ways of reading the Scriptures, of understanding the mind of Christ, is strained. It is characterised by conflict as well as by complementarity. At the same time, every Christian community must deal with issues which are raised by intellectual, social and political developments in that part of the world in which it is set. Its response to these issues is also a part of its interpretation of the Scriptures and of the Word that the Scriptures mediate. Inevitably, then, the operation of authority in the Church involves conflict and disagreement. Indeed it would probably be true to say that authority in the Church works *through* rather than in spite of disagreement. Its primary function is not, then, to provide ahead of time answers to all possible questions, but to assure that when disagreement occurs it is settled in accord with the principles according to which Christians normally discern the mind of Christ for them: that the solution is rooted in Scripture, consonant with the mind of the Church, and 'reasonable' in the sense that it speaks a language the world can understand – that it makes 'good sense' even if the sense it makes is unexpected. At this level, authority in the Church refers not

so much to an absolute right to decide, vested in some particular individual or group, as it does to a right to orchestrate argument and consultation with a view to guaranteeing that what emerges from disagreement will be an understanding that grows out of the authentic sources of the Church's life. One inevitable result of such a process will be the exclusion of teachings or forms of behaviour seen at length to be inconsistent with Christian faith.[13]

90   Here lies the answer to the frequently asked question whether there are no limits to the plurality of interpretations of the Gospel. The fact that the Church uses the traditional Creeds at all establishes the fact that there is a boundary between what is true and what is false or heretical. But tradition contains an astonishing variety of possibilities, and with each new development of interpretation precise discrimination between what is 'within' and what is 'outside' the boundary may be very difficult. But the fact that difficulties may arise in some cases does not mean that there are no boundaries, nor that most Christians may not hold with confidence to the point where the centre lies, which is Jesus Christ himself.

91   Once we raise the issue of how conflict and disagreement are to be handled, however, we move into a new realm of discourse: that which concerns *structures* of consultation and decision.

BEING IN COMMUNION

92   The Anglican Communion consists of a family of Churches which say of themselves that they are in communion with each other. At a time when there is debate and disagreement in the family, it is essential to set all consideration of what it might mean to be Anglican in the wider context of the familiar and ancient (indeed biblical) word 'communion'. The fundamental theological question about the identity of Anglicanism is what it means for a Christian to be in communion.

93   In the Apostles' Creed we say, 'I believe... in the communion of saints' (*communio sanctorum*). In the Collect for All Saints' Day widely used throughout the Anglican world we hear of the whole Church in heaven and on earth being bound together in 'one communion and fellowship'. What *is* that communion? It is, fundamentally, the redemptive gift of incorporation into Christ, into our crucified, risen and ascended Lord. 'God is faithful, by whom you were called into the fellowship of his Son, Jesus Christ our Lord' (1 Cor. 1.9). It is a fellowship both of affliction, a sharing in Christ's sufferings, and also of comfort, a participation by hope in the resurrection of Christ (2 Cor. 5.3-11). Because it is a communion which sustains us throughout our life in which we are given the first-fruits of our eventual redemption (Rom. 8.9-25), it is spoken of by St Paul as 'fellowship of the Holy Spirit' (2 Cor. 13.14). Communion with Christ is communion in the Spirit.

94   This has the consequence that we are drawn into the very life of the Divine Trinity. 'Our fellowship is with the Father and with his Son Jesus Christ' (1 John 1.3). Father and Son will make their home with those who love the Son (John 14.23), and there will be a mutual indwelling of the Son in us, and we in the Son. By being drawn into the divine life the whole created order is brought into relation with the Father who creates, the Son who creates and redeems, and the Holy Spirit who creates and sanctifies. Human life and the whole natural order is therefore set within the horizon of creation and consummation.

95   Communion with Christ also means communion with all those who belong to Christ. Through the response of faith and of baptism, Christians enter a living Body, the Church, of persons committed to relationship with one another. In the New Testament the implications of this are spelt out realistically and concretely. It implies the task of the overcoming of divisions imposed by culture, whether of race, class or caste, or sexual discrimination (Gal. 3.28, 'You are all one in Christ Jesus'). It means giving material help to those in need (Rom. 15.27). It means esteeming each and every believer for the gift which the Holy Spirit has bestowed, to be used for the benefit of the whole body (1 Cor. 12.12-30). Thus the Gospel establishes as the normative pattern of the life of the community a relationship of interdependence, of mutuality between persons.

RELATIONSHIP AND GROWTH

96   As a consequence, the characteristic quality of a life lived in such communion is relationship and growth. This is true both of an ever-deepening relationship of our love towards, and confidence in God, and of spiritual growth in the quality of our relationships with one another. Those who are baptised are called upon to reflect the glory of the Lord as they are transformed into his likeness by the power of the Holy Spirit with ever-increasing splendour (2 Cor. 3.18). To sustain us in this growth the Church has been given the gift of Holy Communion, sacramental fellowship in the body and blood of Christ. To share in that gift by faith with thanksgiving, is to be strengthened and nourished in the body of Christ, to be built up as an integral part of a spiritual house and a holy priesthood (1 Pet. 2.1-6).

97   We are brought by the eucharist, the sacrament of unity, into a relationship with creation and all humanity. The eucharistic horizon is that of a new heaven and a new earth in which the nations will be gathered together to feast in a messianic kingdom. It is the eucharist which 'opens up the divine rule which has been promised as the final renewal of creation, and is a foretaste of it'[14] and which 'signifies what the world is to become: an offering and a hymn of praise to the Creator, a universal communion in the body of Christ, a kingdom of justice, love and peace in the Holy Spirit'.[15]

106

98 Furthermore, we are brought by the promise of eucharistic fellowship into a relationship of longing and desire with those Christians with whom we do not yet fully enjoy institutional communion, because of prohibitions contained in canon law or imposed by conscience. Here we confront a paradox, in that by mutually recognised baptism we share in a basic bond of incorporation into Christ, a transition and conversion of such momentous importance as to overshadow all our other divisions. 'Our one baptism into Christ constitutes a call to the Churches to overcome their divisions and visibly manifest their fellowship'.[16] This is the ecumenical context in which we have to set all disagreement between Christians who nonetheless seek to realise their unity in Christ.

99 We are challenged by the eucharist to an ever-deepening quality of spiritual union, a union of heart and mind, with those with whom we have institutional communion. It is of this that St Paul speaks when he pleads with his congregation in Philippi to display in their life together a unity and humility of mind – the very mind of Christ himself – each counting another to be better than him- or her-self. (Phil. 2.1-11).

100 Such quality of relationship is a radical 'being with' the other, a new pattern of life in which the healing, forgiving and liberating deeds of Jesus are continued by his disciples.

101 It is essential to observe that the growth of which we have spoken is not to be thought of as an undeviating upward progress. Failure, repentance and renewal are an integral part of the lives of Christians and of Churches. Growth, therefore, includes both advance and the possibility of learning through suffering, conflict and setback.

102 In the paschal mystery, which establishes the definitive victory of Christ's resurrection among us, we are constantly called to repentance and to new life through death to sin.

COMMUNICATION

103 In order that communion with God and with one another may be realised in history, in time and space, Christians are commanded and empowered to communicate the liberating gift of the Gospel in word and deed. To do so requires the use of human symbols bearing meanings in specific cultures. As we have already said (see para. 12), the Church itself has a 'language' and a 'culture', so that it can never fully be assimilated to any society in which it finds itself. But it also uses pre-existing languages and expresses itself in terms of existing cultural symbols. Ambiguity and the possibility of misunderstanding belong, therefore, to the very act of communicating the Gospel.

104   If, therefore, the truth of the Gospel is to be preserved, and its message to be clear and intelligible, all the symbolic means used in proclaiming and embodying it need to be consistent with one another. There is thus a special task which is both the responsibility of the whole Church, and especially of those ordained as its pastors, to ensure, so far as possible, the consistency of the message.

KINGDOM AND CULTURE

105   The Gospel is not a human invention, nor is it at human disposal. It is the Gospel of the kingdom, that reign of God which embraces the whole world, which has come true in Jesus Christ and can even now be tasted and experienced in the Spirit. The kingdom is the reality which frames the world, and gives an account both of its origin and of its destiny. It is the world's *'transcendent* horizon'.[17]

106   There is, therefore, both a 'Yes' and a 'No' to human culture. Because the natural world with all its potential, and human beings with their manifold abilities, are the good creation of God, culture, the human creation of a secondary environment, must be affirmed. Yet at the same time, because of sin and alienation from God, human culture is also in bondage and in need of liberation.[18]

DECISION BY PROVINCE

107   The Church is inevitably called upon to make decisions of great difficulty and complexity in discriminating between what must be affirmed and what denied. It is essentially a learning community. It has not arrived at a final perception or understanding; its belief is always being discovered and relearned in different generations and setting. Contexts and settings change, and meanings carried by culture change with them.

108   The history of Christian doctrine suggests that being faithful to what has been known and revealed in the past often involves us in saying something new – because to go on saying or doing exactly the same thing in a different context is actually to *change* the meaning of what was said or done before.

109   At the time of the Reformation, the Anglican Church wanted to be faithful to the tradition of the threefold ministry, but recognised that to reproduce the patterns of mediaeval or even patristic ministry would be an inadequate response to the needs of the sixteenth century in terms of education and pastoral care. In the nineteenth and early twentieth centuries, the Church wanted to be faithful to the authority of the Bible, but recognised that scholarly and critical questions had made it impossible simply to repro-

duce what earlier ages had said about its literal meaning: even a conservative believer would now have to respond to new challenges and say things in a different way. There is more to faithfulness than repetition and preservation. Faithfulness goes hand-in-hand with learning and discovery because faithfulness is loyalty to Jesus by *being with* the realities of the particular human beings to whom Jesus is being preached or who are seeking to open their lives to him.

110 In the light of this complexity it is justifiable that most decisions relating to the Church's communication of the Gospel should be taken by those familiar with the meanings learned by symbols in their own culture. This is the theological root of Anglicanism's unsatisfactorily expressed concept of provincial 'autonomy'. The Anglican Communion's strength still lies in what some see as weakness: its suspicion of centralised authority, of anything or anyone claiming an absolute power of veto on what a local church (within the one discipline of sacramental fellowship) does. This must be seen as a great gift, enabling the process of Christian learning, because it authorises local churches to take responsibility in clear and bold ways for what they do – to be themselves, in other words. And – as was said earlier – if a church can explain that its decisions arise out of the pressure to make the Gospel more clearly heard in its mission, other churches have a responsibility to listen, to take this seriously, to give thanks, whether or not they feel the same pressures to take such steps. And conversely, a church which does not take the same decision on the grounds that in *its* context such a move would make the preaching of the Gospel less, not more, accessible must also be heard and taken seriously.

111 As a concrete expression of the Church's mission in a particular region, meetings might usefully be convened, with clerical and lay representation where appropriate and desirable, to plan for its effective expression. There must therefore be sufficient provision for a process of discernment and for effective decision-making in specific contexts, combined with a real care to perceive the impact of a proposed course of action in one context upon another part of the world. Decision-making may lead to anomalies. Throughout the history of the Church, beliefs and practices, which have originated in one part of the Church but which have had implications for other parts of the Church, have only gradually been received or rejected by the whole Church. The principle of reception is not, therefore, a modern invention. The Church has experience of tension and plurality, and truth is often discerned in the midst of such tension and plurality.[19]

112 But at the same time, and inseparable from the responsibilities of particular Provinces or regions, the Gospel must be seen to be good news for *all* humanity and its proclamation must express its universal coherence. Care needs to be taken to prevent a local church from becoming bound by its cul-

ture. The corrosive effects of particular environments are often not perceptible to those who are immersed in them.[20]

EMBODIMENTS AND AGENTS OF UNITY [21]

113   Anglicans are not alone in needing sufficient provision for a process of mutual consultation, discernment and criticism, and for effective decision-making at a universal level. In a state of division between Churches which indubitably enjoy with us communion with the crucified, risen and ascended Lord (see para. 93), Anglicans judge that the unity of the world-wide Church is best served by processes of mutual consultation within world Communions as well as between separated Churches.

114   In the Anglican Communion, four particular embodiments or agents have developed to make provision for our own process of consultation, by which both the institution and juridical communion are preserved:

The Archbishop of Canterbury
The Lambeth Conference
The Anglican Consultative Council
The Meeting of Primates

115   Historically the *Archbishop of Canterbury* has been the personal focus of unity and communion at the universal level. The Lambeth Conference of 1978 in a statement on the basis of Anglican unity said *inter alia:*

> It [unity] is personally grounded in the loyal relationship of each of the Churches to the Archbishop of Canterbury who is freely recognised as the focus of unity.[22]

116   Being in communion with the See and the Archbishop of Canterbury has been a visible sign of the membership of bishops and of their Churches in the Anglican Communion. The Archbishop of Canterbury's task has been described as involving 'in a particular way, that care of all the Churches which is shared by all the bishops', and also as a task 'not to command, but to gather' the Communion. Clearly, the emphasis is upon service and caring and not upon coercive power.

117   The *Lambeth Conference* since 1867 has provided a consultative forum for each of the dioceses of the Anglican Communion through its Bishop. Archbishop Longley called the first Lambeth Conference in 1867 for 'brotherly counsel and encouragement'. In his opening address to the Conference he denied that the Conference could assume the functions of a general synod for the Communion, or that it could enact canons that could bind the Provinces. 'We merely propose to discuss matters of practical interest and pronounce what we deem expedient in resolutions which may serve as safe guides to future actions', he said.[23] Subsequent Lambeth Conferences have supported the principle of the autonomy of the Provinces. But from time to time the Conferences have passed resolutions that serve as 'safe guides' to future actions in the Communion.

118   In an encyclical letter, the 1920 Lambeth Conference described its status in this way:

> The Lambeth Conference ... does not claim to exercise any powers of control or command. It stands for the more spiritual and more Christian principle of loyalty to the fellowship. The Churches represented in it are indeed independent but independent with the Christian freedom which recognises the restraints of truth and love. They are not free to deny the truth. They are not free to ignore the fellowship ... the conference is ... a fellowship in the Spirit.[24]

119   The Lambeth Conference has proved a valuable meeting to discern and to express the mind of the Churches. ACC-5, for example, looked forward to the Conference 'pronouncing the consensus of the Communion' in the matter of the ARCIC agreed statements.[25] The Lambeth Conference thus plays an important role in expressing the mind of the Communion on particularly crucial issues.

120   The *Anglican Consultative Council* was instituted by the agreement of the Provinces on the recommendation of Lambeth 1968. In one sense it is less representative than the Lambeth Conference, where every diocese is represented by its Bishop. The inclusion of lay women and lay men, and of clergy other than bishops, however, gives it a dimension of wider representation. Its greater frequency of meeting gives it more continuity of life and thought. Its role and its relationship with other organs of the Communion are still in the process of being worked out.

121   The calling of regular *Primates' Meetings* was endorsed by Lambeth 1978. This reflected the need for a more effective means of exercising episcopal collegiality through the consultations of the Primates. These meetings, at regular intervals, are a 'meeting of minds' through which individual provincial and international concerns can be tested by collective discussions between acknowledged leaders who will attempt to reach a common mind. The Primates' Meeting has already shown itself to be a flexible instrument of consultation: for example, in dealing with practical questions about authority and the possibility of the consecration of women as bishops in some Provinces.

122   These *four* institutions – *the Archbishop of Canterbury, the Lambeth Conference, the ACC, the Primates' Meeting* – are the ways by which the autonomous Provinces of the Anglican Communion express their unity and communion and live out their interdependence today. They may not, either individually or together, take decisions on behalf of the whole Communion. They *do* provide means of consultation, places in which to search for a common mind, and they provide the means for expressing the mind of the Communion. They serve to develop and to sustain Anglican cohesion and unity.

FURTHER DEVELOPMENT OF EMBODIMENTS AND AGENTS OF UNITY

123 There remains a need to evaluate the work of these agents of communion and to see how this work can develop.

124 We consider that the Archbishop of Canterbury should continue to hold the 'primacy of honour' which he presently has within the Anglican Communion. We acknowledge his leadership; we express our gratitude for the unstinting way in which the present Archbishop has sought to build up and deepen his relationship with other Provinces. We record our desire that this *personal* ministry of the Archbishop should continue among us.

125 There is every indication that the present Lambeth Conference is proving to be as significant and strategic as any previous Conference. Bishops meeting in personal relation not only are made aware of their collegiality but also of their representative role in bringing and reflecting the mind of their dioceses. We are firmly of the view that the future meeting of Lambeth Conferences is a crucial element in the continuing life of the Communion.

126 We recognise the valuable and necessary work carried out by the Anglican Consultative Council. We do not, at present, envisage any general enlargement of the Council's advisory role. We are aware that the secretariat of the Council also functions as an inter-Anglican secretariat for the Lambeth Conference and for the Primates' Meeting. An enhanced role for the Primates' Meeting may well call for additional resources for the secretariat.

ENHANCED ROLE OF THE PRIMATES [26]

127 The need for increased commitment to the interdependence of the Churches of the Communion suggests that encouragement be given to a developing role for the Primates' Meeting under the presidency of the Archbishop of Canterbury. In the general context of the Church's mission to preach the Gospel to every person, the Primates should take special care for the universal coherence of the Communion in major questions affecting its unity.

128 For Anglicans, who have always related true doctrine to the worship of the Church, this will involve special attention to the liturgies of the Churches. Encouragement, support and advice should be given to the Churches of the Communion in their work of liturgical revision. Mutual consultation regarding liturgical development and common reviews of the Prayer Books in use in the Communion should be envisaged. This should be a particular concern of the Primates in their collegial exercise of *episcope*. This is no new responsibility, but one which is inherent in the episcopal

office as such, and is therefore to be shared with episcopal colleagues. (See Resolution 18.6.)

129   Consideration should also be given to the development of a common declaration of faith and practice to be used at major events in the life of the Churches of the Communion. (See Resolution 19.)

130   In view of the symbolic role of the Archbishop of Canterbury in the life of the whole Communion, it would be altogether appropriate and highly desirable for the Primates of the Churches to be brought into the process of consultation at the time of the Archbishop's appointment. (See Resolution 18.2b.)

131   In view of the strengthening of provincial consultation processes, the position of extra-Provincial dioceses needs urgent consideration in order that they may be fully incorporated into the existing structures.

TWO QUESTIONS BEFORE ANGLICANS

132   The structures through which the Anglican Communion works are at present being tested and developed by the way in which decisions are being made in two important areas. One is the procedure by which, as a worldwide Communion, Anglicans make their *response to the Final Report of ARCIC and to the Lima text*. The other is the way by which the matter of *the ordination of women* is handled. Not only are these issues testing the existing structures of authority in the Anglican Communion, they are also providing a creative opportunity to realise hitherto unrecognised possibilities of communion.

133   In 1981 the ACC asked the question: 'How is it possible for a Communion of autonomous Provincial Churches to come to a common acceptance of an ecumenical agreement?'[27]

134   It was recognised that the formal acceptance of such an agreement as is expressed in the *Final Report* must remain with the provincial synods of the Communion but that only an inter-Anglican body could articulate the common mind of the Communion as a whole. The ACC saw the Lambeth Conference, to which each Bishop is able to bring the mind of his diocese, as the body best able to discover and pronounce a consensus, and this will be the responsibility of Lambeth 1988. But the decision of the Lambeth Conference follows an exhaustive process of response to the ARCIC Report by the Provinces, not only by provincial synods but in widespread consideration at every level of the Church's life, involving clergy and laity.[28] The pronouncement of any consensus which may emerge by the Lambeth Conference will not be the end of the matter. That pronouncement must then undergo a process of reception in the Provinces, and provincial synods will need to act

upon it so far as any consequences flowing from agreement might require legislative initiative or sanction.

135   It is important that during any such process of reception the Provinces be able to continue in consultation with each other over any subsequent developments or decisions. This would be one of the responsibilities and functions of the Primates' Meeting.

136   In the other matter of the *ordination of women to the presbyterate and the episcopate,* the process of discovering a common mind is similar but has some differences in detail. What is clear is that a lengthy and widespread consultation has been, and still is, going on. The Lambeth Conference in 1968 passed the following resolution:

> The Conference requests every national or regional Church or Province to give careful study to the question of the ordination of women to the priesthood and to report its findings to the Anglican Consultative Council which will make them generally available to the Anglican Communion.

The Conference further resolved:

> That, before any national or regional Church or Province makes a final decision to ordain women to the priesthood, the advice of the Anglican Consultative Council be sought and carefully considered.[29]

137   Some two and a half years later, the first meeting of the ACC was held at Limuru, Kenya. Although eight Churches had begun the consultative process none had sent results of their study. The Bishop of Hong Kong asked for advice on what course to follow since his diocesan synod had voted in principle to ordain women. The ACC passed, with a narrow margin of support, the following resolution:

> 28(b) this Council advises the Bishop of Hong Kong, acting with the approval of his synod, and any other Bishop of the Anglican Communion acting with the approval of his Province, that, if he decides to ordain women to the priesthood, his action will be acceptable to this Council; and that this Council will use its good offices to encourage all Provinces of the Anglican Communion to continue in communion with these dioceses.[30]

138   The 1978 Lambeth Conference was important in furthering the direction of developments in the decade leading to 1988. Resolution 21 noted that since Lambeth 1968 *four* Provinces had proceeded to ordain women to the presbyterate and eight other member Churches had 'either agreed or approved in principle or stated that there are either no fundamental or no theological objections to the ordination of women to the historic threefold ministry of the Church'. The resolution can be thought to envisage the possibility of ordination to the episcopate. Indeed this would be in line with the view held by many in the 1970s that, once women were ordained to the presbyterate, there were no further arguments to preclude consecration to the episcopate. However, Resolution 22, devoted to *Women in the episcopate,*

clearly hinted at an implied difference between ordination of women to the presbyterate in a Province and consecration to the episcopate:

> While recognising that a member Church of the Anglican Communion may wish to consecrate a woman to the episcopate, and accepting that such a member Church must act in accordance with its own constitution, the Conference recommends that no decision to consecrate be taken without consultation with the episcopate through the Primates and overwhelming support in any member Church and in the diocese concerned, lest the bishop's office should become a cause of disunity instead of a focus of unity.[31]

139   The development of opinion since Lambeth 1978 on the question of the ordination of women to the episcopate is outlined in detail in the Report of the Primates' Working Party, *Women and the Episcopate*. What is of importance for us is that the matter was taken up by the Primates' Meeting in Toronto in 1986 and a process of consultation in, and between, the Provinces was undertaken by the Primates' Meeting in preparation for Lambeth 1988.

140   The Report of the Primates' Working Party, *Women in the Episcopate,* examines how the Communion might discover a mind on this issue which affects the nerve centre of the Communion. It considered both the decision-making process in the fellowship of the Anglican Communion and the process of decision-making where there is division in the universal Church. Throughout this report the Primates show concern for a process of listening to one another and understanding what is being said by those who hold the opposite view.

> [Provinces] may be persuaded by compelling doctrinal reasons, by their experience of women in ordained ministry and by the demands of the mission of the Church in their region to proceed to the ordination of a woman to the episcopate. This would only be done with overwhelming support in the diocese and Province concerned. Such a step could only be taken within an over-riding acknowledgement of the need to offer such a development for reception, or indeed rejection, by the worldwide Communion and by the universal Church and with care and support for the women so ordained'.

Were a Province to ordain a woman as Bishop:-

> The development should be offered to the Anglican Communion in an open process of reception.

> The development could not be expressed as the mind of the Church until it were accepted by the whole Communion. Even then there would necessarily be a tentativeness about it until it were accepted by the universal Church.

> Consideration of the ordination of women to the presbyterate and episcopate within the Communion would need to continue with Provinces listening to one another's thoughts and experiences, aiding one another in theological reflection and exercising mutual sensitivity and care.

Debate in the wider fellowship of the Churches ought to be encouraged, particularly within existing bilateral and multi-lateral dialogues. [32]

141   On the question of the ordination of women to the threefold ministry, the important issues are whether the move to ordain women (especially to the episcopate) can be set forth in terms of the will to pursue the mission of Jesus within the common framework of sacramental and scriptural discipline, and whether resistance to such a move can likewise be defended in such terms. As a matter of bare fact, no Province that ordains women has seen such action as a complete breach with the past: i.e., no Province has argued its case as part of a wider rejection of the disciplines of Scripture and sacramental order, whatever individual theologians may occasionally have said. The arguments have been recognisably Christian arguments, and recognisably Anglican arguments. No official representative Anglican body has promulgated a clear and unambiguous theological case against women's ordination. At the level of its official voice, Anglicanism as such does not hold this development to be so damaging to the common discipline of Scripture and sacraments that it cannot be lived with, though individual theologians, once again, are free to dissent.

142   It is also a recognisably Anglican argument, however, to say that the Church in some cultural contexts would unhelpfully distance itself from the society to which it ministers if it were to ordain women. This case is grounded in the priorities of mission, and it must be taken seriously. A Church advancing this argument must be wary, however, of assuming too quickly that it knows exactly how its cultural context is operating and changing. Churches need to retain their flexibility in the face of a rapidly changing world. Whether a local church is 'for' or 'against' is, in this perspective, more than just a matter of cultural convenience: the considerations involved, about mission, about the Church's freedom to be both with a culture and over against it, are essentially theological.

143   So, on the difficult issue of the interchangeability of ministries between Churches that have different policies, we suggest two considerations. A Church that has ordained women should not seek *by itself* to define the terms on which its ministers shall be received elsewhere, as this would be to side-step the need for a real engagement with the particular needs of another setting. But equally, a Church that has not ordained women has a responsibility to a Church that has done so – not just as a courtesy to ecclesiastical guests, though that is not unimportant, but to make the experience of that other Church accessible and intelligible in its own setting. Such a responsibility has to be exercised in an appropriate way, so that the life and witness of another and very different Christian community may assist the growth and understanding of the local church, even if the latter is not committed to moving towards similar policies.

144   Because the ordination of women is everywhere acknowledged to be one of the major questions affecting the unity of the Communion, it follows that the Primates have a continuing responsibility in the matter. (See Resolution 1.3.)

145   Should the action of any Province result in a further rupture of juridical communion, that would undoubtedly be a setback to unity and deeply to be regretted. Yet there is the possibility of learning through conflict and the recall to new life through repentance.

146   The wider ecumenical issues cannot be treated in detail here; but we wish to commend to our partners in ecumenical dialogue the theology of plural ecclesial practice here outlined, a pluralism within a common scriptural and sacramental discipline. Such a theology would make it possible for us to give thanks for the variety and distinctiveness of local expressions of a common discipline. We suggest that the idea of a Church characterised by mutual learning and mutual thanksgiving gives an appropriately dynamic dimension to the goal of unity, a unity of active relation, not institutional conformity.

TWO EMPHASES IN ANGLICAN DECISION-MAKING

147   There are clearly *two* emphases in Anglican decision-making. The *first* is the place of *reception*. Decisions taken by provincial synods still have to be 'received' in the life of the people of that Province. That reception is not simply about response and affirmation in word but entails embodying what is affirmed in the lived experience of the community. In the same way, the mind of the Communion expressed by the Lambeth Conference still has to be received by the fellowship of Churches in the Anglican Communion and by the *whole Church*. Reception is a gradual and dynamic process. It means the way by which the people of God as a whole actively respond to decisions made by synods and councils. This is a process which takes time and is always open to the guidance of the Holy Spirit within the community. Until such a process is complete there is necessarily a 'provisionality' about decisions taken by synods and councils of the Church. A matter cannot be deemed to be settled without reception. It is still possible for those decisions to be modified, or even reversed, even though they have been accepted and even acted on by provincial synods and endorsed by a majority of bishops at the Lambeth Conference.

148   Closely related to the matter of reception is a *second* issue which needs further exploration. We have spoken of the importance of discovering 'the mind of a Province', 'the mind of the Anglican Communion', 'the mind of the Church'. What is it that constitutes *the mind of a Province, Communion or the whole Church?* On the one hand the expression of 'consensus' will

117

involve the achieving of certain thought out and stipulated majorities in synods at the appropriate level: for the mind of a Province, in provincial synod; for the mind of the Communion, at the Lambeth Conference, in the Primates' Meeting and in meetings of the ACC; and in the context of the whole Church, at a truly ecumenical council. A synodical majority on its own, however, cannot be deemed to constitute the mind of a Province or Communion or of the whole Church. Consensus must involve and ensure that all arguments have been put to the community and heard by it, that people are not swept forward without understanding the implications of what is being agreed, and that there is indeed secure maximum agreement. On the one hand it must be possible for a Province or a Communion to have confidence in its decisions, even though individuals or groups continue to express views contrary to those declared by synods. On the other hand, it is important to make room for dissent within the reception process. We need to satisfy one another that the exercise of authority through the structures of our Communion and the pronouncing of decisions do indeed carry weight, but also that there is a place for continuing debate, even conflict.

THEOLOGICAL CONCERN AND PASTORAL CARE

149 Both theological and pastoral care are related to the exercise of authority within the Anglican Communion. These apply particularly in situations where actions of individual Provinces might threaten the unity of the Communion. They are also involved where the unity of a Province might be threatened by a crisis within its own life or where an action by the Communion as a whole threatens our relations with sister Churches. We have to bear witness to Christ not only in words but also in our lives. This involves the way in which we make decisions, and the love, care and concern we show for those whose views differ from our own. The way we go about decision-making, especially over issues which touch us all at a deep level, will be a sign of our Christian maturity. The bishops have a particular role in maintaining theological unity and in the pastoral care of the whole Communion.

150 Theological concerns are addressed by scholars, by individual bishops, by provincial synods and provincial bishops' meetings and their associated theological commissions. In the Communion as a whole we have the Inter-Anglican Theological and Doctrinal Commission. In these different ways, theological opinion as well as the practice of the Church are being continually tested. We believe it important that pastoral care and practice be in the context of continuing theological exploration undertaken, at different levels, throughout the Communion.

151 Pastoral care involves ensuring that the reception process is an open one and there should be provision of pastoral care along the following lines:

    a. Each Province should develop a process within its life with respect to disputed matters which ensures that there is dialogue leading to a resolution of the matters in question.

b. The process should assure those who have not accepted a decision of the Province that they will not be excluded or marginalised; the gifts and insights of all groups must continue to be welcome.

c. Practical pastoral arrangements will need to be made both at provincial and diocesan levels for those who are conscientiously unable to accept a decision made at the Provincial level. (In this respect, we call attention to the provisions for 'episcopal visitors' adopted by the 1988 General Convention of ECUSA.)[33]

d. The Anglican Consultative Council and the Primates' Meeting should be understood as overseeing the continuing process of interchange among Provinces on disputed matters. They should be available to give counsel and advice where continuing divergences persist in and among Provinces.

152   In both theological concerns and pastoral care we need, more than anything else, to declare our belief in the promise of the Holy Spirit to lead us into all truth and to bind us together in the love of Christ.

NOTES

[1] Rowan Williams, *Resurrection,* Darton, Longman and Todd, London, 1982.

[2] See further David Paton and Charles Long (eds.), *A Roland Allen Reader: The Compulsion of the Spirit,* Eerdmans, Grand Rapids, 1983; also G.C. Davis (ed.), *Setting Free the Ministry of the People of God: The Report of a Pacific Inter-Anglican Conference on the life and work of Roland Allen,* Forward Movement, Cincinnati, 1984, Michael Nazir-Ali, 'Church, Culture and Change', in *Communion and Episcopacy,* Cuddesdon, 1988, pp.93f. Gustavo Gutierrez, *We Drink from Our Own Wells:* The Spiritual Journey of a People, SCM Press, 1984.

[3] *Towards a Theology for Inter-Faith Dialogue,* ACC, London, 1986.

[4] Kenneth Cracknell, *Towards a new Relationship,* Epworth Press, London, 1986, pp.98f. See also Michael Nazir-Ali, 'That which is not to be found but which finds us', *Towards a Theology for Inter-Faith Dialogue,* pp.40f.

[5] See, for example, J.N.D. Anderson, *Christianity and Comparative Religion,* Tyndale Press, 1970, pp.91f; *God's Law and God's Love,* Collins, London, 1980; D.L. Edwards and J.R.W. Stott, *Essentials,* Hodder, London, 1988, pp.320f.

[6] See further *Guidelines on Dialogue,* WCC, Geneva, 1979.

[7] e.g. Klaus Klostermaier, *Hindu and Christian in Vrindaban,* SCM Press, London, 1969; Roger Hooker, *Uncharted Journey,* CMS, London, 1973; George Appleton, *On the Eightfold Path,* SCM Press, London, 1961; Raymond Hammer, *Japan's Religious Ferment,* SCM Press, London, 1961.

[8] An example of this is to be found in D. Cohn-Sherbok's *On Earth as it is in Heaven: Jews, Christians and Liberation Theology,* Orbis, New York, 1987.

[9] See further Michael Nazir-Ali, *Islam: A Christian Perspective,* Westminster Press, Philadelphia, and Paternoster Press, Exeter, 1983, and *Frontiers in Muslim-Christian Encounter,* Regnum, Oxford, and Paternoster Press, Exeter, 1987. The Conference received and commended the document *Jews, Christians and Muslims: The Way of Dialogue,* printed as Appendix 6 of this Report.

[10] *For the Sake of the Kingdom: A Report of the Inter-Anglican Theological and Doctrinal Commission, ACC, London, 1986, pp.38f.

[11] ibid., pp.39f.

[12] J. Marshall, The Tablet, 28 July 1988.

[13] Many of the issues related to the sources and exercise of authority are discussed in Stephen Sykes (ed.), Authority in the Anglican Communion, Anglican Book Centre, Toronto, 1987.

[14] Baptism, Eucharist and Ministry, Eucharist, para.22.

[15] ibid., para.4.

[16] ibid., Baptism, para.6.

[17] For the Sake of the Kingdom, p.23.

[18] ibid., pp.50f.

[19] On reception see further Mary Tanner, 'Communion, Episcopacy and the Ordination of Women', and Michael Nazir-Ali, 'Church, Culture and Change', both in Communion and Episcopacy, pp.88f and pp.97f.

[20] The Conference resolved that an Inter-Anglican Commission be asked to undertake, as a matter of urgency, a study of the meaning and nature of communion (Resolution 18.1.).

[21] The following discussion has arisen out of consideration of a draft document entitled Instruments of Communion and Decision-Making: The Development of the Consultative Process in the Anglican Communion, circulated to conference participants at the very beginning of the Conference. The document is printed as Appendix 5 of this Report.

[22] Report of the Lambeth Conference 1978, p.98.

[23] Five Lambeth Conferences 1867-1908, Macmillan New York, 1920, SPCK, London, 1948, p.8.

[24] Six Lambeth Conferences 1867-1930, SPCK, 1948, pp.26f.

[25] ACC-5 – Newcastle-upon-Tyne, p.44.

[26] See Resolution 18.2a.

[27] ACC-5, p.43.

[28] Cf. *The Emmaus Report: A Report of the Anglican Ecumenical Consultation 1987, ACC, London, 1987.

[29] The Lambeth Conference 1968, SPCK/Seabury, 1968, pp.39-40.

[30] The Time is Now: ACC-1, Limuru, Kenya, SPCK, London, 1971, pp.38f.

[31] Report of the Lambeth Conference 1978, pp.45f.

[32] Women in the Episcopate, p.45. See Resolution 1.

[33] These provisions enable parishes, unable to accept the ministry of a woman bishop or a bishop who has consented to the election of a woman bishop, to ask for an Episcopal Visitor from a panel of such visitors appointed by the Presiding Bishop of ECUSA with the concurrence of the House of Bishops.

* indicates a title published through the Inter-Anglican Publishing Network.

RESOLUTIONS

Resolutions 18-23 and Resolution 66 deal with matters within the purview of the Section on Dogmatic and Pastoral Concerns.

BIBLIOGRAPHY

Rowan Williams, *Resurrection,* Darton, Longman & Todd, London, 1982.

David Paton and Charles Long (eds.), *A Roland Allen Reader: The Compulsion of the Spirit,* Eerdmans, Grand Rapids, 1983.

Gerald C. Davis (ed.), *Setting Free the Ministry of the People of God: Report of a Pacific Inter-Anglican Conference on the life and work of Roland Allen,* Forward Movement, Cincinnati, 1984.

Michael Nazir-Ali, 'Church, Culture and Change', in J. Draper (ed.), *Communion and Episcopacy,* Cuddesdon, 1988.

* *Towards a Theology for Inter-Faith Dialogue,* ACC, London, 1986.

Kenneth Cracknell, *Towards a New Relationship,* Epworth Press, London, 1986.

J.N.D. Anderson, *Christianity and Comparative Religion,* Tyndale Press, 1970.

J.N.D. Anderson, *God's Law and God's Love,* Collins, London, 1980.

D.L. Edwards and J.R.W. Stott, *Essentials,* Hodder, London, 1988.

Guidelines on Dialogue, WCC, Geneva, 1979.

Klaus Klostermaier, *Hindu and Christian in Vrindaban,* SCM Press, London, 1969.

Roger Hooker, *Uncharted Journey,* CMS, London, 1973.

George Appleton, *On the Eightfold Path,* SCM Press, London, 1961.

Raymond Hammer, *Japan's Religious Ferment,* SCM Press, London, 1961.

D. Cohn-Sherbok, *On Earth as it is in Heaven: Jews Christians and Liberation Theology,* Orbis, New York, 1981.

Michael Nazir-Ali, *Islam: A Christian Perspective,* Westminster Press, Philadelphia, and Paternoster Press, Exeter, 1983.

Michael Nazir-Ali, *Frontiers in Muslim-Christian Encounter,* Regnum, Oxford, and Paternoster, Exeter, 1987.

For the Sake of the Kingdom, A Report of the Inter-Anglican Theological and Doctrinal Commission, ACC, London, 1986.

Stephen Sykes (ed.), *Authority in the Anglican Communion,* Anglican Book Centre, Toronto, 1987.

Baptism, Eucharist and Ministry: The Lima Report, WCC, Geneva, 1982.

Mary Tanner, 'Communion, Episcopacy and the Ordination of Women', in J. Draper (ed.), op. cit.

SECTION REPORTS

Five Lambeth Conferences 1867-1908, Macmillan New York, 1920, SPCK, London, 1948.

Six Lambeth Conferences 1867-1930, SPCK, 1948.

ACC-5 – Newcastle-upon-Tyne, ACC, London, 1981.

The Emmaus Report: A Report of the Anglican Ecumenical Consultation 1987, ACC, London, 1987.

The Lambeth Conference 1968: Resolutions and Reports, SPCK, London, Seabury Press, New York, 1968.

The Time is Now: ACC-1, Limuru, Kenya, SPCK, London, 1971.

Report of the Lambeth Conference 1978, CIO Publishing, London, 1978.

* indicates a title published through the Inter-Anglican Publishing Network.

Ecumenical Relations

Chairman	The Most Revd Michael Peers (Primate of Canada)
Vice-Chairman	The Rt Revd Edward Buckle (Assistant Bishop of Auckland, New Zealand)
Secretary	The Revd Canon Martin Reardon
Staff	The Revd Geoffrey Brown
	Dr Gillian Evans
Communicator	Mrs Nicola Currie

Assistant to the Chaplain: Mother Janet OHP

INTRODUCTION

STORIES OF HOPE ...

1   Bishops came to the Lambeth Conference from all the continents and from a great variety of local circumstances. Those assigned to the Ecumenical Relations Section came to reaffirm their commitment to the search for the full, visible unity of the Christian Church. They began by telling one another their stories, and many of these testified to heartening progress in the ten years since the last Lambeth Conference. In some places there are exciting new developments in the search for Christian unity, and a new impetus.

2   A few bishops had shared in international theological discussions with representatives of other Churches. Six such theological discussions had taken place with six different partner Churches or groups of Churches. They showed how much these Churches shared with Anglicans in the way of a common faith, one baptism, and a growing agreement on the eucharist, on ministry and on authority.

3   For the first time bishops from the united Churches of Bangladesh, India and Pakistan, where Anglicans have united with Christians of other traditions, were welcomed as full members of the Conference (Resolution 12). They were able to testify to the strength that Christian unity brings to formerly divided Churches. Bishop K.H. Ting was also present as Chairman of the Chinese Christian Council. This is the first stage on the way to a 'post-denominational' Church in China. It includes Anglicans. After a period of persecution it is growing rapidly in size, coherence and vigour within an ancient and dynamic culture.

4   Other bishops told of their participation in national Conferences or Councils of Churches, some of these recently or currently being renewed by the full participation of Roman Catholics and other Christians who until now had not been members. Some bishops from the United States of America told of developments in the consultation on Church Union there. Those from Wales spoke of further developments under the Welsh Covenant, and those from Namibia and Tanzania of increasing unity with Lutherans.[1]

5   Many bishops were able to tell of improved relationships with the leaders of other Churches in their dioceses. Some met and prayed with them regularly, and jointly exercised pastoral oversight over people involved in local ecumenical work. We heard in particular from Merseyside in England. Not many years ago Liverpool had been the scene of Protestant-Catholic violence not dissimilar to that happening in parts of Ireland. Today, however, the Anglican and Roman Catholic bishops and the leaders of the Free Churches have committed themselves and their Churches to work very closely together. They are careful always to make public statements jointly.

Their Churches have established a joint Assembly, and they work together extensively in the area. In this way they try to fulfil the request of the Lund Conference of 1952 'that Churches should do together all those things that deep differences of conviction do not compel them to do separately'.

6 These same bishops and other members of the Conference were able to tell of the formation and development of 'co-operating parishes' in Australia and New Zealand, 'shared ministries' in Canada, 'local ecumenical projects' in England, Scotland and Wales, and 'communities of reconciliation' in Ireland. The Church of England was altering its canon law in order formally to permit this increase in ecumenical co-operation. In many places Christians of some Churches were going beyond their own Church's rules in sharing in worship, including communion, with those of other traditions. In several places Christians of different Churches have joined together in evangelism.

... AND DISMAY

7 Some bishops, however, had sad stories to tell. They spoke of their own sorrow and penitence that, in England, New Zealand and Southern Africa, after giving initial encouragement, their Churches had finally rejected or shelved national union schemes or proposals for a covenant of union with Methodist and Reformed Churches.

8 Several bishops from small Anglican Churches in parts of Latin America and other places, where a Church of another tradition dominated the community, spoke of the immense difficulty of developing any serious ecumenical contact with it, especially if there was also a difference in racial origin between the members of the two Churches.

9 Several African bishops complained that the struggle of the Western Churches to come to an agreement in faith meant little to African Christians when they saw actions contradict beliefs. Years ago, when new townships were springing up around mines in Africa, men from many different tribes and speaking many different languages came to live in the townships without their families. They were in desperate need of help in building a sense of community. All that the (Western) Churches could do was to establish different Churches belonging to competing denominations and so create more division than before. For these African bishops, many of the divisions of the Churches in Africa had been imported from Europe and North America. Those Churches which had caused the divisions in Europe and North America should heal the divisions. This would help to heal the same divisions in Africa and free the Africans to deal with their own more urgent problems from within a united Church. At the same time, it was realised that not *all* divisions originate in Europe and North America. There are ancient divisions in India, the Middle East and even parts of Africa.

10   In what follows we try

to show the essential relationship between the unity of the Church and the unity of the whole human race;

to examine the motivation for the search for Christian unity;

to paint afresh a vision of the goal of unity;

to point to steps which will take us some way towards that goal.

CHRISTIAN UNITY AND HUMAN UNITY

11   The connection between the search for Christian unity (with its questions about the faith and ordering of the Church) and the search for human unity between people of different colours and races, rich and poor, men and women ... is vital.

12   In parts of the world where the struggle for survival is a daily reality Christians are often united in their perception of human need. But their desire for concerted prayer, witness and action is frustrated all too often by the fact that they are divided into separate denominations. This is one factor that makes the necessity of reconciliation among the historic Churches so urgent. These Churches, European, Asian and African, must take a particular responsibility for working for Christian unity so that the Churches to which their missionary labours gave rise may no longer be impeded in their combined Christian witness and service by denominational divisions. The importance of the search for agreement in faith ought not to be minimised. Without it the witness and service of the Church is everywhere impeded. However, the insights and perspectives of all Christians have to be brought into the expression of the agreement in faith, if that agreement is to speak not only to the divisions of the past, but also to the life and work of the Church today. We would be wrong to think that there were two agendas, one concerned with matters of faith, order and worship, the other with the struggle for justice.

13   Those who teach that all people are united in baptism must learn to prove in their life that people of different races, cultures and sexes are equal before God. One of the issues held before the 1988 Lambeth Conference has been how we can move towards a more whole community of women and men in the Church, so that the Church may witness before the world to the overcoming of that division. Similarly those who receive communion at the Lord's Table with someone who is in need cannot rightly then refuse to share their resources with the poor. In the search for Christian unity and human unity, right belief and worship (orthodoxy) and right practice (orthopraxy) must be kept together.

14   Christians will be of service to the world at large in its injustices and divi-

sions only if those same injustices and divisions are being overcome *within* the Christian Church.

MOTIVATION FOR THE SEARCH FOR UNITY

15 The bishops observed that what is often lacking in ecumenical relations is a lively motivation to reach towards unity. Too often preoccupation with negotiations to restore the institutional union of denominations, separated in the distant past, has failed to capture the imagination and fire the enthusiasm of Anglicans. We need to ask what the Church is for; and only if its purpose demands closer unity will we be moved to work actively for such unity.

16 For some Christians the Church is seen in too passive and individualistic terms, as a haven in the storms of life, as a ship to carry the individual to harbour in heaven – or rather as a flotilla of different kinds of ships among which each person is free to choose the one in which he or she feels most comfortable on. If the Church is seen in this way it is understandable that there is little or no motivation or enthusiasm for closer unity. For other Christians the Church is a kind of club for like-minded people. If the Church is seen in this way, then the greater the variety of clubs the more likely each person is to find a suitable one.

17 These descriptions of the Church's purpose, set out above, are caricatures. We set them here in contrast to what we believe to be a fuller and more adequate description of the purpose of the Church - to reflect the unity and love of God, Father, Son and Holy Spirit, and to be God's agent of evangelism and reconciliation in a lost and divided world. Christians cannot credibly preach the gospel of reconciliation in Christ to others if they themselves are unreconciled. It is only as the nature and purpose of the Church is understood in this way that we shall discover the necessary motivation for Christian unity.

THE VISION OF THE GOAL OF UNITY

IN SCRIPTURE

18 In the beginning God created the heaven and the earth, and the Spirit of God moved over the waters, bringing order out of chaos. The world was made to live in harmony with itself and to fulfil the loving and life-giving purpose of its creator. But in their God-given freedom men and women have sinned and rejected God's plan; both as individuals and as groups they have sought their own private or sectional advantage; they have fought, and spoilt their relationship with God and with one another, and they have damaged the environment in which they live. In their attempt to become gods themselves they have built their Tower of Babel.

19   God chose a people, Israel, and through Moses led them out of slavery into the promised land. He made a covenant with them: 'I will be your God and you shall be my people'. Yet Israel, sharing in the fallenness of the whole of humankind, broke God's law again and again, and rejected the prophets that he sent to them. God, however, was patient with them and continued his work among them.

20   As a definitive disclosure of himself, God sent his Son, born of Mary his human mother, to save men and women from their sin, and to bring them fullness of life and peace. In a life of total obedience to his Father, and in sacrificial love of men and women, Jesus showed what God is like by preaching the good news of freedom from sin and oppression, by healing the sick and forgiving the repentant sinner, and above all by allowing himself, out of love for them, to be crucified for their salvation, like a lamb led to the sacrifice. God vindicated his way of love by raising Jesus from the dead. He appeared to Mary Magdalene, and to the other disciples. He sent them out in the power of the Holy Spirit to preach the good news to the whole creation.

21   The early Church had a vision of the world restored at the end of time as God intended. As the Archbishop of Canterbury reminded us at the beginning of this Conference:

> In the Book of Revelation we are given a vision: a new heaven and a new earth, and the holy city, New Jerusalem, coming down from God out of heaven. Here is God's disclosure of the unity of the whole human family. The Lord God Almighty and the Lamb are the central focus of the holy City. All the nations shall walk in the light of the glory of God and of the Lamb. The Kings of the earth shall bring with them the glory and honour of the nations. *And the gates of the city shall not be shut* (Rev. 21.22-27). Exclusiveness is not a characteristic of the City of God.

> In this vision there is ultimately no difference between the quest for the Church's unity and the quest for human healing in the widest sense. The Church is the model towards which the whole human family will look for its healing and reconciliation. To the degree that the Church is effectively gathered in unity in the assembly of worship around God and the Lamb, it is the sign of hope and the bearer of good news to the whole world.

The Reconciliation of All Things in Christ

22   Reconciliation and unity is also a constant theme of the Pauline writings in the New Testament. The author of the Letter to the Ephesians tells his readers of the mystery of God's plan for the fullness of time, to unite all things in Christ, things in heaven and things on earth (Eph. 1.10).

A Reconciled and Worshipping Church

23   In his letter to the Romans, St Paul describes the Church as 'one body in Christ' (Rom. 12.5). He appeals to them to live in harmony with one another so that they may praise God together (Rom. 15.5, 6).

The Church as a Reconciling Community

24   St Paul writes to the Corinthians to say that God was in Christ reconcil-

ing the world to himself, and that he has committed to them, his followers, the continuing work of reconciliation (2 Cor. 5.19).

The Source of Unity - One God in Three Persons

25   The biblical passage which most clearly illuminates the theme of Christian unity is Jesus' prayer in John 17. In this prayer we are privileged to overhear the Son speaking with the Father. There are three interlocking themes in the prayer – unity, truth and holiness. The unity for which Jesus prays is unity in truth and in holiness.

26   Jesus prays that his disciples 'may all be one; even as thou, Father, art in me, and I in thee, that they may also be *in us,* so that the world may believe...' (John 17.21). He prays that all who follow him should be drawn into that unity which exists between Father and Son (and Holy Spirit). Here is the secret and key to our unity with one another. It is grounded in the life of unity and communion of the Godhead. The eternal, mutual, self-giving and receiving love of the three persons of the Trinity glimpsed in the prayer is not simply an inspiring model for us. It is the source and ground of our communion, of our fellowship with God and with one another. We are to be drawn into and locked together in his life. This is the vision of Christian unity we seek to convey. And that, of course, carries with it implications for our vision of a visibly united Church. It is precisely because the Trinity, the source of the Church's unity, is a unique unity of purpose and also a diversity of ways of being and of function, that the Church is called to express diversity in its own life – diversity held in unity.

27   But we have not begun to grasp the heart of the matter unless we have understood, through the inter-relation of the parts of John 17, that to share in the unity of the Godhead is to discover a cross at its heart. To enter into that unity is the willing acceptance of a cross at the heart of all our living and loving in God and with one another. The vision of unity is of a community called to be always prepared to walk together the way of glorification, the way of the cross. Only in this act of obedient self-offering can Christians be united with God in Christ. Only then are they conformed to the glory of the crucified one. Only then will the love of God shine through them 'so that the world may believe'. Moreover, the Church, which takes its identity from the God in whom it lives, should embody in its own life that mixture of pain and glory that belongs to the incarnation of the Son. Part of its cross will be the bearing of conflict in its own life without breaking the unity. We have discovered something of the pain and cost as we try to hold our Anglican Communion together in love, despite serious differences over the ordination of women.

28   Since Christian unity is the gift of God, fervent and persistent prayer in union with Christ's own prayer in John 17, and preferably in the company of Christians of other traditions, should be a universal and fundamental

response of all Christian people. It is in common worship and prayer that we come closer to the Father, and so to one another in Christ through the Holy Spirit. In union with this prayer the Church becomes an instrument of God in bringing unity to the world.

The Final Goal of Unity

29   The ultimate goal is not simply the unity of the Church. It is a gift which comes into the world from God and which will be completely revealed only at the end of time. It is the perfect reign of God over a reconciled, restored and transformed creation. It will be a kingdom in which what has been broken, distorted or disordered by the sin of men and women will be mended and put right through the life, death and resurrection of Jesus Christ. What will be put right is not only a shattered humanity – 'the leaves of the tree are for the healing of the nations' (Rev. 22.2) – but also the whole universe. The environment, polluted and misused by men and women, will be restored. Its 'groaning' will cease as a result of the redemption of men and women in Christ (Rom. 8.18-25). However, it is not to be simply a return to the Garden of Eden. It is to be a consummation of the work of Jesus Christ. In his earthly ministry Jesus released people from slavery, healed the sick, forgave sins, fed the hungry, cast out devils, and pointed to these actions as signs that the final victory over the powers of evil was assured and that the Kingdom or rule of God had already begun. The Kingdom which he inaugurated in his earthly ministry will be completed at the end of time. The goal of the unity we seek as Christians may never be less than the unity of all things in heaven and on earth which is God's plan for the fullness of time.

THE CHURCH IN THE WORLD ON THE WAY TO THE KINGDOM

30   The Church, then, is called to be united both because God, its source, is one, and also because the goal to which it journeys is the reconciliation of the whole creation to God in Christ. The unity of the Church is not an end in itself. The Church, as it is now, belongs to the interim – to the time between the coming of Christ in Palestine and his coming at the end to bring in the final rule of God. God longs for the whole world to be transformed and brought into his Kingdom. His Spirit is already at work in the world wherever the values of the Kingdom are upheld and lived. Wherever the Holy Spirit breathes life, breaks down hostility, brings freedom from oppression, heals and reconciles, there is a taste of the coming Kingdom. However, God has called his Church and sent it into the world to be a particular sign, instrument and first-fruits of his Kingdom here and now on earth:

– as Sign

31   The Church is called to be a sign of the Kingdom because all it says, does and is, should show the self-sacrificing life in Christ, and should point to the coming of his kingly rule. The Church is like a mirror held up to the face of God in the world. It is intended perfectly to reflect the image of God. How-

ever, if a mirror is broken or cracked, it distorts what it reflects. So a divided Church distorts the image of God's love held out to the world.

– as Instrument
32   The Church is called to be an instrument of the Kingdom. All it says and does should help to bring near God's reign of justice and peace. Christians are called to work together in service and prophetic witness in the world, and to be good stewards of the environment.

– as First-fruits
33   Because the very life of God himself is flowing in its fellowship, breaking down the barriers which men and women have erected against God and against one another, the Church is intended here and now to be a kind of first-fruits of God's Kingdom of love. In the Church, people and relationships are transfigured. Changed lives and changed relationships provide a hint or foretaste of a world in which all hatred and alienation will be overcome.

– as Provisional Embodiment
34   However, in this sinful world the Church, which is the body of Christ, will never be a perfect embodiment of God's Kingdom. It will always be provisional, awaiting the final coming of God at the end of time, its own and all creation's transformation.

35   The Church is provisional in two senses:

(a) Only part of the human race has been brought into the Church's life – hence the continuing demand to preach the Gospel to every creature of every race and culture and in every place. Christian unity and Christian mission can never be separated, for it is Christ's will that the whole inhabited world be reconciled to God and brought into his Kingdom.

(b) Those who have been brought into the Church's life are only gradually being conformed to God's purpose. If they were fully conformed, they would be fully reconciled to one another. The search for unity within the Church is part of the prayer: 'Your Kingdom come'.

CELEBRATING UNITY IN CULTURAL VARIETY
36   In the Pentecost story, people belonging to different language groups all understood what was being said. For the first time at a Lambeth Conference it has been possible for those who speak French, Japanese, Korean, Khumi (Burma), Spanish or Swahili to speak in their own language and to be interpreted and understood.

37   When the Gospel is first preached in a different language and the Church established in a different culture, new words, new ideas, new customs and traditions have gradually to be adopted. For effective missionary penetration the Gospel and the Church have to be embodied in a new way

appropriate to the particular culture. The reconciliation of all people to God does not mean the suppression of cultural diversity, for this enriches humanity and can create a deeper harmony and unity. However, there must be limits to diversity if the Church is to witness effectively to Christ's reconciliation in a divided world.

38 There are two dangers to be avoided when the Gospel and the Church come to be immersed in many, different cultural forms, in countries widely separated from one another:

(a) The Gospel and Church may be radically distorted by adaptation to a particular culture, so that the Church in that place becomes heretical or schismatic, and no longer witnesses to the truth of the reconciliation of all people to God in Christ.

(b) Though faithful to Scripture and tradition, the Church in different places may take on such different forms that it is hard to find and express a substantial unity with the Churches in other cultural contexts; and so it is unable to witness effectively to the unity of all people in the world.

39 One of the primary ways in which the Church has tried to preserve unity amid cultural diversity has been through meetings of bishops. The Lambeth Conference itself fulfils something of this function. The bishops have brought the cultures, races and languages of their dioceses with them, and have been able to exchange insights with bishops from other places. Amid the inevitable tension and conflict that ensue, they search for ways of expressing their fundamental unity in the Gospel in the service of the reconciliation of the world. Bishops from Southern Africa, Iran, and other places where there is conflict have testified to the great support they have found in belonging to a world-wide Christian fellowship.

40 Within his diocese, the bishop is the focus of unity. The ideal for Anglicans and for many other Christians is that there should be one bishop in each place. The Lambeth Conference in 1908 stated:

> the principle of one bishop for one area is the ideal to be aimed at as the best means of securing the unity of all races and nations in the Holy Catholic Church.

There has, traditionally, been a dislike of 'parallel' or 'overlapping' episcopates.

41 In recent times, however, movements of population have led to people of different races, cultures and languages settling down side by side. Often these movements have been the result of wars, famines, oppressive governments or the need to find work. Sometimes they have been voluntary, or the result of improved communications. Increasingly, migrants cherish, and wish to conserve, their cultural heritage. In these circumstances the Church has to find ways of ministering to people in a particular situation or in their diversity, while retaining the fundamental unity of the whole people of God

in that place. Cultural, ethnic or non-territorial bishoprics are being developed in Australia, New Zealand, Southern Africa and the United States of America in order to try to achieve this. In these experiments bishops are appointed to look after particular cultural, ethnic or racial groupings, and they work across the boundaries of existing territorial bishops.

42   As indicated in para. 40, such experiments run counter to traditional Anglican ideals, but they respond to pastoral needs which are increasingly felt. As early as 1968 the Lambeth Conference recognised that special reasons might 'make it necessary to bear the anomaly of two overlapping communities in the same area, for a greater or lesser time'.[2]

43   Facing these situations, Provinces have to weigh up two conflicting concerns.

(a) The need to minister effectively to a particular cultural or ethnic group.

(b) The need to embody in the Church the fact that in Christ all ethnic and racial divisions are overcome.

Where more weight is given to the former concern, it is important that unity is maintained among the bishops through some collegial arrangement. Indeed, without the episcopal link the maintenance of unity in these circumstances would be very difficult.

44   The ecumenical impact should be noted: where the Anglicans of a particular race are given a non-territorial bishop, it is not unknown for people of the same race, but belonging to different denominations, to regard this man as 'our bishop'. The implications of this for ecumenical relations need to be sensitively and creatively explored.

UNITY WITHIN THE ANGLICAN COMMUNION

45   We have already begun to touch on the way in which unity is preserved within the Anglican Communion. During the last 120 years, since the first Lambeth Conference, the Anglican Communion has expanded from a few mainly white and predominantly English-speaking Churches and their missions, without any global organisation, into a world-wide Communion. This Communion is held together by its foundation upon Scripture, tradition and reason, by having a common baptism, eucharist and ministry, and by a common history. At the same time, many of the other particular cultural bonds, which helped to hold it together in the past, are weakening – Anglo-Saxon culture, the British Empire, the English language and, in particular, the King James Bible and the traditional Book(s) of Common Prayer.

46   At least four issues which call for decision by the whole Communion have been presented to this Conference: How can we maintain communion in the face of our different practices over the ordination of women? How do

we pronounce the consensus of the Communion on *the Final Report* of the Anglican-Roman Catholic International Commission?[3] How do we respond to *Baptism, Eucharist and Ministry*[4] as a Communion and not simply as Provinces? How do we respond to the Orthodox request that we remove the Filioque clause from the Nicene Creed. In short, how can the Anglican Communion, which has no central legislative body to make decisions, come to a common mind on these issues?

47   In his opening address to the first Lambeth Conference in 1867 Archbishop Longley rejected any suggestion of establishing a general synod of the Communion, and successive Conferences have maintained that position. Each Province remains autonomous. The establishment of the Anglican Consultative Council and the Primates' Meeting has not altered the fact that the authority exercised by these two bodies and by the Archbishop of Canterbury is moral and not legislative.

48   It is, however, significant that in the last few years the word 'interdependent' has begun to replace the word 'independent' as the appropriate description of the position and attitude of Provinces. As early as 1920 the Lambeth Conference emphasised that legal independence was not the same as licence for independent action in a Christian Church. It recognised that the Lambeth Conference had no power to command, but emphasised

> the far more spiritual and more Christian principle of loyalty to the fellowship. The Churches represented in it are indeed independent, but independent with the Christian freedom which recognises the restraints of truth and love. They are not free to deny the truth. They are not free to ignore the fellowship ... the Conference is ... a fellowship in the Spirit.[5]

49   What is of ultimate Christian significance in the Anglican Communion is not that, where there is conflict, decisions are made in a particular way, but that they are made in the spirit of the prayer of Christ in St John's Gospel, (John 17), with a fearless regard for truth and holiness in Christ, and with a Christ-like, self-sacrificing, concern for the unity of all Christians in one God, and for their *visible* unity, so that the world might believe. The picture of a bitter and bickering Church, at odds with itself, contradicts and destroys the Gospel. However, conflict is bound to come, and the picture of a Church living with conflict in a Christ-like way, painfully struggling to find the truth in Christ, can itself be a witness to the Gospel of reconciliation.

50   One of the most difficult tasks is to discern the issues which concern the whole Communion, and which therefore need to be decided on a worldwide basis, and to distinguish them from issues which may properly be decided on a Provincial basis without consultation with other Provinces.

THE ANGLICAN COMMUNION TRANSCENDED?

51   A study of earlier Lambeth Conference Reports shows that the bishops

have thought of the Anglican Communion as only a relatively small part of the whole Church of Christ. The bishops have also

> forecast the day when the racial and historical connections which at present characterise (the Anglican Communion) will be transcended and the life of our Communion will be merged in a larger fellowship in the Catholic Church.[6]

The presence of bishops from the united Churches of Bangladesh, North and South India and Pakistan, where Anglicans have entered into union with other Christians, as full members of our Conference is a pointer to the coming of that day, as is the presence of representatives of other Churches in full communion, and of observers from the Churches with which we are in dialogue.

52 As we have already seen, successive Lambeth Conferences have rejected all suggestions that the Conference should become a general synod of the Anglican Communion with legislative powers. It is all the more significant, therefore, that successive Conferences have also looked forward to the time when it may be possible to participate in a 'true general council' of *all* the Churches of Christ.

There has been a concern that the strengthening of worldwide Anglican unity should not prove a hindrance to the growth of the worldwide unity of all Christians.

THE NATURE OF THE UNITY WE SEEK WITH OTHER CHRISTIANS

53 There is a close relationship between Anglican attempts to understand, maintain and develop our own unity in the Anglican Communion, and our search for a wider unity with other Christians. The wider unity we seek is not simply the Anglican Communion writ large. We are learning and developing all the time. Our own unity within the Anglican Communion is developing. An example of this has been our search for appropriate means of consultation between Provinces. Our understanding of wider Christian unity has also been developing since the Lambeth Conference 1888 when the Bishops affirmed what came to be known as the Chicago-Lambeth Quadrilateral.

THE CHICAGO-LAMBETH QUADRILATERAL

54 Indeed, the Quadrilateral itself was intended not primarily to describe internal Anglican unity, but as the basis on which to express the nature of the unity we seek with other Christians. The four elements of the Quadrilateral, affirmed one hundred years ago, were:

> (a) The Holy Scriptures of the Old and New Testaments, as 'containing all things necessary to salvation', and as being the rule and ultimate standard of faith.

> (b) The Apostles' Creed, as the Baptismal Symbol; and the Nicene Creed, as the sufficient statement of the Christian faith.

(c) The two Sacraments ordained by Christ Himself – Baptism and the Supper of the Lord – ministered with unfailing use of Christ's words of Institution, and of the elements ordained by Him.

(d) The Historic Episcopate, locally adapted in the methods of its administration to the varying needs of the nations and peoples called of God into the unity of His Church.

55   The Quadrilateral is not a catalogue of four separate and unrelated items which, added together, create a united Church. It is an attempt to describe four inter-related elements used by the Spirit of God to hold together a body of diverse men and women in Christ. Nor is the Quadrilateral a static list. At various points in the last hundred years (notably in 1920 and in 1968) the fourth element in particular has been modified in relation to the ecumenical situation of the time. The Quadrilateral has profoundly shaped the attitudes of Anglican Churches as they have entered into dialogue with other Churches, and indeed it has influenced the thought of other Churches too.

56   It can be thought of as a skeleton, which, if it is to live, needs to be embodied in a community and breathed on by the Spirit in a life of fellowship in worship and service. Within an already existing Communion the body and the Spirit are taken for granted, and the four elements of the Quadrilateral can serve as a shorthand description of a Church. But when it is used as a basis for discussions with another Communion about unity, then we have to explore with those Christians the elements of the Quadrilateral to discover if indeed we share the same faith, whether there is consonance in our celebration and understanding of the Sacraments and whether we can recognise one another's ministries as authentically apostolic. How then are we learning to understand the elements of the Quadrilateral through our theological conversations with other Christians?

INTERNATIONAL THEOLOGICAL CONVERSATIONS

57   We have had the privilege of studying the reports which have come from five different sets of theological conversations since the last Lambeth Conference.[7] These are the multilateral conversations carried on between many different Churches under the auspices of the World Council of Churches, and the bilateral dialogues which have taken place between the Anglican Communion and respectively the Lutheran, Orthodox, Reformed and Roman Catholic Churches. In addition, we learnt of the beginning of a new dialogue with the Oriental Orthodox Churches.[8] Representatives of all these Churches were present and contributed much to our understanding.

A COMMON EXPRESSION OF FAITH

58   In these dialogues we can see how our understanding of each of the elements of the Quadrilateral has been expanded. For example, the World

137

Council of Churches, formed forty years ago, has in its work filled out and extended the characteristics briefly set down in the Quadrilateral. It has sent to its member Churches for their preliminary consideration a report, *Towards a Common Expression of the Apostolic Faith.* This treats the same themes as the first two articles of the Lambeth Quadrilateral, but in a more dynamic way. The faith of the Scriptures and the Creeds, while remaining normative for the Church, is seen to be in need of fresh expression in every age and culture. Churches on the way to unity are called upon to confess that faith *together.*

59   Other dialogues too have examined the faith we share with other Christians. The early discussions with the Orthodox considered our knowledge of God and the inspiration and authority of Scripture. The *Anglican – Reformed Report* is founded on the doctrine of the grace of God.[9] The Second Anglican – Roman Catholic International Commission has recently produced *Salvation and the Church.*[10] This tackles the most controversial issue of the Reformation, the doctrine of justification by faith. All these dialogues should be studied together, for they illuminate one another and build up our confidence that we, together with all our partner Churches in these dialogues, believe the same thing about the faith which the Church has held through the ages. The World Council of Churches challenges us to express that faith not only in a spoken creed but also embodied in our life, which is set in so many different cultural contexts throughout the world.

SACRAMENTS

60   The other two articles of the Quadrilateral have been taken up and reflected upon creatively in *Baptism, Eucharist and Ministry,* the work of the Faith and Order Commission of the World Council of Churches. They have also been tackled, at least in part, in all the other dialogues. There is a remarkable agreement on the meaning of baptism, which is recognised as a fundamental bond of unity. However, there is no consensus on the practice of Christian initiation and the relationship between baptism, confirmation and first communion. (Resolution 3.)

61   The deepest agreement can be discovered in what the various dialogues say about the eucharist. Moreover, both *Baptism, Eucharist and Ministry* and the *Anglican – Reformed Report* lay stress upon the ethical implications of the celebration of the eucharist. In the eucharist the Church is not only expressing its faith in, and feeding upon, its risen Lord. It is also driven out by the same Lord to feed his hungry world.

MINISTRY

62   Much progress towards agreement on ministry has been registered since the fourth element of the Quadrilateral was described in 1888. All the

dialogues affirm that no single pattern of ministry, as it exists today, can be traced back to the New Testament. Nevertheless, in *Baptism, Eucharist and Ministry* the ministry of bishops, presbyters and deacons is put forward as a pattern agreeable to the Word of God and appropriate to the unity of the Church and also a means of achieving it. The way that pattern is exercised in the Anglican Communion is challenged by the insights and experience of others, and we should look for the re-examination and renewal of our ministry. The *Anglican – Reformed Report* challenges our lack of a real diaconate. The Anglican – Lutheran *Niagara Report* raises pertinent questions about our exercise of episcopacy.[11]

63   The recognition and reconciliation of the ministry of one Church by another has always been a difficulty for Anglicans. In its 1920 form, the commentary on the fourth element of the Quadrilateral recognised the 'spiritual realities of the ministries of those Communions which do not possess the Episcopate', and acknowledged that they were an 'effective means of grace'. However, it saw the only way to the reconciliation of the ministries of those who had not received it to be by episcopal ordination. We have had before us two reports, *Ministry in a Uniting Church: From Recognition to Reconciliation* from the Covenanted Churches in Wales[12] and the Anglican – Lutheran *Niagara Report*. The former is modelled on the North India and Pakistan Union Scheme, and we see no difficulty insofar as that is the case, in maintaining full communion with the Uniting Church, should the Church in Wales decide to go forward to union on that basis. The latter presents a more gradual way forward for reconciliation with Lutheran Churches, and we commend this to the Provinces of the Anglican Communion for study and synodical reception. (Resolutions 4, 12, 13.)

64   The Chicago-Lambeth Quadrilateral says nothing explicitly about the structures of unity that hold the Church together. However, we cannot reflect long on the ministry without acknowledging the fact that the ministry is one of the indispensable, instrumental signs of the Church's communion. The ordained ministry, especially the episcopal ministry, has a particular responsibility for maintaining and focusing the communion and unity of the Church. *Baptism, Eucharist and Ministry* says that personal (e.g. the bishop), collegial (e.g. all the bishops acting together, and also the bishop acting with his presbyters), and communal (synodical) ministry must be exercised at every point in the Church's life. This creative proposal remains undeveloped in *Baptism, Eucharist and Ministry,* but it is taken up and developed in the *Anglican – Reformed Report*. The ministry of oversight, particularly the inter-relation of primacy and collegiality, is most fully treated in the work of the Anglican – Roman Catholic International Commission (ARCIC I) whose *Final Report* looks at ministry at the world level. There it envisages a universal primate exercising a personal ministry. But this is held together with the collegial ministry of the bishops, and these two

ministries are never exercised apart from one another.[13] The question which Anglicans are asking is what place there is for the communal role of the laity in what this dialogue has to say about the Councils of the Church (conciliarity). The Anglican – Orthodox dialogue describes the office of 'seniority', an office of encouragement which is exercised collegially.[14] It is not an office of arbitrary intervention or universal jurisdiction or infallibility. The Anglican – Orthodox and Anglican – Roman Catholic dialogues, with their distinctive contributions on this point, need now to be considered by all three partners together.

65   All that is said about the elements of the Quadrilateral is integral to the nature of the unity we seek with other Christians, and cannot be separated from it. How then do we envisage the goal of unity – short of the perfect Kingdom of God to come at the end of time? Is the goal of unity, as it is envisaged in each conversation or dialogue, compatible with the goals set out in the others? It is vital that it should be, because there can be only one ecumenical movement. We shall trace different descriptions of the goals and see how they relate to one another.

ORGANIC UNITY

66   In their struggle to develop and maintain unity within their own Communion, Anglicans believe that they have something valuable to share with other Christians in the search for a wider Christian unity. Anglicans have always valued St Paul's picture of the Church as the body of Christ. We have used it as the basis of what has been our commonest description of unity – *organic unity*. This image emphasises the corporate and interdependent nature of unity – the diverse parts of a body are inter-related in organic life, not simply cogs in a machine, and all the parts have their particular and diverse roles to play in obedience to the head, who is Christ. Anglicans have distinguished organic unity, which provides scope for flexibility and growth, from uniformity or mere organisational unity. We have also distinguished it from a loose federation. It is of the nature of an organism that it is bound together throughout its whole extent by ligaments and channels of communication.

67   It has to be admitted that the organic nature of Anglican unity is much more evident within a diocese and within a Province than it is between the Provinces. It is only relatively recently that continuing bonds have begun to emerge at that level.

ALL IN EACH PLACE UNITED WITH THOSE IN ALL PLACES AND AGES

68   The World Council of Churches has also done much work on the nature of the unity we seek, and has added much to the rather static formulation of

the Quadrilateral. At the New Delhi Assembly in 1961 it evolved a classic statement describing the growth of unity as 'all in each place' being united in 'one fully committed fellowship', and at the same time being united with 'the whole Christian fellowship in all places and in all ages'. This statement showed that, beyond the four elements of the Quadrilateral, a united Church would need to have bonds between local Churches so that they could make decisions together and preserve universal communion with one another.

CONCILIAR FELLOWSHIP

69   Later the World Council of Churches described this as *conciliar fellowship:* 'conciliar' because this unity was held together by representative councils which could express the consensus of the local Churches; 'fellowship' because that network of councils was only the outward expression of an inner communion grounded in the love of God.

70   The report of the Anglican – Reformed dialogue, *God's Reign and Our Unity,* builds on the insights developed in the World Council of Churches, and lays great emphasis on the necessity of having only one Church in each place. The permanent existence of our separated Churches, as they are, with all their differences of faith and practice, each acting independently of the others without consultation, but technically 'in communion' with one another, would not fulfil our Lord's will for unity. A mere federation of coexisting denominations, living side by side with one another in the same city or town, whose members were free to receive communion in one another's Churches, would not be a satisfactory instrument or sign of God's reconciling power in society.

71   'Hence we seek the emergence of reconciled local communities, each of which is recognisable as "church" in the proper sense: i.e. communities which exhibit in each place the fullness of ministerial order, eucharistic fellowship, pastoral care and missionary commitment, and which, through mutual communion and co-operation, bear witness on the regional, national and even international levels. Such churches would express both the unity to which God calls his whole creation in Christ and the diversity which properly characterises the human family as God intends it to be.'[15] A small Anglican working party summed up this view of the goal of unity succinctly in the following words: 'We believe that the organic union of all Christians and all Churches in each place, and of each place with every other, is the will of Christ.'[16]

FULL COMMUNION BETWEEN AUTONOMOUS CHURCHES

72   At first sight the various reports emanating from Anglican – Lutheran discussions seem to present a different vision of the goal of unity. In particu-

lar, the report *Anglican – Lutheran Relations* appears to envisage the continuance of our two Communions side by side, perhaps having churches of the two bodies in the same town or even street. It looks

> forward to the day when *full communion* is established between Anglican and Lutheran Churches. By full communion we here understand a relationship between the two distinct Churches or communions. Each maintains its own autonomy and recognises the catholicity and apostolicity of the other, and each believes the other to hold the essentials of the Christian faith...'[17]

73   A number of factors, however, suggest that this could be a complementary and not a contradictory goal. A significant factor in Europe, though not elsewhere, is that Anglican and Lutheran Churches tend to be geographically separated, with minimal overlapping. The relationship of full communion proposed, therefore, would not lead to two distinct Churches in each place in Europe, but would be more like the present relationship between distinct Provinces of the Anglican Communion.

74   A more significant factor, because it would apply everywhere, is the determination that both Churches should work very closely together, and possibly unite in one local Church if two congregations find themselves in the same geographical area.

75   *Anglican – Lutheran Relations* goes on to say:

> To be in full communion implies a community of life, an exchange and commitment to one another in respect of major decisions on questions of faith, order and morals. It implies, where churches are in the same geographical area, common worship, study, witness, evangelism and promotion of justice, peace and love. It may lead to a uniting of ecclesial bodies if they are, or come to be, immediately adjacent in the same geographical area. This should not imply the suppressing of ethnic, cultural or ecclesial characteristics or traditions which may in fact be maintained and developed by diverse institutions within one communion.[18]

76   Ethnic and cultural diversity will rightly continue to be a feature of a united Church. But what is meant by 'ecclesial' traditions, and is it right that they should be retained in 'diverse institutions'? If this is merely a perpetuation of existing denominations continuing to live side by side, it should be rejected. However, it is more likely to be a concern to preserve valuable church traditions which have sometimes been lost when a hasty merger of a small Church with a larger one has occurred. Many of our Churches have lived in separation from one another for centuries. In their separation they have developed different traditions of worship, even distinctive theological emphases, which should not be wantonly lost in a hasty attempt to create an artificial uniformity. It may be that as a stage towards closer unity such Churches may coexist, while committing themselves to explore and enter into one another's traditions and so to discover which are of continuing value and which are not.

77   However, perhaps the most significant factor which suggests that the goal of the Anglican – Lutheran dialogue need not be incompatible with that of the others is its commitment to the notion of unity by stages. Perhaps its description of full communion should be seen as a stage on the way to an even deeper unity. (Resolution 4.)

78   In the *Niagara Report,* to which we have already referred, the Anglican – Lutheran International Continuation Committee specifically commit themselves to 'rethinking our goals', since 'questions have surfaced about the way full communion is described'. We look forward to their clarification.

79   We have mentioned three pictures which have been used to describe the visible unity of Christ's Church: organic unity, conciliar fellowship, and full communion between autonomous Churches. These are not the only pictures used. Each tends to give a different emphasis. However, they should be regarded as complementary and not contradictory. It may be significant, for example, that the *Final Report* of the Anglican – Roman Catholic International Commission uses both organic unity and full communion to describe its vision of the goal. The pictures supplement and correct one another as we try to glimpse the goal ever more clearly.

UNITY BY STAGES

80   In the Anglican – Roman Catholic International Commission, and more particularly in the conversations between Anglicans and Lutherans, there has been support for the idea that unity should proceed by stages. This proposal is warmly to be accepted, since unity should be considered a process of growth. The stage of growth will depend upon how much the participating Churches have in common and what is their level of commitment to one another.

81   The idea of growth into unity by stages is important because it shows that progress towards full, visible unity does not have to wait for complete agreement on every aspect of faith and order. Each level of such agreement can be expressed in a corresponding growth in relationship and co-operation.

82   The stages have been set out in detail as follows:

(a) *Fellowship in faith and mission*
Agreement in the faith, expressed in teaching and in practice, strengthens co-operation in mission and service, which in turn encourages growing agreement in faith.

(b) *Limited sharing of communion*
When Churches have sufficient agreement in faith and are committed to proceed ultimately to full communion, then members of Churches are

admitted to communion at one another's altars. *Anglican – Lutheran Relations* also commends what it calls 'interim sharing of the eucharist' in which two whole congregations come together for what is called 'a common, joint celebration' of the eucharist. At this stage there has as yet been no reconciliation of the ordained ministries of the two Churches (Resolution 4 : 6b iia).

(c) *Full communion*

Full communion should imply that the ordained ministers and members of two Churches are interchangeable – that is, fully accepted in one another's Churches. It should also imply that the two Churches have regular means of consulting and making decisions together on matters of common concern. We shall return to the meaning of 'full communion' shortly. Some interpret it as the final goal of Christian unity, short of the Kingdom of God. Others envisage a distinct, fourth stage.

(d) *Organic unity*

Those who distinguish organic unity from full communion would claim that it implies an organically united structure of Church life at every point. This would include an organic structure (possibly with a general council and a universal primate) to bind the national or provincial Churches together.

83   We wish to commit ourselves to the idea of unity by stages. Throughout history Christian divisions have developed gradually and untidily. We should not expect the healing of these divisions to happen tidily or all at once.

COMMUNION

84   Following the early tradition of the Christian Church, Anglicans use the word 'communion' (Greek *koinonia*, sometimes also translated as 'fellowship' or 'sharing') in two senses. It is used to describe the relationship which exists between Anglicans all over the world. We call our worldwide body 'the Anglican Communion'. It is also used of the act of sharing together in the eucharist, the Holy Communion.

85   The *Final Report* of the Anglican – Roman Catholic International Commission encourages us to meditate more deeply on this term, which is seen as fundamental to an understanding of the true nature of the Church, and describes the mystery underlying it:

> Union with God in Christ Jesus through the Spirit is the heart of Christian *koinonia*. Among the various ways in which the term *koinonia* is used in different New Testament contexts, we concentrate on that which signifies a relation between persons resulting from their participation in one and the same reality (cf. 1 John 1.3). The Son of God has taken to himself our human nature, and he has sent us his Spirit, who makes us so truly members of the body of Christ that we too are able to call God 'Abba, Father' (Rom. 8.15; Gal. 4.6). Moreover, sharing in the same Holy Spirit, whereby we become members of the same body of Christ and

adopted children of the same Father, we are also bound to one another in a completely new relationship. *Koinonia* with one another is entailed by our *koinonia* with God in Christ. This is the mystery of the Church.[19]

86   To understand the Church as a shared fellowship *(koinonia)* acknowledges both the diversity of Christian experience and the need for an order which maintains the different local Churches and dioceses in truth and mutual love. Order is dependent upon a life grounded in the communion of God the Holy Trinity, and the ministerial office is subordinate to the sovereignty of the Word of God.

87   Bishops, presbyters and deacons are to be seen as serving the fellowship *(koinonia)* in Christ, and a universal primate, as envisaged in the ARCIC I *Final Report,* has the role of focusing the fellowship *(koinonia)* in Christ. To understand ministry in this way is to reject the hierarchical pattern of authority, by which juridical decisions are simply passed down from the top of a pyramid to its bottom.

88   Moreover, this understanding of the Church as a shared fellowship, sacramentally expressed in Holy Communion, leads us to see that the Church looks to an end beyond itself. The presence of the Kingdom is in part realised when the Word is faithfully preached, and the sacraments rightly administered, in the continuing life of the community. But the eucharist is a foretaste of the heavenly supper of the Lamb; and the Church celebrating it is not an institution finding its end in itself.

89   Central to the Church as a sharing fellowship is personal encounter with God and acceptance of his commission and gift to serve him in the world. To understand the Church as *koinonia* brings out the full force of the apostolic theme of the people of God as constituting a body of which Christ is head. Through him and with him and in him (and only in him) it is possible for us to offer ourselves to the Father.

90   Christian unity is fundamentally a personal relationship in God. The sharing of bread and wine in the eucharist is a profound but not the only effective sign of communion in the Church. Christian communion cannot be *fully* expressed without such a eucharistic sharing together, and our communion is impaired where that sharing is not possible. In this Lambeth Conference we have sadly experienced the impairing of our own communion between Provinces because of our different practice on the ordination of women. But our communion with God and therefore with one another is also profoundly expressed in other ways – in sharing a common baptism, in studying the Scriptures together, in sharing our resources (as St Paul's Churches did with the poor in Jerusalem), in engaging together in common service and evangelism, and in all forms of joint worship and prayer.

91   In the early centuries a sharp distinction was made between being in communion with another Christian or Christian group and being out of communion with them. This came to be used narrowly of eucharistic communion, and was designed to safeguard the truths of the Gospel when they were threatened by heresies, and to signal the vital importance of maintaining a united Church in the face of schism.

92   Today, however, circumstances have changed. We no longer attack one another polemically, nor do we define ourselves any longer by the things on which we disagree. We are able to regard communion as a flexible and growing relationship. We already have fundamental communion with one another in that we all share the same personal relationship with God in Christ through the grace expressed in baptism; and we are summoned to accept one another as freely as God in Christ has accepted us.

FULL COMMUNION

93   The united Churches of the Indo-Pakistan sub-continent are full members of the Anglican Consultative Council, and those of their Bishops who have been present with us have been voting members of this Lambeth Conference. Membership of the Meetings of Primates for their moderators would place these Churches in a similar position to that of the various Anglican Provinces. We welcome this development, which appears to be the logical conclusion of our describing these Churches as being in full communion with us, but which does not prevent them from relating to the other Christian world communions with which their Churches are also linked. (Resolution 12.)

94   The phrase 'full communion' has been much used by Anglicans, although its meaning has not always been consistent. Until 1958 it seems most commonly to have been used to describe the close relationship which existed between Churches of the same confessional family, and was particularly used in this way by the Churches of the Anglican Communion of their own relationship with one another. The 1958 Lambeth Conference, however, defined its meaning more precisely as the relationship between Churches in which there is a mutual acceptance of ministers and members, so that the ministers of one Church can preside at the sacraments in and for the other Church; and that the bishop of the one Church can take part in the ordination of bishops in and for the other Church. This more precise definition of full communion made it possible to claim that the Provinces of the Anglican Communion were in full communion not only with the emerging united Churches of what were to become Bangladesh, India and Pakistan, where Anglicans had entered or were about to enter into union with other Churches, but also with the Old Catholic, Mar Thoma and Philippine Independent Churches. This has been how Anglicans have generally described such relationships since 1958.

95   However, it should be noted that the Bonn Agreement established with the Old Catholic Church in 1931 spoke of 'intercommunion' between the two Churches or Communions, and *not* of 'full communion'. Moreover, the Anglican – Old Catholic agreement of 1947 specifically encouraged the two Churches to maintain their own distinct life, with their own bishops and clergy, where they were working in the same locality. Agreements with the Philippine Independent Church and with the Mar Thoma Church have been based upon the Bonn Agreement, although they also are generally described as relationships of 'full communion'

96   The definition of 'full communion' established in 1958 has recently been criticised as being inadequate. If communion has a much wider meaning than just sacramental sharing, then full communion must imply more than the ability of the ministers and members of one Church to share in the celebration of the eucharist and in other sacramental acts in the other Church. Should it not also require at least a commitment by the Churches not to take decisions on matters which affect the other Church without consultation? Such consultation would require a regular process of communication between the Churches. Such a process now exists with the united Churches.

97   The Anglican Communion now has no presence in Bangladesh, India and Pakistan except through the united Churches. They, therefore, hold a position in the Anglican Communion analogous to all the other Provinces. However, the Church of England (and to a lesser extent the Episcopal Church in the United States of America) has a diocese and chaplaincies on the continent of Europe parallel to the dioceses and parishes of the Old Catholic Church. Similarly, the Episcopal Church has dioceses in the Philippines, even though for the most part the Churches are not in the same areas as those of the Philippine Independent Church. The Mar Thoma Church exists alongside the Church of South India. If the goal of unity is one Church in each place, full communion should at least imply that Churches in the same country and area should have means of regular consultation and of sharing in one another's life, with a view to growth into closer unity. Were such consultations and sharing totally absent, 'full communion' would not have been the correct description of the relationship. However, such consultation has grown in recent years. Some of the bishops of these 'full communion' Churches have been present at the Lambeth Conference, as they were at the last meeting of the Anglican Consultative Council. There has also been an increase in contact and consultation in those areas where these Churches exist alongside Anglican or united Churches. All this is to be encouraged and welcomed. Nevertheless, the question should perhaps be asked again whether the proper description of the relationship between the Anglican Communion and these Churches should be 'intercommunion', as agreed at Bonn in 1931, or 'full communion', as decided on the Anglican side at the Lambeth Conference in 1958.

MOVING GRADUALLY INTO FULLER COMMUNION

98   Whatever the appropriate description should be of the relationship of two Churches at any particular moment, it is far more important that those Churches find ways of moving gradually into deeper and deeper communion with one another. Growth into unity is a flexible process, since initiatives may be taken in different places at different times and at different levels of the Churches' life.

99   What is certain is that there is only one ecumenical movement. Just as the international theological conversations should not be played off against one another, but should be seen as part of the same process of growth in theological understanding between all Christian Churches, so every true work for unity at every point in the Churches' life contributes to the whole.

ECUMENISM IN ALL AREAS AND ASPECTS OF THE CHURCH'S LIFE

100   Christian unity is fundamentally about the redemptive love of God the Father in Christ through the Holy Spirit, and so it concerns human persons in relationship with God and with one another wherever they are and whatever their roles. And so it affects every *area* of the Church's life (in families, small groups, congregations and parishes, dioceses, Provinces, nations, regional groupings, and worldwide), and also every *aspect* of the Church's life (its education, administration, law and pastoral care, as well as its theology, evangelism, service and prophetic witness).

Internationally
101   We have already noted the enormous work and progress of the various *international* theological dialogues. The resolutions passed by the Conference as a whole show our commitment to pursuing these dialogues as well as beginning new ones. We have also committed ourselves to the continuing work of the World Council of Churches. (Resolutions 3 to 12.)

Nationally
102   For many years a major focus of the ecumenical movement was upon the discovery of sufficient theological agreement to achieve *national* schemes of union between Anglican and various other Churches. One of those is at present under discussion by the Covenanted Churches in Wales. There is also the Consultation on Church Union in the United States of America. However, perhaps the most widely notable development in work for unity *nationally* has been in the changing role of national Conferences or Councils of Churches. In a number of countries the role of these national bodies has been under scrutiny and revision, partly so as to include the full participation of Roman Catholic and various Evangelical and Pentecostal Churches where it did not previously exist, and partly to try to find an ecumenical instrument through which the various Churches could feel more

deeply committed to one another and their joint mission in society. We commit ourselves to search for ways to make these bodies even more effective. (Resolution 14.)

Locally

103   For most people, however, Christian unity becomes real only locally. There, actual relationships between Churches in different parts of the world vary enormously on a developing scale, from conflict or competition or mere coexistence, through co-operation, mutual commitment or covenant, to communion.

104   In many places Christians have begun to learn to trust one another by engaging together in mission and social witness. As we do so we discover the impetus and motive to advance towards closer unity.

We also discover our need of ecumenical education. Such education can be gained in three ways. Primarily, it is learned through the experience of meeting, praying, living and working with Christians of other traditions. There is no substitute for such direct, ecumenical encounter. Such encounter is valuable for everyone, but it is particularly necessary for those training for ordination to the ministry. Secondly, it is learned by theological reflection, both upon such direct experience and also on the work, for example, of the international theological dialogues. Unfortunately in many places the reports of these dialogues have proved generally too difficult for the members of congregations. There is a great need for simple guides and courses which will make theological concepts accessible to Christians generally. Thirdly, we are challenged to make our whole Church and school education programme ecumenical, so that Anglicans from a young age may grow up learning about their faith alongside Christians of other traditions, and using educational materials in common with them.

105   In some parts of the world this growth in practical co-operation has led to a much greater depth of understanding and mutual commitment and has resulted in the development of co-operating parishes, shared ministries, local covenants or local ecumenical projects (the designation varies in different parts of the world). The reality is a mutual commitment of local congregations to share in one another's life, ministry and mission in their particular locality. These local ecumenical projects or parishes are often in the vanguard of the ecumenical movement and are given insights which should be shared with their parent Churches. (Resolution 15.)

106   Also in the ecumenical vanguard are those interchurch marriages where Anglicans married to Christians of another Communion, often a Roman Catholic, have tried to remain faithful to their own tradition, while bringing up their children to share in the riches of the traditions of both parents. In some countries, such as Canada, and some dioceses, for example in the United States of America and Ireland, the bishops of Anglican and

Roman Catholic Churches have jointly established public guidelines for the pastoral care of interchurch families. In many places also, such as England, France, Ireland and Scotland, interchurch families have formed themselves into groups for mutual support and Christian formation.

107 However, both local ecumenical projects and interchurch families, where they have been left alone to pursue their own goals, are sometimes in danger of losing their close connections with their parent denominations. Where the diocesan bishops and similar authorities from other local Churches have maintained a continuing interest in these families or local projects, they have sometimes found ways of jointly exercising oversight. (Resolution 13.)

108 Indeed, one of the most recent developments in some areas has been regular meetings of bishops and their equivalents in other denominations to pray together, and to review the problems and opportunities presented by increasing ecumenical co-operation in mission. Some of these problems can be overcome and opportunities grasped by decisions taken jointly by leaders of local, regional or national Churches. (Resolution 13.)

CONCLUSIONS

109 We, the bishops assembled at this Lambeth Conference, have been aware of the importance of our role as signs of Church unity, and therefore of our special responsibility to work for the unity of all Christians. We therefore commit ourselves vigorously to pursue the search for the visible unity of the Church in our dioceses and throughout the world. We wish to encourage every member of our dioceses to join us in the search for the unity Christ wills. By learning from members of other traditions, in joint study, in shared evangelism and acts of service and witness in the world, and above all in prayer and worship, may we grow together into that fellowship *(koinonia)* in God, Father, Son and Holy Spirit, in which we may all be one to the glory of God's holy name, that the world may believe.

NOTES

[1] For the list of Reports from these discussions, see Bibliography.

[2] *The Lambeth Conference 1968 : Resolutions and Reports,* SPCK/Seabury, 1968.

[3] *The Final Report,* Anglican – Roman Catholic International Commission (ARCIC), CTS/SPCK, London, 1982.

[4] *Baptism, Eucharist and Ministry,* WCC, Geneva, 1982.

[5] *Lambeth Conference Report, 1920,* SPCK, London, p.14.

[6] *Lambeth Conference Report, 1930,* SPCK, London, p.153.

[7] See Bibliography.

[8] See Bibliography.

[9] *God's Reign and Our Unity,* Anglican–Reformed International Commission, SPCK/St Andrew Press, London and Edinburgh, 1984.

[10] *Salvation and the Church* (ARCIC II), CTS/CHP, London 1987.

[11] *The Niagara Report : Anglican–Lutheran Consultation on Episcope,* ACC/LWF, London and Geneva, 1988.

[12] *Ministry in a Uniting Church: From Recognition to Reconcilation,* Swansea, 1986.

[13] *The Final Report,* ARCIC I, pp.53f.

[14] *Anglican–Orthodox Dialogue: The Dublin Agreed Statement 1984,* SPCK, London 1984, pp.15f.

[15] *God's Reign and Our Unity,* para. 110.

[16] *Full Communion: A Study Paper for the Anglican Consultative Council* (2189), ACC, 1981, p.3.

[17] *Anglican–Lutheran Relations: A Report of the Joint Working Group,* ACC/LWF, London and Geneva, 1983, para.25, p.13.

[18] ibid., para.27, p.14.

[19] *The Final Report,* ARCIC I, para.5.

* indicates a title published through the Inter-Anglican Publishing Network.

RESOLUTIONS

Resolutions 3 to 17 of the Conference fall within the purview of the Ecumenical Relations Section.

BIBLIOGRAPHY

I   INTERNATIONAL THEOLOGICAL DIALOGUES

Baptism, Eucharist and Ministry, WCC, 1982.

Anglican–Lutheran Relations, Report of the Anglican–Lutheran Joint Working Group, ACC, LWF, 1983.

* *Niagara Report* of the Anglican–Lutheran Consultation on Episcope, CHP, 1987.

Anglican–Orthodox Dialogue, the Dublin Agreed Statement, SPCK, 1984.

God's Reign and Our Unity, the Report of the Anglican–Reformed International Commission, SPCK, 1984.

The Final Report of the Anglican–Roman Catholic International Commission, CTS/SPCK, 1982.

* *Salvation and the Church,* An Agreed Statement by the Second Anglican–Roman Catholic International Commission ARCIC II, CTS/CHP, 1987.

Light from the East, A Symposium on the Oriental Orthodox and Assyrian Churches, compiled and edited by the Rt Revd Henry Hill, Toronto, 1988.

* indicates a title published through the Inter-Anglican Publishing Network.

II   PREPARATORY FOR LAMBETH

The Emmaus Report, A Report of the Anglican Ecumenical Consultation 1987, ACC, 1987.
Steps Towards Unity, Documents on Ecumenical Relations presented to ACC-6, ACC, 1984.

III   ALSO CONSIDERED BY THE ECUMENICAL RELATIONS SECTION AT LAMBETH

Ministry in a Uniting Church: From Recognition to Reconciliation, Commission of the Covenanted Churches in Wales, 1986.

Youth Consultant: Miss Vanessa Mackenzie,
Church of the Province of Southern Africa

Christianity And The Social Order

Chairman	The Most Revd John Habgood (Archbishop of York, England)
Vice-Chairman	The Most Revd Desmond Tutu (Archbishop of Cape Town, Southern Africa)
Secretary	The Ven. Richard Randerson
Staff	Prebendary John Gladwin
	The Revd Charles Cesaretti
	The Revd Canon Na'im Ateek
Communicator	Mrs Ruth Nicastro

PROLOGUE – A WORLD OF HOPE AND FEAR

1   The social problems of our world which we set out in this report are so overwhelming that it is easy to become hopeless about their resolution. Christians, however, can never be without hope. We believe God has a plan for his world in which all men, women and children are to have adequate care and sustenance for their bodies, and a relationship with him that brings joy in their lives. We yearn for the fulfilment of the purpose of God in the prayer 'Thy Kingdom come, thy will be done' and in seeking to create the social and political will to obey God. What is required of political, economic, social and religious leaders is the prior determination and will to make things change according to this purpose. But first we must ask, what kind of world is it that we live in?

2   An English priest, recently arrived in the Diocese of Kuching, was attending a local festival in a Dyak longhouse. The forest surrounded the remote human settlement. The generator broke down, leaving the celebrations to continue by torchlight. Late into the night the headman invited the guest to his own quarters for a special treat. There he switched on a battery-operated TV set at the precise moment for the guest to enjoy the kick-off of the World Cup relayed by satellite.

3   In this incident are revealed a number of elements in the modern world: the mixture of cultures, the confusion of values, wider horizons of information, expectations and ambitions for a changed lifestyle.

4   Increasingly, human invention has made possible achievements that were previously inconceivable. Medicine has lowered the rates of infant mortality and increased the overall life expectancy of human beings. Technology applied to communication has brought each part of the world into an immediate awareness of every other. The potential is there for all to be freed from many of the ills which have, in the past, limited human life. We are able in principle to understand and manage our environment. We can look forward to the removal of other obstacles that impede human welfare.

5   All these achievements give hope on the one hand, hope of what can be accomplished in the future; but they also bring with them a fear that their misuse could be destructive, and an uncertainty about our ability to handle what our science has created.

6   The problem begins with the overload of information. We are rightly aware of the way in which our whole world is an interactive system in which change in any part affects the whole. Economically, politically, and environmentally we depend upon one another. But so complex is that relationship that it becomes virtually impossible to be sure of the outcome of any courses of action. Governments necessarily pursue the immediate advantage of their own nation. Yet, by the same action, they compound world problems which then adversely affect the original situation.

The way forward will not be found only through a better use of the existing processes of planning and prediction, whether socialistic or capitalistic, but in new forms of mutual interdependence and the sharing of power between the individual and society, whereby society works for the good of the individual and the individual works for the good of society.

7   The mission of the Church is twofold: to seek the renewal of society by the spiritual renewal of the individual, and to seek the renewal of the individual by the spiritual renewal of society. Words of Christ's Gospel, such as repentance, forgiveness, love and hope, will thus have implications both for individual and social renewal.

8   It will be the role of the Church, locally, regionally and internationally, to become prophet to itself, seeking the embodiment in its own being of mutual interdependence as a sign of God's kingdom of power through love. It will also be the role of the Church to speak prophetically to the world, to call for mutual interdependence in all personal and social relationships, to oppose all misuse of power whether by individuals, the tribe, the party, the majority or the minority. Mutual interdependence within the Body of Christ is the Church's own ideal of just and loving relationships. Mutual interdependence is God's way for society generally. This is the Christian vision of society, a new and living way. Our hope is in God, in whose Kingdom the oppressed are set free, the hungry are fed and children inherit a world made whole.

9   Such a vision must not be constructed from our fantasies but be based for us, as Christians, upon our understanding of God as he has been declared in Jesus. We do not find in the Gospel the expectation of steady progress through history, but rather the promise of God's presence discovered paradoxically on the margins of society. There is a continual corrective to human pride and triumphalist institutions by the surprising invasion of divine revelation summed up in the living, dying and rising of Jesus. Therefore, as we strive to be loyal citizens, we are also aware of an obedience which transcends and sometimes challenges judgements which depend upon an unquestioning acceptance of the prevailing assumptions of society.

10   We have talked of problems and opportunities created by the revolution in communications. Satellite TV can bring the event of the World Cup directly to the Borneo longhouse. The western visitor arrives there in less than twenty-four hours by air. In the meeting there is the negative potential for envy, rivalry and exploitation, as much as the positive opportunity to meet and share. It will depend upon the fundamental assumptions of the representatives of the two cultures whether they become competitors or collaborators.

11   In this report we examine a variety of issues where there is a choice for

individuals or societies to go the way of hope or fear, life or death. Two convictions determine our approach. The first is that, underlying the record of human achievement and the experience of overwhelming change, it is God who has called his creation into being and who is at work in its history. In this is involved our understanding both of the doctrine of Creation and of the doctrine of the Incarnation.

12   The Bible begins with the story of God's primeval awakening of the universe, and 'Behold, it was very good'. God gave dominion to the first created human pair. The second creation story describes how Adam and Eve, tempted to be like God by eating of the tree of knowledge, were driven out of innocence to alienation from their environment. In this state of alienation their son Cain killed his brother Abel, denying responsibility and saying 'Am I my brother's keeper?' So Genesis sets a scene of lost innocence, from which men and women fall into alienation from their environment, from their brothers and sisters, and from God.

13   It was to this alienated and disfigured human race that God sent his Son – the new Adam (Rom. 5.17). Undefeated by temptation to be like God, he gave his life in sacrificial love. By taking on himself the alienation, he offered a new covenant. By his victorious and obedient humanity, he gave us the potential to live with the truth without alienation, to live as brothers and sisters without fear and envy, and to love God and his creation without idolatry.

14   Secondly, the way in which we approach our fellow human beings and, indeed, our total environment must reflect the pattern of Christ's self-offering, by which he restored the relationships that sin had broken. Without such an overall sense of meaning and direction, the decisions which have to be made could overwhelm our humanity as we move from one desperate expedient to another. If, on the other hand, we can acknowledge our weakness and corruptibility and yet find security in the love and forgiveness of God, there is a hope that all our powers can be deployed in God's service to make possible a new way forward in human history.

RESPONDING IN FAITH

OUR RIGHT TO SPEAK AND ACT

15   The right and duty of Christians to speak and act on problems of social order needs no defence. It follows directly from our belief that this is God's world, and that he has shown his care for it in creation, incarnation, and redemption, and in his promise that all things ultimately will be brought to fullness in himself.

16   Many of the most serious national and international conflicts have an obvious and strong religious or ideological dimension. Many of the most

serious issues of social policy raise questions about the nature of human life, and about ultimate aims and values. For Christians not to play a part in the attempts to confront such issues would imply that the religious dimension is irrelevant. That would be a surrender to secularism.

17   It is right to affirm the valuable social role which Christians may perform individually, especially the role of the laity as they seek to exercise their Christian vocations as 'the Church scattered' in the workplace, in the home and as citizens. It is right also to affirm the role in social concern of 'the Church gathered' whether locally, regionally or internationally. Thus the task of the Church will be unavoidably both individual and corporate.

18   Arguments that seek to affirm the Church's mission of individual renewal but deny its mission to seek social renewal, or arguments which affirm the Church's mission to seek social renewal at the expense of individual renewal, are both distortions of how God has created us. We are created in and through each other, and can only be redeemed in and through each other – a new creation. We must carry out God's mission individually and together.

19   What particular Churches may be able to do in terms of social witness and action will vary enormously in relation to their resources and circumstances. There is no single pattern. Most Churches are conscious of being minority groups in cultures which may be friendly, hostile or indifferent. Some issues may be more readily acceptable than others. Not only are the main social issues different in different cultures, but the scope for action is widely different too. In most circumstances it is unwise for a Church to link itself with a particular political party. But there are occasions when a political commitment to a particular policy becomes inescapable.

20   A Lambeth Conference cannot, therefore, lay down guidelines about what all Churches should be doing in every place. But it can assert on behalf of all that no part of human life is excluded from God's care and concern. It can reaffirm moral principles for the guidance of communities and peoples, as well as for individuals. It can remind the world that there is much to be concerned about in the way human beings hurt each other and exploit God's creation. It can go on asserting, in the face of so much which seems to deny it, that the reconciling power of Christ's love and the motivating power of the Holy Spirit are available to heal, restore and renew a world in which we are promised that 'sin shall not have dominion over you' (Rom. 6.14).

21   These are not just tasks for Christian individuals, but for Christians witnessing and acting together. Bishops have a special prophetic, pastoral and teaching responsibility to lead, and need to maintain the difficult balance between speaking in the name of the Church as it is, and imperilling its unity by becoming wedded to a particular point of view not shared by all their

people. They may need to arouse the Church to a greater sense of social commitment. On some occasions this will arise directly out of Gospel imperatives and on other occasions it will be a contribution to responsible citizenship. But it is also important to safeguard oneself against self-deception. It is all too easy to claim a Christian basis for a particular stance when the real, but unperceived, motives may owe little or nothing to the Christian Gospel. Furthermore, Churches need to recognise that they are not separate from the societies in which they exist, that they share the same problems and internal tensions, and that they can only to a very limited extent stand over against their social settings and judge them from an external standpoint. Indeed in many circumstances the Churches are themselves part of the problem. The question of the basis for our speaking and acting on social matters is therefore crucially important.

OUR BASIS FOR SPEAKING AND ACTING

22   The basis is the same as the basis for all Christian speaking and acting; in our own Anglican tradition this is articulated as the threefold basis of Scripture, tradition and reason. The way in which these three guide us and constitute our authority is set out in other parts of the report of this Lambeth Conference. Here it is only necessary to pinpoint some special considerations affecting questions of social order.

23   We find in the Bible helpful guidance on many of the difficult moral, social and political problems of our day. However, this guidance usually takes the form of broad principles rather than specific, detailed solutions. Particular Bible stories may be illuminating and may serve to prick consciences as they have always had the power to do. The parable of Dives and Lazarus, for instance, may offer few direct parallels with the complexities of international debt, but should rightly haunt the minds of those who try to wrestle with the problem in practical economic terms. Where, though, can one look in the Bible for evidence on genetic engineering, or environmental pollution or on the intricate balance of factors involved in development? Connections, when made, can often seem forced and arbitrary.

24   Our age is characterised by bewildering and rapid change. This change comes to regions at a different pace and sometimes in different forms. This means that one area of our Communion will pose different questions to the Bible and to our faith when compared to another. This should not frighten us, but should, in dialogue, be a way of understanding better the eternal will of God. Different parts of the world must contribute to the vision of God's hope for his creation. We shall discover the riches of the Bible by letting its light shine through our diverse experience, because Christ is contemporary with us all through the Spirit (John 14.16-17). New secular knowledge inevitably changes our world for good or ill. Our different understandings of that knowledge can help us to evaluate it in the light of our faith.

25   The radical difference between our own world and that of the Bible can highlight the need to concentrate on basic biblical principles. It is the great themes of creation – redemption, sin, judgement, glory and hope, human dignity and worth, the need for human community, and other central truths of our faith – which need to inform and guide us. The witness of the Bible, in the face of problems considered in this section, is made by opening up these great theological themes in different human contexts.

26   Our second basis, tradition, has two aspects. There is a long-term aspect, demanding that we take seriously the facts of Christian history. It points us to a long tradition of Christian ethical and social thinking which is often overlooked in the search for answers to new problems. In a rapidly changing world it is possible for Churches to lose their memories, and constantly to be doing all over again work which was well done by previous generations. A Lambeth Conference, in particular, needs to ask itself how far it is building on work done by earlier Conferences.

27   There is also a short-term aspect to tradition, perhaps better described as 'experience'. Part of the basis for authentic Christian response to social issues has to lie in acknowledging the validity of first-hand experience, the living witness of those actually engaged in the issues under discussion. Not all first-hand experience is experience of the truth. Some, however, does embody genuine moral insight through its appeal to common humanity. *The Family in Contemporary Society*, a report prepared for the 1958 Lambeth Conference, gained much of its credibility, and wielded much of its subsequent influence, by its careful study of what contemporary families were then experiencing.[1] In our own day we are sharply conscious of the experience of those who are the victims of social change. It is in this context that the voices of the poor, the oppressed and the marginalised gain their special authority. What is said 'out of the depths' may lack subtlety and may ignore many of the factors evident to those who stand outside some painful situation. But in our Christian response the voice from the depths may have to be heard as the voice of God.

28   Reason, our third basis for speaking and acting, also draws deeply on human experience. It is based upon the belief that God's wisdom is discernible in the world he has created (Rom. 1.20). Without his Word, nothing was made (John 1.3). The poet, the artist, the psychologist, the economist, the philosopher and the scientist can contribute to this discernment, and especially at our time, through the scientific approach. This is not to claim that science is a pure expression of reason, nor that reason is found only in science. But it is to recognise that in all human endeavour, and despite many mistakes and disasters, science can claim to provide rational knowledge about important aspects of our world, and has been one of the most effective means of actually changing the material conditions of human life.

29   In applying scientific knowledge, the fallen nature of humanity can lead to distortion and misuse, e.g. the pollution of our atmosphere, the abuse of animals and even human beings for experimental purposes, the unjust distribution of knowledge and technology, and above all its use for purposes of war and greed. Nevertheless, we rejoice that the days when science and Christianity were seen as in conflict with one another are now past, though creative tension still exists. Both have learnt the folly of making inappropriate claims for themselves, and the way is open for a fruitful partnership. This is all the more important in a world where relativist thinking is widespread, and where the notion of ultimate truth is discarded in favour of mere 'opinion', or feeling, or even pseudo-scientific superstition. In such a world true science and true religion are both threatened.

30   Within the context of the great truths of Scripture interpreted through continuing tradition and tested by first-hand experience we can recognise that truth, as apprehended by human reason, is provisional and open to criticism and correction. The reasoning mind needs to assert that there is an ultimate truth towards which all our valid but partial knowledge converges.

31   Science and Christianity need to see themselves, therefore, as allies; not uncritical ones, but part of the same human quest. Each can gain courage from the other in a world where much is bewildering, many problems seem insoluble, and much goes tragically wrong.

32   In accepting this partnership, Christians seeking effective action will see more clearly the need for the disciplined study and principled interpretation of facts, for the openness of mind to accept unwelcome facts as well as those which support our preferred solutions, and for the critical spirit which refuses to rush to conclusions and which tries to assess actual results.

33   Such an approach should remind us of the limitations of our knowledge. It should also provide a sympathetic understanding of the huge difficulties faced by people of integrity in all walks of life who have to provide leadership and make decisions in highly complex situations.

34   Reason, understood in this sense, enables us to pass moral judgement and to make moral decisions in the daily demands of life. St Paul validated its exercise in the argument of Romans 1.18ff, as we have seen. By moral reasoning we work out our duty when faced with conflicting moral claims. By moral reasoning, we test what appear to be intuitive moral insights, or claims based on experience, to decide whether they are valid claims or not. To moral reasoning we submit the moral judgements of the past, even the Christian past, to determine whether they must be revised. By moral reasoning we have to commend our moral intuitions and judgements to others, if we would have them accepted. The appeal to conscience – 'What do you think?' as Jesus said, or 'Judge for yourselves' in St Paul – is in fact an appeal

to the God-given rational capacity, distinctively human, passing moral judgement.

35   Because human reason shares in the 'fallenness' of human beings, it must always be employed by the Church along with an acknowledgement of the revelation of God in the Scriptures and of the working out of this revelation in the lives of Christians of past ages, preserved for us in tradition. In the sections which follow we try to allow Scripture, tradition and reason to guide our judgement. Sometimes more has to be said than cool analysis can offer. Sometimes it is necessary to speak and act knowing that what is said and done may be mistaken. We are deeply conscious of the inadequacy of our knowledge and the fallibility of our judgement, but there are times when God makes it impossible for us to keep silent.

LIVING TOGETHER IN A DIVIDED WORLD

HUMAN RIGHTS AS A SAFEGUARD AGAINST INJUSTICE

36 Nasser and his wife tell of standing in the street looking at the ruins of their home. During the night soldiers came and evicted the family and destroyed the house. The soldiers said that their teenage son was a terrorist.

Another Palestinian family has lost a home and a son since he has fled from the West Bank to safety abroad. Having no place to go, the family seeks shelter and comfort within the dwindling Christian community and joins the ranks of bitter refugees in their own homeland.

37   Conflict and struggles between peoples are persistent throughout human experience. Our own contemporary world is no exception. Communities view each other with deep suspicion across historic divisions. Whether we are facing the issues of the struggle for self-determination by excluded peoples in our world, the evil of racism in multi-ethnic societies or conflicts which arise because of tribalism, we face a common question: how are people to relate to one another, affirming their common life as human community, across such harsh and bitter divisions?

38   The Gospel gives us a vision of unity in human life but also of a God-given freedom to choose death or life. The Church is called to witness to this unity and to this freedom. This Christian theme starts in creation, where we come to terms with the givenness of our humanity. God created us in his image with a unique individuality which finds its fulfilment in a shared humanity. In the creation story we read of the God who gave the world almost infinite diversity of creatures, including human beings, but with harmony and unity. As human beings we rejoice in our fundamental unity with all others as God's human creatures and also in the wonderful diversity which is God's gift.

39   We seek no uniformity of individuals, of society or of culture which

detracts from God's gift of diversity, but we recognise that in a fallen world humanity has spoilt God's unity in diversity through the abuse of freedom. It is when one individual group or culture seeks to coerce into conformity or subjugate another individual, group or culture that God's freedom is abused and disunity created. When individuals, groups and cultures choose to exercise their freedom to deny freedom to others, they must be called to correct their behaviour both by word and, if necessary, by deed. To individuals, societies and cultures the Church proclaims redemption and seeks thereby to embody in herself the Gospel of the Kingdom, the Gospel of personal and social renewal and of our deliverance into a final liberty of unity in diversity.

40   This theological tradition helps us face contemporary reality with all its bewildering complexities. The many struggles for existence, for quality of life, or for power in our world, have led to conflict, the destruction of families and communities and to some serious and persistent injustices. Peoples have either moved or been driven from their home and land, and are now refugees, outcasts or alienated in record numbers in our world. Power married to prejudice has led to the institutionalisation of racism and division. Tribalism threatens the unity of nations unable to resolve the power struggle between different regions, languages, or races. Tribalism within the Church itself (our Christian disunity) has hindered our witness to the Gospel vision of the unity of human life in Jesus Christ.

41   We have started by reminding ourselves of the Christian vision of unity in diversity. Self-worth and the worth of others derive from each human person being created in the image of God. Redeemed humanity in Christ is specifically required to seek the restoration of the divine image impaired by human fallenness, and to live by Christ's Golden Rule of human relationship: namely, to love one's neighbour as one loves oneself. In attempting to translate this vision into practice many Christians increasingly use the language of Human Rights. We wish to stress that the advocacy of human rights must be understood in terms of mutual interdependence and not merely the self-assertion of individual rights abstractly. To claim human rights for oneself is to claim the same rights for others. Thus, rights, responsibilities and duties must be kept in balance.[2] With this theological understanding, Christians can affirm support for statements such as the United Nations Universal Declaration on Human Rights, recognising that these are not only rights one may claim for oneself but rights one has a duty to seek for others even at the cost of personal suffering. The language of human rights is one of the few universal languages available to all, regardless of religious allegiance, as a means of affirming human value and dignity. Human rights offer a base line by which the performance of any group, community or state can be judged. Implicit in them are certain clear duties and responsibilities. The rights of others define our obligations. Because they are universal they remind us of our responsibility for all peoples irrespective of their state of life.

164

42   The UN Declaration of Rights falls into four categories:

(a) *Moral rights*   These pertain to the integrity and liberty of the individual person. They protect the life, liberty and security of the person. They affirm the basic freedoms of conscience and religion, of movement within states and out of them. They protect the right to married and family life and protect people from discrimination on the ground of race, colour, sex, language, religion, political or other opinion. They make concrete the sanctity of the individual.

(b) *Civil rights*   These concern membership withinparticular states and nations. They affirm the rights of all to participate in government, freedom of association, democratic rights, freedom for cultural and scientific pursuits, the rights to nationality and to the ownership of land and property.

(c) *Legal rights*   These protect people before the law of the country. They concern equality before the law, recognition by the law, protection against arbitrary arrest, detention and exile. They affirm the innocence of the person until proven guilty by due, fair and impartial procedures of law. They offer protection of personal and family privacy.

(d) *Social and economic rights*   These affirm the right of everyone to social security, to work and liberty of choice in employment, to an adequate standard of living, adequate shelter and to educational provision.

The Lambeth Conference adds its support to these by once again endorsing these rights and asking the Provinces of the Anglican Communion to support all who are working for their implementation. (Resolution 33.)

THE DENIAL OF RIGHTS

43   The denial of these basic human rights in our world leads straight to the struggle for freedom and liberation by those so denied. The urgency of this theme is raised in many parts of our world. It has come to the forefront of Christian thought and action in Latin America, which has made a major contribution to the development of the theme of liberation in Christian theology: in the midst of the struggle of the oppressed for their freedom, there is the joyful and hopeful discovery of God as the one who liberates the oppressed. We are faced with a particular challenge for liberation by the struggles of the excluded peoples in South Africa. (Resolutions 31, 35, 37, 38 and 39.)

44   In a Bantustan homeland resettlement camp, a little girl emerged from a shack she shared with her widowed mother and sisters.

'Does your mother get a grant or something?'
'No.'
'What do you do for food?'
'We borrow food.'

'Have you ever returned food that you borrowed?'
'No.'
'What do you do when you can't borrow food?'
'We drink water to fill our stomachs.'

This in a country that boasts of feeding its starving neighbours.

45   This family has been dumped in a Bantustan resettlement camp as part of the white minority government policy of forced population removal. Hardly any work is available there, and very little food. Every member of the family suffers. Father would be expected to leave his family and work on the white man's farm as a migrant worker. Here he would live an unnatural existence in single-sex hostels, prey to sexual abuse, prostitution and drunkenness. The children are starving and are exposed to the hazard of diseases (many of which, such as kwashiokor, can be prevented) and malnutrition. They can be seen standing around, pot-bellied victims of the policy of apartheid, their emotional, physical and intellectual growth permanently stunted. The father will see his wife and children once every eleven months. For the women the scene is a grim illustration of the feminisation of poverty. It is the womenfolk who bear the brunt of the struggle to make ends meet and sustain themselves and their children in this hostile environment.

46   Over three million Black people have been deprived of their citizenship under the Bantustan policy, by which they have been made aliens in the land of their birth. Their land has been carved up and fragmented by the South African Government to create 'homelands' to which they have been assigned. Thirteen per cent of the land has been allocated to 73 per cent of the population. The White 16 per cent of the population own 87 per cent of the land. The 1984 constitution excludes the 73 per cent from participation in the processes of power.

47   The oppressed want to be free from poverty, ignorance and disease, free to be able to take responsibility for their lives in a proper exercise of self-determination, free to be able to choose where they can live, free to express themselves without undue restriction, free to associate with whomever they wish, free to marry whomever they choose, free to own their own homes and land, free to be able to choose the sort of education their children should have, free to travel without undue let or hindrance – in short, free to be truly human in an environment that is not hostile to the attainment of worthwhile human ideals and vision. They want to be free from arbitrary arrest, especially where the writ of *habeas corpus* is ignored as in the practice of detention without trial. They want to be free from the arbitrary use of power by those in authority when the rule of law is abrogated. This is what is entailed in appealing for the observance of the Universal Declaration on Human Rights of the UN.

48   There are many other stories of oppression and injustice from across the globe. ACC-7 drew particular attention to the struggles of the Palestinian people in the Middle East for liberation and self-determination.[3] In many places we are confronted by racism, the denial of people's rights for self-determination, and new forms of colonialism, where people's land is expropriated and where humans including infants and children are tortured. Indigenous peoples are made aliens in their own countries, and others are driven out or reduced to a lower status of citizenship. The list can be much extended. The essence of the matter is that the forces of evil are everywhere strong and growing rampant. The tragedy is that many people of good will either remain silent or for one reason or another align themselves with those who have the power to change things but do not. Some even stand with racists, exploiters and dehumanisers.

49   The need to speak and to act is urgent. Christians are called to be faithful to Christ and to the Word of God where he always and unconditionally stands alongside the poor, the disadvantaged, and the oppressed. The people of God ought, therefore, to be the voice of those whose voice has been silenced and suppressed, speaking and acting not necessarily on a political party platform but out of Christian conviction about the God who demands justice and whose will is peace and reconciliation.

50   Resolutions presented to this Conference express this concern for justice, liberation and peace. (Resolutions 35, 36 and 58.) We end this section by quoting the words of some bishops from the Pacific Islands, which express in a very personal way the impact of great powers on small ones.

> The countries in the South Pacific consist of many tiny coral and volcanic islands which are surrounded by the warm sea. Our livelihood depends on the crops of the land and sea food, fresh streams to drink from, and sea water for bathing and washing.
>
> Our littleness has the beauty of nature and a real closeness to the land, the sea and the rivers. Our dependence on these will be everlasting.
>
> Today we are being threatened by superpowers who, for their greed and pride, come to exploit our total livelihood.
>
> For example, in New Caledonia the French Government killed 19 Kanaks (natives) who wanted to lead their people to self-determination. Why should we struggle to get independence when we were independent in the first place? We had our own leaders and chiefs, so this should be recognised by the superpower nations.
>
> In Murorua Atoll, the French continue testing bombs in the Pacific Ocean. The nuclear weapons, as we all know, are deadly, but the superpowers seem to turn a deaf ear.
>
> In the Marshall Islands, the Government of the United States of America is also testing its nuclear weapons and some islands have been abandoned as the result of pollution. The air, plants, sea-food and human life are all affected.
>
> In the Solomon Islands, our clams and shellfish are taken by the Taiwanese,

Japanese and Koreans. The Americans do not respect the 200-mile zone limit, and fish illegally in our waters, taking our tuna fish.

Our beautiful local woods are being taken by foreign countries, destroying our land by heavy machines and paying only a small amount of money to the local people while the companies make millions of dollars.

These are the evils done to our nation – to our land, seas, plants and fresh water. These are the burning issues that are affecting our people *now*.[4]

SHARING OUR RESOURCES

51   We live on a planet rich with resources. The world of nature teems with variety and beauty. Life seems to have almost infinite potential for growth and change. Humanity can boast of enormous achievements in the arts and sciences, in harnessing nature for human purposes and in realising its possibilities. We have developed unprecedented powers.

52   Yet the world is haunted by the knowledge of powers put to waste, of an earth ravaged and threatened, and of an environment whose potential is being diminished rather than enhanced. 'The earth is the Lord's and the fullness thereof' (Ps.24.1), but when human beings selfishly regard it as their own, things begin to go wrong. The environmental crisis is part of a much larger crisis in human affairs about the way we treat all the gifts and resources which God has entrusted to us.

53   Nowhere is this more clearly seen than in what we do to our fellow human beings. Poverty may be as old as humanity, but desperate poverty in the face of affluence is an offence against God.

54   We may approach this issue by considering the question of power, the problem of poverty, the need for development, the contribution of technology, and the effect of technology on the environment.

POWER AND POWERLESSNESS

Powerlessness in my diocese means having no project, no ideas, no thinking … having no wisdom means powerlessness. Conversely power is to be seen in things being done. (From an African bishop).

55   Power may be described as the capacity to make and enforce decisions both for oneself and for others. In personal terms it is to be in control of one's life. In social and political terms it is to be in control of and to manage the institutions that affect the lives of others. This includes the transmission and perpetuation of the binding myths and traditions of culture. Those in power are the keepers of the symbols of authority. To have power is to be at the centre of the decision-making process.

56   Powerlessness may be described as the loss or inability to exercise personal or communal control over decisions. Perhaps more accurately, there is powerlessness where the possibilities of making decisions are limited and

where legitimate authority is denied or restricted by force, fear or social convention. To be powerless is to be outside, or on the margins of, the decision-making process.

57 From every part of the world we hear reports of the growing sense of separation between the 'haves' and 'have nots', between the rich and the poor, between the North and the South, between the industrial and developing countries, between the superpowers and their allies and the non-aligned.

58 We hear also reports of tension between Church and State, between majority and minority populations, and between racial majorities in subjection to a minority. In other forms, the issue of power and powerlessness has expressed itself in terms of sexism, elitism or classism, and racism.

59 Although power tends to become concentrated and institutionalised, in areas such as governments and military and financial institutions, the power of ideas, especially of religious ideals, is often overlooked.

60 At the same time the power of one terrorist can paralyse a world that has become focused only on the systemic aspects of power. The powerlessness of a superpower in the face of one airplane hijacker is but one symptom of the paradox of power in contemporary society.

61 The issue of power and powerlessness exists for the wealthy nations as it does for the mother on welfare. What has Christianity to say to both? And, what roles has the Christian Church to play in each case?

62 The Church is called to embody the good news. It includes the powerful and the powerless, the rich and the poor, within its life. In solidarity with the poor, it is called to bring power to the powerless. In solidarity with the rich, it is to raise a new consciousness of powerlessness. This is the message of the cross.

63 To the powerful – be they in the structures of government, of academia, of science and technology, of the military, of finance or of the media – the Church is called to be a disturber of conscience.

64 To the poor, to the oppressed, to the homeless, to the unemployed and to those on the margins of society, the Church is to be voice and servant.

65 In its own life and structure the Church needs to exemplify what it is asking of others. The question of power and powerlessness is to be addressed to the Church in its response to disadvantaged minorities and majorities within its own membership. We are concerned that if we are to address with credibility the world problem of powerlessness and poverty, Anglicans as a world Communion must set their own house in order. We must find new ways of sharing more generously and more effectively the Communion's

resources and of meeting the needs of the materially poorer Churches. At the same time, we recognise that they may have many spiritual and cultural riches to share with the materially prosperous Churches.

66 To all – the powerless and the powerful – the Church is to bring the sacramental ministry of Christ in challenging, comforting and healing society's divisions.

POVERTY

Every morning I get up at 4.30 am, lock the door to keep the children safe inside, and take several buses to the downtown market. I buy one crate of lemons and start out on the return trip. I arrive home early in the afternoon. I distribute the lemons among the children and we all set out to sell them in the streets. It is important that we sell every lemon so that a profit is made and we can live another day. If it rains, or if I'm sick, or if the public transportation breaks down, my family will go hungry. (Story reported by a South American bishop)

Twelve English youths visiting my diocese came to a coffee farm at harvest time. For two days they joined the pickers and filled two tins. A workman fills 22 tins a day. I said to the young people, 'Go home and tell them how much you think coffee should cost!' (A Tanzanian bishop)

67 Some 800 million or more individuals continue to be trapped in absolute poverty, a condition of life so characterised by malnutrition, illiteracy, disease, squalid surroundings, high infant mortality and low life expectancy as to be beneath any reasonable definition of human decency. As Jesus said, quoting Deuteronomy, 'The poor you will always have with you' (Mark 14.7; cf. Deut.15.11). This is not a call to complacency or indifference but a sober reminder of the persistence of the battle to overcome poverty.

68 The current phrase 'feminisation of poverty' has highlighted the researched and undeniable truth that mothers with sole responsibilities for dependent children constitute the group of greatest need and social deprivation. Unemployment and lower wages for women, and their exclusion from social security systems, all contribute to the unacceptable level of poverty experienced by huge numbers of women in our world.

69 It is important to grasp that this has nothing to do with the 'Lady Poverty' of St Francis of Assisi. The feminisation of poverty is involuntary. There is a material poverty of the destitute and powerless which is a social evil. This is a poverty that degrades and stunts the image of God in the human being. We reject this poverty utterly.

70 It is important to recognise that poverty is relative as well as absolute. It varies from one part of the world to another. Ten thousand may sleep out in the streets of London whilst a quarter of a million are homeless in Calcutta. However, the real and unacceptable scandal is the cruel contrast bet-

The Compasrose in Canterbury Cathedral

'Look up and you see the pillars converting into arches which are upheld, not by independence, but through inter-dependence.' (Address at the Inaugural Eucharist of the Lambeth Conference 1988.)

The Archbishop of Canterbury on the throne of St Augustine, flanked by the Primates of the Anglican Communion
(Photograph: Rex Features Ltd)

An unexpected, but welcome, visitor joins the Melanesian bishops as the procession enters Canterbury Cathedral for the Opening Eucharist.
(Photograph: Ben May)

The Archbishop of Canterbury with Ecumenical Observers
(Photograph: Ben May)

The Conference Consultants with the Archbishop of Canterbury
(Photograph: Robert Miles)

A Bible Study Group (Photograph: Ben May)

A sea of hands on the vote on Resolution number 1
(Photograph: Stephen Webb)

Final rehearsal for the Group Photograph
(Photograph: Stephen Webb)

Following a Service of Light and to mark Hiroshima Day, a cherry tree was planted near the Senate Building of the University by the Primate of the Nippon Sei Ko Kai, The Most Revd Christopher Kikawada. Extreme left is the Primate of Burma, the Most Revd Andrew Mya Han
(Photograph: Robert Miles)

Worship in the Plenary Hall
(Photograph: Ben May)

The Wives' Conference in Plenary Session
(Photograph: Ben May)

ween luxurious affluence and extreme poverty within and between nations. The rich man has little excuse to be ignorant of or indifferent to the human story behind his cup of coffee or the slice of lemon in his cocktail.

71 The response called for in the face of persistence of such poverty has to be made at all levels. At the level of political and economic structures, there are serious imbalances and injustices in the distribution both of the opportunities for creating wealth and of the wealth so created. The present structures of international trade and finance are manifestly not meeting the need. At the local level there is need for development of the grass roots economy and systems of welfare. At the personal level there is need of a sense of responsibility, particularly by the rich, for one's own personal lifestyle in the face of such desperate poverty. The symbolic witness of a disciplined lifestyle should not be underestimated. The spiritual testimony of this can be powerful.

72 At all levels we are being faced with the need for some fundamental changes, be they of the major structures of finance or of the personal choices about our own lives. We recognise that there can be no effective change without cost. Those of us who have benefited most from the present order should be ready to meet the costs of the changes necessary for a better order for our world.

73 The particular problem of the present level of international debt has been reported by ACC-7 and by many of the responses of the Anglican Provinces.[5] Crippling levels of debt – amounting to some $1,000 billion – which add intolerable burdens to the poorer nations of our world, raise sharp moral questions. Debt of this nature creates unhealthy dependencies of the weak upon the powerful, leads to the breakdown of the life of poor communities and threatens the relationships of international politics and finance. It is urgent to find new ways of relieving the problem without crippling the world economy. The practice of borrowing at this level needs boundaries set by moral values. Christians need to recall the meaning of forgiveness and those parts of their history where the Church has sought to protect the poor from exploitation by the rich in matters of debt. (Resolution 36.)

74 How is the Church to respond in its proclamation of the Gospel among the poor? As Gustavo Gutierrez expressed it, our problem is not Bonhoeffer's, how to talk of God to a person 'come of age' in the twentieth century, but how to proclaim the living God in a situation of death. The poor die before their time. The Bolivian may on average expect to live 58 years while the West German can expect a life-span of 75 years.

75 In view of the present situation there have been many advocates of 'a preference for and solidarity with the poor'. There is no favouritism here, no

glorification of the poor as if they were innocent of sin, but a genuine recognition that they have been sinned against, which justifies the need for positive discrimination in witness to the inauguration of the Kingdom.

76 Poverty in my life is my material problem. Poverty in the lives of 800 million human beings is my moral and spiritual problem. Affluence should not be allowed to stifle our conscience or sap our wills in the work for the eradication of poverty.

COMMUNITIES OF SELF-HELP

77 Major questions have been put before us about how local communities can gain greater control over their own lives and circumstances. There are many aspects to the issues of development in our world. All of them raise questions about how communities which have been relatively powerless can be strengthened from within. The development of participatory styles of community life is crucial to the recovery of worth.

78 The story of one South American country is of the phenomenal growth of informal, unplanned and illegal economic and social development to the extent that government cannot ignore it. It is the spontaneous grass roots response of the poor to the failures of local and national government. This informal, hidden and marginal activity includes business life, housing and transportation. Between 1960 and 1984, for example, one South American city managed to construct $173 million worth of public housing. At the same time the informal sector achieved a staggering $8,319 million worth of unauthorised housing. Rather than fight official bureaucracies, people are taking action for themselves. The hopes, the skills and ingenuities of the poor are being harnessed to the development of their own communities, and governments are having to accept it. These communities have disregarded ideologies and political platforms as they have sought to construct their homes and to open markets, bypassing the legal process on the way.

79 What is the reason for this? It may have to do with corruption by State politicians and officials. It may be the result of the effect of foreign debt or of the arms race on public resources. Bureaucracy may have become so complex and stifling as to be of no effective value. Population growth may have outstripped the capacity of the system to cope. Ideological terrorism may have fractured the community, absorbing its energies and resources. Whatever the reasons, the public sector has been unable to 'deliver the goods' to the poor, and the virtual breakdown of the centres of power has in this instance released remarkable energies.

80 Perhaps there is a lesson here for community development. This issue has surfaced in the responses coming from the Anglican Provinces and is documented in *Transforming Families,* the report of the International Pro-

ject on Family and Community.[6] We urge the Churches to assist the development of the resources and skills already present in local communities of the poor and so to help bring a new sense of self-esteem in the attack on poverty.

TECHNOLOGY AND THE ENVIRONMENT

81   We take serious note of the fact that the United Nations has designated the next decade as being for the repair of the earth. This provides the clearest possible indication of the mounting concern about the way human beings are exploiting the environment. Among other factors, this is leading to the permanent loss of non-renewable resources, the non-replacement of renewable resources, soil erosion, the pollution of air, sea and rivers, and the damage to the ozone layer. Taken together, these now pose a serious threat to the whole ecosystem.

82   We believe, therefore, that any consideration of the environment must also examine the impact of technology, because the two are now inextricably related to one another. Yet there has been very little debate on these crucial matters within the Churches, possibly because insufficient attention has been paid to the doctrine of creation and to the ethical implications of technology within the natural order.

83   Christians must recognise that concern for the environment is concern for God's world both for its own sake and for the capacity of human beings to flourish in it. The world has come into being by the creative act of God and is therefore a gift to us to be revered and cared for as his, not ours. It may even be called our sacrament of creation, which is to be received and shared, enjoyed and celebrated, and used in such a way that its benefits can be passed on to our children. For this to occur, we must all recognise that we live in a highly sensitive, single, interlocking system which demands from all of humanity a high level of reverence, respect and responsibility. Together with all people of good will, Christians must learn again to cherish the God-given resources of the earth, through responsible stewardship of technology and of the environment.

84   Technology is also a gift from God who has implanted in us the gift of creative vision and inventive skill, calling us to be partners and co-creators with him. In these times it is critical that we now find ways of participating in the creative process that will nourish rather than damage the environment.

85   As the Church proclaims that God is reconciling the world to himself, so it has a responsibility to see that people do not become alienated from the life of God and his world by the misuse of technology and the destruction of the environment.

173

86   A proper understanding of the doctrine of creation carries with it important ethical considerations about the behaviour of humanity in relation to technology and the environment. These are embraced in the principles of accountability, the separation of means and ends, conservation, equity and, by implication, the avoidance of the exploitation of people.

87   In the first instance it is important to remind nation states, transnational corporations and the people who work for them that they are accountable to God and humanity for all their actions. One important implication here is that they must be much more willing to carry out rigorous social and environmental audits in addition to those routine financial audits that are required of them.

88   Secondly, there is an important educational task in helping people to distinguish between technological means and ends. In the West especially, people must discriminate between necessity and luxury. As most of us seek a more comfortable lifestyle, we are caught up in the lure of technology as the means. Yet media advertising subtly turns its possession into an end in itself. The other discernible trend in the West is to love technology and to use people, rather than loving people and using technology to achieve appropriate human ends.

89   Thirdly, conservation policies must distinguish between the resources that are necessary to the good life and those used purely for luxury purposes, and then make conscious decisions when releasing and allocating those resources for public consumption.

90   Fourthly, the issue of equity needs to be addressed more strongly. Those who possess technology have the means of using and controlling the earth's resources and of determining the quality and direction of people's lives. Those who have access to the most highly developed technologies make the most money from them, whilst the poorest people are the losers. Thus, access to new technology is now a major factor in widening the gap between the rich and poor nations of the world.

91   Finally, there is the problem of exploitation, when the poorer nations are sold suspect technological products, or have industrial waste dumped on their lands or in their seas, or are forced into growing certain crops for export at the expense of growing their own food crops. Those corporations owning the technology capable of producing needed products often have monopoly control and so set price levels that poor people cannot afford. (Resolution 40.)

92   To illustrate these issues, the following examples were offered by Conference participants arising from their own local experiences:

Nigeria reported on the dumping of highly toxic waste materials in its coastal areas by Italy as part of a joint financial arrangement. It is likely that the long-term environmental damange will far outweigh the short-term financial benefit to that country.

Uganda expressed concern that DDT continues to be exported to it as a viable and safe chemical substance long after western countries have acknowledged its harmful properties.

Another report from the Pacific expressed widespread concern about the environmental and social health effects of nuclear testing, storage and the dumping of nuclear waste. One island has already been declared perm- anently unfit for human habitation. This example is set against such recent disasters and ecological threats as occurred at Chernobyl in the Soviet Union, Bhopal in India, and Three Mile Island in the USA, where insufficient control and care was taken in technological processes involv- ing highly dangerous products.

The Philippines, in welcoming a new strain of disease-resistant grain, noted with concern that the product was under the total control of one company which set such exorbitant prices that local farmers could not afford to buy the grains, even though they needed it for economic survi- val.

Canada reported on the activities of some logging and mining companies that had taken over the traditional lands of aboriginal people where there was no treaty, destroying their traditional livelihood.

Inducements have been offered to many Kenyans to plant pineapple, cof- fee and sugar export crops, thereby replacing traditional staple food crops needed for domestic consumption. Instead of meeting their own food requirements, the local people now have to purchase food at a much higher cost, to the point where their overall economic position has worse- ned considerably.

South Africa reported on the forced dislocation and resettlement of people on to small and isolated plots, where they can neither grow food nor develop industries typical of other parts of their country, without proper regard for people's social and economic needs.

93   The Church must remind itself once again that as God is the true and liv- ing God of the whole earth, Christians are called to know him in the name of Jesus Christ through the Spirit and must see him and serve him as Lord of the environment and its people. So the fight against pollution, erosion, waste, and all devastation of natural territories and human communities, is a necessary and direct expression of their faith in God. It is a part of the Church's prophetic role to proclaim that faith cannot be disembodied and Christians may not behave as if such evils did not exist in the world.

94   The Church can also exercise an important role in practical sharing as

part of its worldwide fellowship in Christ. Member Churches within the Communion can be of great assistance to each other through both co-ordinated and bilateral programmes. For example, one English diocese has helped an African diocese by being involved in a tree-planting scheme.

95   The Church has also a pastoral role in helping those people who are caught up at all levels of corporate and national decision-making on technological and environmental matters. It can support them by providing forums where the ethical implications of decision-making can be discussed in depth and where they can feel free to share their hopes and fears for creation.

96   Finally, the Church can exercise an educational role in promoting holistic approaches to education, so that future decision-makers will be not only technical experts but also people capable of wrestling with and resolving the complex social, political and ethical outcomes of the decisions they may take.

97   All this is summed up by saying that it is better to work with the grain of nature than against it; for there is only one earth given to us by our God, and if we destroy it, we destroy ourselves. (Resolution 40.)

LIVING TOGETHER IN PEACE

98   The awfulness of war and violence has been persistent in human history. Our own generation is no exception. Many of us come from communities torn by violence and civil war. All of us face the realities of domestic violence in our countries and all live under the threat of nuclear war. Lambeth Conferences have discussed some of these matters before. In 1930 the Lambeth Conference passed a famous resolution stating that 'War as a method of solving international disputes is incompatible with the teaching and example of our Lord Jesus Christ'.[7] Successive conferences have reaffirmed this resolution. We emphatically wish to do the same. (Resolution 27.) The vision of ultimate peace held up to us in the Gospel, and our Lord's own method of reconciliation through sacrificial love, remain the basis of our Christian thought and action. Love seeks the affirmation of the dignity of all and the liberation of their gifts and possibilities in community with one another. This goal is denied by war; it is denied also by those structures which prevent the liberation of people. Peace and justice belong together in the ultimate vision of the Kingdom, and both spring from the love of God for his creation.

99   We are conscious, however, that wars have continued. We are faced, across the world, with new kinds of military violence as more powerful weapons are introduced and by a proliferation of violence within nations as human communities and families become less stable. While we want to

affirm again the fundamental teaching of the Gospel as a means of settling disputes and of achieving political goals, we believe we need to examine more closely why communities and nations try to resolve their problems by violent means. Therefore, we wish to suggest some searching questions by which Christians in situations of conflict can develop a response that seeks to minimise the coercion and violence that surrounds them (see para.103).

100   Many Christians are caught up in the midst of these conflicts. It is not our purpose to condemn or condone those who in conscience can see no other way to defend themselves and their communities from the violence done to them except by acts of violence and war. We have a responsibility to try and understand their dilemmas and to pray for them. We also have a duty to participate with them in working through the moral dilemmas they face in making their choices. Christian leaders have particular responsibilities to promote negotiations between parties caught in the midst of conflict.

COERCION

101   When we use the term 'coercion', we mean no more than the attempt to force people to do what they do not wish to do. In this very general sense, coercion is a feature of all social life. Its justification is dependent upon answers to a range of questions concerning the basis, aims and means of acts of coercion. Violence is only one of the means that may be used to seek to coerce others to accept what they otherwise might resist. In a world in which states are so often tempted to abuse their power through indiscriminate violence, and in which it is vital to distinguish between acts of terrorism and the legitimate struggle for liberation, we believe we might be helped by a close examination of these two themes of coercion and violence.

102   No Christian can avoid conflict. Some Christians renounce the use of violence in all circumstances. All will wish to place limits on the extent and on the kind of violence which may be justified in any situation. No one will want to use coercion where consent and participation in decision-making is possible. We suggest that in any kind of conflict these are some of the questions which need to be considered before deciding what is the response closest to the mind of Christ:

103   What is the moral case on both sides of the conflict?

What possibilities are there for the peaceful redress of grievances and changes in the balance of power? Have they been attempted?

What is the degree of suffering and injustice being experienced; how much is anticipated if the present situation continues; and how much if violent change is attempted?

What is the danger of violent change leading to anarchy or even more violent action?

On what side of the conflict do we find more morally acceptable purposes expressed by a sufficiently representative authority?

Would the coercion or violence proposed be proportional to the end desired?

Does the action proposed aim to be discriminating in the suffering that may be caused to non-combatants?

Have the resources of the non-violent process been exhausted?

What are the prospects of achieving the desired objectives?

What effect will the action have on the possibility of reconciliation at the end of the conflict?

104   The Church should honour those whose commitment to reconciliation through self-sacrifice is absolute in all circumstances. It should maintain and strengthen its witness to the cross and the resurrection of Jesus as the ultimate demonstration of the powerlessness of the powers of this world, and to the danger that a last resort to violence may simply give a further twist to the downward spiral of futility and self-destructiveness.

105   There are no easy answers to questions about the right use of force. Discussions about violence in recent decades have been complicated by the recognition of 'structural violence' – the constraints exerted by social, economic and political systems, and experienced by some of their members as violent. Sometimes the constraints entail the use of physical force; sometimes they are psychological; sometimes legal; sometimes the use of the word 'violence' in such contexts is rejected as misleading.

NUCLEAR WEAPONS

106   It is very difficult to reconcile possession of nuclear weaponry with the Christian insistence on limits and proportion when having recourse to violence. For that reason many Christians, though by no means all, have come to reject nuclear weapons, if not modern war in general, as incompatible with the teaching of our Lord Jesus Christ. The nuclear powers claim that nuclear weapons are essential for their security. This means, in effect, that they apply one standard to Third World conflicts and another to their own defence policies.

107   We are concerned at the growing insensitivity to violence which we find among both children and adults. We believe that the media, by presenting vivid details of violent happenings in both news and entertainment, must accept much responsibility for the numbing of our consciences. There is also much evidence that the existence of the nuclear stock-pile encourages a moral indifference and fatalism, especially among young people. Governments, which have become aware of the need for moral strengthening of national life, must take note of the relationship between national defence policies and personal morality.

108   It is inherent in the nature of nuclear weapons, as in the nature of many conventional weapons, that they are undiscriminating in their effects and that the evil consequent on their use would be disproportionate to any conceivable desired result. Moral thinkers in many different traditions have repeatedly made these points. We simply reaffirm them. We continue to press them on those who bear responsibility for these weapons, while continuing to work and pray for the success of negotiations aimed at reducing the nuclear threat.

109   We wish to pay tribute to the various forms of the Peace Movement which have kept before us in recent years the moral issues arising from the growing militarism of the world. We call on the Church to continue to wrestle with these issues and to support those sister Churches and individual members who have felt called to a public witness to the Christian imperative of peace-making, including those who have turned to civil non-violent disobedience as an act of conscientious objection to military solutions of world problems.

110   The magnitude of the nuclear threat is sometimes in danger of obscuring the threat from new generations of sophisticated non-nuclear weapons. The same criteria apply. Who is using these weapons? On what authority? For what purpose? With what effect? And do the means match the end?

OTHER USES OF COERCION

111   The state has the responsibility of protecting all its citizens. We are concerned, therefore, when large and powerful states (often with an allegedly Christian tradition) impose their policies and their military bases on smaller and weaker states. We suggest that the time is past when any nation, large or small, is justified in developing its own defence policies without regard to the common security of other nations and to the ecological care of the planet. 'My country right or wrong' is neither morally acceptable nor does it make sense in the global village in which we all live.

112   We are similarly concerned about those states which have institutionalised violence towards those among their own peoples who have legitimately claimed their basic human rights. The right of the state to use the power of coercion cannot, in the light of traditional moral values, be stretched to justify such oppressive abuses. In some parts of the world the state has lost its moral authority, at least in the eyes of its opponents, who then feel justified to rebel. Sometimes the state has lost its effective power, with the result that other power centres can claim to represent the true interests of either the nation or some major group within it. The state which is so challenged will believe that it has a right to resist with physical force if necessary.

179

113   The criterion that the force used should be proportional to the end desired or to the threat encountered has obvious applications. Most guerrilla operations are small scale. To wipe out whole villagers in retaliation, or to threaten whole populations by the poisoning of water supplies, for example, is clearly immoral. If a choice has to be made, attacks on property create fewer moral problems than attacks on people, though even this distinction does not hold in all cases, especially when people's livelihoods are at stake. To some, those fighting for their rights are freedom fighters, to others they are terrorists. We can only decide which description is most accurate by considering the searching questions set out in para.103.

THE PREVENTION OF CONFLICT

114   The asking of such questions is only a very small part of the Church's task when faced with conflict either internally or in the world around. People get more and more extreme in their attempts to gain a hearing when they are ignored or excluded. The last stage is violent action when dialogue has broken down. Terrorists or freedom fighters are motivated either by a sense of injustice or fear of what violence may be done to them.

115   At that point external standards will make little impact. Therefore, work needs to be done before a sense of human community is lost. Everyone involved needs to be shown the meaning of God's universal love. All must be called to repentance and be assured that they can be forgiven. Christians must try to discover how they can follow the way of their crucified Lord in being agents of the Kingdom which includes peace.

116   Matched with that theology there must be an honest and rigorous analysis of the situation so that threat or injustice can be faced responsibly and reality disentangled from imaginary fears.

117   Where the process breaks down, the Church must stand beside all who suffer and work to re-establish dialogue. In particular it should try to identify the powers at work which distort and pervert human life. By its example it must encourage the powerful to share power and make sure that those who speak out against unjust structures are heard.

118   The practical steps which each situation requires will be different. The wider Church can continue to provide prayer, support appropriate direct action and friendship for those involved, and bring to bear the broad principles of what must be decided locally.

119   To be credible as peacemakers in this way, every Christian needs to examine her or his own society to see where it is directly or indirectly involved in the support of unjust structures or regimes (as in the supply of arms) and so pushes the opposition to acts of violence.

SOCIAL COERCION

120 The consequences of applying questions about coercion to family life could be dramatic. Parents have responsibilities for their children and hence, during their upbringing, have a legitimate authority to coerce them into doing what they believe is best for them. But this authority has limits: it is to be exercised for the good of the children themselves; the degree of coercion is not to be excessive; it has to be fair and appropriate; an innocent child is not to be punished in order to shame a guilty one into acknowledging guilt. The rights of the parents in relation to their children do not include the right to abuse or exploit them. Parental responsibility, in other words, is to be exercised on behalf of those for whom it is given. Domestic violence, whether towards children or between parents themselves, is a wholly illegitimate use of the power to coerce, sometimes made worse by inappropriate ideas about authority in the family.

121 Other types of political or quasi-political coercion may usefully be analysed in the light of the same criteria. The burden of debt loaded upon the poor, the diversion of world resources to the arms trade, the dumping of nuclear and toxic waste, and the testing of nuclear weapons constitute grave coercive disruption of the economies and ecologies of many Third World countries. The Church cannot remain silent, faced by the evidence. The devastating effect of such coercion on the lives of innocent people is not discriminatory or proportionate to any alleged benefit in terms of world peace or prosperity.

MILITARISM AND OUR ROLE AS PEACEMAKERS

122 Militarism is the tendency in many nations for the military apparatus to assume ever-increasing control over the lives and behaviour of citizens. When this occurs, military goals and values increasingly dominate nation, culture, education, politics, the media and even religion, at the expense of civilian institutions. Resources needed for development are ploughed into weapons. Some are killed in battle; others starve; babies die; poverty becomes feminised and basic human needs go unaddressed.

123 In many cases, major powers and corporations contribute to this by engaging in massive arms sales, profiting by discord and violence in smaller nations. Where corporate greed interlocks with military interests, the making of profit displaces national well-being. Large numbers of people are drawn into the employ of the arms industry, which in turn sustains increasing military strength and power in the world. A good deal of the trade takes place by covert means outside effective political control. The growth of both military power and this covert trade undermines the authority of democratic forms of accountability. Third World dignity and development suffer, the burden of debt increases, and the poor become poorer.

124   There is an encouraging sign of hope in the effort being made in the Soviet Union to reorder its priorities in the direction of development and in its withdrawal from Afghanistan. The recent intermediate nuclear forces treaty between the USA and the USSR is a constructive step back from the brink of war. (Resolution 32.)

125   However, the continued existence of nuclear arms adds opportunities for some nations to dominate others and creates an all-pervading threat which can be morally destructive.

126   Worldwide religious bodies such as the Anglican Communion are well placed to address the task of peace-making. We must rise above the temptation to be only chaplains to our nations. We are blessed by God with spiritual and material resources. We have the opportunity to:

share these resources with one another;

strive for arms reductions, nuclear non-proliferation, and the elimination of nuclear testing;

invite corporate leadership to address these concerns; work for regional co-operation, more balanced trading relationships, and constructive development policies;

urge our leaders and peoples away from militarism and toward those things that lead to justice, peace, and fullness of life, especially for the poor.

As bearers of hope in a world shadowed by suffering and war in many areas, we can communicate by symbols, liturgy, and significant social action the vision of Shalom, God's peace for all people on earth. That which will most effectively disinfect the fear and selfishness lying at the heart of the world's turmoil will be a Church living the Gospel of our crucified and risen Saviour. (Resolution 40.)

LIVING TOGETHER IN FAMILIES

MARRIAGE

127   We reaffirm the statement on marriage of the Lambeth Conference 1978, which declares marriage to be sacred, instituted by God and blessed by our Lord Jesus Christ.[8]

128   The definition of marriage set forth in the canons of the Scottish Episcopal Church is representative of all the Provinces of the Communion:

The doctrine of this Church is that marriage is a physical, spiritual and mystical union of one man and one woman created by their mutual consent of heart and mind and will thereto and is a holy and lifelong estate instituted by God.

This union signifies to us the mystery of the union between Christ and his Church.

129   Anglican formularies have traditionally taught that the union of husband and wife in heart, body and mind is intended by God for their mutual joy; for help and comfort of one another in both prosperity and adversity; and, when it is God's will, for the procreation of children and their nurture in the knowledge and love of the Lord. They have gone further to state among the purposes of marriage the safeguarding and benefit of society.

130   We believe that marriage is a vocation to which many but not all persons are called, and also a gift from God to all of humanity. Marriage is not a private matter but is rooted in the community, and all persons, single as well as married, have an obligation to uphold and support marriage.

131   'The ingredients of Christian marriage', as noted in the booklet, *Transforming Families and Communities,* 'are fidelity, trust, acceptance, an intention of permanence, mutual service and empowerment'.[9] These ingredients describe the nature of the relationship between husband and wife which should exist in order to fulfil the purpose of marriage; they are also precisely those which mark that bond of union between Christ and his Church, of which marriage is the sign.

132   Yet, while throughout our Provinces millions of couples strive to live out this standard of Christian marriage, reports from across the Anglican Communion demonstrate that in every Province marriages are experiencing many stresses – economic, political, social, religious. These vary in particulars but are present in virtually all cultures. Among them are the changing roles of men and women in all cultures, the rise of individualism and materialism in many.

133   Such stresses have caused rapid increases in divorce rates and unfaithfulness and the almost total breakdown of the extended family in the West.

134   The Church needs to affirm and support those marriages which are striving to embody the values and behaviour of Christian marriage reflecting the union between Christ and his Church; and the Church needs to work in society, as well, for social conditions and government policies that uphold the dignity and integrity of marriage for all couples.

135   Through its liturgical, pastoral, educational and social work, the Church needs to prepare couples for marriage. Pre-marital counselling should be over a period of several months and should involve not only the priest but laity as well.

136   The counselling should include not only explanations of the theology and sacramental understanding of Christian marriage, but also specific preparation for married life including sexual union, standards of fidelity, financial budgeting, living with stress, and obligations to community. Requirements for counselling should be the same for all churches within the diocese,

and diocesan leaders should seek ecumenically for a common standard of preparation for marriage. This is particularly important when the couple to be married are from different traditions, so that the integrity of each is respected.

137   Recognising that in many cultures young people are marrying at much older ages than was previously typical, and that they may have lived for many years far away from their families, we believe that all congregations should include in their religious education programmes for young people, discussion and affirmation of Christian marriage. Such programmes should build in correctives to the existing ethos that may be detrimental to marriages.

138   Support for couples getting married should not end with the wedding, but should continue, especially during the first five years, with other married couples directly involved as counsellors to the newly married. Anniversaries should be occasions for congregational recognition and celebration.

139   Special support should be provided for clergy marriages, which are subject to the same social pressures as other marriages and are often further strained by the particular requirements of the ordained ministry. The Church must provide particular and confidential opportunities for counselling, help and support for clergy families.

140   The Church needs to discern the reality concerning the current state of marriage. Social pressures do affect marriages; marriages respond to crises in the society around them. There needs to be careful analysis, however, about where the crisis is and what role the marriage has in it. The point is made in the next section that despite the strains upon it, marriage has remained a strong, resilient institution. In some cases it is upholding and providing the ideas necessary to combat tendencies towards social disintegration.

141   The Church needs to challenge those governments, institutions and corporate policies that undermine family life. This includes directly and forthrightly challenging those governments that speak of the importance of traditional values and family life while promoting legislation that in fact undermines family life. Particularly, the Church must challenge any policies, governmental or corporate, which are disruptive of family life, such as those which require separation for long periods of wage-earners from their families and migrant worker policies. (Resolution 34.)

THE FAMILY

142   Everyone belongs, or at some time has belonged, to a family. There are different understandings of what a family is. The way one thinks about family often determines how one approaches the issues facing family life.

143   As Christians, we view the family theologically and we affirm that in the social ordering instituted by God the family structure is a basic element. A statement from the Report of ACC-6, 1984, reminds us that the family

> is the social unit by which values are nurtured and conveyed to succeeding generations. Even more important for the Judeo-Christian tradition, it has been the human institution on which the Church has relied for the development of the faith and of personal spirituality.[10]

144   We hold that no human institution is more important in all cultures than the family. The family is where one can begin to experience and understand love, compassion, and deep personal relationship with God. It is where individuals – brothers, sisters, parents and other members – learn to grow and work together. Here one can gain a foretaste of all the peoples of God's creation coming together to achieve a unity of mutual purpose and service. The family is where one can be fed, sheltered, clothed and educated. Here individuals should understand the eternal ministry of Jesus as he feeds us with the bread of life, shelters us as children in his arms, teaches his faithful disciples and, having taken on human nature, ennobles all humanity.

145   Together with our understanding of the family from primary experience, there is a growing body of literature about family life as a social institution. The family is recognised as the place where roles are defined, where the lines of responsibility and freedom are drawn, where sexual relationships are modelled, where mutual respect, order and discipline are taught. In this view the family acts as the agent of socialisation for society. Thus, families that are emotionally and spiritually healthy contribute richly to the health and stability of society. In a section of the Report of ACC-7, 1987, it is observed that

> since children learn by observing, parents need to provide models of tenderness and care-giving, and the Church should be encouraging this; otherwise, we will raise generations unable to be fully human.[11]

146   Families around the world experience stresses. While the particular sources of stress may differ from country to country because of different national conditions, we perceive common pressures on family life from economic factors, changing social roles for men and women, political forces that denigrate the value of family life, and an isolating and excessive individualism that devalues the dignity of family life. Many stresses on family life are internal, and there are sad instances where family life can be destructive rather than life-giving. Excessive expectations of the family may lead to disappointment and disintegration within, and to an inappropriate reliance on government or other external institutions beyond the family.

147   We recognise that many families experience grave burdens and that

women and children suffer under those burdens to a disproportionate degree. We further recognise that these pressures diminish the economic wellbeing and status of women. We therefore welcome the World Council of Churches' programme 'Decade for Solidarity with Women'. We encourage dioceses to consider how they might through their theological, structural and pastoral approaches achieve a fuller recognition of the contribution and status of women in both Church and society.

148　We believe that the family, whether a unit of one parent and children, an adult child and an elderly parent, adult relatives, a husband, wife and children, or whatever other shape, is the fundamental institution of human community. Other institutions, whether government or private, have important supportive functions, but must be seen as secondary and supportive of the primary family unit. In healthy families, children and adults are nourished and cherished; dependent members, whether disabled children or adults, are protected and valued; the wisdom and experience of the elderly is cherished and utilised; and individuals experience in family life nothing less than the love of the Father, 'from whom every family in heaven and earth is named' (Eph. 3.15). (Resolution 34.)

149　In various parts of the Anglican Communion there is an emphasis toward strengthening the parish as a 'family'. It is important that this image should not be used in an exclusive sense, but inclusively by giving a welcome to persons of all ages and races, children and adults, married and single persons, disabled and homeless persons. Where that welcome occurs, we demonstrate the gracious hospitality of the Reign of God. We need to affirm more fully in word and deed that inclusive character of the Body of Christ. We call upon our people to recognise that everyone has a place in the family of the Church as we minister to one another. We affirm the centrality of the family, sustained by the Church, as a foundational community for human growth.

150　We ask our Churches around the world to support families through practical programmes in the local congregation and through advocacy in communities and nations of social and political programmes that protect and enhance family life.

151　The International Family Network is being developed by the ACC as a result of its International Project on Family and Community, to whose report *Transforming Families and Communities* we have already referred.[12] This project has identified both urgent needs facing family life throughout the world and programmes which have been developed to meet these needs. We commend the Network to our Churches and invite co-operation and support.

152   We are encouraged and challenged by some words of Bishop David Gitari from Kenya:

> Liberating the Church means freeing the Christians to be a community of believers that serves as an agent of the Kingdom of God. As the Church becomes a community in the New Testament sense, it is able to create community and to enhance existing community not only among Christians but in society at large. With so many fractured and lonely families in cities and so many people living alone, the Church should see itself as an extended family, where every believer finds a home, not just figuratively but literally. The Church must work to build strong homes, exploring extended family models, so that each home truly is a Church and the Church is truly a family.[13]

SEXUAL ORIENTATION

153   Despite its basic assertions about marriage and family, there is much confusion in the area of the Church's doctrine and teaching about sexuality. *Transforming Families and Communities* witnesses to this on the basis of extensive Communion-wide consultations. Thus, on the vexed question of sexuality, it reports:

> The question of sexual orientation is a complex one which the Church is still grappling with: many Provinces have traditionally maintained that homosexuality is a sin whilst others are responding differently to the issue. As sexuality is an aspect of life which goes to the very heart of human identity and society it is a pastorally sensitive issue which requires further study and reflection by Church leadership.[14]

154   We recognise that this issue remains unresolved, and we welcome the fact that study is continuing. We believe that the Church should therefore give active encouragement to biological, genetic, and psychological research, and consider these scientific studies as they contribute to our understanding of the subject in the light of Scripture.

155   Further study is also needed of the socio-cultural factors which contribute to the differing attitudes towards homosexuality, mentioned above, in the various Provinces of our Church. We continue to encourage dialogue with, and pastoral concern for, persons of homosexual orientation within the Family of Christ. (Resolution 64.)

SEXUAL ABUSE

156   There is universal agreement that respect, reverence and mutuality are necessary in all human relationships. This agreement about the fundamentals of human relations, including sexual relations, leads to a firm judgement and condemnation of sexual abuse and exploitation. This is a challenge to all irrespective of sexual orientation. Again, the Family Network reports:

> Domestic violence must be looked at as a community and structural problem as well as the problem of each individual family. Violence in the home helps to perpetuate the status quo acquiesced in by wider society: the dominance of the male

187

over the female, the dominance of men in highly paid or powerful positions, and the dependence of women on men for general protection, income and/or shelter. Similarities occur in the case of child sexual abuse.[15]

157 The Church in every community is called to share in a holistic approach to the problems of domestic violence. By co-operating with social service agencies, medical and psychological personnel, governments and volunteer groups, a united programme of physical, spiritual and psychological healing could be offered. The Church should play an important role in the counselling of both the victims of abuse and the abusers as well, and in sponsoring sheltered care for abused children and adults. Church-sponsored support groups for admitted spouse and child abusers can provide a healing touch to their self-esteem and to their ability to control their actions.

158 Sexual abuse is self-gratification by exploitation. It makes an impersonal object of the other person, abusing both the person and sexuality itself. Abuse occurs in a wide range of sexual activities: always in rape and child molestation, usually in adultery and prostitution, and sometimes even in marriage. Sexual abuse also occurs in the socially subtle aspects of sexism, as noted by the Family Network above, and in sexual harassment of employees in the workplace. The Church must be clear about these violations of sexual intimacy. It must be explicit in its teaching about these particular aberrations of sexual relations, aggressively proactive about its social policy and action touching on these areas, and forthright in dealing with violations in its own community. It should be aware of the programmes of sex education given to the young in school or home. Such programmes should help persons discern between normal sexual expression and sexual abuse in order that they may express their sexuality appropriately. (Resolution 28.)

159 In some African and Asian countries represented among us, the traditional cultures have been more supportive of families, and fewer problems of both heterosexual and homosexual abuse have appeared. The Church everywhere can approach these problems positively by acting to strengthen family structures and the bonds of marriage. Each diocese should have a commission on family life that would initiate appropriate preventative programmes.

160 With the 1987 General Synod of the Church of England and the 1988 General Convention of the Episcopal Church in the USA, we affirm: 'The biblical and traditional teaching on chastity and fidelity in personal relationships is a response to, and expression of, God's love for each one of us, and … that all Christians are called to be exemplary in all spheres of morality, including sexual morality, and that holiness of life is particularly required for Christian leaders'. (Resolution 28.)

AIDS – A MAJOR THREAT

161   AIDS is a disease which confronts all people with immense challenges of care and responsibility. Any response to these demands requires that we should know and understand the facts about the virus, about its transmission, and about the extent of its spread in different parts of the world. Though the greatest number of deaths have so far occurred in the USA among identifiable social groups, the incidence of infection is very much more widespread, both geographically and socially. In some parts of Africa, for instance, random tests suggest that between 10 and 30 per cent of the young adult population may be infected, and that among the professional classes the incidence is even higher. In New York 8,000 people have already died, and 38,500 in the USA as a whole. Fifty per cent of these deaths are drug-related. Even in parts of the world which have so far seen very few AIDS-related deaths, the incidence of infection may be much greater.

162   The facts make it clear that although AIDS, in one sense, resembles any other epidemic, it differs from other epidemics in a number of ways. The scale of it could be immense. The fact that it attacks young people in their most productive years greatly increases its social impact. The long delay between the onset of infection and the appearance of symptoms makes it difficult for people to relate cause and effect. It can spread rapidly, particularly in a world of easy mobility. Its association in the majority of cases with sexual or drug-related behaviour makes it especially difficult to face the implications of the disease objectively.

163   Christians have no option but to be in the forefront of those committed to care and education. The Churches have often had a crucial part to play in the development of health care and education in many parts of the world, and they continue to make major contributions to those ministries. In relation to AIDS, we recognise with gratitude the efforts contributed by many caring agencies, both voluntary and governmental. But we also recognise that much more remains to be done.

164   Acknowledging that there are different theological presuppositions and different interpretations of Scripture about this matter, the Church must not wait to settle these differences before proceeding to bring the compassion of Christ and the renewal of the Holy Spirit to those in need and distress.

165   It is important to remember that the world has had plagues of 'incurable' disease before. The bubonic plague is perhaps the best-known example. It is not known why it ebbed and flowed and eventually disappeared. AIDS may disappear ultimately, but there is no prospect of its doing so in the near future. Meanwhile, we must pray earnestly for God to guide us to a cure and not lose hold of our Christian hope both for this world and the next.

EPISCOPAL RESPONSIBILITIES

166   The role of bishops in influencing opinion, within the Church and outside it, should not be underestimated. Fear and condemnation have been the prevailing responses to AIDS, and bishops need to counter hysteria and irrational behaviour. Inspired and inspiring leadership is urgently required. In particular, the bishops should lead the *whole* Church into the living and proclaiming of the Christian way, with its particular values and compassion, and in making this way apparent in society at large.

167   The Christian response to AIDS needs to be theological, educational, pastoral, practical and political.

First, the Church is required to avoid fear-inspired and judgemental responses which deny the theology of hope and betray the true ministry of compassion and service.

168   *Secondly,* the Church has a role in changing social attitudes from fear to compassionate love. We must assist in all efforts aimed at preventing the spread of the virus, especially by encouraging changes in behaviour among those people most at risk.

169   *Thirdly,* pastoral ministry means helping, without judgement, those whom AIDS leaves helpless and hopeless.

170   *Fourthly,* there is a role for the Church in providing care for people at home, as well as in developing residential alternatives. All this involves financial commitments which must be faced.

171   *Fifthly,* there will be circumstances in which political action is needed, whether by co-operating in government initiatives or by calling for more effective and humane government action.

172   We call on each Province and diocese to develop its own strategy, since circumstances differ so widely; and to find practical ways of expressing our interdependence as a Communion, especially since the heaviest burden in terms of medical, social and pastoral care will probably fall on those countries least able to bear it.

173   We need theologically informed studies of the problems of human experience which lead people to seek fulfilment in drug abuse and sexual promiscuity, and of community attitudes which isolate people into minority groups. These are some of the conditions which make people vulnerable to the AIDS virus.

THEOLOGICAL AND ETHICAL RESPONSES

174   It is important to distinguish between the theological arguments about the way in which the disease is acquired and those which relate to pastoral response. To confuse the two may well identify the spread of AIDS with

homosexual practices (despite the fact that in many countries the virus is spread in heterosexual relations) and with drug abuse. In this way, important factors affecting the spread of the disease – such as poverty, war and deprivation – are ignored. AIDS exposes the vulnerable places and people in our society, and our negligence towards our neighbours. AIDS is a challenge to the Church and the whole of society.

175   Disease of any kind poses difficult theological questions. Christians believe that God created a world that is good. It is too simple to suggest that all disease is the result of sin, although some patterns of behaviour can be identified as likely to lead to sickness of mind or body, or both. AIDS has been especially associated by some with the 'judgement of God', but there is no more reason to think of it in these terms than any other disease, though the social factors which have encouraged its spread point to specific problems in all societies. It requires a special sensitivity in pastoral care to exhibit God's love to persons living with AIDS who need not only the assurance of God's love and close identification with them in their suffering, but the immediacy and reassurance of physical human contact in their inevitable fear. The ministry of God's healing will need to be intense, accepting, and full of hope for the ultimate future of the individual. The Church needs to develop specific forms of prayer and liturgical rites to assist in the ministry to those living with AIDS. Examples are available in the Dioceses of New York, California and Los Angeles.

176   AIDS has reinforced the need for human beings to observe faithfulness and permanence in sexual relationships, as the Christian Church has always taught. Nevertheless, such an approach to human relationships is by no means universal. In the present state of emergency the Church should support those governments and medical agencies seeking to prevent the spread of AIDS by making clean needles available to certain drug users and encouraging the use of condoms in both heterosexual and homosexual activities. Such support should be given in a way which makes it clear that the Church is not condoning the practices involved.

177   People with AIDS, their families and friends, will experience a wide range of emotional response to the circumstances in which they find themselves. Among these emotions, anger, outrage, guilt, remorse, recrimination and a sense of injustice are likely to be dominant. In its supportive ministry the Church will need to offer the good news of God's loving acceptance and forgiveness of every human being and encourage the same loving response in others. In particular, church members will need to be trained to understand and express this love in word and action.

EDUCATIONAL AND PASTORAL RESPONSES

178   Education about AIDS begins with us, and should include an understanding of sexuality, disease and death, deprivation and drug abuse.

179   Diocesan strategies should make every effort to ensure that AIDS is discussed everywhere – within church organisations, youth clubs, at synods, from the pulpit – as well as in special meetings. AIDS is a preventable disease, and much of the prevention lies in education and consequent behavioural change. It is vital that people understand how it is spread and how it is *not* spread.

180   The Church must lead the way in articulating images and symbols of hope that survive in the face of disaster. Art, drama and music are important allies, which should be deliberately cultivated in support groups and symbolic liturgical rites.

181   Diocesan and parish strategies should work through marriage preparation programmes and community organisations to create understanding for every generation of the forces in contemporary society which disrupt and destroy families and wholesome relationships. Children need to develop healthy attitudes about themselves and their sexuality before their patterns of behaviour are established, and families need to develop understanding of attitudes and practices which are constructive to human relationships. Different cultures will need different approaches. It may often be necessary to support and work through educational programmes which exist independently of religious structures. Certain initiation rituals (for instance circumcision for both males and females) provide particular dangers of infection in certain cultures.

182   The Church should be vigilant in 'redeeming' the vocabulary of AIDS. It is better to speak of people with AIDS rather than victims of AIDS; and living with AIDS rather than dying with AIDS.

183   The Church has special responsibilities for developing new ways and extra dimensions of caring. In particular, it needs to create an atmosphere in which AIDS can be discussed and in which people can state openly, should they so wish, that they have AIDS and can expect to be accepted and loved.

184   Great attention must be paid to provide proper support for the caregivers who attend persons living with AIDS.

185   Many examples of good practice exist already in developing new methods of home care and personal friendship, known in one culture as 'the buddy system'. For instance, the Presiding Bishop of ECUSA has suggested that each bishop of that Province should act as such a 'buddy' to a person living with AIDS, developing a personal pastoral relationship with that person and his or her family.

186   Particular problems arise within prison systems. Certain Provinces already have an entrance into this system but all Provinces and dioceses are

urged to establish support ministries, sensitive pastoral care and educational programmes for those in prison as well as for prison officials and staff.

187   The Church needs to be aware of the civil liberties that are presently under threat. Those living with AIDS have difficulty in obtaining insurance, mortgages, employment and housing. They also have difficulty in protecting confidentiality of material and records relating to themselves. Civil liberties vary greatly in different parts of the world; but in all places the Church should be vigilant and sensitive to all threats to human liberty and dignity, and must oppose discrimination on grounds of infection, disease, national origin, race or sexuality.

188   Diocesan strategies should recognise the disruption of family life caused by AIDS; they should support the families of those with AIDS, and be aware of the possible need to establish new forms of family support for those whose own families or friends have abandoned them.

189   The Church should also be highly sensitive to the very particular distress caused by the transmission of the HIV virus through blood transfusions using contaminated blood stock. Although this has affected people with haemophilia in particular, it has been a more general problem (for instance, in surgical procedures) in developing countries.

ADMINISTRATIVE ACTION

190   The Church has two urgent practical tasks: to establish solidarity with those affected, and to start preventative programmes in parts of the world where the disease has not yet spread.

191   Resources should be shared within and beyond the Church, whether those resources be financial, human, or the possession of information. The AIDS epidemic is causing immeasurable personal suffering and grief and, as it spreads throughout the general population, especially in developing countries, it has the potential of doing unimaginable damage to the social fabric by killing the most productive age group. The current costs of medical care alone are a terrible warning of what is to come.

192   The Church must be challenged to use its financial resources and property in the present crisis by, for instance, making available capital or certain properties for the development of hospices or housing and for the equipping and running of such places.

193   The Church should challenge governments to devote greater community resources to preventing the spread of AIDS, to the treatment and support of those living with AIDS, and to research.

194   The circumstances of AIDS are different in each part of the world and what is appropriate to one area (for instance, where AIDS has not yet man-

ifested itself) will not be appropriate to another (for instance, where the epidemic is extensive). We believe we must learn from each other and that some mechanism is necessary which will enable the exchange of information and practical assistance. We believe that the ACC should be invited to co-operate with the WCC and WHO in exploring ways in which efforts can be co-ordinated on a global basis. (Resolution 29.)

CONCLUSION

195   The stories of the bishops gathered at Lambeth 1988 have made us more aware of the issues of social order facing the Church at this time. As we worshipped and prayed together, studied the Scriptures in groups and wrestled with the perplexing problems of today's world, we sought to understand what God would have us do and say. The basic response 'thus says the Lord' is inescapable in the face of the profound social injustices of our time. Similarly, there is no alternative to seeking to share in the confusions and complexities of many of today's issues. The search for practical and attainable ways forward is rarely easy and never without cost. In all our work we are called to keep before us the vision of God and of a transformed humanity which both challenges our present experience and offers us hope in the task.

NOTES

[1] *The Family in Contemporary Society,* SPCK, London, 1958.

[2] *Peace and Justice: A Working Paper for Lambeth 1988,* Cincinnati, 1986.

[3] *Many Gifts, One Spirit: Report of ACC-7, Singapore 1987,* ACC, London, 1987, p.111(d).

[4] From a presentation made at the Lambeth Conference 1988.

[5] *Many Gifts, One Spirit,* pp. 100f.

[6] A. Nichols, J. Clarke and T. Hogan, *Transforming Families and Communities,* Anglican Information Office, Sydney, for ACC, 1987.

[7] *Report of the Lambeth Conference 1930,* SPCK, London, 1930, Resolution 25.

[8] *Report of the Lambeth Conference 1978,* CIO Publishing, London, 1978, p.62.

[9] op. cit., p.64.

[10] ACC-6, *Bonds of Affection,* 1984, p.120.

[11] *Many Gifts, One Spirit,* p.118.

[12] See paras. 80, 131 of this Section report.

[13] *Transforming Families and Communities,* pp. 79f.

[14] ibid., p.64.

[15] ibid., p.46.

* indicates a title published through the Inter–Anglican Publishing Network.

RESOLUTIONS

Resolutions 24 to 40 and Resolutions 56, 58, 62, 64, 68 and 73 deal with matters within the purview of the Section on Christianity and the Social Order.

BIBLIOGRAPHY

ACC, *Peace and Peacemaking,* 1984.

Board for Social Responsibility (C of E), *AIDS: Some Guidelines for Pastoral Care,* Church House Publishing, London, 1986.

A. Nichols, J. Clarke and T. Hogan *Transforming Families and Communities,* ACC, 1987 (International Project on Family and Community).

Peace and Justice, A Working Paper for Lambeth 1988, Cincinnati, 1986.

The Lambeth Conference 1958, SPCK, London, 1958.

The Family in Contemporary Society, SPCK, London, 1958.

ACC-6 *Bonds of Affection,* 1984.

ACC-7 *Many Gifts, One Spirit,* 1987.

Michael Nazir-Ali and W D Pattinson (eds.), *Working Papers for the Lambeth Conference 1988,* London 1987.

* indicates a title published through the Inter-Anglican Publishing Network.

RESOLUTIONS

List of Resolutions

1   The Ordination or Consecration of Women to the Episcopate
2   (Consecration of Women Bishops – failed)
3   'Baptism, Eucharist and Ministry': Report of the Faith and Order Commission of the World Council of Churches
4   Anglican–Lutheran Relations
5   Anglican–Oriental Orthodox Relations
6   Anglican–Orthodox Relations
7   Anglican–Reformed Dialogue
8   Anglican–Roman Catholic International Commission (ARCIC)
9   Methodist Church
10   Baptist World Alliance
11   Pentecostal Churches
12   United Churches in Full Communion
13   Unity: Locally, Nationally and Internationally
14   Councils of Churches
15   Local Ecumenism
16   Theological Education
17   Steps Towards Unity
18   The Anglican Communion: Identity and Authority
19   Draft Common Declaration
20   Inter-Faith Dialogue
21   Inter-Faith Dialogue: Jewish/Christian/Muslim
22   Christ and Culture
23   Freedom of Religious Activity
24   Palestine/Israel
25   Iran
26   Church and Polygamy
27   War, Violence and Justice
28   Sexual Abuse
29   Acquired Immune Deficiency Syndrome (AIDS)
30   Conscientious Objection – **see page 345**
31   Voiceless Minority
32   World Peace
33   Human Rights
34   Marriage and Family
35   Concerns of South Pacific Islands
36   Poverty and Debt
37   Latin America
38   Namibia
39   South Africa
40   Environment, Militarism, Justice and Peace
41   Training of Bishops
42   Ministry of Lay People

RESOLUTIONS

1 THE ORDINATION OR CONSECRATION OF WOMEN TO THE EPISCOPATE

This Conference resolves:

1   That each Province respect the decision and attitudes of other Provinces in the ordination or consecration of women to the episcopate, without such respect necessarily indicating acceptance of the principles involved, maintaining the highest possible degree of communion with the Provinces which differ.

2   That bishops exercise courtesy and maintain communications with bishops who may differ, and with any woman bishop, ensuring an open dialogue in the Church to whatever extent communion is impaired.

3   That the Archbishop of Canterbury, in consultation with the Primates, appoints a commission:
   (a) to provide for an examination of the relationships between Provinces of the Anglican Communion and ensure that the process of reception includes continuing consultation with other Churches as well;
   (b) to monitor and encourage the process of consultation within the Communion and to offer further pastoral guidelines.

4   That in any Province where reconciliation on these issues is necessary, any diocesan bishop facing this problem be encouraged to seek continuing dialogue with, and make pastoral provision for, those clergy and congregations whose opinions differ from those of the bishop, in order to maintain the unity of the diocese.

5   Recognises the serious hurt which would result from the questioning by some of the validity of the episcopal acts of a woman bishop, and likewise the hurt experienced by those whose conscience would be offended by the ordination of a woman to the episcopate. The Church needs to exercise sensitivity, patience and pastoral care towards all concerned.

Voting: *For:* 423
         Against: 28
         Abstentions 19

(See further paras. 132-150 of the Report on **Mission and Ministry**.*)*

3 'BAPTISM, EUCHARIST AND MINISTRY': REPORT OF THE FAITH AND ORDER COMMISSION OF THE WORLD COUNCIL OF CHURCHES

This Conference:

1   Welcomes the text *Baptism, Eucharist and Ministry* (BEM) as a con-

tribution of great significance in the search for the visible unity of the Church and notes that the ecumenical climate has already been much improved by it in many places. It recognises this text to be one part of a wider agenda in which the Faith and Order Commission of the World Council of Churches is engaged. It values the consonance between BEM and the bilateral and other multilateral dialogues in which Anglicans are engaged and the fact that BEM enables us to see a convergence towards substantial agreement in faith and practice between many Communions.

2   Endorses the view of the provincial responses that Anglicans can recognise to a large extent in the text *Baptism, Eucharist and Ministry* 'the faith of the Church through the ages'.

3   Considers that Anglicans can draw important consequences from *Baptism, Eucharist and Ministry* for their relations with other Churches, particularly with those Churches which also recognise the text as an expression of the apostolic faith.

4   Recommends that Provinces take guidance from the text for their worship, educational, ethical and spiritual life and witness.

5   Encourages the Faith and Order Commission of the World Council of Churches to pursue its work to develop the convergences of *Baptism, Eucharist and Ministry* and the study on *Towards the Common Expression of the Apostolic Faith Today* within the context of the study on *Unity and Renewal*. Anglicans urge the Faith and Order Commission to resume its work on structures of authority and decision-making in order that the work of the bilateral dialogues may be seen in a broader context.

6   Recommends that formal response be sought from those Provinces that have not yet replied to the World Council of Churches; asks the Anglican Consultative Council to find ways of promoting a continuing reception of the BEM text in all Provinces of the Anglican Communion; and hopes that sufficient finances and personal resources will be set aside for this to be carried out effectively.

EXPLANATORY NOTE

The Four BEM Questions

The Faith and Order Commission of the WCC asked the Churches to prepare an official response to BEM at the highest appropriate level of authority. Four questions were to be answered:

1   *the extent to which your Church can recognise in this text the faith of the Church through the ages.*

In the light of the provincial responses it is clear that Anglicans can recognise to an impressive degree the faith of the Church through the ages. BEM is found to be a positive document, balanced and comprehensive, in the subjects it treats. In each of the three areas of baptism, eucharist and ministry we look forward to an even greater development of the convergence. In the area of baptism more work needs to be done on the inter-relationship of the various parts of the initiation process and the strengthening of the theme of covenant in relation to baptism. In the area of eucharist we should like to ensure that the *anamnesis* of the mighty acts of God in Christ remains focused upon his saving death and resurrection, and that while at every eucharist the true president is Christ, an ordained priest ought to preside. In the area of ministry we look for a fuller treatment of the ministries of all the baptised and clarification of the nature of priesthood and the respective roles of bishops, presbyters and deacons. In particular we think it important to develop work on the personal, collegial and communal forms of ministry exercised at every point in the Church's corporate life. It would be helpful to Anglicans if work on the ordination of women to the priesthood was developed in the context of the multilateral dialogue.

The responses from the Provinces detect three underlying issues of a more general nature that need continuing exploration: the relation between Scripture, Tradition and traditions; the nature of the Sacraments, their efficacy and their relation to the Word; the ecclesiology implicit in the text of BEM.

2 *the consequences your Church can draw from this text for its relations and dialogues with other Churches, particularly with those Churches who also recognise the text as an expression of the apostolic faith.*

We should like to develop the ecumenical consequences of the fact that our common baptism is a basic bond of unity. The responses of the Provinces to BEM encourage us to take up specific matters with particular partners in dialogue: the theology and practice of baptism with those who practise only 'believers' baptism; the question of eucharistic hospitality with Churches with whom we have no eucharistic fellowship; the mutual recognition of ministries, and particularly the role of the episcopate as a sign of unity and continuity.

3 *the guidance your Church can take from this text for its worship, educational, ethical, and spiritual life and witness.*

We recognise that BEM brings to expression the fruits of recent liturgical revision in our Communion and in others. The text challenges Anglicans to reform their own lives and practice in the areas of: preparation for baptism, and the continuing nurture of the baptised; the eucharist as the centre from which Christians go out to work as reconcilers in a broken world; the theology and practice of the diaconate, the complementarity of women and men in ministry, and the exercise of episcopacy.

4 *the suggestions your Church can make for the ongoing work of Faith and Order as it relates the material of this text on* Baptism, Eucharist and Ministry *to its long-range research project* Towards the Common Expression of the Apostolic Faith Today.

We look forward to the developing study on *Towards the Common Expression of the Apostolic Faith Today.* In light of the work of the bilateral dialogues on authority, Anglicans encourage the Faith and Order Commission to resume as soon as possible the earlier study *How does the Church Teach Authoritatively Today?* The study on the *Unity of the Church and the Renewal of Human Community* will help to locate the search for the visible unity of the Church in the proper context of God's mission to the world for the sake of the Kingdom.

(See further paras. 60-64 of the Report on **Ecumenical Relations***.)*

4 ANGLICAN–LUTHERAN RELATIONS

This Conference:

1   Receives with gratitude the *Cold Ash Report* (1983) of the Anglican–Lutheran Joint Working Group and approves its recommendations (see *Emmaus Report,* pp.82-84).

2   Welcomes the *Niagara Report* of the Anglican–Lutheran Consultation on *Episcope* (1987), recognises in it a substantial convergence of views, and commends it to the member Churches of the Anglican Communion for study and synodical reception.

3   Recommends that the permanent body already established by the Anglican Consultative Council and the Lutheran World Federation to co-ordinate and assess developing Anglican–Lutheran relationships (the Anglican/Lutheran International Continuation Committee) be renamed as the Anglican–Lutheran International Commission; and asked to undertake the following tasks in addition to its existing terms of reference:

  (a) to integrate in a broader document the theological work already accomplished in international, regional and local dialogues;

  (b) to explore more thoroughly the theological and canonical requirements that are necessary in both Churches to acknowledge and recognise the full authenticity of existing ministries (see *Niagara Report,* para. 94);

  (c) to advise with sensitivity on the actual pastoral practices of our Churches in regard to the celebration of God's Word and Sacraments, especially the Holy Eucharist;

  (d) to produce a report which will indicate the degree of convergence of views on the ordained ministry of bishops, presbyters and deacons.

4   Recognises, on the basis of the high degree of consensus reached in international, regional and national dialogues between Anglicans and Lutherans and in the light of the communion centred around Word and Sacrament that has been experienced in each other's traditions, the presence of the Church of Jesus Christ in the Lutheran Communion as in our own.

5   Urges that this recognition and the most recent convergence on apostolic ministry achieved in the *Niagara Report* of the Anglican–Lutheran Consul-

tation on Episcopacy (1987) prompt us to move towards the fullest possible ecclesial recognition and the goal of full communion.

6 Recommends to member Churches, subject to the concurrence of the Lutheran World Federation, that:

(a) Anglican and Lutheran Churches should officially establish and encourage the practice of mutual eucharistic hospitality – if this is not already authorised – where pastoral need exists and when ecumenical occasions make this appropriate;

(b) The Provinces of our Communion should make provision for appropriate forms of 'interim eucharistic sharing' along the following lines:

   (i) They should by synodical action recognise now the member Churches of the Lutheran World Federation as Churches in which the Gospel is preached and taught;

   (ii) They should encourage the development of common Christian life throughout their respective Churches by such means as the following proposals of the *Niagara Report:*

      (a) Eucharistic Sharing and Joint Common Celebration of the Eucharist;
      (b) meetings of Church leaders for regular prayer, reflection and consultation, thus beginning joint *episcope;*
      (c) mutual invitation of Church leaders, clergy and laity, to synods, with a right to speak;
      (d) common agencies wherever possible;
      (e) exploring the possibility of adjusting boundaries to assist local and regional co-operation;
      (f) Covenants among Church leaders to collaborate in *episcope;*
      (g) joint pastoral appointments for special projects;
      (h) joint theological education and training courses;
      (i) sharing of information and documents;
      (j) joint mission programmes;
      (k) agreed syllabuses for Christian education in schools, joint materials for catechesis and adult study;
      (l) co-operation over liturgical forms, cycles of intercession, lectionaries and homiletic materials;
      (m) welcoming isolated clergy or diaspora congregations into the life of a larger group (see ALERC *Helsinki Report,* 5);
      (n) interchange of ministers to the extent permitted by canon law;
      (o) twinning (partnership) between congregations and communities;

> (p) joint programmes of diaconal ministry and reflection on issues of social responsibility;
>
> (q) joint retreats and devotional materials.

(iii) they should affirm by synodical action now on the basis of the consensus documents of Anglican–Lutheran International Conversations that the basic teaching of each respective Church is consonant with Scripture and that Lutheran teaching is sufficiently compatible with the teachings of the Churches of the Anglican Communion so that a relationship of *Interim Sharing of the Eucharist* may be established between these Churches under the guidelines appended.

APPENDIX

GUIDELINES FOR INTERIM SHARING OF THE EUCHARIST

(a)   The Churches of the Anglican Communion extend a special welcome to members of the Lutheran Churches to receive Holy Communion on the understanding that the Lutheran Churches will do likewise. This welcome constitutes a recognition of eucharistic teaching sufficient for Interim Sharing of the Eucharist.

(b)   Bishops of dioceses of the Anglican Communion and bishops/presidents of Lutheran districts and synods may by mutual agreement extend their regulations of church discipline to permit common, joint celebration of the Eucharist within their jurisdictions according to guidelines established by respective synods.

In this case:

When a joint Eucharist is held in an Anglican church an Anglican bishop or priest should preside, using an Anglican liturgy, with the Lutheran preaching; when a joint eucharist is held in a Lutheran church a Lutheran should preside using a Lutheran liturgy, with the Anglican preaching. This is not concelebration, nor does it imply rejection or final recognition of either Church's eucharist or ministry. The liturgical arrangements, including the position of the ministers in relation to the altar, should take into account local circumstances and sensitivities.

*(See further paras 72-78 and para. 82b of the Report on **Ecumenical Relations**.)*

5   ANGLICAN–ORIENTAL ORTHODOX RELATIONS

This Conference:

1   Warmly welcomes the renewal and development of relationships between the Anglican Communion and the Armenian Apostolic, Coptic Orthodox, Ethiopian Orthodox, Syrian Orthodox and Indian Orthodox Churches.

2   Warmly welcomes the renewal of relationships between the Anglican Communion and the Holy Apostolic Catholic Assyrian Church of the East.

3   Particularly welcomes the presence of more Observers from these Churches than at any previous Lambeth Conference, thus regaining the momentum of the Conferences of 1908 and 1920.

4   Notes with satisfaction the visits to these Churches made before and since the WCC Assembly at Vancouver in 1983 by Bishop Henry Hill, the meeting of the Anglican–Oriental Orthodox Forum held at St Albans in 1985 and the subsequent publication of the symposium *Light from the East,* as well as the meetings between the Archbishop of Canterbury and the Patriarchs of these Churches, including that with Pope Shenouda III in 1987 resulting in their Joint Declaration.

5   Affirms our friendship with these two families of Churches, and recognises the severe difficulties and challenges faced by them through war and persecution, through the growth of secularism and militant atheism, and also recognises the challenge presented by the interface with Islam.

6   Recognises that we are present together in many parts of the world, and offers our hopes for the development of friendship, fellowship and support wherever we find ourselves side by side.

7   Values greatly the rich contribution that these Churches have made to the spirituality of the Church as a whole throughout the centuries.

8   Affirms and supports the work of the Anglican–Oriental Orthodox Forum, and commits itself to the task of the forum in developing areas of possible co-operation, particularly:

   (a) The development of dialogue on matters of common theological interest and concern.

   (b) The establishment of theological scholarships mainly for postgraduate study for students who have completed their basic training in their own institutions and the possibility that some Anglican students spend some time in Oriental Orthodox theological institutions and monasteries as part of their regular training for the ministry.

   (c) The hope that theological seminaries of the Oriental Orthodox Churches can be assisted, especially in the building up of libraries, in the supply of new books, and in subscriptions to scholarly journals, with journals and magazines published by the Churches of the two Communions being exchanged on a more systematic basis.

   (d) The need for regional co-ordinating bodies for promoting understanding and co-operation among the Churches especially in the USA and Canada, in the Middle East, in Australia and New Zealand, and in the United Kingdom.

9   Desires that in view of the importance of Anglican–Oriental Orthodox relations, the Anglican Consultative Council enter into consultation with

the relevant Oriental Orthodox authorities with a view to the Forum being upgraded to a formally recognised Commission.

(See further para. 57 of the Report on **Ecumenical Relations.***)*

6   ANGLICAN–ORTHODOX RELATIONS

This Conference:

1   Remembers with gratitude the long history of cordial relations between Anglicans and Orthodox, not only in Europe but throughout the world, and records our sense of privilege at sharing in the celebrations of the Millennium of the Baptism of Kievan Rus, and the enrichment of the Conference by the presence of Orthodox Consultants and Observers who have shared with us in our life and worship; and values the dialogue between our Communions not only because it transcends East–West divisions (theological, cultural and political) but also because it stimulates and aids our own internal reflection on important issues.

2   Warmly welcomes the Dublin Agreed Statement of 1984 as an important successor to the Moscow Agreed Statement of 1976 and notes with particular pleasure the measure of theological agreement which the Dublin Statement records, the honesty with which it expresses divergences of outlook, and its special emphasis on prayer and worship as the context in which doctrinal discussion must be pursued.

3   Commits itself to drawing the attention of all the Provinces of our Communion to the contents of the Dublin Agreed Statement, hoping to see it given the serious discussion which it deserves, especially in those Provinces where there is a strong Orthodox presence and where there has hitherto been too little fraternal contact, and asks further all the Provinces to submit to the Secretary General of the ACC, by a date to be specified by that body, their responses to the Dublin Statement, such responses as far as possible to be expressed after conversation with local Orthodox Christians.

4   Welcomes the resumption of the Anglican–Orthodox Joint Doctrinal Discussions (AOJDD) and encourages the work of that Commission towards the restoration of that unity for which Christ prayed, particularly noting its intention to address the question of ecclesiology which it is hoped will include the increasingly significant concept of 'reception', the issue of ecclesial diversity and the inter-relationship between faith and the culture in which it is expressed; believing that these are pressing issues which affect both our Communions, and at the same time urging that the AOJDD take into its consideration other dialogues in which both Anglicans and Orthodox separately are involved.

5   Asks that further thought be given to the Filioque Clause, recognising it

to be a major point of disagreement, (a) recalling Resolution 35.3 of the Lambeth Conference 1978 and the varied, and on the whole positive response from those Provinces which responded to ACC-4's request to consider the removal of this clause from liturgical texts, (b) noting that the Report of the Faith and Order Commission of the WCC 'Ecumenical Explication of the Apostolic Faith as expressed in the Niceno-Constantinopolitan (381) Creed' bases itself on the original text, (c) believing that it may be possible to achieve unity of action on the part of all the 'Western Churches' to adopt the original form of the Creed without any betrayal of their theological heritage, (d) recommending to the Provinces of the Anglican Communion that in future liturgical revisions the Niceno-Constantinopolitan Creed be printed without the Filioque clause.

6 Noting the forthcoming Pan-Orthodox Consultation on Women and Ordination, requests that the results of its deliberations be circulated to the Provinces of the Anglican Communion and urges that ecumenical theological dialogue ensue on this issue.

7 Notes with gratitude to God the increasing openness towards the Orthodox Churches in the Soviet Union and encourages the Provinces of the Anglican Communion:

  (a) to explore increased contact, co-operation and exchanges;
  (b) to offer such theological literature and other aid as may be practicable.

8 Welcomes the various international exchange programmes and study visits that are taking place between Anglicans and Orthodox and hopes that more such opportunities will be created.

9 Welcomes the many examples of friendship, hospitality, co-operation and participation in each other's worship that already exist at the local level and urges the Churches of the Anglican Communion to be more active in such endeavours, noting with particular thanksgiving the influence of Orthodox spirituality and iconography on contemporary Anglicanism and asking Anglicans to share with Orthodox their experience of witness and ministry in secular contexts.

(See further paras. 57 and 59 of the Report on **Ecumenical Relations**.*)*

7 ANGLICAN–REFORMED DIALOGUE

This Conference:

1 Impressed by the insight of the Report of the Anglican–Reformed Conversations, *God's Reign and our Unity,* particularly of the way in which the unity and mission of the Church and the quest for human unity are set within

the context of the kingdom of God, commends this text for widespread study and synodical reception throughout the Anglican Communion.

2 Notes with satisfaction that the dialogue helps both Anglicans and Reformed to recover together a reformed pattern of the threefold ministry; and that Anglicans are challenged to consider the expression of diaconal ministry, the Reformed the expression of the personal dimension of oversight (*episcope*) at the regional level.

3 Endorses the stress on the need for personal, collegial and communal expressions of ministry exercised at every level of the Church's life.

4 Recommends that the ACC collects from the Provinces responses to the dialogue and any implications that have resulted; and requests the ACC to consult with the World Alliance of Reformed Churches (Presbyterian and Congregational) over the setting up of a small continuation committee to encourage wider study and implementation in life of the insights of this dialogue as a contribution towards growth in unity;

5 Acknowledging that this is the only dialogue which deals at any length with the ordination of women to the threefold order, notes that it is suggested that 'it is clearly impossible for churches which exist in the same geographical area but which take different stands on this issue to enter into complete union'; recommends further study on this issue in the light of the remaining differences of opinion and practice in both traditions.

6 Affirms the concept promoted in this dialogue: that orthopraxis (right action) is as important in ecumenical conversations as orthodoxy (right belief), and therefore urges that adequate attention be given to orthopraxis in all ecumenical dialogue.

*(See further paras. 59, 61, 64, and 70 of the Report on **Ecumenical Relations**.)*

8 ANGLICAN–ROMAN CATHOLIC INTERNATIONAL COMMISSION (ARCIC)

This Conference:

1 Recognises the Agreed Statements of ARCIC I on *Eucharistic Doctrine, Ministry and Ordination,* and their *Elucidations,* as consonant in substance with the faith of Anglicans and believes that this agreement offers a sufficient basis for taking the next step forward towards the reconciliation of our Churches grounded in agreement in faith.

2 Welcomes the assurance that, within an understanding of the Church as communion, ARCIC II is to explore further the particular issues of the reconciliation of ministries; the ordination of women; moral questions; and continuing questions of authority, including the relation of Scripture to the

Church's developing Tradition and the role of the laity in decision-making within the Church.

3   Welcomes *Authority in the Church (I and II)* together with the *Elucidation,* as a firm basis for the direction and agenda of the continuing dialogue on authority and wishes to encourage ARCIC II to continue to explore the basis in Scripture and Tradition of the concept of a universal primacy, in conjunction with collegiality, as an instrument of unity, the character of such a primacy in practice, and to draw upon the experience of other Christian Churches in exercising primacy, collegiality and conciliarity.

4   In welcoming the fact that the ordination of women is to form part of the agenda of ARCIC II, recognises the serious responsibility this places upon us to weigh the possible implications of action on this matter for the unity of the Anglican Communion and for the universal Church.

5   Warmly welcomes the first Report of ARCIC II, *Salvation and the Church* (1987), as a timely and significant contribution to the understanding of the Churches' doctrine of salvation and commends this Agreed Statement about the heart of Christian faith to the Provinces for study and reflection.

EXPLANATORY NOTE

This Conference has received the official responses to the *Final Report* of the Anglican–Roman Catholic International Commission (ARCIC I) from the member Provinces of the Anglican Communion. We note the considerable measure of consensus and convergence which the *Agreed Statements* represent. We wish to record our grateful thanks to Almighty God for the very significant advances in understanding and unity thereby expressed.

In considering the *Final Report,* the Conference bore two questions in mind:
(i)   Are the *Agreed Statements* consonant with Anglican faith?
(ii) If so, do they enable us to take further steps forward?

Eucharistic Doctrine

The Provinces gave a clear 'yes' to the statement on *Eucharistic Doctrine.*

Comments have been made that the style and language used in the statement are inappropriate for certain cultures. Some Provinces asked for clarification about the meaning of *anamnesis* and bread and wine 'becoming' the body and blood of Christ. But no Province rejected the Statement and many were extremely positive.

While we recognise that there are hurts to be healed and doubts to be overcome, we encourage Anglicans to look forward with the new hope which the Holy Spirit is giving to the Church as we move away from past mistrust, division and polarisation.

While we respect continuing anxieties of some Anglicans in the area of 'sacrifice' and 'presence', they do not appear to reflect the common mind of the Provincial responses, in which it was generally felt that the *Elucidation* of *Eucharistic Doctrine* was a helpful clarification and reassurance. Both are areas of 'mystery' which ultimately defy definition. But the Agreed Statement on the Eucharist *sufficiently* expresses Anglican understanding.

Ministry and Ordination

Again, the Provinces gave a clear 'yes' to the Statement on *Ministry and Ordination*.

The language and style have, however, been a difficulty for some Provinces, especially in the Far East. Wider representation has also been called for from Africa. Though this has now been partially remedied in ARCIC II, there is still currently no representation from Latin America, a subcontinent with very large Roman Catholic populations.

An ambivalent reply came from one Province which has traditionally experienced a difficult relationship with the Roman Catholic Church. This seems to reflect the need for developing deeper links of trust and friendship as ecumenical dialogue goes forward.

While some Provinces asked for a clarification of 'priesthood' the majority believed this had been dealt with sufficiently – together with the doctrine of the eucharist – to give grounds for hope for a fresh appraisal of each other's ministries and thus to further the reconciliation of ministries and growth towards full communion.

Authority in the Church

The Responses from the Provinces to the two Statements on *Authority in the Church* were generally positive.

Questions were, however, raised about a number of matters, especially primacy, jurisdiction and infallibility, collegiality, and the role of the laity. Nevertheless, it was generally felt that *Authority in the Church* (I and II), together with the *Elucidation*, give us real grounds for believing that fuller agreement can be reached, and that they set out helpfully the direction and agenda of the way forward.

(See further paras. 59, 64, 80, 85-89 of the Report on **Ecumenical Relations***.)*

9 METHODIST CHURCH

This Conference:

1   Gives thanks to Almighty God for the 250th Anniversary of the conversion of John and Charles Wesley, and for the influence and witness of the Methodist Church.

2   Recognises with regret that at this time there is no international theological dialogue between the Anglican Communion and the World Methodist Council.

3   Requests the Anglican Consultative Council to initiate Conversations with the World Methodist Council with a view to the beginning of such a dialogue.

10 BAPTIST WORLD ALLIANCE

This Conference:

1   Gives thanks for the many dialogues which are taking place between the Anglican Communion and other Christian Churches and for the closer fellowship which these dialogues have enabled between us.

2   In the light of the growing reception of *Baptism, Eucharist and Ministry*, believes that the time is ripe for a dialogue between the Anglican Communion and the Baptist World Alliance.

3   Requests the Anglican Consultative Council to initiate Conversations with the Baptist World Alliance with a view to the beginning of such a dialogue.

11 PENTECOSTAL CHURCHES

This Conference notes the rapid growth of Pentecostal Churches in many parts of the world, and encourages where possible the initiation of personal contact and theological dialogue with Pentecostal Churches especially at the local level.

12 UNITED CHURCHES IN FULL COMMUNION

This Conference:

1   Expresses its gratitude for the presence of bishops from the Church of South India, the Church of North India, the Church of Bangladesh and the Church of Pakistan, acknowledging that their presence reminds us that our commitment as Anglicans is to the wider unity of the Church.

2   Affirms the request of ACC-7 (Resolution 17, p.97) that all United Churches with which the Churches of the Anglican Communion are in full communion be invited to accept full membership in the Lambeth Conference and the Primates' Meeting (as is already the case with the Anglican Consultative Council).

3   Welcomes the proposals entitled *Ministry in a Uniting Church* of the Covenanted Churches in Wales, and insofar as the Welsh proposals are similar to the North India and Pakistan Scheme, sees no difficulties in relation to the question of full communion if such proposals are brought to fruition.

4   Encourages the development of similar proposals in other parts of the world.

EXPLANATORY NOTE

The term 'united Churches in Full Communion' is used of those Churches where Anglicans have entered into union with Christians of other traditions. These Churches are in full communion with the Churches of the Anglican Communion.

(See further paras. 3, 51, 93-97 of the Report on **Ecumenical Relations***.)*

13 UNITY: LOCALLY, NATIONALLY AND INTERNATIONALLY

This Conference, acknowledging that the withdrawal of Anglicans from several previous covenanting proposals and schemes of unity with Methodist, Reformed and other Churches is a cause for sorrow and repentance, nevertheless is encouraged by:

1   the continuing unity conversations in the Consultation on Church Union (USA) and the Welsh Covenanting Proposals:

2   the developing partnership in oversight of ecumenical ventures which is being shared by bishops with the leaders of other Churches;

3   the local unity developing in various countries, such as the co-operating parishes in New Zealand, the 'Shared Ministries' in Canada and the Local Ecumenical Projects (with the proposed new Canons) in England.

4   Recognises the special pastoral needs of interchurch families and wishes to express its support and encouragement for the work of associations of interchurch families and all forms of work locally and internationally which seek to help them.

(See further paras. 2-9 and 102-108 of the Report on **Ecumenical Relations***.)*

14 COUNCILS OF CHURCHES

This Conference:

1   Recognises the World Council of Churches as a special instrument of God in bringing into fuller unity and mission those Churches that confess 'the Lord Jesus Christ as God and Saviour according to the Scriptures, and therefore seek to fulfil together their common calling to the glory of the one God, Father, Son and Holy Spirit', and in expressing their commitment to justice, peace, and the integrity of creation.

2   Encourages the Provinces of the Anglican Communion to fuller commitment to the work of the WCC as well as other councils.

3 Recommends that all such councils be as inclusive of the baptised as possible and that all Churches be encouraged to contribute to the life and witness of such councils as fully as possible.

4 Expresses the hope that, through the councils, the Churches are helped to function as closely as possible in accordance with the Lund Principle, viz. that Churches should do together all those things that deep differences of conviction do not compel them to do separately.

(See further paras. 101 and 102 of the Report on **Ecumenical Relations.***)*

15 LOCAL ECUMENISM

This Conference:

1 Believes that the significance and value of the bilateral and multilateral conversations which Anglicans continue to have with other Churches depends in large part on a parallel movement of growth in unity at the local level, and therefore commits itself to work at this at Provincial, diocesan and parish level, and in particular to share in fellowship, discussion, study, worship, mission and action with fellow Christians of other traditions, in order that the unity which our Lord has given to all who believe in him may be more generally experienced and more visibly realised.

2 Requests that special attention be given to the ways in which bishops may share with the leadership of other Churches in the pastoral oversight of all Christians in ecumenical projects.

(See further paras. 102-108 of the Report on **Ecumenical Relations.**)

16 THEOLOGICAL EDUCATION

This Conference notes with gratitude the numerous experiments in joint education with other Churches which are being made all over the world, and recommends the extension of such work beyond the training of those who are to be ordained both in order to meet the needs of the whole people of God for a better understanding and fuller knowledge of their faith, and to foster the development of ecumenical theology and catechetics.

17 STEPS TOWARDS UNITY

This Conference recognises that the growth of Christian unity is a gradual and costly process in which agreement in faith, sharing in prayer, worship and pastoral care, and co-operation in mission all play their part and recommends to the Churches in their own particular situations that they progress from mere coexistence through to co-operation, mutual commitment or covenant and on to full visible unity with all their brothers and sisters in Christ.

(See further paras. 80-108 of the Report on **Ecumenical Relations.***)*

18 THE ANGLICAN COMMUNION: IDENTITY AND AUTHORITY

This Conference:

1 Resolves that the new Inter-Anglican Theological and Doctrinal Commission (or a specially appointed Inter-Anglican Commission) be asked to undertake as a matter of urgency a further exploration of the meaning and nature of communion; with particular reference to the doctrine of the Trinity, the unity and order of the Church, and the unity and community of humanity.

2 (a) Urges that encouragement be given to a developing collegial role for the Primates' Meeting under the presidency of the Archbishop of Canterbury, so that the Primates' Meeting is able to exercise an enhanced responsibility in offering guidance on doctrinal, moral and pastoral matters.

(b) Recommends that in the appointment of any future Archbishop of Canterbury, the Crown Appointments Commission be asked to bring the Primates of the Communion into the process of consultation.

3 Resolves that the Lambeth Conference as a conference of bishops of the Anglican Communion should continue in the future, at appropriate intervals.

4 Recommends that Regional Conferences of the Anglican Communion should meet between Lambeth Conferences as and when the Region concerned believes it to be appropriate; and in the event of these Regional Conferences being called, it should be open to the region concerned to make them representative of clergy and laity as well as bishops.

5 Recommends that the ACC continue to fulfil the functions defined in its constitution (developed as a consequence of Resolution 69 of the 1968 Lambeth Conference) and affirmed by the evaluation process reported to ACC-6 (see *Bonds of Affection,* pp.23-27); in particular to continue its consultative, advisory, liaison and communication roles within the Communion (and to do so in close co-operation with the Primates' Meeting).

6 Requests the Archbishop of Canterbury, with all the Primates of the Anglican Communion, to appoint an Advisory Body on Prayer Books of the Anglican Communion. The Body should be entrusted with the task of offer-

ing encouragement, support and advice to Churches of the Communion in their work of liturgical revision as well as facilitating mutual consultation concerning, and review of, their Prayer Books as they are developed with a view to ensuring:

(a) the public reading of the Scriptures in a language understood by the people and instruction of the whole people of God in the scriptural faith by means of sermons and catechisms;

(b) the use of the two sacraments ordained by Christ, baptism with water in the threefold Name, and Holy Communion with bread and wine and explicit intention to obey our Lord's command;

(c) the use of forms of episcopal ordination to each of the three orders by prayer with the laying-on of hands;

(d) the public recitation and teaching of the Apostles' and Nicene Creeds; and

(e) the use of other liturgical expressions of unity in faith and life by which the whole people of God is nurtured and upheld, with continuing awareness of ecumenical liturgical developments.

EXPLANATORY NOTE

On 1 above   If there is the possibility of ordination of women bishops in some Provinces, it will throw into sharper focus the present impaired nature of communion. It is a matter of urgency that we have a further theological enquiry into and reflection on the meaning of communion in a Trinitarian context for the Anglican Communion. Such an enquiry should relate to ecumenical discussions exploring similar issues. This, more than structures, will provide a theological framework in which differences can be handled.

On 2 above   We see an enhanced role for the Primates as a key to a growth of inter-dependence within the Communion. We do not see any inter-Anglican jurisdiction as possible or desirable; an inter-Anglican synodical structure would be virtually unworkable and highly expensive. A collegial role for the Primates by contrast could easily be developed, and their collective judgement and advice would carry considerable weight.

If this is so, it is neither improper nor out of place to suggest that part of the consultative process prior to the appointment of a future Archbishop of Canterbury should be in consultation with the Primates.

On 3 above   We are convinced that there is considerable value in the bishops of the Anglican Communion meeting as bishops, both in terms of mutual understanding and as an effective agent of interdependence.

On 4 above   Regional issues need regional solutions. Regional conferences can also provide for wider representation.

On 5 above   We value the present work of the ACC. We do not see, however, that it ought to move beyond its present advisory role.

217

On 6 above   Concern for how the Church celebrates the sacraments of unity and with what consequences is a central expression of episcopal care and pastoral oversight in the Church of God. As bishops of the Anglican Communion we have a particular responsibility for securing those elements in worship which nurture our identity and unity in Christ and which therefore have an authority for us as Anglicans. (A parallel but significantly different resolution has been proposed by the Anglican Consultative Council: Resolution 12 of ACC-7.)

(See further paras. 113-152 of the Report on **Dogmatic and Pastoral Concerns**.*)*

19   DRAFT COMMON DECLARATION

This Conference resolves that the Inter-Anglican Theological and Doctrinal Commission consider paragraph 20 of the paper 'Instruments of Communion and Decision-Making' (Draft Common Declaration) and report to the Primates' Meeting.

(See further para. 129 of the Report on **Dogmatic and Pastoral Concerns** *and Appendix 5.)*

20   INTER-FAITH DIALOGUE

This Conference commends dialogue with people of other faiths as part of Christian discipleship and mission, with the understanding that:
(1)   dialogue begins when people meet each other;
(2)   dialogue depends upon mutual understanding, mutual respect and mutual trust;
(3)   dialogue makes it possible to share in service to the community;
(4)   dialogue becomes a medium of authentic witness.

Acknowledging that such dialogue, which is not a substitute for evangelism, may be a contribution in helping people of different faiths to make common cause in resolving issues of peace-making, social justice and religious liberty, we further commend each Province to initiate such dialogue in partnership with other Christian Churches where appropriate.

(See further paras. 55-58 of the Report on **Dogmatic and Pastoral Concerns**.*)*

21   INTER-FAITH DIALOGUE: JEWISH/CHRISTIAN/MUSLIM

This Conference:

1   Commends the document *Jews, Christians and Muslims: The Way of*

Dialogue for study and encourages the Churches of the Anglican Communion to engage in dialogue with Jews and Muslims on the basis of understanding, affirmation and sharing *illustrated* in it.

2   Recommends that the Anglican Consultative Council gives consideration to the setting up of an Inter-Faith Committee, which Committee, in the interest of cost and in practical pursuance of our commitment to ecumenism, would work in close co-operation with the Inter-Faith Dialogue Committee of the WCC; and that this Committee, amongst its other work, establishes a common approach to people of other faiths on a Communion-wide basis and appoints working parties to draw up more detailed guidelines for relationships with Judaism and Islam and other faiths as appropriate.

3   Recommends that Provinces initiate talks wherever possible on a tripartite basis, with both Jews and Muslims.

4   Urges Provinces to support those institutions which are helping Christians towards a more informed understanding of Judaism and Islam.

(See further paras. 63 and 64 of the Report on **Dogmatic and Pastoral Concerns** *and Appendix 6.)*

22   CHRIST AND CULTURE

This Conference:

(a)   Recognises that culture is the context in which people find their identity.

(b)   Affirms that God's love extends to people of every culture and that the Gospel judges every culture according to the Gospel's own criteria of truth, challenging some aspects of culture while endorsing and transforming others for the benefit of the Church and society.

(c)   Urges the Church everywhere to work at expressing the unchanging Gospel of Christ in words, actions, names, customs, liturgies, which communicate relevantly in each contemporary society.

(See further paras. 23-40 of the Report on **Dogmatic and Pastoral Concerns.***)*

23   FREEDOM OF RELIGIOUS ACTIVITY

This Conference calls upon all governments to uphold religious freedom, including freedom of worship and freedom to teach and evangelise, as a fundamental human right, the denial of which threatens all other liberties.

EXPLANATORY NOTE

We are concerned for minority religious groups, but have a special concern for those in Islamic States.

(See further para. 68 of the Report on **Dogmatic and Pastoral Concerns.***)*

24 PALESTINE/ISRAEL

This Conference, saddened by the present suffering in the West Bank and Gaza Strip:

1   Affirms the importance of the Church in the exercise of its prophetic role by standing on the side of the oppressed in their struggle for justice, and by promoting justice, peace and reconciliation for all peoples in the region.

2   Affirms the existence of the state of Israel and its right to recognised and secure borders, as well as the civic and human rights of all those who live within its borders.

3   Affirms the right of the Palestinians to self-determination, including choice of their own representatives and the establishment of their own state.

4   Supports the convening of an international conference over Palestine/ Israel under the auspices of the UN and based on all the UN resolutions in relation to this conflict, to which all parties of the conflict be invited.

5   Commits itself to continued prayer for Israelis and Palestinians, for Muslim, Jew and Christian, for the achievement of justice, peace and reconciliation for all.

(See further paras. 36 and 48 of the Report on **Christianity and the Social Order.***)*

25 IRAN

This Conference, recognising the positive development of recent events in Iran, and in the light of a declared policy of religious tolerance in that land, respectfully requests the Islamic Republic of Iran to facilitate a positive response to the many requests, sent on behalf of the Diocese of Iran, the Primates of the Anglican Communion, and the President Bishop of the Episcopal Church in Jerusalem and the Middle East, concerning all the claims of the Church in Iran.

26 CHURCH AND POLYGAMY

This Conference upholds monogamy as God's plan, and as the ideal relationship of love between husband and wife; nevertheless recommends that a polygamist who responds to the Gospel and wishes to join the Anglican Church may be baptised and confirmed with his believing wives and children on the following conditions:

(1)   that the polygamist shall promise not to marry again as long as any of his wives at the time of his conversion are alive;

(2)   that the receiving of such a polygamist has the consent of the local Anglican community;

(3)   that such a polygamist shall not be compelled to put away any of his wives on account of the social deprivation they would suffer;

(4)   and recommends that Provinces where the Churches face problems of polygamy are encouraged to share information of their pastoral approach to Christians who become polygamists so that the most appropriate way of disciplining and pastoring them can be found, and that the ACC be requested to facilitate the sharing of that information.

27   WAR, VIOLENCE AND JUSTICE

This Conference:

1 (a)   Reaffirms the statement of the 1930 Lambeth Conference that war as a method of settling international disputes is incompatible with the teaching and example of Our Lord Jesus Christ;

   (b)   Affirms also that there is no true peace without justice, and reformation and transformation of unjust systems is an essential element of our biblical hope;

2 (a)   Supports those who choose the way of non-violence as being the way of Our Lord, including direct non-violent action, civil disobedience and conscientious objection, and pays tribute to those who in recent years have kept before the world the growing threat of militarism;

   (b)   Understands those who, after exhausting all other ways, choose the way of armed struggle as the only way to justice, whilst drawing attention to the dangers and injustices possible in such action itself; and

3   Encourages Provinces and dioceses to seek out those secular and religious agencies working for justice and reconciliation, and to make common cause with them, to ensure that the voice of the oppressed is heard and a response is made so that further violence is averted.

(See further paras. 98-126 of the Report on **Christianity and the Social Order.***)*

28 SEXUAL ABUSE

This Conference:

1   Expresses deep concern about the frequency of domestic violence and the sexual abuse of children.

2   Asks Christian leaders to be explicit about the sinfulness of violence and sexual abuse whether of children or adults, and to devise means of providing support for the victims and perpetrators of such exploitation to enable them to break the cycle of abuse.

3   Reaffirms the traditional biblical teaching on the value of the human person who, being made in the image of God, is neither to be exploited nor abused.

(See further paras. 156-160 of the Report on **Christianity and the Social Order**. *See also Resolution 13.)*

29 ACQUIRED IMMUNE DEFICIENCY SYNDROME (AIDS)

This Conference:

recognising (a) that the disease AIDS poses a catastrophic threat to every part of the world, and (b) that unless preventative measures are taken, the disease can spread rapidly (though the long latency period may mask its presence, thus giving a false sense of security), asks bishops to accept their responsibility to witness to Christ's compassion and care, in response to this crisis, by giving a lead in:

1   The promotion of, and co-operation with, educational programmes both of Church and State concerned with the cause and prevention of the disease, in a loving and non-judgemental spirit towards those who suffer.

2   The development of diocesan strategies
   (a) to train and support pastoral helpers;
   (b) to give direct personal support to those living with AIDS;
   (c) to identify and try to resolve the social problems leading to and arising from the disease;
   (d) to reaffirm the traditional biblical teaching that sexual intercourse is an act of total commitment which belongs properly within a permanent married relationship.

3   The need to work together
   (a) to encourage global co-operation between Churches, governments and non-government agencies in the fight against the disease;
   (b) to develop ways in which the Churches can share information and resources;

(c) to press where necessary for political action;

(d) to promote prayer for all concerned, not forgetting those active in research to discover a cure.

(See further paras. 161-194 of the Report on **Christianity and the Social Order**.*)*

31 VOICELESS MINORITY

This Conference conscious of the work in many dioceses with deprived minorities in developed, affluent countries, such as native Americans and Canadians, Australian aborigines and Islanders, ethnic Koreans in Japan, and black urban communities in Britain, asks the relevant Anglican provinces to support work among such minorities who have difficulty in making their plight known in national and world forums.

(See further paras. 55-65 of the Report on **Christianity and the Social Order**.*)*

32 WORLD PEACE

This Conference:

1   Welcomes recent new directions in Soviet policy as a constructive contribution to world peace;

2   Urges the leaders of the Western nations to review their foreign and defence policies to allow for new opportunities for co-operation with the Soviet Union;

3   Appeals to all governments with nuclear forces to cease the production of nuclear weapons and to plan together an international programme for the dismantling of such weapons;

4   Urges the major world powers to recognise and respect the self-determination of smaller states and not to penalise them when their decisions conflict with the foreign policies of these major powers.

(See further paras. 122-126 of the Report on **Christianity and the Social Order**.*)*

33 HUMAN RIGHTS

This Conference:

1   Endorses the UN Universal Declaration of Human Rights, and asks the Provinces of the Anglican Communion to support all who are working for its implementation.

2 Commends to all Churches the good practice of observing 'One World Week' in proximity to United Nations Day, October 24th, as a means of highlighting human interdependence and the need to eliminate exploitation.

3 Urges the Church to speak out against:

(a) torture, used as a cruel, inhuman and degrading treatment of prisoners, burning down of people's homes, granaries, and the confiscation of livestock and denial by governments of supplies of medical facilities and relief food by international organizations to people in areas of armed conflict;

(b) all governments who practise capital punishment and encourages them to find alternative ways of sentencing offenders so that the divine dignity of every human being is respected and yet justice is pursued;

(c) the incarceration of prisoners of conscience, challenging governments to search for treatment and punishment of convicted persons in accordance with internationally accepted standards;

(d) any denial of the principle that a person is innocent until proven guilty by due, fair and impartial procedures of law.

4 Commends the work of various international human rights organisations campaigning to support the freedoms set out in the Universal Declaration of Human Rights, and their work on behalf of human rights activists throughout the world who are persecuted for their defence of those fundamental freedoms.

(See further paras. 36-50 of the Report on **Christianity and the Social Order.***)*

34 MARRIAGE AND FAMILY

This Conference:

1 Reaffirming the 1978 Lambeth statement on marriage and the family, calls the Churches of the Anglican Communion to ministries that prepare couples for marriage, sustain them throughout their lives together with the spiritual, pastoral, and community life of the Church and, in the face of increasing stresses, encourage and support them with the resources of the Church as an extended family.

2 Recognises that the same range of pressures no less affect clergy marriages and families and recommends that each diocese identify some means of providing confidential counselling and support services for clergy families.

3 Noting the gap between traditional Christian teaching on pre-marital sex, and the lifestyles being adopted by many people today, both within and

outside the Church:

(a) calls on Provinces and dioceses to adopt a caring and pastoral attitude to such people;

(b) reaffirms the traditional biblical teaching that sexual intercourse is an act of total commitment which belongs properly within a permanent married relationship;

(c) in response to the International Conference of Young Anglicans in Belfast, urges Provinces and dioceses to plan with young people programmes to explore issues such as pre-marital sex in the light of traditional Christian values.

4 Recognising the political, economic and social pressures on family life:

(a) affirms the family in its various forms, as the fundamental institution of human community;

(b) calls our Churches to the development of support systems for families at every level within the Church and to the advocacy of public policies supportive of family life;

(c) commends in particular the developing family network inaugurated by the Anglican Consultative Council and encourages participation in the continuing educational and pastoral work of the network;

(d) recognises that these pressures serve to diminish the economic well-being and status of women, welcomes the World Council of Churches 'Decade for Solidarity with Women', and encourages dioceses to consider how they might through their theological, structural and pastoral approaches help to achieve a fuller recognition of the contribution and status of women in the Church and society.

5 Affirms that effective ministries to families and to individuals, who are thereby enabled to experience the Church as an extended family, are signs of life and hope and are central to evangelism that proclaims and models the oneness that Christ wills for all people.

(See further paras. 127-152 of the Report on **Christianity and the Social Order.***)*

35 CONCERNS OF SOUTH PACIFIC ISLANDS

This Conference, noting that in Churches of the South Pacific there is deep pain and anxiety about many tiny island sovereign nations in the region regarding the abuse and exploitation of their lands and seas by powerful external political and economic forces:

1 Affirms the desire of many indigenous peoples in the region to self-determination and to be in control of their own affairs and especially of the use of the vital resources of their lands and seas.

2   Supports them in their opposition to the testing of nuclear weapons, the dumping of nuclear waste and the establishment of further military bases in the region, and calls on France and the superpowers to cease these activities forthwith.

3   Further supports them in their resistance to all those powerful states and multinational corporations who, for immediate economic and political gain, rape and destroy the forests, fisheries and mineral deposits in the region.

4   Wishes to be identified with the stand of the Churches in Australia, New Zealand and Japan in support of these concerns and requests the member Churches of the Anglican Communion to make these matters known in their own countries and congregations as a matter of urgency, to pray for them and to press their governments for action.

(See further para. 50 of the Report on **Christianity and the Social Order.***)*

36   POVERTY AND DEBT

This Conference:

1   Calls attention to the life-and-death urgency of the problems of world poverty.

2   Salutes the courage and solidarity of poor people who, at great personal cost, are struggling to achieve their own liberation from poverty and oppression.

3   Calls for an international, co-operating settlement, negotiated by both industrial and developing countries, that will establish policies to reduce interest charges and the level of indebtedness, based on shared responsibility for the world debt and in accordance with Christian and humanitarian principles of economic justice and social and ecological interdependence.

4   Calls on national governments, transnational corporations, the International Monetary Fund and the World Bank together, to re-examine all principles governing trade relationships, the transfer of technology and resources and all loan and aid policies in order to improve the economic viability and local autonomy of developing countries.

5   Requests these bodies to consider these and other creative ways of involving the global economy over time by

    (a) (i) correcting demand imbalances;

        (ii) reducing protectionism;

      (iii) stabilising exchange rates;

      (iv) increasing resource transfers;

    (b) offering relief from debt incurred with commercial banks in ways that will not leave debtor economies vulnerable to foreign manipulation, by

(i)   lending directly to developing countries at reduced and subsidised interest rates;

(ii)   improved rescheduling of existing debt repayments;

(iii)   debt conversion arrangements;

(iv)   establishing a multilateral body to co-ordinate debt relief;

(c) offering relief from official debts incurred with the World Bank and the International Monetary Fund through

    (i)   improved rescheduling of existing debt repayment;

    (ii)   lending on conditions oriented to development objectives;

    (iii)   refraining from making demands on debtor countries which would endanger the fabric of their national life or cause further dislocation to their essential human services.

(See further para. 73 of the Report on **Christianity and the Social Order.***)*

37 LATIN AMERICA

This Conference:

1   Affirms that self-determination is a fundamental human right based on the freedom which God has given to us, and to which every person, nation and region is entitled.

2   Commends and supports the Church in Latin America as it seeks ways and means of helping their people to develop a higher standard of living and to motivate their governments to provide greater freedom and justice for their people.

3   Urges those governments whose military policies inhibit self-determination to refrain from unjust political manipulation of Latin American countries and from military interference in their lives.

4   Urges the lifting of the sanctions imposed upon Nicaragua, Panama and Cuba by the United States of America.

5   Urges the industrial countries of the world to cease all military aid to combatants in Latin American countries and to give them economic and humanitarian assistance so as to end the suffering of the people.

6   Commends the peace effort of the Central American countries and the support given by other Latin American nations.

38 NAMIBIA

This Conference, bearing in mind the tenth anniversary of the United Nations Resolution 435, and being deeply aware of the protracted suffering of the Namibian people at the hands of the South African regime:

1 Expresses support for the people in their struggle for independence, and pays tribute to the Anglican Diocese and the Council of Churches in Namibia for their courageous witness;

2 Calls on the South African Government
   (a) to withdraw from Angola;
   (b) to implement Resolution 435.

3 Asks the Anglican Provinces of Canada, the United Kingdom and the United States of America to press their governments to fulfil their obligations as members of the Contact Group of nations.

39 SOUTH AFRICA

This Conference:

1 *Reaffirms* its belief that the system of apartheid in South Africa is evil and especially repugnant because of the cruel way a tyrannical racist system is being upheld in the name of the Christian faith.

2 *Condemns* the detention of children without just cause.

3 *Calls* upon the Churches to press their governments to

   (a) bring the maximum pressure to bear on the South African regime in order to promote a genuine process of change towards the establishment of democratic political structures in a unified state;

   (b) institute forms of sanction calculated to have the maximum effect in bringing an end to the evil dispensation, and in establishing a just peace among all citizens;

   (c) give direct aid to anti-apartheid organisations within South Africa particularly with a view to assisting the unemployed and persecuted;

   (d) give effective practical support to the Frontline States in order to ensure their economic survival and welfare, as well as their military protection from the threat of South African aggression;

   (e) push for the release of Nelson Mandela and all other political prisoners and detainees in South Africa, and the unbanning of organisations like the African National Congress and the Pan Africanist Congress which represent the majority of citizens;

   (f) give direct moral and humanitarian support to such organisations in the pursuit of a just order which reflects Gospel values and urges the Churches to ensure that none of their own financial resources is used to support the present regime in South Africa and for this purpose to disinvest from all corporations which have a significant financial stake in South Africa (ACC-7, Resolution 24.)

4   *Believes* that to work for a just peace in South Africa is to work for the true liberation of all peoples of the region, black and white.

NOTE

The Lambeth Conference agreed to the request by Bishop D. Sengulane (Diocese of Lebombo, Mozambique) that he be dissociated from this motion.

40   ENVIRONMENT, MILITARISM, JUSTICE AND PEACE

This Conference:

1   Identifies four inter-related areas in which the misuse of people or resources pose a threat to the life system of the planet, namely

(a) unjust distribution of the world's wealth,

(b) social injustice within nations,

(c) the rise of militarism,

(d) irreversible damage to the environment,

and therefore

2   Calls upon each Province and diocese to devise a programme of study, reflection and action in which the following elements should play a part:

(a) as a matter of urgency, the giving of information to our people of what is happening to our environment, and to encourage them to see stewardship of God's earth for the care of our neighbours as a necessary part of Christian discipleship and a Christian contribution to citizenship;

(b) actively to support, by public statement and in private dialogue, the engagement of governments, transnational corporations, management and labour in an examination of what their decisions are doing to our people, and our land, air and water;

(c) opposition to the increase in the arms trade; questioning both excessive expenditure of scarce resources on weapons and trade policies which look upon arms sales as a legitimate source of increased export revenue;

(d) the encouragement of Christians to re-examine the currently accepted economic policies which operate to the disadvantage of those with less bargaining power at every level from international to personal, and to use God's gifts of technology for the benefit of all;

(e) the critical examination of the exercise of power, first within congregations and all other church bodies, and then in secular institutions which affect the lives of all. Insofar as the aim is to achieve a just and sustainable society worldwide, priority must be given to those modes which nurture people's gifts and evoke responsible participation rather than those which dominate and exclude.

3 (a) Commends, in general, the participation by every Province in the WCC's programme for 'Justice, Peace and the Integrity of Creation';

(b) Urges Churches, congregations and individual Christians to actively support all other agencies which share this urgent concern. In particular we commend a widespread study of the United Nations report *Our Common Future* and a participation by church bodies in the local responses it requires;

(c) Recommends that, in view of the resolutions passed by ACC-7, information concerning local needs and initiatives be shared throughout Provinces, possibly by extending the terms of reference for the existing Peace and Justice Network;

(d) Encourages people everywhere to make changes, personal and corporate, in their attitudes and lifestyle, recognising that wholeness of living requires a right relationship with God, one's neighbour, and creation.

EXPLANATORY NOTE

Some effects, like famine, can be recognised immediately; some, like pollution, are a creeping crisis which is nonetheless deadly. These major threats to the earth's future cannot be averted by action in one region of the world alone, nor by focusing on a single issue. Everything connects.

*(See further paras. 36-50, 81-97 and 122-126 of the Report on **Christianity and the Social Order**.)*

41 TRAINING OF BISHOPS

This Conference:

Congratulates African Provinces for having made provisions for the training of newly consecrated bishops as recommended by Lambeth 1978 (Resolution 19).

Resolves that every Province implement programmes of initial preparation and in-service training for the episcopate, and accordingly that:

1 A duration of one month, at least, be set aside for preparation, which should include instruction regarding the tasks and functions of a bishop, finance and management control; such training being in the language and culture of the bishop concerned.

2 After six years in office, all bishops should be encouraged to have a

period of sabbatical leave for study and refreshment; and that financial support for such a period should be available from appropriate sources within the Province concerned.

3   Where appropriate, preparation, training and support should also be made available to the spouse.

4   In view of the stress factor within the life of the bishop, bishops should present themselves for a medical examination at least once a year.

(See further paras. 160-174 of the Report on **Mission and Ministry.***)*

42   MINISTRY OF LAY PEOPLE

This Conference recommends that Provinces and dioceses encourage, train, equip and send out lay people for evangelism and ministry.

(See further paras. 87-110 of the Report on **Mission and Ministry.***)*

43   DECADE OF EVANGELISM

This Conference, recognising that evangelism is the primary task given to the Church, asks each Province and diocese of the Anglican Communion, in co-operation with other Christians, to make the closing years of this millennium a 'Decade of Evangelism' with a renewed and united emphasis on making Christ known to the people of his world.

(See further paras. 14-23 of the Report on **Mission and Ministry.***)*

44   EVANGELISM IN THE ANGLICAN COMMUNION

This Conference:

1   Calls for a shift to a dynamic missionary emphasis going beyond care and nurture to proclamation and service;
and therefore

2   Accepts the challenge this presents to diocesan and local church structures and patterns of worship and ministry, and looks to God for a fresh movement of the Spirit in prayer, outgoing love and evangelism in obedience to our Lord's command.

(See further paras. 10-13 of the Report on **Mission and Ministry.***)*

45 MISSION AND MINISTRY OF THE WHOLE CHURCH

This Conference:

1 Acknowledging that God through the Holy Spirit is bringing about a revolution in terms of the total ministry of all the baptised, thus enriching the Church and making Christ known to men and women as the hope of the world;

2 Urges each bishop with his diocese to take the necessary steps to provide opportunities, training and support to ensure that this shared style of ministry becomes a reality.

*(See further paras. 70-75 of the Report on **Mission and Ministry**.)*

46 MINISTRY OF ALL BISHOPS

This Conference resolves that each Province re-examine the position and work of all bishops active in full-time diocesan work, including those known in the various Provinces as suffragan, assistant, assisting, area or regional bishops, to ensure that all bishops have a true *episcope* of jurisdiction and pastoral care and are seen as belonging fully to the local college of bishops.

*(See further paras. 156 and 157 of the Report on **Mission and Ministry**.)*

46A MINISTRY OF ALL BISHOPS

This Conference resolves that each Province re-examine the principle that all bishops active in full-time diocesan work be made full members, with seat, voice and vote, of all provincial, national and international gatherings of Anglican bishops.

*(See further para. 157(b) of the Report on **Mission and Ministry**.)*

47 LITURGICAL FREEDOM

This Conference resolves that each Province should be free, subject to essential universal Anglican norms of worship, and to a valuing of traditional liturgical materials, to seek that expression of worship which is appropriate to its Christian people in their cultural context.

*(See further paras. 181-186 of the Report on **Mission and Ministry**.)*

48   MISSION TO YOUTH

This Conference:

1   Encourages every diocese to conduct an evaluation of existing mission and ministry among its youth,* as far as possible in co-operation with other Churches, which should include an examination of the current nature and extent of youth involvement in the life of the diocese and Provinces and at every level.

2   Suggests that this should include the following questions to be investigated:

(a)   What occasions or venues for meeting are provided for young people who have no contact whatever with the Church or the Christian faith?

(b)   What proportion of diocesan and parish budgets is set aside for youth ministry, compared with other activities?

(c)   What relationships exist between the diocese and its clergy on the one hand, and the local schools and state education authorities on the other, if any?

(d)   How are the dioceses and parishes making use of the skills and gifts of local Christian teachers, youth leaders, young people who have a ministry among their peers, and what opportunities for encouragement and training in Christian witness are being provided?

* Known elsewhere as a 'Mission Audit': see ACC-6, Resolution 11, p.60, for suggested Guidelines.

(See further paras. 32-35 and 75 of the Report on **Mission and Ministry.***)*

49   SUPPORT FOR FRENCH-SPEAKING DIOCESES

This Conference draws the attention of the whole Anglican Communion to the problems faced by the Province of Burundi, Rwanda and Zaire and other French-speaking dioceses, so that they can be supported by their Partners-in-Mission and other parts of the Communion with an aim of helping them to obtain self-sufficiency in fulfilling their mission in terms of training manpower, transport and financial support.

(See further para. 159 of the Report on **Mission and Ministry.***)*

51   ELECTION AND RETIREMENT OF BISHOPS AND ARCHBISHOPS

This Conference:

1   Urges all Provinces to ensure that their provincial provisions for election

and retirement of bishops and archbishops are unambiguous and are adhered to.

2   Recommends that, where problems arise regarding implementation of such provisions, and where such problems cannot be solved at the provincial level, the Regional Conferences of Primates should be called upon to advise, and if such Conferences fail to solve the problem, the matter is referred to the meeting of the Primates of the Anglican Communion.

52   PRIMATES' MEETING AND ACC

This Conference requests the Primates' Meeting and the Anglican Consultative Council to give urgent attention to implementing the hope expressed at Lambeth 1978 (and as confirmed by recent Provincial responses) that both bodies would work in the very closest contact.

53   ANGLICAN COMMUNICATIONS

This Conference:

(a)   Directs the ACC to explore the establishment of a telecommunication network linked to every Province in order to improve the communication and consultation process throughout the Anglican Communion and to ensure that accurate information is available to the Churches.

(b)   Urges the creation of a telecommunication centre for the Communion through the sharing of resources between Provinces and building on the experience of the Inter-Anglican Information Network (IAIN).

54   INTER-ANGLICAN BUDGET

This Conference, recognising that there is a common Secretariat for meetings of the Primates, the Lambeth Conference, and the ACC, endorses the concept of an inter-Anglican budget and requests the ACC to consult with the Provinces about the best way in which this is to be achieved.

EXPLANATORY NOTE

Resolution 34 of ACC-7 asks for a response from the Lambeth Conference on the subject of an inter-Anglican budget about which Provinces are being consulted. In addition resolutions will be passed by the Lambeth Conference which have financial consequences and it is desirable to remind the Conference that when they ask for work to be done the consequential bill falls upon the Provinces.

55   CONFERENCE TRANSLATION

This Conference warmly appreciates arrangements made for simultaneous translation of Conference deliberations into French, Spanish, Japanese and Swahili, and requests that the final Conference report be translated into these Conference languages.

56   REFUGEES

This Conference commends to the members of the Communion the report of the ACC Refugee and Migrant Ministry network meeting held at Harare for study and action.

(See further paras. 40 and 41 of the Report on **Mission and Ministry**.*)*

58   CIVIC AND LAND RIGHTS FOR INDIGENOUS PEOPLE OF THE AMERICAS

This Conference supports all efforts being made for the procuring of land and civic rights for native indigenous people of the Americas, specially in the light of the forthcoming celebrations of the 500th anniversary of the arrival of Columbus in the New World in 1992.

EXPLANATORY NOTE

In 1992 a great celebration is being proposed to commemorate the arrival of Europeans and their culture, specially the Spanish Conquest. That arrival meant the destruction of many indigenous cultures and peoples as the Spanish, British, French, Portugese and Dutch colonizers arrived. Efforts are being made to highlight this suffering. Traditionally, Anglicans have taken the side of the Indians throughout the Americas and a lot of our work has been to improve their lot.

This resolution is backed by:

The Primate of the Southern Cone of South America
The Bishop of Honduras (ECUSA)
The Bishop of Guatemala (ECUSA)
The Bishop of Western Mexico (ECUSA)
The Bishop of South Dakota (ECUSA)
The Rt Revd Robert Townshend, Suffragan Bishop of Huron (Canada)
The Primate of Brazil
The Rt Revd Martiniano Garcia-Montiel, Suffragan Bishop of South and Central Mexico (ECUSA)

(See further paras. 40 and 92 of the Report on **Christianity and the Social Order**.*)*

235

59 EXTRA-PROVINCIAL DIOCESES

This Conference requests the Primates' Meeting and ACC to give urgent consideration to the situation of the Extra-Provincial dioceses, that they may be fully part of the structures of the Anglican Communion.

60 RECOGNITION OF SAINTS

This Conference:

1 Welcomes the proposal by Africa Region that the Anglican Communion should recognise men and women who have lived godly lives as saints by including them in the calendars of the Churches for remembrance; and

2 Recommends that the Anglican Consultative Council discusses this matter and advises the Provinces on the procedure to follow in recognition of such saints.

61 ISLAMIC FUNDAMENTALISM

This Conference:

1 Expresses concern that the emergence of Islamic religious fundamentalism has resulted in serious violation of fundamental human rights, including the right of religious belief, practice and propagation, as well as destruction of property of Christian Churches in such places as Northern Nigeria and the Sudan.

2 Urges the ACC to find ways and means of bringing these concerns to international Islamic organisations and the United Nations, and encourages dialogue with countries where pursuit of Islamic religious fundamentalism has led to such violations of human rights.

EXPLANATORY NOTE

This is a real issue in Sudan and Nigeria.

62 PEACE IN THE SUDAN

This Conference:

1 Commends the effort of the Christian Churches in the Sudan in seeking peace and reconciliation between southern and northern Sudan.

2 Urges the government of the Sudan to take the initiative in beginning negotiations with the Sudan People's Liberation Army as a first step towards peace in the Sudan, and further

3   Urges the Sudanese Government to consider accepting a third party to initiate peace talks, e.g. World Council of Churches and the All Africa Conference of Churches.

63   SHARÎ'A LAW IN THE SUDAN

This Conference:

1   Notes with great concern that the Government of the Sudan wishes to reintroduce Sharî'a Law and impose it upon the people of the Sudan.

2   Respectfully requests the Government of the Sudan to reconsider its decision on this matter and replace Sharî'a Law with some other more humane legislation for punishing offenders.

64   HUMAN RIGHTS FOR THOSE OF HOMOSEXUAL ORIENTATION

This Conference:

1   Reaffirms the statement of the Lambeth Conference of 1978 on homosexuality, recognising the continuing need in the next decade for 'deep and dispassionate study of the question of homosexuality, which would take seriously both the teaching of Scripture and the results of scientific and medical research'.

2   Urges such study and reflection to take account of biological, genetic and psychological research being undertaken by other agencies, and the socio-cultural factors that lead to the different attitudes in the Provinces of our Communion.

3   Calls each Province to reassess, in the light of such study and because of our concern for human rights, its care for and attitude towards persons of homosexual orientation.

(See further paras. 153-155 of the Report on **Christianity and the Social Order.***)*

65   MISSIONS TO SEAMEN

This Conference thanks God for the worldwide Missions to Seamen, which began its work in 1856. It supports and endorses the remarkable way in which the Society has adapted its ministry to changed circumstances, acknowledging the fact that there is no part of the Church which has greater ecumenical involvement and experience; that it is deeply involved in dialogue with people of other faiths every day; and that through the Centre for Seafarers' Rights and through almost every member of staff, it is daily involved in issues of social justice. The Conference, encouraged by the appointment of Liaison Bishops throughout the Anglican Communion, accepts the ministry and mission of the Society as the mission of the Church to all seafarers, regardless of creed, class or colour.

66 HANDBOOK OF ANGLICAN SOURCES

This Conference encourages the publication of the proposed Handbook of Anglican Sources, which will reflect the catholicity of our tradition from the beginning and the concerns of the worldwide Anglican Communion today.

EXPLANATORY NOTE

Plans are in hand for SPCK to publish such a handbook, to be edited by J. Robert Wright and G.R. Evans, with a consultative editorial board drawn from the Anglican Provinces. It will involve no cost to the Church. It will be useful for encouraging understanding of Anglicanism, both among Anglicans and people of other traditions.

67 YOUTH NETWORK

This Conference:

1 Endorses the recent developments that have taken place concerning the youth of the Anglican Communion, particularly the establishment of a youth network and the holding of the first International Conference of Young Anglicans in Belfast in January 1988.

2 Urges each diocese to ensure that the momentum created by these developments is continued.

68 THE GULF AND LEBANON

This Conference:

1 Views with grave concern the continued conflict between Iran and Iraq, with its very dangerous consequences not only for all the Gulf states and for the Middle East as a whole, but also for the world at large.

2 Welcomes Iran's acceptance of Security Council Resolution 598 and looks to Iraq to honour its commitment to do so, and calls upon all countries which have influence to use it to bring an end to the conflict on that basis.

3 Condemns the use of chemical weapons in any circumstances and urges

that any further use by any country should immediately be met by punitive sanctions; and calls upon the international community to take steps to prevent the sale and supply of such chemical weapons.

4   Urges that all countries involved should respect property rights and contractual obligations.

5   Recognises that the grief of the families of hostages is universal, knowing no boundaries of religion or nationality.

6   Conveys its deep sympathy to the families of all hostages and to all the people of Lebanon who have suffered for so long the brutal savagery of civil war.

7   Calls upon all states with influence to use their good offices to secure the release of all hostages in Lebanon of whatever nationality; and

8   Prays earnestly for peace and tranquillity in the region.

69   ADMISSION TO COMMUNION

This Conference requests all Provinces to consider the theological and pastoral issues involved in the admission of those baptised but unconfirmed to communion (as set out in the Report of ACC-7), and to report their findings to the ACC.

EXPLANATORY NOTE

This resolution does what ACC-7 expected to be done, and is in line with a draft statement from 'Mission and Ministry'. Whilst it comes as a private member's resolution, it comes with the good will of the 'Mission and Ministry' Section.

(See further para. 194 of the Report on **Mission and Ministry***.)*

71   1988 LAMBETH CALL TO PRAYER

This Conference calls upon individuals, prayer groups, congregations, devotional organisations, and Religious Communities to give renewed emphasis to the work of prayer. We call upon the bishops of the Anglican Communion to give a strong lead in the ministry of prayer in all its forms, so that we may know God's will for our time and be empowered for the mission of the Lord Jesus Christ.

EXPLANATORY NOTE

A Call to Prayer has been issued by the last two Lambeth Conferences. This encouragement for prayer is even more essential as we meet the challenges of the coming years in the Anglican Communion.

72 EPISCOPAL RESPONSIBILITIES AND DIOCESAN BOUNDARIES

This Conference:

1 Reaffirms its unity in the historical position of respect for diocesan boundaries and the authority of bishops within these boundaries; and in light of the above

2 Affirms that it is deemed inappropriate behaviour for any bishop or priest of this Communion to exercise episcopal or pastoral ministry within another diocese without first obtaining the permission and invitation of the ecclesial authority thereof.

EXPLANATORY NOTE

With the number of issues that could threaten our unity it seems fair that we should speak of our mutual respect for one another, and the positions we hold, that serves as a sign of our unity.

73 NORTHERN IRELAND

This Conference:

1 Expresses solidarity with fellow Anglicans and with all the people of Northern Ireland in their suffering.

2 In the circumstances of Northern Ireland condemns all violence.

3 Urges all political and community leaders to seize every opportunity to work together to bring about a just and peaceful solution.

PARTICIPANTS

Conference Steering Committee

Chairman:
The Most Revd and Rt Hon Robert Runcie,
Archbishop of Canterbury
Secretary:
The Revd Canon Samuel Van Culin,
Secretary General of the Anglican Consultative Council
Deputy Secretary:
Mr David Long
Chairmen and Vice-Chairmen of Sections
The Rt Revd James Ottley
The Rt Revd David Sheppard
The Most Revd Keith Rayner
The Rt Revd Mark Dyer
The Most Revd Michael Peers
The Rt Revd Edward Buckle
The Most Revd John Habgood
The Most Revd Desmond Tutu
Chaplain to the Conference
The Rt Revd Alastair Haggart
Co-ordinator of Studies
The Rt Revd Michael Nazir-Ali
Co-Editors of the Report
The Rt Revd Michael Nazir-Ali
Mr Derek Pattinson
Episcopal Co-ordinator of Communication
The Rt Revd Ronald Bowlby
Theological Consultant
The Rt Revd Frederick Borsch
Consultant in Design
The Rt Revd Patrick Kalilombe

The Steering Committee was for the day-to-day work of the Conference.

The Primates of the Anglican Communion

Australia	The Most Revd John B. Grindrod
Brazil	The Most Revd Olavo Luiz
Burma	The Most Revd Andrew Mya Han
Burundi, Rwanda and Zaire	The Most Revd Samuel Sindamuka
Canada	The Most Revd Michael G. Peers
Central Africa	The Most Revd W.P. Khotso Makhulu
East Asia	The Rt Revd Tan Sri John G. Savarimuthu Chairman, The Council of the Churches of East Asia
England	The Most Revd and Rt Hon. Robert Runcie
Indian Ocean	The Most Revd French K. Chang-Him
Ireland	The Most Revd Robert H.A. Eames
Japan	The Most Revd Christopher Kikawada
Jerusalem and the Middle East	The Most Revd Samir Kafity
Kenya	The Most Revd Manasses Kuria
Melanesia	The Most Revd Amos Waiaru
New Zealand	The Most Revd Brian N. Davis
Nigeria	The Most Revd Joseph A. Adetiloye
Papua New Guinea	The Most Revd George Ambo
Scotland	The Most Revd Edward Luscombe
Southern Africa	The Most Revd Desmond M. Tutu
South America	The Rt Revd David Leake
Sudan	The Most Revd Benjamin Yugusuk
Tanzania	The Most Revd John Ramadhani
Uganda	The Most Revd Yona Okoth
USA	The Most Revd Edmond L. Browning
Wales	The Most Revd George D. Noakes
West Africa	The Most Revd George D. Browne
West Indies	The Most Revd Orland U. Lindsay

Participants

ANGLICAN PROVINCES AND DIOCESES

† Principal Archbishop and Primate
* Head of Internal Province
( ) Not attending Lambeth Conference

Assistant Bishops: only those attending the Conference are named.

The number after the name of each participant indicates the Section to which the participant was assigned, viz.

1 **Mission and Ministry**
2 **Dogmatic And Pastoral Concerns**
3 **Ecumenical Relations**
4 **Christianity and the Social Order**

THE ANGLICAN CHURCH OF AUSTRALIA

Internal Provinces:

New South Wales *NSW*
Queensland *Q*
South Australia *SA*
Victoria *V*
Western Australia *WA*
Extra-Provincial *EP*

Diocese/Province	*Bishop*	*Section*
Adelaide *SA*	* K. Rayner	2
Armidale *NSW*	P. Chiswell	2
Ballarat *V*	J. Hazelwood	2
Bathurst *NSW*	H.A.J. Witt	2
Bendigo *V*	O. Heyward	3
Brisbane *Q*	† J.B.R. Grindrod	2
Bunbury *WA*	H.T. Jamieson	1
Canberra & Goulburn *NSW*	O.D. Dowling	1
Carpentaria *Q*	A.F.B. Hall-Matthews	4
Gippsland *V*	C.D. Sheumack	1
Grafton *NSW*	B.A. Schultz	4
Melbourne *V*	* D.J. Penman	1
The Murray *SA*	R.G. Porter	3
Newcastle *NSW*	A.C. Holland	4
North Queensland *Q*	J. Lewis S.S.M.	3
Northern Territory *Q*	C.M. Wood	4
North West Australia *WA*	G.B. Muston	1
Perth *WA*	* P.F. Carnley	3
Riverina *NSW*	B.R. Hunter	1
Rockhampton *Q*	G.A. Hearn	4
Sydney *NSW*	* D.W.B. Robinson	2
Tasmania *EP*	P.K. Newell	2
Wangaratta *V*	R.G. Beal	4
Willochra *SA*	W.D.H. McCall	1

IGREJA EPISCOPAL DO BRASIL
(THE EPISCOPAL CHURCH OF BRAZIL)

Brasilia DF	A.G. Soria	2
Central Brazil	S.A. Ruiz	4
Northern Brazil	C.E. Rodrigues	1
South Central Brazil	S. Takatsu	1
South Western Brazil	† O.V. Luiz	3
Southern Brazil	C.V.S. Gastal	3

THE CHURCH OF THE PROVINCE OF BURMA

Mandalay	T. Mya Wah	2
Myitkyina	A.U. Hla Aung	3
Pa'an	G. Kyaw Mya	2
Rangoon	† A. Mya Han	1
Sittwe	B.T. Theaung Hawi	3

THE CHURCH OF THE PROVINCE OF BURUNDI, RWANDA AND ZAIRE

Diocese/Country	Bishop	Section
Boga-Zaire *Zaire*	B. Njojo	1
Bujumbura *Burundi*	† S. Sindamuka	3
Bukavu *Zaire*	B.J. Dirokpa	1
Butare *Rwanda*	L.J. Ndandali	1
Buye *Burundi*	S. Ndayisenga	4
Gitega *Burundi*	J.W. Nduwayo	3
Kigali *Rwanda*	A. Sebununguri	4
Kisangani *Zaire*	S.T. Mugera	3
Shaba *Zaire*	E. Kolini	3
Shyira *Rwanda*	A. Nshamihigo	3

THE ANGLICAN CHURCH OF CANADA

Internal Provinces:

British Columbia *BC*
Canada *C*
Ontario *O*
Rupert's Land *RL*

Primate	† *M.G. Peers*	3

Diocese/Province	Bishop	Section
Algoma *O*	L.E. Peterson	4
The Arctic *RL*	J.R. Sperry	4
Athabasca *RL*	G.F. Woolsey	4
Brandon *RL*	J.F.S. Conlin	1
British Columbia *BC*	R.F. Shepherd	2
Caledonia *BC*	J.E. Hannen	2
Calgary *RL*	J.B. Curtis	1
Cariboo *BC*	J.S.P. Snowden	3
Central Newfoundland *C*	M. Genge	2
Eastern Newfoundland & Labrador *C*	M. Mate	4
Edmonton *RL*	K. Genge	1
Fredericton *C*	* H.L. Nutter	3
Huron *O*	D.D. Jones	4
Keewatin *RL*	H.J.P. Allan	1
Kootenay *BC*	R.E.F. Berry	1
Montreal *C*	R. Hollis	1
Moosonee *O*	C.J. Lawrence	2
New Westminster *BC*	* D.W. Hambidge	1
Niagara *O*	* J.C. Bothwell	1
Nova Scotia *C*	A.G. Peters	2
Ontario *O*	A.A. Read	2
Ottawa *O*	E. Lackey	4
Qu'Appelle *RL*	E. Bays	4
Quebec *C*	A. Goodings	3

Rupert's Land *RL*	W. Jones	3
Saskatchewan *RL*	T.O. Morgan	1
Saskatoon *RL*	R.A. Wood	3
Toronto *O*	(L.S. Garnsworthy)	
Western Newfoundland *C*	S.S. Payne	4
Yukon *BC*	R.C. Ferris	1

THE CHURCH OF THE PROVINCE OF CENTRAL AFRICA

Diocese/Country	*Bishop*	*Section*
Botswana *Botswana*	† W.P.K. Makhulu	2
Central Zambia *Zambia*	C. Hlanya-Shaba	4
Harare *Zimbabwe*	R.P. Hatendi	4
Lake Malawi *Malawi*	P.N. Nyanja	3
The Lundi *Zimbabwe*	J. Siyachitema	3
Lusaka *Zambia*	S.S. Mumba	4
Manicaland *Zimbabwe*	E.M.P. Masuko	2
Matabeleland *Zimbabwe*	T.T. Naledi	2
Northern Zambia *Zambia*	J. Mabula	
Southern Malawi *Malawi*	B.N. Aipa	1

THE CHURCH OF ENGLAND

Internal Provinces:

Canterbury C
York   Y

Diocese/Province	*Bishop*	*Section*
Bath and Wells *C*	G.L. Carey	3
Birmingham *C*	M. Santer	2
Blackburn *Y*	(D.S. Cross)	
Bradford *Y*	R.K. Williamson	1
Bristol *C*	B. Rogerson	2
Canterbury *C*	† R.A.K. Runcie	
Carlisle *Y*	H.D. Halsey	1
Chelmsford *C*	J. Waine	3
Chester *Y*	M.A. Baughen	2
Chichester *C*	E.W. Kemp	3
Coventry *C*	S. Barrington-Ward	1
Derby *C*	P.S. Dawes	3
Durham *Y*	D.E. Jenkins	4
Ely *C*	P.K. Walker	2
Exeter *C*	G.H. Thompson	1
Gibraltar in Europe *C*	J.R. Satterthwaite	3
Gloucester *C*	J. Yates	1
Guildford *C*	M.E. Adie	2
Hereford *C*	J.R.G. Eastaugh	2
Leicester *C*	(C.R. Rutt)	4
Lichfield *C*	K.N. Sutton	4

Lincoln *C*	R.M. Hardy	1
Liverpool *Y*	D.S. Sheppard	1
London *C*	G.D. Leonard	1
Manchester *Y*	S.E.F. Booth-Clibborn	4
Newcastle *Y*	A.A.K. Graham	
Norwich *C*	P.J. Nott	1
Oxford *C*	R.D. Harries	2
Peterborough *C*	W.J. Westwood	1
Portsmouth *C*	T.J. Bavin	3
Ripon *Y*	D.N. de L. Young	4
Rochester *C*	M. Turnbull	
St Albans *C*	J.B. Taylor	3
St Edmundsbury & Ipswich *C*	J. Dennis	3
Salisbury *C*	J.A. Baker	2
Sheffield *Y*	D.R. Lunn	1
Sodor and Man *Y*	A. Attwell	
Southwark *C*	R.O. Bowlby	
Southwell *Y*	P.B. Harris	
Truro *C*	P. Mumford	3
Wakefield *Y*	D.M. Hope	2
Winchester *C*	C.C.W. James	1
Worcester *C*	P.H.E. Goodrich	2
York *Y*	* J.S. Habgood	4

THE CHURCH OF THE PROVINCE OF THE INDIAN OCEAN

Diocese/Country	*Bishop*	*Section*
Antananarivo *Madagascar*	R.J. Rabenirina	4
Antsiranana *Madagascar*	K.J. Benzies	3
Mauritius *Mauritius*	L.R.V. Donat	1
Seychelles *Seychelles*	† F. Chang-Him	2
Toamasina *Madagascar*	F. Razakariasy	1

THE CHURCH OF IRELAND

Internal Provinces:

Armagh	A
Dublin	D

Diocese/Province	*Bishop*	*Section*
Armagh *A*	† R.H.A. Eames	4
Cashel and Ossory *D*	N.V. Willoughby	3
Clogher *A*	B.D.A. Hannon	3
Connor *A*	S.G. Poyntz	4
Cork, Cloyne and Ross *D*	R.A. Warke	2
Derry and Raphoe *A*	J. Mehaffey	1
Down and Dromore *A*	G. McMullan	2
Dublin *D*	* D.A.R. Caird	3
Kilmore, Elphin and Ardagh *A*	W.G. Wilson	3
Limerick and Killaloe *D*	E.F. Darling	1

Meath and Kildare *D*	W.N.F. Empey	3
Tuam, Killala and Achonry *A*	J.R.W. Neill	1

NIPPON SEI KO KAI
(THE HOLY CATHOLIC CHURCH IN JAPAN)

Chubu	S. Hoyo	3
Hokkaido	A.H. Amagi	2
Kita Kanto	(J.T. Yashiro)	
Kobe	P.K. Yashiro	1
Kyoto	J. Yagi	4
Kyushu	J.N. Iida	3
Okinawa	(P.S. Nakamura)	
Osaka	† C.I. Kikawada	4
Tohoku	C.Y. Tazaki	2
Tokyo	J.M. Takeda	3
Yokohama	R.S. Kajiwara	1

THE EPISCOPAL CHURCH OF JERUSALEM AND THE MIDDLE EAST

Cyprus and the Gulf	J.E. Brown	2
Egypt	G. Abdel Malik	3
Iran	H.B. Dehqani-Tafti	1
Jerusalem	† S. Kafity	2

THE CHURCH OF THE PROVINCE OF KENYA

Eldoret	A. Muge	4
Machakos	B.P. Nzimbi	1
Maseno North	J.I. Mundia	2
Maseno South	J.H. Okullu	4
Maseno West	J.D. Omolo	1
Mombasa	C.D. Nzano	3
Mount Kenya Central	J.S. Mahiani	2
Mount Kenya East	D.M. Gitari	4
Mount Kenya South	G.M. Njuguna	4
Nairobi	† M. Kuria	3
Nakuru	L.K. Mbiu	1
Nambale	I. Namango	3

THE CHURCH OF THE PROVINCE OF MELANESIA

Central Melanesia	† A.S. Waiaru	1
Malaita	W.A. Pwaisiho	1
Temotu	L.S. Munamua	1
Vanuatu	H.S. Tevi	4
Ysabel	E. Pogo	2

THE CHURCH OF THE PROVINCE OF NEW ZEALAND

Aotearoa	T.W. Vercoe	4
Auckland	B. Gilberd	4

Christchurch	M.J. Goodall	2
Dunedin	P.W. Mann	2
Nelson	P.E. Sutton	3
Polynesia	J.L. Bryce	4
Waiapu	P.G. Atkins	1
Waikato	R.A. Herft	1
Wellington	† B.N. Davis	1

THE CHURCH OF THE PROVINCE OF NIGERIA

Aba	A.O. Iwuagwu	1
Akigwe/Orlu	S.C.N. Ebo	4
Akoko	J.O.K. Olowokure	4
Akure	E. Gbonigi	2
Asaba	R.N.C. Nwosu	3
Awka	M.S.C. Anikwenwa	1
Benin	J.K. George	3
Egba-Egbado	T.I. Akintayo	4
Ekiti	C.A. Akinbola	1
Enugu	G.N. Otubelu	4
Ibadan	G. Olajide	
Ijebu	I.O.B. Akintemi	2
Ijebu Remo	E.O.I. Ogundana	3
Ilesa	*vacant*	*1*
Jos	T.E.I. Adesola	2
Kaduna	T.Ogbonyomi	1
Kano	B.B. Ayam	3
Kwara	H.Y. Haruna	2
Lagos	† J.A. Adetiloye	2
The Niger	J.A. Onyemelukwe	4
The Niger Delta	S.O. Elenwo	3
Ondo	S.O. Aderin	4
Osun	S.O. Fagbemi	3
Owerri	B.C. Nwankiti	1
Owo	A.O. Awosan	1
Warri	J.O. Dafiewhare	2

THE ANGLICAN CHURCH OF PAPUA NEW GUINEA

Aipo Rongo	P. Richardson	2
Dogura	R.E. Sanana	1
New Guinea Islands	B. Meredith	3
Popondota	† G. Ambo	1
Port Moresby	I.R. Gadebo	2

THE SCOTTISH EPISCOPAL CHURCH

Aberdeen and Orkney	F.C. Darwent	3
Argyll and the Isles	G.K.B. Henderson	4
Brechin	† L.E. Luscombe	1
Edinburgh	R.F. Holloway	2
Glasgow and Galloway	D.A. Rawcliffe	1
Moray, Ross, and Caithness	G.M. Sessford	3
St Andrews, Dunkeld and Dunblane	M. Hare-Duke	4

THE CHURCH OF THE PROVINCE OF SOUTHERN AFRICA

Diocese/Country	Bishop	Section
Bloemfontein *South Africa*	T.S. Stanage	1
Cape Town *South Africa*	† D.M. Tutu	4
George *South Africa*	D.G. Damant	2
Grahamstown *South Africa*	D. Russell	4
Johannesburg *South Africa*	G.D. Buchanan	2
Kimberley and Kuruman *South Africa*	G.A. Swartz	3
Lebombo *Mozambique*	D.S. Sengulane	1
Lesotho *Lesotho*	P.S. Mokuku	4
Namibia *Namibia*	J.H. Kauluma	3
Natal *South Africa*	M. Nuttall	1
Niassa *Mozambique*	P.T. Manhique	2
Port Elizabeth *South Africa*	B.R. Evans	4
Pretoria *South Africa*	R.A. Kraft	1
St Helena *St Helena and Ascension*	J.N. Johnson	1
St John's *South Africa*	J.Z.B.D. Dlamini	3
St Mark the Evangelist *South Africa*	R.P.J. Le Feuvre	1
Swaziland *Swaziland*	B.L. Mkhabela	2
Zululand *South Africa*	L.B. Zulu	2
Order of Ethiopia	S. Dwane	2

IGLESIA ANGLICANA DEL CONO SUR DE AMERICA (THE ANGLICAN CHURCH OF THE SOUTHERN CONE OF AMERICA)

Argentina and Uruguay	R.S. Cutts	1
Chile	C.F. Bazley	1
Northern Argentina	† D. Leake	3
Paraguay	J.A. Ellison	2
Peru and Bolivia	R.J. Evans	4

THE CHURCH OF THE PROVINCE OF THE SUDAN

Bor	N. Garang	2
Juba	† B.W. Yugusuk	4
Khartoum	B.T. Idris Tia	1
Rumbek	G.R. Jur (Acting)	3
Yambio	D. Zindo	4

THE CHURCH OF THE PROVINCE OF TANZANIA

Central Tanganyika	Y. Madinda	4
Dar es Salaam	(C. Mlangwa)	
Kagera	C. Ruhuza	4
Mara	G.O. Nyaronga	3
Masasi	C.R. Norgate	3
Morogoro	D. Mageni	2
Mount Kilimanjaro	A.F. Mohamed	4
Ruvuma	M.D. Ngahyoma	2

South West Tanganyika	C.J. Mwaigoga	2
Victoria Nyanza	J.O. Rusibamayila	2
Western Tanganyika	G.E. Mpango	4
Zanzibar and Tanga	† J.A. Ramadhani	3

THE CHURCH OF THE PROVINCE OF UGANDA

Bukedi	N.E. Okille	4
Bunyoro-Kitara	Y.K. Rwakaikara	1
Busoga	C. Bamwoze	1
East Ankole	A. Betungura	4
Kampala	† Y. Okoth	3
Karamoja	P. Lomongin	4
Kigezi	*vacant*	
Lango	M. Otim	3
Madi and West Nile	E. Adrale	2
Mbale	A. Wesonga	1
Mityana	Y. Mukasa	3
Mukono	L. Nkoyoyo	4
Namirembe	M. Kauma	3
North Kigezi	Y. Ruhindi	2
Northern Uganda	B. Ogwal-Abwang	2
Ruwenzori	E. Kamanyire	4
Soroti	G. Ilukor	2
South Ruwenzori	Z. Masereka	4
West Ankole	Y.K. Bamunoba	2
West Buganda	D.C. Senyonjo	4

THE EPISCOPAL CHURCH IN THE UNITED STATES OF AMERICA

Presiding Bishop	† E.L. Browning	1

Diocese/Province	*Bishop*	*Section*
Alabama *IV*	F.C. Stough	1
Alaska *VIII*	G.C. Harris	1
Albany *II*	D.S. Ball	2
Arizona *VIII*	(J.T. Heistand)	4
Arkansas *VII*	H.A. Donovan Jr	3
Atlanta *IV*	C.J. Child	1
Bethlehem *III*	M. Dyer	2
California *VIII*	W.E. Swing	1
Central and South Mexico *IX*	(J.G. Saucedo)	
Central Florida *IV*	W.H. Folwell	2
Central Gulfcoast *IV*	C.F. Duvall	4
Central New York *II*	O. Whitaker	2
Central Pennsylvania *III*	C.F. McNutt	3
Central Philippines *VIII*	M.C. Lumpias	1
Chicago *V*	F.T. Griswold	2
Colombia *XI*	B. Merino	2
Colorado *VI*	W.C. Frey	2
Connecticut *I*	A.E. Walmsley	2

253

Dallas *VII*	D.D. Patterson	3
Delaware *III*	C.C. Tennis	3
Dominican Republic *IX*	T.A. Isaac	1
East Carolina *IV*	B.S. Sanders	4
East Tennessee *IV*	W.E. Sanders	1
Eastern Oregon *VIII*	R.R. Kimsey	2
Easton *III*	E.L. Sorge	1
Eau Claire *V*	W.C. Wantland	3
Ecuador *IX*	A.D. Caceres	1
El Camino Real *VIII*	C.S. Mallory	1
El Salvador *IX*	*vacant*	
Florida *IV*	F.S. Cerveny	1
Fond Du Lac *V*	W.L. Stevens	4
Fort Worth *VII*	C.C. Pope	3
Georgia *IV*	H.W. Shipps	3
Guatemala *IX*	A.R. Guerra-Soria	2
Haiti *II*	L.A.J. Garnier	1
Hawaii *VIII*	D.P. Hart	2
Honduras *IX*	L. Frade	4
Idaho *VIII*	D.B. Birney	1
Indianapolis *V*	E.W. Jones	3
Iowa *VI*	W.C.C. Righter	3
Kansas *VII*	R.F. Grein	3
Kentucky *IV*	D.B. Reed	3
Lexington *IV*	D.A. Wimberly	3
Litoral Ecuador *IX*	L.E. Caisapanta Bedon	2
Long Island *II*	R.C. Witcher	2
Los Angeles *VIII*	F. Borsch	2
Louisiana *IV*	J.B. Brown	3
Maine *I*	E.C. Chalfant	4
Maryland *III*	A.T. Eastman	3
Massachusetts *I*	D.E. Johnson	4
Michigan *V*	H.C. McGehee	4
Milwaukee *V*	R.J. White	3
Minnesota *VI*	R.M. Anderson	3
Mississippi *IV*	D.M. Gray	4
Missouri *V*	W.A. Jones	4
Montana *VI*	C.I. Jones	1
Navajoland *VIII*	*vacant*	
Nebraska *VII*	J.D. Warner	2
Nevada *VI*	S.C. Zabriskie	2
New Hampshire *I*	D.E. Theuner	4
New Jersey *II*	G.P.M. Belshaw	4
New York *II*	P. Moore	4
Newark *II*	J.S. Spong	2
Nicaragua *IX*	S. Downs	3
North Carolina *IV*	R.W. Estill	1
North Dakota *VI*	H.A. Hopkins Jr	2
Northern California *VIII*	J.L. Thompson	4
Northern Indiana *V*	F.C. Gray	3
Northern Luzon *VIII*	R. Abellon	3
Northern Mexico *IX*	G. Martinez	2
Northern Michigan *V*	T.K. Ray	2
Northern Philippines *VIII*	R.L. Longid	4

Northwest Texas *VII*	S.B. Hulsey	1
Northwestern Pennsylvania *III*	D.J. Davis	1
Ohio *V*	J.R. Moodey	4
Oklahoma *VII*	G.N. McAllister	1
Olympia *VIII*	R.H. Cochrane	4
Oregon *VIII*	R.L. Ladehoff	2
Panama *IX*	J.H. Ottley	1
Pennsylvania *III*	A.L. Bartlett	4
Pittsburgh *III*	A. Hathaway	1
Quincy *V*	E.H. MacBurney	2
Rhode Island *I*	G.N. Hunt	1
Rio Grande *VII*	(R.M. Trelease Jr)	
Rochester *II*	W.G. Burrill	3
San Diego *VIII*	C.B. Morton	3
San Joaquin *VIII*	V.M. Rivera	2
South Carolina *IV*	C.F. Allison	2
South Dakota *VI*	C.B. Anderson	4
Southeast Florida *IV*	C.O. Schofield	4
Southern Ohio *V*	W.G. Black	2
Southern Philippines *VIII*	N.V. Ticobay	1
Southern Virginia *III*	C.C. Vache	1
Southwest Florida *IV*	*vacant*	
Southwestern Virginia *III*	A.H. Light	1
Spokane *VIII*	L.A. Wallace	2
Springfield *V*	D.M. Hultstrand	2
Taiwan *VIII*	J.C.T. Chien	1
Tennessee *IV*	G. Reynolds	2
Texas *VII*	M.M. Benitez	1
Upper South Carolina *IV*	W.A. Beckham	1
Utah *VIII*	(G.E. Bates)	2
Vermont *I*	D.L. Swenson	1
Virgin Islands *II*	D.E. Taylor	4
Virginia *III*	P.J. Lee	4
Washington *III*	J.T. Walker	4
West Missouri *VII*	A.A. Vogel	2
West Tennessee *IV*	A.D. Dickson	1
West Texas *VII*	J.H. MacNaughton	3
West Virginia *III*	R.P. Atkinson	4
Western Kansas *VII*	J.F. Ashby	1
Western Louisiana *IV*	W.R. Henton	3
Western Massachusetts *I*	A.F. Wissemann	3
Western Mexico *IX*	S. Espinoza	1
Western Michigan *V*	*vacant*	
Western New York *II*	D.C. Bowman	4
Western North Carolina *IV*	W.G. Weinhauer	3
Wyoming *VI*	B.G. Jones	1

Extra-Provincial

Costa Rica *IX*	C.J. Wilson	4
Europe (Convocation of American Churches in Europe)	(M. Bigliardi)	
Puerto Rico *IX*	F. Reus-Froylan	1
Venezuela *IX*	O. Soto	2

255

THE CHURCH IN WALES

Bangor	J.C. Mears	4
Llandaff	R.T. Davies	1
Monmouth	R.C. Wright	1
St Asaph	A. Rice Jones	2
St Davids	† G. Noakes	3
Swansea and Brecon	D.M. Bridges	4

THE CHURCH OF THE PROVINCE OF WEST AFRICA

Diocese/Country	Bishop	Section
Accra *Ghana*	F.W.B. Thompson	3
Bo *Sierra Leone*	M.M. Keili	4
Cape Coast *Ghana*	*vacant*	
Freetown *Sierra Leone*	P.E.S. Thompson	1
Gambia *Gambia, Senegal & Cape Verde*	*vacant*	
Guinea *Guinea & Guinea Bissau*	*vacant*	
Koforidua *Ghana*	R.G.A. Okine	4
Kumasi *Ghana*	E.K. Yeboah	1
Liberia *Liberia*	† G.D. Browne	2
Sekondi *Ghana*	T.S.A. Annobil	3
Sunyani/Tamale *Ghana*	J.K. Dadson	3

THE CHURCH IN THE PROVINCE OF THE WEST INDIES

Barbados	D.W. Gomez	4
Bélize	*vacant*	
Guyana	R.O. George	1
Jamaica	N.W. de Souza	1
Nassau and the Bahamas	M.H. Eldon	3
North Eastern Caribbean and Aruba	† O. Lindsay	4
Trinidad and Tobago	C.O. Abdulah	2
Windward Islands	P. Elder	2

EXTRA-PROVINCIAL

Diocese/Country	Bishop	Section
Bermuda *Bermuda*	C.C. Luxmoore	3
Colombo *Sri Lanka*	J.J. Gnanapragasam	1
Cuba *Cuba*	E.J. Hernandez	1
Hong Kong & Macao *Hong Kong & Macao*	P. Kwong	4
Kuching *Malaysia*	J.L. Chee Yun	3
Kurunagala *Sri Lanka*	A.O. Kumarage	2
Lusitanian Church *Portugal*	F. da L. Soares	1
Pusan *Korea*	B.C.H. Kim	3
Sabah *Malaysia*	L. Chhoa Heng Sze	2
Seoul *Korea*	S.S. Kim	4
Singapore *Singapore*	M. Tay	1
Spain *Spain*	A. Sanchez	2
Taejon *Korea*	P. Yoon	1
West Malaysia *Malaysia*	† J.G. Savarimuthu	2

Suffragan or Assistant Bishops Attending the Lambeth Conference 1988

AUSTRALIA

G.H. Walden (Ballarat)	3
B.W. Wilson (Canberra & Goulburn)	4
J.C. Stewart (Melbourne)	1
A.A. Malcolm (North Queensland)	3
B.R. Kyme (Perth)	4
E.D. Cameron (Sydney)	Consultant
J.R. Reid (Sydney)	1

BRAZIL

L.O. Prado Pires (Southern Brazil)	4

BURUNDI, RWANDA AND ZAIRE

D. Nduhura (Butare)	1

CANADA

C.R. Townshend (Huron)	4
C.M. Mitchell (Niagara)	3
T.E. Finlay (Toronto)	2
A.D. Brown (Toronto)	2

ENGLAND

C.O. Buchanan (Birmingham)	1
R.H.M. Third (Canterbury)	1
J.W. Roxburgh (Chelmsford)	1
P.J. Ball (Chichester)	2
P. Coleman (Exeter)	4
D. Tustin (Lincoln)	3
M. Henshall (Liverpool)	3
T.F. Butler (London)	4
B.J. Masters (London)	4
J.L. Thompson (London)	4
C.J.F. Scott (Manchester)	3
T. Dudley-Smith (Norwich)	1
S.H. Burrows (Oxford)	3
E.N. Devenport (St Edmundsbury & Ipswich)	4
J.D.G. Kirkham (Salisbury)	2
W.M.D. Persson (Sheffield)	2
W.D. Wood (Southwark)	4
T.R. Hare (Wakefield)	2
M.R.J. Manktelow (Winchester)	3
A.C. Dumper (Worcester)	4
G. Bates (York)	4
C.C. Barker (York)	4
I. Harland (Blackburn)	3

NEW ZEALAND

E.G. Buckle (Auckland)	3
G.E.A. Wilson (Auckland)	4

SOUTHERN AFRICA
C. Albertyn (Cape Town)	4
J.S. Nkoane C.R. (Johannesburg)	3
A. Mkhize (Natal)	4

SOUTHERN CONE OF AMERICA
H.W. Godfrey (Argentina and Uruguay)	3

SUDAN
M.B. Dawidi (Juba)	2
J. Marona (Maridi Area)	1
S. Solomona (Yei Area)	4

TANZANIA
D.L. Mtetemela (Central Tanganyika)	1

USA
R. Haines (Washington)	3
M. Garcia-Montiel (Central & South Mexico)	3
W.H. Wolfrum (Colorado)	2
C.N. Coleridge (Connecticut)	4
V.K. Pettit (New Jersey)	1
W.D. Dennis (New York)	4
F.H. Vest Jr (North Carolina)	4
A.B. Williams Jr (Ohio)	3
R.S. Harris (Upper South Carolina)	4
W.F. Carr (West Virginia)	4
E.N. McArthur (West Texas)	2

UGANDA
W. Rukirande (Kigezi)	1
G.A. Oboma (Northern Uganda)	1

WEST AFRICA
E.D. Neufville (Liberia)	1

WEST INDIES
W.A. Murray (Jamaica)	3

258

PARTICIPANTS FROM UNITED CHURCHES IN FULL COMMUNION*

Alphabetical by Church and Diocese

* Those Churches where Anglicans have entered into union with Christians of other traditions.

† Moderator
( ) Not attending Lambeth Conference

PARTICIPANTS

THE CHURCH OF BANGLADESH
Dhaka   B.D. Mondal   3

THE CHURCH OF NORTH INDIA
Agra   (W.O. Simon)
Amritsar   (A. Chandu Lal)
Andamans & Nicobar Islands   (E. Matthew)
Assam   (E.W. Talibuddin)
Barrackpore   (S. Bairagi)
Bhopal   (M.B. Singh)
Bombay   (S.B. Joshua)
Calcutta   (D.C. Gorai)
Chandigarh   (M.A.Z. Rolston)
Chota Nagpur   (Z.J. Terom)
Cuttack   (J.K. Mohanty)
Darjeeling   J.E. Ghose   1
Delhi   (M. Caleb)
Durgapur   (S.K. Kisku)
Gujarat   (P. Chauhan)
Jabalpur   F.C. Jonathan   1
Kolhapur   I.P. Andrews   1
Lucknow   † Din Dayal   2
Nagpur   (V. Peter)
Nasik   (D.J. Vairagar)
Patna   (N.M. Bagh)
Rajasthan   (E.C. Anthony)
Sambalpur   L. Tandy   1

THE CHURCH OF PAKISTAN
Faisalabad   (Z. Mirza)
Hyderabad   B. Jiwan   1
Karachi   A. Rudvin   3
Lahore   † A.J. Malik   3
Multan   (J.V. Samuel)
Peshawar   (K.U. Din)
Raiwind   S. Azariah
Sialkot   S. Pervez

CHURCH OF SOUTH INDIA
Coimbatore   *vacant*
Dornakal   (D.N. Samuel)
East Kerala   (K.M. John)
Jaffna   (D.J. Ambalavanar)
Kanyakumari   G. Christdhas   2
Karimnagar   *vacant*
Karnataka Central   C.D. Jathanna   1
Karnataka North   (V.P. Dandin)
Karnataka South   *vacant*
Krishna-Godavari   T.B.D. Prakasa Rao   3
Madhya Kerala   (M.C. Mani)
Madras   S. Clarke   2
Madurai-Ramnad   (D. Pothirajalu)
Medak   † V. Premasagar   2

Nandyal	(B.R. Devapriyam)	
North Kerala	(K.T.C. Seth)	
Rayalaseema	(L.V. Azariah)	
South Kerala	I. Jesudasan	3
Tiruchirapalli-Thanjavur	(R. Paulraj)	
Tirunelveli	(J.S. Dharmaraj)	
Vellore	*vacant*	

Bishops from Churches in Communion

MAR THOMA SYRIAN CHURCH OF INDIA

P. Mar Chrysostom	(Suffragan Metropolitan of Hermon – invited but unable to attend	
J. Mar Irenaeus	(Trivandrum-Quilon)	

PHILIPPINE INDEPENDENT CATHOLIC CHURCH (P.I.C.)

N.F. Canlas	(Chairman of the Supreme Council of Bishops)	4
E.D. Coronado	(Lucena City)	4
P. de la Cruz	(Cebu and Bohol – invited but unable to attend)	
†S. Ganno	(Supreme Bishop, P.I.C.)	4
J.O. Juanitez	(East Pangasinan; National Program Director)	4
R.B. Tiples	(Negros)	4

THE OLD CATHOLIC CHURCHES

H. Gerny	(Old Catholic Bishop of Switzerland)	2
†A.J. Glazemaker	(Primate and Archbishop of Utrecht)	2
S. Kraft	(Bishop of the Old Catholic Church of Germany, Western)	2
†J.F. Swantek	(Prime Bishop of the Polish National Catholic Church)	3

Participants from the Anglican Consultative Council

Episcopal members of the Anglican Consultative Council at the Conference have been included within the foregoing list of bishops. The following clerical and lay members of the ACC were also appointed as participants and were present at the Conference:

The Hon. Mr Justice Abimbola	Nigeria	2
The Very Revd Walter Asbil	Canada	2
Mrs Patricia Bays	Canada	3
Mr David Benjamin	West Indies	3
Mr Edgar Bradley	New Zealand	3
Mr Gervase Chidawanyika	Zimbabwe	1
Mrs Pamela Chinnis	USA	3
The Revd Canon Simon Chiwanga	Tanzania	4
Mrs Ruth Yangsoon Choi	Korea	1
The Revd Canon Colin Craston	England	1
(Vice-Chairman)		
Mr Barry Deane	Ireland	4
The Very Revd Robert Ewbank	Zimbabwe	3
The Ven. Ian George	Australia	4
Mrs Betty Govinden	South Africa	4
Mr César Guzman	Chile	1
Miss Lorna Helen	Ireland	2
Dr Margaret Hewitt	England	1
Mr Max Horton	Australia	1
The Very Revd Samuel Johnson	Nigeria	1
The Revd John Kanyikwa	Sudan	1
The Revd Benezeri Kisembo	Uganda	4
Mrs Rhoda Lusaka	Kenya	2
Mr David McIntyre	Wales	1
The Revd John Makokwe	Burundi	2
Mrs Faga Matalavea	Samoa	4
The Revd Canon Winston Ndungane	South Africa	1
Prof. Enoka Rukare	Uganda	3
The Revd Gideon Waida	Papua New Guinea	2
The Ven. Robert Wainwright	USA	2
Mr Ibrahim Wakid	Egypt	3
The Revd Canon Ian Watt	Scotland	1
The Ven. Yong Ping Chung (Chairman)	Malaysia	2
Mrs Alice Yuk Tak-Fun	Hong Kong & Macao	4

Consultants

The Rt Revd John Baycroft	Canada	Gen
The Ven. Enrique Brown	USA	1
The Rt Revd Don Cameron	Australia	3
The Revd Canon Prof. Henry Chadwick	England	Gen
The Revd Edmundo Desueza	Costa Rica	4
The Revd Canon Prof. Gordon Dunstan	England	4
Mr Matt Esau	South Africa	3
Miss Ruth Etchells	England	1
The Rt Revd Henry Hill	Canada	3
Dr Janet Hodgson	South Africa	1
The Rt Revd Peter Hollingworth	Australia	4
Miss Vanessa Mackenzie	South Africa	Gen
The Revd Prof. Jaci Maraschin	Brazil	2
The Rt Revd Kenneth Mason	Australia	1
Mr Andrew Masterton	Australia	Gen
The Revd Prof. Richard Norris	USA	2
Mar Gregorios Paulose	India	3
The Revd Nan Peete	USA	Gen
Mr John Rea	England	4
The Rt Revd Alfred Reid	West Indies	Gen
The Revd Canon Stanford Shauri	Tanzania	4
The Revd Canon Prof. Stephen Sykes	England	2
Dr Mary Tanner	England	3
Mrs Elizabeth Templeton	Scotland	3
The Revd Canon Prof. Rowan Williams	England	2
The Revd Margaret Wood	New Zealand	Gen

Observers from other Churches

Armenian Apostolic Church	The Most Revd Nerses Bozabalian
	The Most Revd Datev Sarkissian
Assyrian Church of the East	The Ven. Yonan Yonan
Baptist World Alliance	The Revd Dr David S Russell
British Council of Churches	The Revd Dr Philip Morgan
Christian World Communions	Dr Bert Beach
	Dr Paul A. Crow
Coptic Orthodox Church	The Rt Revd Amba Bishoy
Ethiopian Orthodox Church	The Most Revd Abba Garima
Greek Orthodox Patriarchate of Antioch	The Revd Samir Gholan
Lutheran World Federation	The Revd Dr Paul Erickson
	The Revd Dr Eugene L. Brand
	The Rt Revd Sebastian Kolowa
	The Revd Dr Gunnar Staalsett
Orthodox Church	The Most Revd Gregorios of Thyateira and Great Britain
	The Most Revd John Zizioulas
	The Rt Revd Aristarchus of Zenoupolis
Roman Catholic Church	The Rt Revd Cormac Murphy O'Connor
	The Rt Revd Raymond W. Lessard
	The Revd Kevin McDonald
Syrian Orthodox Church	His Eminence Metropolitan Timothios Aphrem Aboodi
World Alliance of Reformed Churches	The Very Revd Prof. Robert Barbour
	The Revd John Marsh/Mrs Julia Gilbey
	The Revd Dr Colin P. Thompson
World Council of Churches	Mrs Nicole Fischer
	The Revd Gunther Gassmann
	Mr William P. Thompson
World Methodist Council	The Rt Revd William Cannon
	The Revd Dr Geoffrey Wainwright

Conference Staff

SECRETARY TO THE LAMBETH CONFERENCE
The Revd Canon Samuel Van Culin
Secretary General ACC

DEPUTY SECRETARY
Mr David Long
Church Commissioners, UK

ARCHIVISTS

Dr Nelle Bellamy	(ECUSA)
Dr Brenda Hough	(C of E)
Mr Edward Pinsent	(C of E)

CHAPLAIN

The Rt Revd Alastair Haggart	(Scotland)
Mother Janet O.H.P.	
(Assistant to the Chaplain)	(C of E)

CO-EDITORS OF REPORT

The Rt Revd Michael Nazir-Ali	
(Co-ordinator of Studies for the	
Lambeth Conference)	(Pakistan/C of E)
Mr Derek Pattinson	(C of E)

COMMUNICATIONS TEAM

Director	Mr Robert Byers	(ACC)
Deputies	The Revd John Barton	(C of E)
	The Revd Peter Davis	(New Zealand)
	Miss Charlotte Rivers	(Australia)

Mr John Allen	(CPSA)
Mr Michael Barwell	(ECUSA)
Miss Alison Brand	(C of E)
Mrs Mary Cates (Wives' Conference)	(C of E)
Miss Julia Cocks	(C of E)
The Revd Canon Cecil Cooper	(Ireland)
Mrs Nicola Currie	(ACC)
Mr Tom Dorris	(WCC)
Miss Amanda Edwards	(C of E)
The Revd Canon Leonard Freeman	(ECUSA)
Mrs Liz Gibson-Harries	(Ireland)
Miss Flavia Gonsalves	(ACC)
Ms Toni Graff	(ECUSA)

Mr Jerrold Hames	(Canada)
The Revd Giles Harcourt	(C of E)
Miss Harriet Harland	(C of E)
Mr Fred Honaman	(NSKK)
Mr John Justice	(ECUSA)
The Revd Dr Roger Kahle	(Lutheran USA)
Mrs Eve Keatley	(C of E)
The Revd Oswaldo Kickhofel	(Brazil)
Mr Alan Kimber (Wives' Conference)	(C of E)
Mrs Mary Lou Lavallee	(ECUSA)
The Revd Charles Long	(ECUSA)
Mrs Nancy Long	(ECUSA)
Mrs Betty McLaughlin	(Ireland)
The Revd Æneas Mackintosh	(Scotland)
The Revd James Massey	(SPCK India)
Mrs Joy Meacham	(C of E)
Mr John Miles	(C of E)
Mr Robert Miles	(C of E)
Mrs Ruth Nicastro	(ECUSA)
The Revd Stanley Nyahwa	(Central Africa)
Ms Winnie Ogana	(Kenya)
Mr Michael Phalatse	(CPSA)
Mr James Rosenthal	(ECUSA)
Father Thomas Ryan	(RC Canada)
Mr Doug Tindal	(Canada)
Mr Stephen Webb	(CCA)

CONFERENCE SECRETARIAT
Director Miss Deirdre Hoban (ACC)

Miss Thelma Abernethy	(Ireland)
Miss Rita Almond	(C of E)
Ms Freda Barrow	(ECUSA)
Mrs Muriel Bartlett	(Canada)
Mrs Helen Bates	(ACC)
Mrs Joan Christey	(ACC)
Mrs Christine Codner	(ACC)
Mrs Elizabeth Coy	(ACC)
Miss Joan Denne	(C of E)
Mr Bert Gorman	(Ireland)
Miss Pat Heaven	(C of E)
Mrs Val Howes	(C of E)
Mrs Doris Kay	(C of E)
Miss Sheila McDonald	(C of E)
Miss Suzanne McKonky	(Ireland)
Ms Pamela Meyer	(ACC)
Mr Ian Rice	(Ireland)

Miss Janice Smith	(ACC)
Miss Brenda Stanley	(C of E)
Miss Juliet Thompson	(ACC)
Miss Sue Waymark	(PWM)
Ms Vanessa Wilde	(ACC)

DEPUTY SECRETARY'S ASSISTANT
Miss Lucy Thirtle	(C of E)

ENQUIRY OFFICE
Director	Col. John Haddon	(C of E)

The Revd Brian Chalmers	(C of E)
The Revd Sheila MacLachlan	(C of E)
Assisted by students from the University and local volunteers	

TREASURER AND REGISTRAR'S OFFICE
The Revd Michael Sams (Treasurer and Registrar)	(ACC)
Mrs Judy Elliott	(ACC)
Miss Sandra Davis	(ACC)

INTER-ANGLICAN INFORMATION NETWORK DEMONSTRATION TEAM
Director	The Revd Kris Lee	(ECUSA)

Mrs Lisa Barnes	(C of E)
Mr Andrew Bessant	(C of E)
Mr Ruben Boiardi	
Mr John Burden	(C of E)
Mr John Crease	(C of E)
Mr Douglas Fryer	(C of E)
The Revd Nigel Hardcastle	(C of E)
The Revd. Roger Hoare	(C of E)
Mr Paul Howarth	(C of E)
Miss Bethany Porter	(Unison)
Mr Tony Potter	(C of E)
Mr Gerry Teague	(C of E)
Mr Hal Whitmore	(ECUSA)

IMPRESARIO
The Revd Canon Austin Masters SSM	(C of E)

ARCHBISHOP OF CANTERBURY'S STAFF
Miss Mary Cryer	(C of E)
The Revd Dr John Fenwick	(C of E)

The Revd Canon Christopher Hill	(C of E)
Miss June Inman	(C of E)
The Revd Graham James	(C of E)
Mrs Eve Keatley	(C of E)
The Revd David Maple	(C of E)
Miss Eleanor Phillips	(C of E)
The Revd Canon Roger Symon	(C of E)
The Revd William Taylor	(C of E)
Miss Anne Tyler	(C of E)

LANGUAGES SECTION
Director Mrs Donata Coleman

The Revd John Ball	Swahili
Mr Beni Chisa	Swahili
Mme Fernanda Comba	Spanish
The Revd Canon E.M. Francis	Asst Burmese Bps
Ms Elizabeth Hale	Japanese
The Revd Michael Ipgrave	Japanese
Dr Lorna Kendall	French
Miss Izumi Kikawada (Wives' Conference)	Japanese
Mrs Ruth Lambert	French
Miss Bridget Lane	Swahili
Mrs Christine Méar	French
Cpt Ray Mills	Spanish
The Revd Daniel Mwailu	Swahili
Mrs Margaret Mwailu	Swahili
Miss Rie Ohno	Japanese
Miss Margaret O'Shea	Swahili
Miss Jenny Siama Paul (Wives' Conference: Asst Sudanese Bps' wives)	
The Revd Peter Potter	French
Miss Madeleine Richter	Spanish
Miss Maria-Lena Sandoz	Spanish
The Revd Clifford Smart	Asst Korean Bps
Miss Keiko Tanaka	Japanese
Miss Colette Terris	French written translation

LONDON DAY CO-ORDINATOR
The Revd Canon Eric Reid	(C of E)

POST LAMBETH CONSULTANT
The Revd Canon Vincent Strudwick	(C of E)

RESOLUTIONS SECRETARY
Mr Derek Fullarton	(C of E)

SECTION CO-ORDINATORS

Sections 2 & 3	The Revd George Braund	(ACC)
Sections 1 & 4	The Revd Canon Martin Mbwana	(ACC)

SECTION SECRETARIES

Section 1	The Rt Revd Pat Harris	(PWM)
Section 2	Prof. John Pobee	(WCC/Ghana)
Section 3	The Revd Canon Martin Reardon	(C of E)
Section 4	The Ven. Richard Randerson	(New Zealand)

SECTION STAFF

Section 1	The Revd Mano Rumalshah	(C of E)
Section 2	The Revd Dr Bert Breiner	(ECUSA)
Section 3	The Revd Canon Howard Root (Anglican Centre in Rome)	(ACC)
Section 3	The Revd Geoffrey Brown	(C of E)
Section 3	Dr Gillian Evans	(C of E)
Section 4	The Revd Preb. John Gladwin	(C of E)
Section 4	The Revd Charles Cesaretti	(ECUSA)
Section 4	The Revd Canon Na'im Ateek	(Jerusalem)

VIDEO CONSULTANTS

Producer	The Revd Robert Browne	(ECUSA)
	Mr Lowell McElvey	(ECUSA)
	The Rt Revd Harold Robinson	(ECUSA)
	Mrs Marie Robinson	(ECUSA)
	Mr Brent Wimberly	(ECUSA)
	Miss Julie Wimberly	(ECUSA)

WIVES' CONFERENCE

Co-ordinator	Mrs Hazel Treadgold	(C of E)
	Mrs Elizabeth Champion	(C of E)
	Mrs Margaret Chapman	(C of E)
	Miss Rosalind Corteen	(C of E)
	Miss Brenda Cowderoy	(C of E)
	Mrs Mary Haggart	(Scotland)
	Mrs Patricia Harris	(C of E)
	Miss Anne Holt	(C of E)
	Mrs Sarah James	(C of E)
	The Revd Rachael Stowe	(C of E)
	Mrs Mary Strutt	(C of E)
	Miss Rita Wilson	(C of E)

APPENDICES

Four Ecumenical Responses to the Archbishop of Canterbury's Opening Address, 'The Nature of the Unity we Seek'

APPENDIX 1

RESPONSE BY THE REVD DR EMILIO CASTRO, GENERAL SECRETARY, WORLD COUNCIL OF CHURCHES
(delivered by Professor John Pobee)

I would like to express my gratitude for the invitation to enjoy your fellowship and to participate in your spiritual and theological search. Let me take this opportunity to greet you in the name of the family of the World Council of Churches, to whose life you contribute so much. We are very thankful to Archbishop Runcie that he has chosen as the topic for the beginning of the Conference, 'The Unity We Seek'. It would be difficult to find a better way to express the ecumenical vocation. We are together trying to respond to the prayer of our Lord, 'that we all may be one, so that the world may believe'.

My comments on the Archbishop's paper are in the direction of underlining certain aspects, or illustrating them, rather than expressing disagreement.

1   It is possible for the purpose of analysis to separate the considerations of confessional unity – in this case Anglican – from the common search for Church unity. In practice, however, in the theological consideration of the topics of the internal life of our Churches today, we are so close to each other that this is impossible. Our readings, our dialogues, our prayers take place today with people from the most diverse confessions. More and more Anglicans – or most Anglicans today! – lead their Christian life and develop their ministry inside united Churches or even in some post-confessional Church. Bishops of those Churches are present here and they are thankful for the Anglican heritage, but they would have great difficulty following an internal Anglican discussion if the same did not take place inside the horizon of the Kingdom, with access to the resources of the whole people of God. It is necessary to recognise a common tradition, a common history and common bonds of intimacy in our belonging to a particular Church family. But we cannot any longer see our own problems separated, isolated or untouched by the problems and perspectives of the others. The only justification for keeping, albeit critically, a confessional identity in this ecumenical era lies in the search for a better contribution to the total mission and unity of the universal Church.

2   We need to be warned not to use the potential consequences of your decisions for the relations with other Churches as a tool, even less a weapon, in the common search for truth, a search that should be carried on its own merit, on the basis of the Bible, tradition, prayer and reason.

What would an eventual decision on the ordination of women mean for Churches which do not ordain or for Churches which ordain? There is a 'no win' situation if we begin to consider these or any other theological or ecclesiological issues from the perspective of the reaction of the others. First, let me recall that the so-called 'other' is a sister Church which is equally interested in going deeper into the truth, into considering seriously the biblical and theological issues. Their challenge to us should help us to go into the depth of the issue; our challenge and response to them should also contribute to their serious handling of the problems with which we are confronted. My ecumenical responsibility inside my Church is first of all to deal with the arguments and secondly, of course, with the sensibilities involved.

Many examples could be given of this kind of dilemma and the positive solutions the Churches have found for themselves. In almost every example of Church union it will be possible to discover small groups of faithful Christians who did not find it possible to integrate into the new Church reality.

In the present internal conflict within the Roman Catholic Church, Rome could not sacrifice among other things its ecumenical vocation in order to keep peace with one sector of its own family. Or, when the Methodist and the Evangelical Churches in Germany came to a reciprocal recognition of pulpit and altar, and when the Evangelical Church in Germany is ready to arrive at the same conclusion with the Old Catholic Church – what does it mean when some people are asking for Orthodox or Old Catholic recognition? There is an unavoidable chain of relations that will be affecting each one of our internal decisions. But the over-riding factor should be the vision of the Kingdom to come, faithfulness to the biblical testimony, and missionary response in the situation in which we find ourselves. Let us be sure that we are able to give account of the dimension of obedience which is present in our decisions. Let us always be accountable, but never hostage one to the other.

We will have difficulties, surely, but the past history of the Church indicates how very often dilemmas that seemed impossible to overcome have become today sources of richness for the life of the Church. Last year, when we were celebrating the 1200th anniversary of the Second Council of Chalcedon, concerning the iconoclast polemic, we gave thanks to God for the way in which, perhaps through the mediation of Orthodox theology and spirituality, almost every sector of the Christian Church is free today to use artistic representations of the Gospel as help to our worship of the Living God. Or we have seen over the last twenty years a growing recognition of justification by faith as expressed by Martin Luther as one of the pillars of Christian faith recognised by all Church families, after having been the symbol of a terrible split in the Western family of Churches. Or we could speak about the tremendous amount of agreement in the perception of the Holy Communion that prevails today in the Christian Churches in terms of the real presence of Jesus Christ in the elements, after so many centuries of heated polemic.

What is necessary today, in the light of this history, is not to blame each other or to separate from each other, but to enter into the theological debate as partners in the search for truth and faithfulness, reciprocally giving the time to grow together in vision and understanding. Only God in God's wisdom knows the way and the moment in which we will recognise the deeper uniting truth inside what seem to be irreconcilable positions.

3   The theme introduced by Archbishop Runcie is the basic challenge and issue in the ecumenical movement. Very rarely is the speech of the head of a Church –

whether the Pope or the president of a local synod – unrelated to the question of Christian unity, the unity we seek. We live in an ecumenical era and cannot escape, even if we wanted to, from this moment. In what direction, then, shall we look for the unity of the Church? In the service of what model shall we devote our endeavours? We are engaged in many bilateral dialogues. Are these exercises in comparison or real negotiations towards unity? There are still many Churches who remain aloof from the conciliar ecumenical movement out of suspicion of imperialistic models of unity, or the assumption that the only possibility for a united Church is a big Church with a big bureaucracy. Others are convinced that they search faithfully for the unity of the Church without realising that they are projecting the model of their own Church as the model which others should follow in order to arrive at a united Church. This is the paradox of the replies that we have received to the document on Baptism, Eucharist and Ministry: many Churches assume the normality of their model and affirm that document out of their 'normality' instead of testing their own being in the light of the common wisdom recognised by theologians from different Churches. This is then the ecumenical challenge and we will follow your discussions of the same with passionate interest.

There are several dimensions mentioned in the Archbishop's paper that are fundamental to this topic:

(a) the acceptance of diversity as demanded by your own Anglican *raison d'être* is a must in any consideration of a united Church. The richness which the Holy Spirit has granted to each one of our Churches, our spirituality, liturgies, theology, cannot be lost. A united Church should be richer in all its expression than the separated Churches. So we need to embrace diversity as we search for the universal Church. One component of that diversity which is clearly developed in the Archbishop's paper is the interaction between the local Church and the universal Church. In your own Anglican terminology you talk about Provinces, and the issue is the relation between provincial autonomy and collegiality, universality, not only in the total Anglican world but also in the total Church of God. There is a serious theological debate that has to do with our understanding of ecclesiology and that comes perhaps to a certain visibility in the dialogue between the Orthodox Churches and the Roman Catholic Church. Is it the local Church, your Province, a total Church with all the elements of catholicity which then searches for a common expression of that catholicity in conciliar structures at the world level, or is the catholicity of the Church in a given place created by the relation to a centre? These are not subtleties but a fundamental debate in the understanding of the unity of the Church which corresponds to our awareness both of the local expression of the Church of Jesus Christ and of the universal vocation of the people of God in the service of the Kingdom to come.

Anglican Provinces are members of the World Council of Churches in their own right. They are recognised as full Churches, and the role of Canterbury is recognised by them as the primacy of love that enables those Churches to consult each other and to increase their service to the total people of God. A constructive solution to the tension between the local, provincial and universal Church will be a breakthrough in the description of a model for unity that could be attractive to all sectors of the Christian Church.

(b) But, not withstanding your Anglican diversity, your tradition seems to demand certain common elements: Creeds, councils, episcopacy, primacy. Archbishop

Runcie reminds us that the function of ecumenical dialogue is to articulate basic unity in faith in diversity of expression. I hope that as Churches come closer to each other, we may learn from the notion of tradition in the Orthodox Church, where the concept does not refer to fixed moments or documents of the past but to the ongoing life of the people of God. The reciprocal recognition is not so much in terms of a commonality of affirmations, but in the common belongings, assuming the ongoing permanent reality and presence of Christ in the life of the people and the world. This notion of living tradition gives continuity and flexibility, recognition and freedom, but our Western-trained minds demand more conceptual clarity and definition. It will be interesting to follow in a few more years the impact of new forms of reasoning coming from the interaction with the cultures of countries in the Third World, liberated from the present slavery to the conceptual-dogmatic mould which is the contribution of the Western world to the Christian Church. The Second Vatican Council coined the expression 'hierarchy of truths', and we need to explore the potential of this concept for the creation of an area of common confession and the recognition of areas of freedom for our local or confessional traditions. Our friends in the Orthodox Churches demand the recognition of the first three universal Councils or of the first seven ecumenical Councils. This is a potential way to affirm a common basis for growing together. Your own Chicago–Lambeth Quadrilateral is also an attempt to underline the common convictions that will facilitate the expression of the unity of the Church. But you will need to allow for the discussion of the notion of episcopacy and the notion of primacy in the light of the experiences of Churches who have been able to preach the Gospel and spread it to the corners of the earth without referring to those offices. Are we ready to discover in collective expressions of the synodal life of other Churches the substance of the office of the bishop as described in the New Testament? Here again, there is an ecumenical exploration to follow through together, always on the basis of our *koinonia* in Christ and inside conciliar structures where we commit ourselves to the others, both in giving and receiving.

(c)   The Archbishop concentrates his attention on demanding some common structures to express unity in diversity: episcopacy, councils and primacy. Perhaps His Grace is right in assuming that in the common celebration of the historical creeds of Christianity we are called to be one and that the real question is our different ecclesiological understanding or perhaps our different ecclesiastical practices. Let us take, for example, the painful awareness of Christian disunity at the Lord's Table. For centuries we thought that the problem was in a different interpretation of the sacrament. Today, for all those Churches who participate in the ecumenical debate, the problem is not primarily there. We confess with the words of our Lord, 'This is my body, this is my blood', the real presence of the crucified and risen Lord in the life of the people of God. After the publication of the Lima liturgy we now have an order of celebration that is practically accepted by all traditions, because all the theological and doctrinal dimensions that are considered necessary for the celebration of the sacrament are fully recognised there. So, we have a commonality of understanding and a potential commonality of practice. But what we do not have yet is the mutual recognition of our ministry. This being the case, we need to speed up urgent theological discussion of this concept. But meanwhile, what could be the obstacle for the opening of our 'confessional' Tables to the participation of Christians from other confessional groups? Even if inter-communion is prevented by the lack of recognition, it could be communion, recognition of the reality that God has already created among ourselves. But it is here where the phrase that 'we have a limited degree of communion but not yet a complete communion' is raised as an explanation of the difficulty. My firm conviction is that our communion is complete because in our baptism we have been immersed in Christ's death, and in prayer we are taken into the mystery of the unity of God (John 17.21). So, if we belong together in Christ, if we join together in prayer in the mystery of God, if we recognise each other as we do, belonging to the same universal Christian tradition of the people of faith by giving to each other honours and recognitions, are we not accepting each other as Christian brothers and sisters? Then the problem is located at the level of ecclesiastical order, but not at the theoretical level of reciprocal recognition of our ordination, but at the practical level of the recognition of the authority of the others. The questions of structures, particularly of authority in the life of the Church, become the fundamental stumbling-block to our unity.

Let us look at a dramatic example: the breaking of communion between the Western and Eastern parts of the Church was consummated with the reciprocal anathemas in the eleventh century. Fortunately, in 1967 Pope Paul VI and Patriarch Athenagoras raised those anathemas in an embrace of love and common belonging. The historical obstacle to communion has been removed; however, communion is not yet a reality between these two Church families. What remains? Where is the obstacle? We need to enter into structures *for* unity that will both oblige us and make it possible for us to confront the real remaining causes of our divisions.

4   The World Council Assembly of Nairobi (1975) developed the image and concept of conciliar fellowship as a step forward in our search for Christian unity: conciliar 'communion'. It is essential to begin with the recognition of the communion that already exists among ourselves. It is only out of the recognition of the grace of God in baptism and in developing bonds of love in the common worship of our Lord that we have the basis to start developing the structures of conciliarity that will be the fruit of that communion and the instrument to enhance it in all aspects of our church life. Nairobi said it in this way:

> The one Church is to be envisioned as a conciliar fellowship of local churches which are themselves truly united. In this conciliar fellowship, each local church possesses, in communion with the other, the fullness of catholicity, witnesses to the same apostolic faith, and therefore the others as belonging to the same Church of Christ and guided by the same Spirit. As the New Delhi Assembly pointed out, they are bound together because they have received the same baptism and share in the same Eucharist; they recognise each other's members and ministries. They are one in their common commitment to confess the Gospel of Christ by proclamation and service to the world. To this end, each church aims at maintaining sustained and sustaining relationships with her sister churches, expressed in conciliar gatherings whenever required for the fulfilment of their common calling (*Breaking Barriers*, p.60).

The Archbishop develops the notion of conciliarity as a fundamental one which should include:

(a)   local churches meeting each other in a universal council (already discussed above);

(b)   the whole people of God participating. The present emphasis of the WCC on the participation of youth and women should be a central component of our search for structures of conciliarity. I quote here a very dear Roman Catholic sister, saying: 'I do not consider the question of women's ordination to be decided until women have access and the right to be in places where it will be discussed and decided'.

(c) the acceptance of other Churches as Churches in their own right, recognising the actions of the Holy Spirit in their midst. The notion of *vestigia ecclesiae* used by Vatican II, that perhaps from a certain ecclesiological *a priori* facilitates co-operation with other communities, unavoidably betrays a certain sense of the patronising, of superiority. It reminds me of some Protestant attitudes in Latin America, when we were discussing whether we could ever conceive of the Roman Catholic Church as a Christian Church while we were obliged to recognise that some individual Catholics may be saved! I think we have progressed enough in the ecumenical movement to eliminate this easy and ambiguous way out of our dilemma, categorising the different collective expressions of the people of God, some as Churches and others as Christian communities. But this of course is part of the debate that is in front of us.

5 I have reserved for the end the main affirmations of Archbishop Runcie, those at the beginning and at the end of his paper. The horizon of the Kingdom of God is fundamental for every discussion of the unity of the Church. The unity that we are searching for should be seen in the participation in the struggle for world liberation and for world reconciliation. The Church exists to be servant of the Kingdom of God, to proclaim, to symbolise, to be an instrument for the unity of all creation. But this general phrase should be brought down to earth in order to give some historical content to the same and to be aware of the conflictual nature of the search for the unity of humankind. Ernst Käsemann, the New Testament scholar, reminds us that the marks of the Church are not only the proclamation of the Word and the administration of the sacraments, but also the presence of the poor, because it is in the poor that Christ has promised to come to our encounter! If our search for the unity of the Church does not confront the conflicts in the world, it is a betrayal both of the Gospel and of the Church. The ecumenical movement has been practically always at the centre of polemic simply because the unity for which we are searching is the unity of the service of reconciliation of all humankind, but in the spirit of the cross which first takes sides with the poor, the sinner, the down-trodden, and from the suffering of solidarity is able to open arms to embrace the world in an offering of sacrificial love and forgiveness.

The Churches of the United States and the Soviet Union, visiting each other over decades, praying with each other for peace, were paving the way for the initial steps of agreement on disarmament which are taking place today. Churches struggling in South Africa to overcome the sin of apartheid give testimony of the power of the Gospel in the confrontation of the powers of this world and are – and should be even more – strengthened by the real unity and solidarity of all those who also struggle against the same enemy inside their nations, challenging the economic and political powers of their countries. I do not want to defend the World Council of Churches. Surely we have made and will make mistakes in trying to be faithful to the Gospel of Jesus Christ in the actual conflicts of the world, but we invite all Churches to share the obligation and privilege of being together at the service of the poor, of the marginal, in challenging structures of oppression, in announcing the new world that is coming from God, which is in confrontation with the prevailing reality of today. The ministry of reconciliation according to Christ's model is the service to be given to the world today, risking even our internal Christian unity for the sake of that unity of love which has been sealed once for ever on the cross.

There is a clear interaction between the unity of the Church and the renewal of humankind, the unity of the world. If we do not advance on the road to Christian unity, how can we pretend to invite the powerful of the world to advance on the road to peaceful solutions of the prevailing conflicts? If we do not put up signs of hope for the unity of our Churches, how could the world believe when we proclaim hope in God for overcoming all hate and division in human history?

And the other way round: when we face the real problems that divide humanity and confront the powers together, we may go to jail together to discover the tragedy of our broken Table! When forty years ago Christians gathered in Amsterdam to establish the World Council of Churches, they were coming from the difficult years of World War II, trying not only to overcome inter-Church differences but to announce to the world dramatically that it was possible to speak of forgiveness, that it was possible to dream of reconciliation. There is a sacramental role, a sacramental reality of the Church, a priestly vocation, *pars pro toto*, assuming our unity as a service to the reconciliation of all things in Jesus Christ. A united Church is better equipped to serve, to announce, to pray for the reconciliation of all peoples and things in Christ. We need a model, we seek a vision. Meanwhile we are searching for the Church which the Bangkok Missionary Conference of 1973 described in this way:

> We are seeking the true community of Christ which works and suffers for his kingdom. We seek the charismatic church which activates energies for salvation (1 Corinthians 12). We seek the church which initiates actions for liberation and supports the work of other liberating groups without calculating self-interest. We seek a church which is the catalyst of God's saving work in the world, a church which is not merely the refuge of the saved but a community serving the world in the love of Christ. (Bangkok Assembly 1973, p.89)

APPENDIX 2

RESPONSE BY THE REVD FR PIERRE DUPREY, OF THE COUNCIL FOR PROMOTING CHRISTIAN UNITY AT THE VATICAN

I wish first of all to thank His Grace the Archbishop of Canterbury for inviting me to respond to his address. His own speech, together with the four responses, should furnish us all with a helpful conspectus of current reflection on ecumenism. This, in itself, seems to me both desirable and timely.

Most of all, however, I wish to thank the Archbishop for his own address, for its breadth of vision and for the lucid and careful way in which he has identified the questions that this assembly must face. Frequently, while he was speaking, I felt myself being drawn and challenged by the questions he raised. For these are not only your questions; they cannot only be your questions. In one guise or another they may well be our questions too. In fact, they are questions that impinge on everyone who is engaged in pastoral ministry. Above all, they are questions which touch everyone who is deeply and earnestly engaged in the service of unity – those, in other words, to whom it has been granted to grasp something of the depth of that prayer of Our Lord which was also a mandate to his disciples: 'may they all be one'.

'May they all be one': concern for unity was powerfully evident in every word of what the Archbishop has said to us. I find it most telling that his opening address is precisely on the theme of unity. The Conference has before it a wide and varied range of pastoral, social and theological issues waiting to be dealt with. There are therefore other themes, other avenues that might have claimed the attention of the Archbishop at this early stage. Yet he spoke about unity. In doing so, however, he has made it clear, and it is a point I strongly corroborate, that the theme of unity bears directly on all the other topics, and all other topics having a bearing on the theme of unity. I want to reflect with you on why this is so.

In about AD 50, Paul pointed out to the Corinthians how shabby their internal divisions really were. He showed them how narrow and how limited was their vision in the face of the reality that has broken into the world in and through the Risen Christ. 'Behold, the new has come. All this is from God, who through Christ reconciled us to himself and gave us the ministry of reconciliation' (2 Cor. 5. 17-18). Paul pleads with the Corinthians to be reconciled with one another. He pleads with us too. He charges us to reconcile humanity in the name of Christ.

This message of reconciliation is perhaps more pressing in the world of today then it was nineteen centuries ago. The ministry of the Church is and must be seen to be a ministry of reconciliation. But for that to be so, must not we be reconciled, and must not we be seen to be reconciled? Reconciled with God and with one another: 'that they all be one, so that the world may believe'.

'Behold, the new has come'; a new reality which is the final reality. The Archbishop, in putting the vision of the apocalypse before our eyes at the very beginning of his address, has confronted us with the vision which rules us on our journey and in all our striving. It is a vision, moreover, which must begin to be a reality on the journey itself. This final reality has already been bestowed on us for the transformation of the world. Even now, in and through the realities of this world, the 'powers of the world to come' (*dunameis tou mellontos aionos*) (cf. Heb 6.5) already engage us and transform us. In this truth lies the whole of the mystery of sacramentality: the mystery of the Church. The Church and its activities have to be signs and means by which the ultimate realities are made present to us, and we in turn are enabled to share in them. 'Behold, the new has come': the new creation is here and it is God working among us.

Above all, that work of God creates a quite new kind of unity: the unity of the members of the risen Christ. A new relationship is forged at the most profound level between those who are born again through baptism and who share in the same Spirit: the communion of the Holy Spirit. And by its very nature this is a relationship which is universal. All those who are baptised through water and the Holy Spirit are caught up in this single new reality which is the work of God. This relationship comes into being and develops in and through the realities of this world: in time and in space. It cannot be otherwise if it is to be proclaimed and to be believed. It is a *new* reality. But how difficult it has been for Christians throughout the centuries to foster and maintain this newness in appropriate forms of community. There was a temptation to fall into the trap of thinking of it or describing it in terms of a monarchy or a parliamentary democracy. It cannot be these or any such thing. No: 'Behold, the new has come', a new reality involving a relationship of total dependence on our One Lord, through the Holy Spirit. That dependence is the crucial relationship in this new work of God. Everything that is in the Church is there simply to serve to announce and to show forth the One Lord who is its saviour and the source of its life. The manifestation of this relationship makes the Church a sign to the nations of the world, that is, the original and ultimate *glasnost*.

Is there not a danger of obscuring this newness with our talk of 'independence' for a Church which cannot have and would not want to have any other relationship than one of total dependence: 'everything comes from God'. He is the source of all, and all the Church's possibilities for being agents of reconciliation and of peace can only come from him (cf. 2 Cor. 3.5); there is no account of the Church that can be given, no portrayal to be made of it except of its relationship to God, just as we can only understand the Son, the Head of the Church, in terms of his relation to the Father.

But precisely here there arises another aspect of the mystery of sacramentality, namely the living presence of Christ and the exercise of the authority of Christ within the Church. Moreover, the deep bond of communion between members of the Church is a profound and objective reality which demands real solidarity and inter-dependence along the local Churches.

Today, the mind of Christians – I won't say of the faithful, since it is precisely fidelity that is at issue here –, the mind of Christians, whatever their role in the Church, risks increasingly being formed by television, radio and the press, rather than by our receiving and our pondering the Word of God which is heard and celebrated in the Church. What is the danger here? The danger is that the newness given in Christ, the newness that is operative in and through the Church, may be discerned only with difficulty, and perhaps with greater difficulty than was the case in the past. The risk we run is that the organisation of the Community, of the society, of the Church, its various services and ministries, the authority exercised within it and for it will be coloured and influenced by the currents and the thoughts of the present world (*tou aionos toutou*). Our vision and understanding risks being shaped by the spirit of this world, a spirit which often runs counter to the Spirit of God.

This is nothing new. We can find this happening in every era and in every division that wounds and isolates. But is it not more dangerous today? Having learned from long experience, must we not be especially attentive today? In the face of new questions which may divide if they are posed, or may divide if they are avoided, must we not urgently ask whether their newness belongs to this world (*to aioni touto*) or to the world to come (*to mellonti aioni*) which is the source of reconciliation, of unity, and of communion. This is a discernment that has to be made by the Church as such.

'Behold, the new has come'. And so, what is involved in the constant reform which the Church as a human institution always needs is an ever deeper fidelity to the new reality. Our renewal must be a striving to take hold of and to hold together all that has been given, all the aspects of God's plan, all the requirements of his Word.

I wish to propose that, for Christians, it can never be 'either ... or'; it must always be 'both ... and'. The new reality is, inseparably, Way, Truth and Life. This is what is transmitted in the Church. We see this very clearly, for example, in the question of apostolic succession. Apostolic succession is succession in ordination because it is also succession in faith. It is succession in faith because it is also succession in ordination. Likewise, the ideal of the Community having but one heart and one mind (*homothumadon*), united in faith, coherent in its evangelical commitment, at the service of all, is not ensured simply either through conciliarity or primacy. Christian primacy only exists within collegiality, and there is no true conciliarity unless each bishop recognises the one who is first among them and unless one does nothing of importance without him (cf. 34 of the Canon of the Apostles). The whole of the Church history teaches us this lesson. All efforts and authentic reform will seek to integrate these two aspects in their vital interaction. May I say how moved I was by what the Archbishop said on this matter?

Is the unity we seek an organic unity? Can it be otherwise? It is the unity of the members of the same body, a unity lived and expressed. It is the unity we have received and continue to receive from the Head of the Body. Sometimes I have the impression – and I had it most strongly of all at the World Council of Churches assembly in 1975 in Nairobi – that people oppose organic unity because they see 'organic' as meaning 'organisation'. Others fear that in describing the unity we seek as a conciliar fellowship of local Churches truly united, one would be abandoning the goal of organic unity. But it is not 'either ... or'. All that was being attempted was to describe progressively together what this organic unity might be like. Since then, and always together, we have been pursuing this study in the context of the Faith and Order Commission, seeking to define the elements that make a local Church truly one. *Baptism, Eucharist and Ministry,* studies on hope, on the profession of faith, on the exercise of authority, all these things help us to make progress in our perception of the different elements which weave the bonds of communion within the local Church and among local Churches.

What we are about, then, is discerning together those things which are given by God to his Church, to enable it to live, to proclaim, to hand on the new reality which is upon us. I am deeply in agreement with the Archbishop when he insists that we must constantly evaluate ecclesial institutions and ecclesial activity in terms of the mission of the Church, in terms of the reason why the Church exists: to reconcile all things with God in Christ, through the Spirit; to make the whole of humanity into a single people united in the unity of the Father, and of the Son, and of the Holy Spirit – to speak in the language of St Cyprian; or, to speak with St Augustine, at the end there will be only one Christ, one Son loving the Father unto all eternity.

It is in this perspective that we must understand the meaning of Tradition. Tradition is the historical dimension of communion, that is the communion through the succession of generations: as the Church pursues its pilgrimage on earth, it is always faithful to what has been given and open to the future, open to new ways of expressing the ancient faith. This involves both continuity and change: they must be kept in balance, and this involves a continuing process of discernment. The whole of the Church is engaged in this process, but at the point of decision on matters of faith and sacramental life, the episcopal college has a responsibility it can never shirk. This brings me back to the balance between primacy and conciliarity.

To be very specific, it is clear to me that among the many fruits of the dialogue that has been pursued between the Catholic Church and the Anglican Communion is that it has enabled us to see clearly and in proper focus the agenda that lies before us. It is really the shared discernment of the gifts of God which are the marks of the new world. We must talk about the Church, about Tradition, about Authority, questions intimately related to one another. Our dialogue on these issues will be a dialogue about the structure, the contours of the communion which is God's work in our midst. Moreover, there is no doubt in my mind that if positive results of our dialogue on eucharist, on ministry, on salvation are to be consolidated it will be in the context of a deeper address to these questions. This study will help both to underpin the agreement already achieved and to resolve differences that are still outstanding. It is clear that this perception is shared by Anglicans. The great amount of discussion and the amount of publications on the question of authority show that Anglicans see this question and the issues relating to it as needing urgent attention. The question of the nature of the unity we seek presses us to ask what are the organs that maintain and deepen unity. In recent years the Anglican Communion has paid serious attention to this issue, and it is in terms of this concern that I see the significance of the Anglican Consultative Council, the meeting of Primates, and the developing role of the Archbishop of Canterbury. In the ARCIC dialogue this concern was taken into a wider context when Anglicans and Catholics discussed together the nature of the universal primacy of the Bishop of Rome. The nature of the universal primacy and the nature of the unity we seek are not issues, surely, that can be kept in isolation from one another. They are one issue and it is a question about which we may earnestly pray together. I wish to recall that last December, Pope John Paul II, in the presence of the Ecumenical Patriarch Dimitrios I, speaking of his own ministry, prayed that the Holy Spirit – and I quote – 'may give his light and illuminate the pastors and theologians of our Churches, so that we may see, together evidently, the forms in which this ministry may be a service of love recognised by both sides'.

The theme of my response, then, is that the purpose of our mission is that humanity may be able to say with St Paul, 'Behold, the new has come'. It is in that perspective that I welcome the third part of the Archbishop's address.

The Church is for mission, for the providing of that reconciliation with God and among men and women for which we all thirst. That mission is to the poor, the hungry, to those on the margins of society; it is to nations and peoples divided amongst themselves and against one another. The Church must be the instrumental sign of the human community that God wishes to bring into being. Men and women, young and old, black and white, rich and poor, are made for communion.

Our anxiety for unity and reconciliation is likewise an anxiety that we should not fail them. I pray that this Conference will bear true fruit and that that fruit may be tasted by all those whose hunger for the Word of Life, even if it is not recognised, is deep and desperate. Christians must help them to understand that 'the new has come'.

APPENDIX 3

RESPONSE BY THE MOST REVD PROFESSOR JOHN D. ZIZIOULAS, METROPOLITAN OF PERGAMOS (ECUMENICAL PATRIARCHATE)

It is a great honour for me to be invited to address this august assembly, the historic Lambeth Conference of Anglican bishops, which for more than a hundred years now has been an event of historic significance not only for the Anglican Church but also for the world-wide Christian community. This invitation constitutes for me a sign of true ecumenical spirit on the part of the Anglican Communion, a most encouraging and hopeful sign for the future of the Church's unity. It indicates clearly that no Christian Church can or does any longer act or speak, or even think and debate – I dare also say *decide* – in isolation. I trust that such an interpretation of this gesture of the Anglican Church on my part, an interpretation, that is, which sees in this gesture far greater and essential significance than a mere act of courtesy, does not sound too presumptuous. Although I should not for a moment forget that I am here as an invited guest to attend as an observer and speaker the proceedings of a body which does not formally belong to my own Church – and I should, therefore, bear in mind all the time that whatever I say should be expressed with the utmost care not to appear as interfering with the affairs of another Church – I nevertheless boldly assume that whatever is being said or even decided in this Conference is a matter of concern for me and for my Church too. After all, our two Churches are engaged in official theological dialogue, and can no longer say to one another on essential matters of faith and order, 'this is *our* business; you keep out of it'. Such an attitude would strongly contradict and even damage the ecumenical spirit lying behind the invitation that has brought me before you today. I should, therefore, like to express my deep gratitude to the Archbishop of Canterbury for this invitation, mainly because it portrays a consciousness of 'interdependence' – a term so central to his address of last night. And I shall try in all humility to submit to your consideration certain thoughts provoked in me by this rich and important address. I beg you to receive these thoughts as coming from a fellow Christian and bishop who has been deeply engaged in ecumenical dialogue for a long time and whose Church treats the Church's unity and its restoration as a matter of greatest importance, indeed as a subject of daily eucharistic prayer.

What can an Orthodox say to an assembly of Anglican bishops? How can the Orthodox tradition be of any relevance to a Church formed historically and spiritually by what is called 'Western Christianity', both Roman and Protestant? We have been accustomed to divide Christendom in two parts – or more recently three: the East, the West, and now also the so-called 'Third World'. While this tripartite division is due mainly to social and political reasons, that of the East-West scheme is not only cultural but to a great extent also theological. It points to a difference in mentality and approach in theology and church life, perhaps also to a different ethos. The Christians of the East have always been preoccupied with different problems from those dominating the Christians of the West. The late Cardinal J. Danielou in his work entitled *The Origins of Western Theology* singles out certain features that make up the typical characteristics of Western Christian thought as early as the time of Tertullian. They include: a strong interest in history, a preoccupation with ethics and a deep respect for the institution, sometimes to the point of being legalistic about it. St Augustine later on, owing to the crisis facing Western civilisation in his time, introduced a dimension that was bound to create a dichotomy within Western Christianity ever since, namely the importance of introspectiveness, of consciousness and the inner man, from which sprang the important mystical, romantic and pietistic movements of the Christian West. The East on the other hand seems to have always been preoccupied with an eschatological, meta-historical outlook that tends to relativise history and its problems. This has sometimes led to an undermining of the historical and political issues or even of missionary activity. But it has also had some positive consequences. The institution has always been central to the Orthodox tradition but has never been conceived purely or primarily in historical and legal terms. Authority in the Church was always placed in the context of worship, particularly the Eucharist, and was thus conditioned by the eschatological outlook in two main respects: through pneumatology, which makes of the institution an event, and through communion which makes the authority of the institution constantly dependent on the community to which it belongs. This preoccupation with eschatology has made it inevitable to look always for the absolute, the ultimate theological *raison d'être* of the institution and never to regard it as a matter of juridical *potestas* transmitted through a code of law.

This has had several concrete consequences in Church life and theology. It has helped the Church, for example, to avoid problems such as clericalism or the clash between charisma and institution. It has made it unnecessary to develop Pentecostalist movements, and, perhaps one may be bold enough to suggest, it has accounted for the fact that a problem so central in the present debate within Anglicanism – and the broader Western Church – as that of the ordination of women, has not been an issue in the Orthodox Church.

All this may imply that there is little or nothing in common between the Orthodox and the Western Churches, and that neither should the Orthodox bother to deal with the problems facing the Western Churches, nor should the Western Christians pay any attention to what 'exotic' Orthodoxy says concerning these problems. In fact there are many, alas too many, on both sides that think in this way. There are many Orthodox, for example, who watch what is happening in Anglicanism with the coolness and the arrogance of the outsider – a sort of 'who has appointed me my brother's keeper?' attitude; and there are many, alas too many, Western Christians who do not give a penny for what the Orthodox think when it comes to their own institutional matters, and who at best allow Orthodoxy to have a say in matters of spirituality and worship.

We thus witness an ecumenical movement still dominated by the past and unable to see that we all – Easterners and Westerners as well as Third World people – live in an increasingly unified world, in a world of interdependence, to use again this important point of the Archbishop of Canterbury's address, in which no geographic part of the Church can be self-sufficient, and no tradition can say to the rest 'I need thee not'. We all have to take *seriously* into account the view of the others, and we all have to think, act and decide on the basis not of what *we* want, but what the world demands and really needs in order to have a future, that future promised by God eschatologically in Christ.

With such thoughts in mind I wish to offer some modest comments on what the Archbishop of Canterbury has so pertinently pointed out in his address. And first I should like to comment on what the Archbishop has called 'internal' matters of the unity of the Anglican Communion. Of these matters, I should like to mention two in particular. They are both interrelated. And they are both far from irrelevant for the Orthodox themselves.

1 THE QUESTION OF CENTRAL AUTHORITY

The Orthodox are known for their decentralised way of church organisation. The system of 'autocephaly' involves an organisation whereby no central authority has the power to dictate to the rest what to do, leaving the final decision to a common agreement between the local Churches, and debating the issues for as long as it is necessary in order to reach unanimity or at least common consensus. I was struck by the Archbishop's reference to a similar attitude he had once observed among the African Christians. It is an interesting indication of how much we need each other and how useful everyone's experience is in the ecumenical movement.

Now, this system of autocephaly and synodical practice is undergoing a certain shift of emphasis in our time. This does not involve any radical departure from Tradition, but rather an application of its most fundamental principles. The 'many' always need the 'one' in order to express themselves. This mystery of the 'one' and the 'many' is deeply rooted in the theology of the Church, in its christological (the 'one' aspect) and pneumatological (the aspect of the 'many') nature. Institutionally speaking, this involves a ministry of primacy inherent in all forms of conciliarity. An ecclesiology of communion, an ecclesiology which gives to the 'many' the right to be themselves, to risk being pneumatomonistic, needs to be conditioned by the ministry of the 'one', just as the ecclesiology of a pyramidal, hierarchical structure, which involves a christomonistic tendency, can undermine the decisive role of the Holy Spirit in the life and structure of the Church and needs the aspect of the 'many'. We need to find the golden rule, the right balance between the 'one' and the 'many' , and this I am afraid cannot be done without deepening our insights into Trinitarianism theology. The God in whom we believe is 'one' by being 'many (three)' and is 'many (three)' 'by being one'.

The question of central authority in the Church is a question of faith and not just of order. A Church which is not able to speak with one mouth is not a true image of the body of Christ. The Orthodox system of autocephaly needs and in fact has a form of primacy in order to function, and I dare think that the same would be true of Anglicanism. The theology that justifies or even (as an Orthodox, and perhaps an Anglican, too , would add) *necessitates* the ministry of episcopacy, on the level of the local Church, the same theology underlies also the need for a primacy on the regional or even the universal level. It would be a pity if Anglicanism were to move in the opposite direction; it would then have to look for a non-institutional kind of identity, and the result would be ecumenically unfortunate, perhaps tragic. The Orthodox need the unity of the Anglican Church, because they have a vision of unity based not on confessionalism (which seeks to profit from the divisions of others), but on the concept of the *Una Sancta* as a reflection and an image of the eschatological unity of all in one body. The unity we seek is neither one of absorption in a confessionalistic sense, in which one Church absorbs another, nor one of a 'reconciled diversity' in which the Church is made up of confessional bodies which bear no structural relation whatsoever with each other. We must work towards a unity in which, in the inspired words of Archbishop Runcie, confessional identities must be ready like tents to dissolve themselves in order to become the One, Holy Catholic and Apostolic Church. But for this it is important not to lose sight of the experience of institutional unity in the present provisional state of confessional existence, for without such an experience no progress towards an organic, visible unity of the Church can be made. Anglicanism has, in spite of its contact with the Reformation, preserved episcopacy as an institution of visible unity. After the surprising experience of BEM we can regard this as a positive factor for the conception of the unity we seek, for it emerges now that episcopacy, properly understood or even, if necessary, reformed, can be the basis of a widely acceptable visible unity. It is in this direction that conciliarity, too, including the function of primacy, can be made into a matter of visible unity. We live at a critical moment in the history of the ecumenical movement, and the direction in which Anglicanism chooses to move with regard to its institutional unity will affect decisively the nature of 'the unity we seek' for all of us. Far from being an 'internal affair' of Anglicanism, its unity is a matter of vital concern for the whole Church.

2 THE ORDINATION OF WOMEN TO THE PRIESTHOOD

This leads me to take the liberty of saying a few words concerning the debated issue of the ordination of women to the priesthood. On this point I should like to begin by speaking bluntly and openly to you. It is no secret that the Orthodox are officially opposed to any decision of the Anglicans to ordain women to the priesthood, let alone the episcopate. Looking at the matter with a confessionalistic spirit, any split in Anglicanism on this matter can 'benefit' the Orthodox (and also the Roman Catholics). But in a non-confessionalistic approach to the ecumenical movement any such split would be extremely undesirable. I personally believe that Orthodoxy is not confessionalistic in its spirit – quite the contrary – and would, therefore, be anxious to see that the unity of the Anglican Church is maintained at all costs. Of course it is not for me, an Orthodox, to say to the Anglican Church how to do this. I can only make a plea and voice my concern on a matter affecting the unity of the entire Church, such as this one. I can, nevertheless, underline what Archbishop Runcie pointed out in his address when he referred to cases of conflict in the early Church, both New Testament and patristic. When conflicts of such acuteness arise, this history of the early Church teaches us that no decision should be reached without an exhaustive *theological* debate of the issue. The letters of St Paul in their majority illustrate this with regard to the issue of the way the Gentile Christians were to be admitted into the Church. And the fourth-century patristic literature speaks clearly of the length of the theological discussion that preceded all final decisions concerning the thorny issues related to Arianism. It took two generations, that of Athanasius and that of the Cappadocians, to clarify the issues theologically. Without an exhaustive theological debate no conflict can be creatively overcome or resolved in the Church.

It seems to me that we have not even begun to treat the issue of the ordination of women as a theological problem at an ecumenical level. Those opposing it have so far produced only reasons amounting to traditional practice, while those supporting it often appear to their opponents to be motivated mainly by sociological concerns.

Before the matter comes to voting it may be wise and more appropriate to the nature of the issue to debate it on an ecumenical level theologically. What is it in the nature of priesthood that prevents women from being ordained to the priesthood? And what is it, apart from perhaps serious and important social reasons, that necessitates the acceptance of women into the priesthood? Theology, being a reflective discipline, may often appear to be an obstacle to quick action. But is this necessarily wrong? Are we to turn theology into a secondary or even irrelevant matter in the unity we seek? Looking at the way the ecumenical affairs are conducted in our time one is sadly forced to think that this is already the case in the ecumenical movement of our days. But the cost of this can be too great for the Church of Christ to pay. As an Orthodox theologian I feel rather strongly about this and I cannot but express this feeling to you on this occasion.

3 But the Archbishop's address was so rich and so broad in the areas it covered that the two points I have just discussed form only a small part of what this address has meant to me as an Orthodox listener. It would not do justice either to the address or to my sensitivities as an Orthodox if I did not say how important I regard the broader perspective in which the Archbishop put the entire question of Church unity. I have in mind in particular two points made so forcefully by the Archbishop. One is the

point that we cannot seek the unity of the Church apart from the broader issue of the unity of humankind, and indeed of the whole created world. Looking at this from the standpoint of the Eucharist – a standpoint that both Anglicans and Orthodox share – one cannot but underline this point very strongly. The Church exists in order to proclaim salvation from all forms of brokenness and division, whether of a social or a natural kind. The catholicity of the Church begins from the Eucharist, where natural and social divisions such as age, sex, race, class, profession, etc are overcome in the body of Christ. The Church does not possess the power to bring about the overcoming of these divisions in history; indeed she believes that no human power whatsoever has such an ability. But this does not excuse her being indifferent to these divisions wherever and whenever they may appear. By word and sacrament, by preaching and not least by her institutions and structures, the Church must proclaim the transcendence of such divisions and be in this way a sign of the Kingdom. It is, therefore, for the sake of the whole world that the Church must be not simply united but form a *visible* unity, based on ecclesial structures which portray and express what the Gospel is about, namely the Kingdom of God. This leads us back to the points we made earlier on: institutional matters are inseparable from theology; Word, sacrament and institution form one unbreakable unity, so that if any one of these is found to be deficient the rest of them are seriously affected. An ecumenism that does not take seriously this unity – and signs of such an ecumenism appear quite often in our day – will not lead us to the right path to unity.

The second point stressed by the Archbishop in his address, which I think deserves underlining, is the one illustrated by the story of reading the story-book from the last page backwards. It took us a long time in theology to cease treating eschatology as the last chapter of dogmatics. Some of us still treat it in this way, but we are all gradually learning that the Omega is what gives meaning to the Alpha, and by having first a right vision of the future things, of what God has prepared for his creation in the end of time, we can see what is demanded of us in the present. Such an eschatological outlook liberates us from the evils of provincialism and confessionalism which threaten our Churches constantly, and broadens our perspective so as not to exclude from our concern for unity people of other faiths and even those who doubt and seek after the unknown God. This makes the Christ whom we regard as the only Saviour the true *anakephalaiosis* of all, and the Church truly Catholic as the eucharistic celebration wants it to be.

Ecumenism needs a vision. We cannot go on seeking unity by treating the Church as a fundamentally social institution. We have to ask ourselves constantly whether what unites or divides us matters eschatologically, whether it affects the destiny of God's world as he has prepared it in Christ. I fear that we often give the impression that we have no vision in our ecumenical endeavours, that we either quarrel about issues of the past or about matters that can make headlines for the news of the day, without asking the question of ultimate significance in these matters. We thus risk seeking a unity different from the one our Lord had in mind when he prayed that we all may be one. For his prayer *did* have a vision and indeed a *theology* behind it. It was a vision of unity modelled on the doctrine of the Holy Trinity.

We have many reasons to be grateful to Archbishop Runcie for giving us so many and such deep insights into the question of the unity we seek. I hope that my modest response to his address has not obscured too much these clear and invaluable insights. This would make it perhaps worth the patience you have shown in listening to me. Thank you.

RESPONSE BY MRS ELIZABETH TEMPLETON, THEOLOGIAN, CHURCH OF SCOTLAND

'Let there be a tree', said God, once upon a time, 'which grows from the birds down.' And the Church came into being. And its branches spread and its trunk grew downwards, till it rooted itself in the dusty ground. And theologians and clergy of many nations rested among its roots.

After a time, a dispute arose among them. 'This tree does not flourish as it should', they said to one another. 'We should pull up our roots, and move to richer soil, for one can see the quality of the earth here is abysmally poor. Other trees are improved by such transplanting. Let us have courage, and follow their example.' (For they saw from other trees that this was so.)

'No! No!' said others. 'We have seen trees wither and die when you tamper with their roots. There are bad years and good ones, and we should take the rough with the smooth. It would be colossal folly to pull up our roots, which give us all our sustenance. Let us wait, and things will improve.' (For they saw from other trees that it was so.)

Meanwhile, the noise of the debate reached some of the birds in the topmost branches, and they were puzzled. 'Do they not know', said one small sparrow, 'that we give this tree its life?' 'No', replied a wise old pigeon. 'We can only sing when we are touched by the sunlight. But we must sing louder, so that they remember the possibilities of birdsong.' And he began to coo with all his might.

It is a great honour to be here, but I do not quite know who I speak for as to the 'unity we seek'. For I am, I suppose, in the context of this Conference, a kind of cut-price bargain specimen of those who are mostly not here – female, lay, Presbyterian and (by the skin of my mother's teeth) post-war. So I will try to respond to the Archbishop's searching paper by speaking for the 'we' who relate to you as 'outsiders'.

There are, of course, many, even more, outside, not only unable to find themselves in any Church, but actively sceptical about the alleged God of love we claim to represent. I speak for them 'by analogy'. Then there are those outsiders, whom many of you rub episcopal shoulders with at home, who, like me, begin their search for unity from a denominational base which is resolutely without bishops.

From such outside positions, any comment at all on the Archbishop's exploration of inter-Anglican unity may be incompetent and presumptuous, but I will, in the end, take the liberty of saying how, from my perspective, what happens to you 'on the inside' has a bearing on us 'on the outside'. So I risk speaking on the nature of the unity 'we' seek in all the Archbishop's three senses, though in the specific Anglican case I use 'we' in that honorary sense which my husband recognises when I say, 'Dear, we must put out the rubbish!'

Of course, in a sense, my first conviction is that there are no outsiders, or that all 'outsiderness' is to be regarded as provisional, since God's lively and inviting love is without bounds. The Church exists to represent, cradle and anticipate the future of *all* our humanness, which is hidden, with the healing of creation, in the love and freedom of God.

Any unity we seek must be to enact and articulate that. It cannot then be the unity of a strong and exclusive club, which makes the outsider more outside, more alien, more at bay. Rather it must be the kind of unity which allows those outside to recognise their own humanness, to glimpse their own future with delight and hope, to get a whiff of their own transformation, their own wholeness. To put it a little provocatively, the Church is the-world-ahead-of-itself. It is not a separate enclave, not separable. As Hooker so gently puts it in his 'Sermon on Pride':

> God hath created nothing simply for itself: but each thing in all things, and of everything each part in each other have such interest, that in the whole world nothing is found whereunto any thing created can say, 'I need thee not'.

This lovely and haunting understanding of the Church, making real and concrete the relatedness of all things in love and freedom, is wonderfully deep in Anglican tradition, and will, I trust, be what sets the agenda for our attempts at inter-Church relations, as well as for our 'mission', our 'ethics' and our 'spirituality'.

That alone will stop us making of the Church yet another apartheid in creation. That alone will give us the courage to keep hearing all the outsiders. For we too rarely acknowledge, we who love this unity of the Church, that it exists in terrible combat with the *actual* Churches so many people encounter, stale, nervous, nostalgic, authoritarian, self-preoccupied in word and deed. Non-Christian credulity, and even Christian credulity, is strained sometimes past breaking-point by the pretensions of such Churches to express the courtesy and refreshingness of God.

Outsiders, too, are properly sceptical about much of our inter-Church activity, recognising in it, better than we may ourselves, the permanent lure of a Superchurch, corresponding to the Superman God of much popular religious longing, and created in his image for our exclusive self-preservation.

Such a Church would speak with one reassuring, unanimous, unambiguous voice on everything: doctrine, sexuality, politics, liturgy. It would have a uniform pattern of ministry. Its authority structures would define and quash heresy and insubordination. This Superchurch tempts many in all our Churches, offering instant relief from panic, from the pain of facing the complexity of life, and the diversity of human responses to it. It even tempts some in the world, battered as they are by the threat of nuclear winter, sexual catastrophe, economic disaster and ideological impasse.

Precisely because we learn from our 'outsiders' how unlovely we can be, it is important that we do not brush aside too quickly their questions about our desire for theological or structural convergence, for clear and unambiguous authority. For at our best we believe the unity we seek is *not* an ecclesiastical protection racket. But we must beware of ourselves at our worst.

One central theological question, which I find deeply embedded in all our internal and ecumenical debates about authority, is what level of *provisionality* we can properly live with together, under a God who is for us, ahead of us, but not within our grasp. I felt this as almost the deepest theological issue when I was privileged to share in a conversation, five years ago, between Cardinal Ratzinger and a group of joint Roman Catholic and British Council of Churches representatives. Finally, in the course of explaining why magisterial encyclicals could not be described as 'approximation to the truth', the Cardinal argued that if God had not disclosed himself and his truth in *absolute, determinate* propositions, then salvation was at risk.

Many a good Calvinist would agree with him, but I do not, and the conversation focused for me the hardest underlying polarity in all our interdenominational and intradenominational battles. There are among us those who believe that the invincibility of God's love discloses itself in some kind of absolute, safeguarded articulation, whether of Scripture, Church, tradition, clerical line-management, agreed reason, charismatic gifts, orthopraxis – or any combination of such elements. And there are those among us who believe that the invincibility of God's love discloses itself in the relativity and risk of all doctrine, exegesis, ethics, piety and ecclesiastical structure, which are the Church's serious exploratory play, and which exist at an unspecifiable distance from the face to face truth of God. What unity is possible in concrete existence between those on either side of the trans-denominational divide seems to me our toughest ecumenical question. If we can find a way through that one, I suspect that all our specific problems of doctrine, ministry and authority will come away as easily as afterbirth. But if we seek in any of our bilateral or multilateral shifts to mask, suppress or smother that divide, our so-called unity will be a disastrous untruth.

While that is my pre-eminent concern about the unity we seek at inter-Church level, I have another shade of worry – the only point where I suspect I reflect my own denomination's self-consciousness. (Since I am well aware of Scottish Anglicanophobia, I hope I speak without Presbyterian huffiness.)

Clearly in the galloping ecumenical progress among Anglicans, Roman Catholics, Orthodox and Lutherans, episcopacy is cherished as a sign (some would say *the* sign) of the apostolicity and catholicity of the whole Church. Now I belong to a denomination which, with some others, like the Archbishop's atheist, not only *happens* not to have bishops, but is so far *determined* not to have them (though, of course, God may surprise even Free Church persons by his future!)

Certainly as a Presbyterian I sometimes entertain the question: 'Was I told the truth at my baptism, that I was now received into the one, living, holy, catholic and apostolic Church? But it is not because we lack bishops that I entertain it, but because we lack, over and over again, love, grace and truthfulness. And surely of all our Churches, episcopal or not, that is true. Indeed, it was partly because at some key points in church history prelates were so unconvincing as custodians of the Gospel that the so-called Protestants thought it better to risk God without bishops than bishops without God! Or to put it more lightly, as Sydney Smith, that devout Anglican, suggests: 'I must believe in the Apostolic Succession, there being no other way of accounting for the descent of the Bishop of Exeter from Judas Iscariot.'

Now much of this is mere historically fossilised resentment, and must be undone. But perhaps it must be gently said, even to a gathering of bishops, that for some Christian bodies within the ecumenical movement, episcopacy itself is a theological problem.

All our denominations have so much to learn, to understand, to forgive, to confess in mutuality, that I rather hope the episcopal Churches will not take off with the collective consciousness of a clump of front-runners, leaving what you perceive as a handicapped assortment of Methodists, Baptists, Presbyterians, Quakers and others hobbling around the back straight! I too celebrate the immense advances made in these rich bilateral encounters between Anglicans and older episcopal Churches. But I hope that it might be your particular gift, after four centuries of 'Reformed Catholicity', to bear into the heart of these encounters the significant absence of the non-episcopal Churches, and to interpret it.

In a way, I am merely reflecting on my experience of BCC or WSCF encounters, where the *lived* working assumption is that all member denominations are equal in their status as 'receiving contributors' to the truth. That, of course, may become bland, evasive, superficial or complacent. It needs constant theological scrutiny. But it is extraordinarily healing as a presupposition. It is, of course, also a procedural necessity. For such federations have no executive authority structures over their members. But precisely that fact actually enacts the hope that the truth is among us, around us and ahead of us, that the truth is our custodian, not we the custodians of the truth. That relaxes us into the real mutuality of those who can risk being ecclesiastically in love.

Finally may I venture an outsider's longing about internal Anglican unity, as you face especially this testing and delicate issue of women's ordination to the priesthood and episcopate?

In preparing for this Conference and reading something of your history as a Communion, I have been constantly struck by the best generosity of your recurrent insistence that across parties, camps, styles and dogmas, you have need of one another. Both internally and in relation to other evolving Christian life-forms, you have been conspicuously unclassifiable, a kind of ecclesiastical duck-billed platypus, robustly mammal *and* vigorously egg-laying. That, I am sure, is to be celebrated and not deplored.

As a guest, I am sad to feel that you are under some pressure to renounce this remarkable openness of being, to tighten up the structures of dogma, ministry, pastoral discipline, to align definitively either with the lions or with the hens. For I find your costly opet to the other Churches and a gift to the world. How you sustain this now, whether you sustain it, seems central to this Lambeth Conference, (though, of course, the survival of formal unity can never properly be used as a blackmailing pistol at the head of perceived truth).

My hope is, at least, that the women's ordination issue does not become a scapegoat for all the questions that potentially divide you in your Communion, though it may be a focus of them. It is, at best, that you can see the issue as a gift, calling us all to earthed exploration of what Christ and culture mean for each other, how a human Church bears God to people, how sacrament and sexuality relate. For these are questions which reach into the wider world, where on the whole people couldn't care less about the ordination of anyone to anything, because they are too busy living and dying.

And if it is gift, it is gift not just because it opens up deep and wide theological questions, but because it also touches the levels of pain and passion which test what it means that we love our enemies.

The world is used to unity of all sorts, to solidarity in campaigns, unity in resistance, communities of party, creed, interest. But it is *not* used to such possibilities as this: that, for example, those who find the exclusion of women from the priesthood an intolerable apartheid and those who find their inclusion a violation of God's will should enter one another's suffering. Somewhere in there authority lies.

I suspect that only from such depth of exploration, which Churches rarely expose themselves to, will unity or authority emerge, at least in any sense which makes us credible as agents of God's 'healing of the nations'.

Instruments of Communion and Decision-Making: The Development of the Consultative Process in the Anglican Communion

A DISCUSSION PAPER FOR THE LAMBETH CONFERENCE, 1988

INTRODUCTION

1   This paper represents the latest stage in a process of discussion and consultation which began many years ago within the Anglican Communion but became prominent at the Lambeth Conference of 1968 and was further crystallised by debates at the meeting of Primates in Washington DC in 1981.

2   During the meeting of the Standing Committee of the Anglican Consultative Council in Toronto in 1986, the question of the inter-relationship of the ACC, the Primates' Meetings and the Lambeth Conference was raised in terms of administrative and financial considerations. On that occasion the Standing Committee was only concerned about questions of servicing these three elements of the Communion and the discussion was confined to sources of administrative support and secretarial assistance. It soon became clear, however, that much more was involved in any analysis of the relationship between the ACC, the Primates and the Lambeth Conference. Support and servicing involved questions of responsibility, leading in turn to matters which touched upon crucial aspects of what holds the Communion together.

3   A group was appointed to prepare a report for ACC-7 in Singapore consisting of: The Archbishop of Armagh, the Most Revd Dr R.H.A. Eames (Chairman); The Rt Revd R. Gordon (Bishop at Lambeth); Canon R.C. Craston (Vice-Chairman of the ACC); Canon S. Van Culin (Secretary-General of the ACC); Mr W.D. Pattinson (Secretary-General of the General Synod of the Church of England); Mr J.W.D. McIntyre (Secretary-General of the Church in Wales); The Revd M.C. Sams (Treasurer of the ACC).

4   The paper prepared by this Group was discussed by ACC-7 in Singapore and a further discussion document was then circulated to the Provinces for comment. This document is to be found in Part 3 of the report of ACC-7 and is entitled *Unity in Diversity within the Anglican Communion: A Way Forward*.

5   The present document is an attempt to place before Lambeth 1988 preliminary considerations on the questions put to the Provinces on authority in the Anglican Communion. It has been drafted by a group consisting of the following:

6   The Most Revd R.H.A Eames, Canon R.C. Craston, Canon S. Van Culin, Canon R. Symon, The Rt Revd M. Nazir-Ali, Mr W.D. Pattinson, Mr J.W.D. McIntyre, Miss D. Hoban, The Revd M.C. Sams.

COMMUNION, CONCILIARITY AND CONSULTATION

7   *Koinonia*, communion or fellowship, is increasingly being recognised as a basic way of speaking about the Church. Each local Church maintains the *koinonia* by a common adherence to the normative authority of Scripture, a common declaration of faith and a common celebration of the sacraments. From the earliest times, eucharistic fellowship with the bishop and with each other has been a sign and focus of *koinonia*.

8   What is true of the local Church is true also of the relationship between local Churches. Communion or *koinonia* between Churches is the result of the recognition of the apostolicity and catholicity by each Church of the others.

9   From time to time, it has become necessary for Churches in communion with each other to come together for mutual consultation and encouragement. Sometimes the common faith which the Churches profess has come under attack and it has been necessary to reaffirm it and to define it more clearly. At other times, a development has taken place in one Church or in certain Churches which is seen to affect the communion between the Churches as a whole. The Churches *in council* have to decide whether such a development is consonant with apostolic faith and practice or not.

10   It should be noticed that although communion and conciliarity are related aspects of the Church's life, they are not identical. Communion is a way of being the Church, whereas conciliarity is simply a way of maintaining and nurturing communion.

11   It has been seen that bishops are a focus of unity in the local Church. They are also a sign of the wider unity of the universal Church. Bishops have always been associated with the teaching office and with guardianship of the apostolic faith. It is entirely natural, therefore, that bishops should come together, from time to time, on a provincial, regional or universal basis, to deepen their knowledge of the faith which they guard and also for fellowship.

12   In the local Church, the clergy and the laity join with the bishop in preserving and promoting *koinonia* for the glory of God and for the sake of mission. At other levels too, priests, deacons and lay people have been associated with the bishops in consultation and decision-making. Over the last two hundred years or so, some Churches have accorded clergy and lay people a constitutional role in the conciliar process.

13   The Anglican Communion consists of a family of Churches each of which recognises the apostolicity and catholicity of the others and is in communion with them. The primatial see of Canterbury is a focus of unity for the family and the Archbishop of Canterbury also exercises a 'gathering' function in his capacity as President of the Lambeth Conference of bishops, the meeting of Primates, and the Anglican Consultative Council.

14   These instruments which maintain and nurture communion, and which may be regarded as the conciliar aspect of Anglicanism, have evolved over a period of time and have now become established.

THE ARCHBISHOP OF CANTERBURY

15   The Archbishop of Canterbury has been regarded as the focal point of the Anglican Communion and, as has been pointed out, exercises a 'gathering' function in the Communion. Communion with the See of Canterbury has been regarded as an essential part of being Anglican. The Archbishop of Canterbury is also becoming important in relations between the Anglican Communion and other world Communions.

THE LAMBETH CONFERENCES

16   From the earliest times, bishops have met as a body at provincial, regional and world levels. They have done this to deepen their knowledge of the faith of which they are guardians and teachers and to crystallise the apostolic teaching in particular contexts and at particular times. Their meeting has also symbolised and promoted the communion that exists between their Churches. The Lambeth Conference has come into being to meet this need for bishops of the Anglican Communion to come together for common counsel, encouragement and fellowship. It has a distinguished history of relating the Christian faith to contemporary issues. It has made notable contributions to the cause of Christian unity, to the ethics of the family and to Christian involvement in urgent social and political concerns. Bishops of the Anglican Communion also meet *as bishops* at regional, provincial and even sub-provincial levels. Provinces fully committed to the involvement of clergy and laity at synodical levels allow, nevertheless, for bishops to meet as a House sometimes when the synod is not even in session! The Lambeth Conference may be regarded as an analogue of such meetings of bishops at the provincial level.

THE ANGLICAN CONSULTATIVE COUNCIL

17   The Lambeth Conference of 1968 proposed the creation of an Anglican Consultative Council. The proposal was approved unanimously by the member Churches of the Communion and the Council came into being. The Council brings together bishops, clergy and laity from the member Churches. The ACC is sometimes described as a quasi-synodical body. Its membership is elected by the separate synods of the member Churches of the Communion to serve a designated term of office. The Council does not consist of separate Houses as most synods do and its decisions do not have binding force on the member Churches until they are ratified by the synods of these Churches. Also, episcopal, clerical and lay membership is not in strict proportion. In most other respects it functions like a synod. It is the one inter-Anglican body at present in which there is full representation from those Churches where Anglicans have entered into union with Christians of other traditions, such as the Church of North India, the Church of South India and the Church of Pakistan. In this conciliar way it implements full communion between these Churches and the Churches of the Anglican Communion.

18   A paper produced by a working group for ACC-7 entitled *Unity in Diversity within the Anglican Communion* proposes that the ACC should be modelled more closely on existing synodical structures within the Anglican Communion. Some provincial responses to this paper have suggested that there should be episcopal representation from every member Church along with clerical and lay representation. Other Provinces have suggested that the Primates could meet at the same time as the

ACC. This would enable them to meet separately as well as in association with the clergy and the laity in the ACC. Either way, the bishops at ACC meetings could function in ways similar to Houses of Bishops in provincial synods. If such changes were to be brought about, it would be necessary to revise aspects of the constitution of the ACC, particularly with respect to the functioning of an episcopal group within the Council, but also with respect to the number and kind of members coming from the Churches.

THE PRIMATES' MEETING

19   This is the latest of the organs of consultation and was established by a resolution of the 1978 Lambeth Conference. It has provided collegial support for individual primates and especially for the Archbishop of Canterbury in his role as a focus of unity for the Anglican Communion. It is yet another sign of communion between the Churches and it has enabled the Communion as a whole to respond quickly to urgent issues raised by the Provinces or by wider society.

20   The working group which carried out the preparatory work for the 'Unity in Diversity' document recommended that the member Churches of the Anglican Communion should adopt a common *Declaration* which would be used at major events in the life of the Church such as the ordination or installation of bishops. This would be a sign of the Church's adherence to apostolic faith and order and would also be a sign of communion between the Churches. *Such a declaration might well become another instrument of communion.* It is necessary, however, to ensure that such a document, while remaining faithful to apostolic faith and order, is as comprehensive as possible and takes full account of the different traditions within Anglicanism. Also, it is undesirable that a declaration based on the Chicago-Lambeth Quadrilateral should be merely about denominational identity. It should be framed in such a way that the involvement of the Provinces in ecumenical activity is not jeopardised. With these factors in mind, the initial draft submitted by the working group was revised. The following is a revised text of the declaration:-

  i.   The Church (of the Province) of .... declares itself to be united under one divine head in the fellowship of the one, Holy, Catholic and Apostolic Church, worshipping the one true God, Father, Son and Holy Spirit.

 ii.   It professes the Faith uniquely revealed in the Holy Scriptures and set forth in the Catholic Creeds, to which faith the formularies of this Church bear witness and which the Church is called upon to proclaim afresh in each generation.

iii.   It celebrates the divinely instituted sacraments, particularly those of Baptism and Holy Communion, as ordinances of the universal Church.

 iv.   It expresses its continuity with the apostolic tradition of faith and witness, worship, fellowship and ministry by means of the historic episcopal order. It is in communion with each of those Churches which preserve the historic threefold order of the ordained ministry and are in communion with the See of Canterbury.

  v.   It looks forward to the unity of all Christians based on a common recognition of the place of the Holy Scriptures, the Catholic Creeds, the dominical sacraments and historic order in the Church of God.

THE CONSULTATIVE PROCESS AND PROVINCIAL AUTONOMY

21   There has been much discussion recently on the relation between the acknowledged autonomy of the Provinces and the consultative process as it has emerged in the Communion. Communion between autonomous Provinces presupposes a certain agreement on matters of faith and practice. These matters are not static and, in a quickly changing world, have to be related to various contemporary situations. This means that if communion is to be maintained and nurtured, there must be frequent consultation between the Provinces. The organs of consultation outlined above seek to serve such consultation.

22   The process of consultation may be understood in the secondary sense of a Province informing the rest of the Communion of what it proposes to do and perhaps seeking advice on the best way to go about doing it. In its primary sense, however, it is to be understood as Provinces seeking counsel together in order to come to a common mind on particular issues. Such a consensus would first become apparent in the organs of consultation but it would also emerge in the pronouncements of particular synods and finally it would become apparent as *consensus fidelium*. Voting on issues at the ACC, the Lambeth Conference and the Provincial and diocesan synods can be significant steps on the way to arriving at a common mind and may be sanction for practical steps to be taken on a particular matter. However, such voting does not, on its own, necessarily represent consensus, which may still need to be sought among clergy and laity in dioceses and Provinces and in the life of the Communion generally.

23   Provinces of the Anglican Communion are certainly autonomous in the legal sense, but exactly how far does autonomy extend in the theological and moral sense?

24   It is clear that if communion between Provinces is to be maintained and nurtured then there must be some limits to autonomy in areas of theological and moral significance. It is true that questions will arise as to which issues are of merely local or provincial significance and which have wider implications.

25   In such cases it would surely be appropriate to say that at the very least the areas covered by the Chicago-Lambeth Quadrilateral and by the proposed declaration should be matters of Communion-wide significance. Significant alteration or adaptation in these by one or more Provinces should have at least the permissive consent of the Communion, apparent first in the organs of consultation. It is sometimes said that if an issue, which is at first an issue only for one or a few of the Provinces, becomes an issue for a significant part of the Communion, it then becomes an issue for the whole Communion.

THE SOURCES AND THE EXERCISE OF AUTHORITY IN THE ANGLICAN COMMUNION

26   The report on 'The Meaning and Unity of the Anglican Communion' which was presented to the 1948 Lambeth Conference acknowledged one Divine Source of authority but pointed out that, as far as the Church is concerned, this authority is found to be distributed among Scripture, tradition, creeds, the ministry of the Word and sacraments, the witness of saints and the *consensus fidelium*. Such a view of authority as dispersed among several elements was held to provide the appropriate checks and balances and to guard against too much reliance on one element alone. What is true of the *sources* of authority is true also of the *exercise* of authority by deci-

sion-making structures in the Communion. Within synods, the different Houses provide the appropriate checks and balances. In Provinces, the relation between diocesan and provincial synods provides a check. In the Communion as a whole, the instruments of communion or the organs of consultation provide the appropriate checks and balances for each other.

27 The Anglican Communion, therefore, seems to have a view of dispersed authority which relates not only to the sources of authority but also to its exercise.

COMMUNION AND CONTEXTUALISATION

28 The existence of instruments of communion and organs of consultation and the necessary limits they place upon Provincial autonomy need not hinder the task of every local Church to incarnate the Christian faith in the idiom and thought-forms of its particular culture. Certainly, the Churches are not free to do absolutely anything. Limits on their autonomy, however, must be very closely related to the safeguarding of that apostolic faith and order which is the basis of communion between the Churches. It is important to note that it is apostolic faith and practice which are being safeguarded not any one cultural expression of them.

AN INTER-ANGLICAN SECRETARIAT AND BUDGET

29 At least three of the four instruments of communion, the Anglican Consultative Council, the Primates' Meeting and the Lambeth Conference, are serviced by the small and under-resourced ACC Secretariat. It is important, if the instruments of communion are to be effective, for the Secretariat to be adequately staffed and equipped. It is vital that the Secretariat should be an efficient channel of communication between the Provinces. It is necessary also for it to be able to provide support for networks and commissions established by the various organs of consultation in the Communion. It is highly desirable that the Secretariat be enabled to sustain a programme of study and research under the direction of the ACC.

30 An effective Secretariat and efficient organs of consultation require funding. ACC-7 requested its Standing Committee and the Archbishop of Canterbury to carry forward proposals for an *Inter-Anglican Budget*, which would incorporate the funding needs of the ACC itself, the Primates' Meeting and the Lambeth Conference. It expressed the hope that, after due consultation with the Provinces and with the agreement of the Lambeth Conference, such a budget might become operational from 1 January 1990.

Jews, Christians and Muslims: The Way of Dialogue

1   Whilst dialogue with all faiths is highly desirable, we recognise a special relationship between Christianity, Judaism and Islam. All three of these religions see themselves in a common relationship to Abraham, the father of the faithful, the friend of God. Moreover these faiths, which at times have been fiercely antagonistic to one another, have a particular responsibility for bringing about a fresh, constructive relationship which can contribute to the well-being of the human family, and the peace of the world, particularly in the Middle East. Dialogue is the work of patient love and an expression of the ministry of reconciliation. It involves understanding, affirmation and sharing.

THE WAY OF UNDERSTANDING

2   The essential condition of any true dialogue is a willingness to listen to the partner; to try to see with their eyes and feel with their heart.. For understanding is more than intellectual apprehension. It involves the imagination and results in a sensitivity to the fears and hopes of the other. Understanding others means allowing them to define themselves in their terms rather than ours, and certainly not in terms of our inherited stereotypes. This means that in dialogue we may have to face some very different understandings of religion.

3   In relation to *Judaism* this means, first of all, recognising that Judaism is still a living religion, to be respected in its own right. The Judaism of today is not that of any one of the sects of first-century Palestine, and certainly not that of the plain text of the Hebrew Scriptures. Its definitive works, such as the Mishnah and the Talmud, as well as its current liturgy, were produced by the post-Pharisee rabbis in the same period, the first to fifth centuries, within which the Fathers of the Church were defining the meaning of Christianity. Great care should be taken not to misrepresent Judaism by imputing to it, e.g., the literal implementation of 'an eye for an eye', which was repudiated by the rabbis, or the denial of life after death. This is also true of the long-standing stereotype of Judaism as a religion of works, completely ignoring the deep Jewish sense of the grace of God. Judaism is a living and still developing religion, which has shown spiritual and intellectual vitality throughout the medieval and modern periods despite its history of being maligned and persecuted. The Middle Ages saw great Jewish philosophers such as Maimonides, Bible commentators such as Rashi, and poets and mystics, such as Moses Ibn Ezra, as well as scientists and interpreters of the Law. Our modern world is inconceivable without the contribution of Jewish thinkers from Spinoza to Büber, scientists such as Freud and Einstein, as well as musicians, artists and others who have helped shape our cultural life; we are, to our loss, less knowledgeable of the creative vitality of such Jewish spiritual movements of recent times as Hasidism and Musar.

4   Secondly, *Judaism* is not only a religion, as many Christians understand the word, but a people and a civilisation. Jews know and define themselves as Jews even

when they do not fully share the religious beliefs of Judaism and though there is ethnic diversity among them. It is against this background, at once secular and religious, that the importance of the land of Israel to the majority of Jews throughout the world needs to be understood.

5   Thirdly, it is necessary for Christians, as well as Jews, to understand the profound changes and potential for good in modern scholarly understanding of the Bible. Modern biblical scholarship is increasingly becoming a joint enterprise between Jews and Christians. Recent Jewish research has shed much light on the complex and varied religious and social situation in Palestine during the first century of the Common Era (i.e. the era common to Jews and Christians). Some Jews have become very aware of Jesus as part of their own history, and their writings have brought home to Christians his Jewishness. Renewed study of Jewish sources by Christian scholars has led them to see first-century *Judaism* in a new and more positive light, and to recognise that the predominantly negative assessment of Judaism in the early Church is far from being the whole story. There were many different groups within Judaism at the time of Jesus, and 'the scribes and Pharisees' reported in the New Testament should be seen as part of a wider discussion within Judaism. The New Testament picture of Judaism needs to be supplemented by expressions of faith by Jews of the time if first-century Judaism is to be properly understood.

6   We now have a far better appreciation than ever before of first-century *Judaism,* and not least of political factors which led events to take the course they did. The trial and execution of Jesus are now recognised by many scholars to have been brought about to serve the political interests of the Roman occupation forces and those Jews who collaborated with them. It was Rome, too, by its destruction of Jerusalem at the end of the Jewish War in 70 CE which forced a reconstruction of Judaism along much narrower and more rigorous lines than had prevailed earlier.

7   This new understanding of events is leading both Jews and Christians also to look at the way in which *Judaism* and Christianity came to part company and go their separate ways. Since many of the factors in this split were contingent on specific historical developments, and events need not necessarily have turned out the way they did, there would seem to be no reason why a new understanding should not develop, based on a reconsideration of what originally drove Christianity and Judaism apart.

8   *Islam,* like Christianity, is a living world religion. Dialogue with Muslims needs to take into account the fact that it has taken root in and shaped a wide range of countries and cultures. Contrary to popular opinion, for example, the largest Muslim country in the world is not in the Middle East. It is Indonesia in South-East Asia. Over the last fourteen centuries, often with vigorous Christian and Jewish participation, Muslims have developed a rich and varied mosaic of cultural patterns, theological schools, mystics and philosophers. While Muslim civilisation developed at first under the influence of the older Christian and Jewish civilisations of the Middle East, its impact, in turn, on the development of both Jewish and Christian thought and civilisation has been profound. Medieval Jewish thinkers like Maimonides and Saadia wrote many of their most influential works in Arabic. The philosophy of Aristotle and the Neo-Platonists came to western Europe largely in translations from Arabic, the translators being in many cases Christians living in the Muslim world. If geometry is a Greek word, algebra, alchemy and chemistry are Arabic. We call our number system Arabic because the Arabs brought it from India and popularised it

throughout the world. The astrolabe and the architectural arch both came from scientists working in the Muslim world. We are sadly unaware of much of Islamic history and thought. So rich and varied is it, that many Muslims are not familiar themselves with some of the thinkers and movements which are historically, geographically or theologically remote from their own experience just as many Western Christians are unaware of Byzantine Orthodox thought or of the life of the Oriental Churches, and vice versa. One of the values of an informed dialogue is that it can help both partners become more aware of some of the riches of their own respective traditions.

9 In understanding *Islam* it is necessary for Christians to grasp the central place of Islamic law in Muslim life. Islamic Law, *Sharî'a,* is based on the belief that God has, as a gracious act of mercy, revealed to humanity basic guidelines to live both individually and in society. Whereas Christians today tend to think of Christian faith as a personal commitment which can be expressed quite happily in a secular society, seeking to influence society but not seeking to impose a 'Christian' system on it, many Muslims believe that God has revealed his will on how the whole of society is to be ordered, from details of banking to matters of public health. Although based on the Qur'ân, the sources of Islamic law are much wider. The picture becomes even more complex if one attempts to include the Shi'ites who are the majority in Iran and form significant minorities in many parts of the Muslim world. A long development independent from the majority Muslim community (*Sunnî*) has resulted in a very different ethos and theology, making blanket statements about Islam almost impossible when Iranian and other Shi'ite thinkers are taken into account. Some non-Muslim communities living under Islamic rule experience the application of Sharî'a law as oppressive and inhumane. Another aspect of Sharî'a law which causes some distress is the treatment of women. We note that in some respects Islamic law has pioneered the rights of women in certain parts of the world. For example, under Islamic law, married women had the right to own property and conduct business in their own names thirteen centuries before these rights were granted in many Western countries. It is hoped that Christians and Muslims may search together for ways in which the position of women may continue to be improved for the benefit of society as a whole. We also need to remember that classical Islamic law provides safeguards for the rights of religious minorities which are not actually being enforced today. Further, in judging, we must always be careful to compare like with like. We must compare the highest and most humane ideals of Islam with the highest and most humane ideals of Christianity and the misuse of power at the hands of Muslims with the misuse of power at the hands of those who call themselves Christians. It is also worth noting that there is a long and distinguished tradition within Islam which seeks to interpret the *Sharî'a* in the light of contemporary conditions. There are many able exponents of this tradition today, and Christians need to affirm their work, particularly in view of the religious fundamentalism ascendent in so many parts of the world.

10 *Islam,* no less than *Judaism,* has suffered from Christian stereotyping. This is especially true of the notion that Islam is a religion committed to spreading its faith by the sword. History shows a much more complex pattern. It is true that the communities of the Middle East, North Africa, Southern and Eastern Europe and the northern half of the Indian subcontinent were originally brought under Islamic rule by military expansion. On the other hand, much of the part of the world which is now predominantly Muslim did not receive its Islam through military conquest. In fact,

the majority of the territory won by Islam in its early advance was taken from it by the Mongols, who already numbered Christians among them and other non-Muslims. Yet Islam converted its Mongol conquerors and much of central Asia remains Islamic to this day.

11   In fact, *jihâd,* usually mistranslated 'holy war', is a complex notion that needs to be seriously explored by Christians in dialogue with Muslims. The word actually means struggle and encompasses everything from spiritual struggle to armed struggle as sanctioned by Islamic law. Although Muslims have, in the course of history, sanctioned aggressive wars in this way, it is important to realise that there are many Muslim views as to what kind of warfare is legal under Islamic law. The existence of such divergent views might be a constructive point of dialogue.

THE WAY OF AFFIRMATION

12   If Christians wish their own faith to be affirmed by others, they themselves must be open to the full force of the attraction of the partner in the dialogue and be willing to affirm all they can affirm, especially when it resonates with the Gospel.

13   For Christians, *Judaism* can never be one religion among others. It has a special bond and affinity with Christianity. Jesus, our Lord and the Christ, was a Jew, and the Scriptures which informed and guided his life were the books of the Hebrew Bible. These still form part of the Christian Scriptures. The God in whom Jesus believed, to whom he totally gave himself, and in whom we believe is 'the God of Abraham, Isaac and Jacob'. A right understanding of the relationship with Judaism is, therefore, fundamental to Christianity's own self-understanding.

14   *Christians and Jews* share one hope, which is for the realisation of God's Kingdom on earth. Together they wait for it, pray for it and prepare for it. This Kingdom is nothing less than human life and society transformed, transfigured and transparent to the glory of God. Christians believe that this glory has already shone in the face of Jesus Christ. In his life, death and resurrection the Kingdom of God, God's just rule, has already broken into the affairs of this world. Judaism is not able to accept this. However, Christian belief in Jesus is related to a frame of reference which Christians and Jews share. For it is as a result of incorporation into Jesus Christ that Christians came to share in the Jewish hope for the coming of God's Kingdom.

15   Christian faith focuses quite naturally on Jesus the Christ and his Church. However, both these realities can and should be seen along with the hope for, and the horizon of, the Kingdom of God. The presence and the hope for the Kingdom of God were central to the preaching and mission of Jesus. Moreover, Christians continue to pray daily 'Your Kingdom come'. Christians and Jews share a common hope for the consummation of God's Kingdom which, for Christians, was inaugurated in the life, death and resurrection of Jesus the Christ. Thus, it is through incorporation into Christ, through membership of the Christian Church, that Christians come to share in the hope for the Kingdom. We believe that if this hope for God's Kingdom was given its central place by both *Jews and Christians* this would transform their relationship with one another.

16   Christians and Jews share a passionate belief in a God of loving kindness who has called us into relationship with himself. God is faithful and he does not abandon those he calls. We firmly reject any view of *Judaism* which sees it as a living fossil,

simply superseded by Christianity. When Paul reflects on the mystery of the continued existence of the Jewish people (Rom. 9-11) a full half of his message is the unequivocal proclamation of God's abiding love for those whom he first called. Thus he wrote:

> God's choice stands and they are his friends for the sake of the patriarchs. For the gracious gifts of God and his calling are irrevocable. (Rom. 11.28-29, NEB)

God continues to fulfil his purposes among the Jewish people.

17   However, with some honourable exceptions their relationship has too often been marked by antagonism. Discrimination and persecution of the *Jews* led to the teaching of contempt; the systematic dissemination of anti-Jewish propaganda by Church leaders, teachers and preachers. Through catechism, teaching of school children, and Christian preaching, the Jewish people have been misrepresented and caricatured. Even the Gospels have, at times, been used to malign and denigrate the Jewish people.

Anti-Jewish prejudice promulgated by leaders of both Church and State has led to persecution, pogrom, and, finally, provided the soil in which the evil weed of Nazism was able to take root and spread its poison. The Nazis were driven by a pagan philosophy, which had as its ultimate aim the destruction of Christianity itself. But how did it take hold? The systematic extermination of six million Jews and the wiping out of a whole culture must bring about in Christianity a profound and painful re-examination of its relationship with Judaism. In order to combat centuries of anti-Jewish teaching and practice, Christians must develop programmes of teaching, preaching, and common social action which eradicate prejudice and promote dialogue.

18   Many Christians would also affirm *Islamic* monotheism and speak approvingly of Islamic devotion to Jesus and to Mary, his virgin mother. Islam stands in a particular relationship to Christianity because of its acceptance of Jesus as the promised Messiah of the Hebrew Scripture. At the same time, however, we note that Muslims do not understand this affirmation to imply a doctrine of the person and work of Jesus as the Messiah which would be acceptable to most Christians. Nonetheless this affirmation of Jesus as the fulfilment of the Messianic promise is unique to Christians and Muslims. The same is true of the Islamic affirmation of Jesus as the 'Word of God', although Islamic Christology does not accept this as implying the Christian doctrine of the Incarnation. Many Muslims, though not all, would confine its significance to the miraculous events surrounding Jesus' conception and birth. At the same time, Islam affirms the Hebrew Scriptures and the special relationship which God had established with the Jewish people 'to whom he had shown his special favour'. While it is currently the majority view among Muslims that the whole Bible has been textually corrupted and is therefore no longer valid, this is not the only view found in either classical or contemporary Islamic thought. Some of Islam's greatest scholars have argued that the 'corruption' of Jewish and Christian scriptures referred to in the Qur'ân is a corruption, not of text, but of interpretation only. Christians in dialogue ought to know the classical Islamic sources which have argued strongly for this view of the Bible.

19   On the other hand, it has been the almost unanimous *Islamic* tradition to reject the crucifixion of Jesus as either historical fact or as theologically significant. The

Qur'ânic material relating to the crucifixion is highly ambiguous and there is the possibility of theological dialogue with Muslims on the interpretation and significance of the Qur'ânic material on Jesus. We need not, however, totally reject the Islamic affirmation of Jesus, even as we challenge it in its rejection of his atoning work upon the cross. It is important to note that the Islamic rejection of the crucifixion is not ultimately based on a rejection of the concept of the suffering of God's righteous prophets. God's power is not perceived in Islam as a magic charm against unjust suffering and persecution. The Qur'ân often refers, as does the New Testament, to prophets of God who have been killed at various times in history. It accepts not only the possibility but the fact of their death at the hands of the wicked. Nor can we say that Islam automatically rejects the positive value of suffering for others or in the cause of God. This it affirms strongly and in the Shi'ite tradition the concept of vicarious suffering is of fundamental importance.

20   Many Christians can also affirm the Islamic struggle to be faithful to the example of Abraham. Islamic tradition traces the descent of the Arabs, and so of Muhammad, to Abraham through Ishmael. Many Christians, among them John of Damascus, and the Arab apologist Ishâq 'Abd al-Masîh al-Kindî, accept this genealogy. This is important for Muslims in their understanding of the prophetic mission of Muhammad and of their relationship with Judaism and Christianity as religions which also have a special connection with the faith of Abraham. Even though most Muslims today are not Arabs, they feel, like Christians, that they are Children of Abraham by faith because of the message of Muhammad, descendant of Ishmael, son of Abraham.

21   Although Luther had already spoken positively about the faith of Ishmael, few Christians have given much thought to this child of Abraham, about whom the Bible says 'God was with the lad and he grew up' (Gen. 21.20). Although rejected from the line of the covenant which God had made with the descendants of Abraham through Isaac, there is no biblical evidence that this child, miraculously saved by God in the wilderness, ever abandoned his faith in the God of his father Abraham. The figure of Ishmael is theologically challenging for, although rejected from the particular covenant made with Abraham, he and his mother were the object of particular and miraculous attention on the part of God. Perhaps we need to challenge the negative assumptions that surround our reaction to this biblical character.

22   Many Christians also often feel challenged to affirm the religious devotion which *Muslims* display in their prayers. This is clear not only in their ritual prayers but in their own personal prayers, such as have been gathered together with Christian prayers by Kenneth Cragg, former Anglican Bishop in Egypt, in his book *Alive to God*.

23   Christians may also affirm the sense of fellowship which *Muslims* often show to each other, regardless of language, race or national origin. They can also affirm early Islamic ideals of religious tolerance. At the same time they would want to challenge Muslims to develop those aspects of their tradition which imply a broader understanding of the unity of all people.

24   Christians would also want to affirm the deep Islamic reliance on the grace and mercy of God. Although often misunderstood and misrepresented by Christian theologians as teaching salvation by works, all schools of Islamic thought are marked

by a deep sense of the gratuitous mercy of God. This mercy cannot be earned by any-one because, in Islamic thought, no one can have any claims against God. All that God gives, he gives not because we deserve it but gratuitously. This emphasis on the gratuitousness of God's gift has led Islamic theology to abandon the doctrine of the atonement as understood in Christianity, although both the word (*kaffârah*) and the concept are known and used in more restricted senses. Islamic theology argues that God needs no sacrifice or atonement in order freely to forgive human sin and aliena-tion. This he may do simply because he is God Almighty. And yet, Islamic thought does not reject the importance of human co-operation with God in working his revealed will here on earth. In this respect the Qur'ân speaks of humanity as God's vicegerent (*khalîfah*) on earth, and this line of thought is developed by many Islamic thinkers. Although some forms of popular Islam may seem to have degenerated into legalism and fatalism, the normative Islamic emphasis on grace and human co-oper-ation should always be borne in mind.

THE WAY OF SHARING

25   Dialogue does not require people to relinquish or alter their beliefs before entering into it; on the contrary, genuine dialogue demands that each partner brings to it the fullness of themselves and the tradition in which they stand. As they grow in mutual understanding they will be able to share more and more of what they bring with the other. Inevitably, both partners to the dialogue will be affected and changed by this process, for it is a mutual sharing.

26   Within this sharing there are a variety of attitudes towards *Judaism* within Christ-ianity today. At one pole, there are those Christians whose prayer is that Jews, with-out giving up their Jewishness, will find their fulfilment in Jesus the Messiah. Indeed some regard it as their particular vocation and responsibility to share their faith with Jews, whilst at the same time urging them to discover the spiritual riches which God has given them through the Jewish faith. Other Christians, however, believe that in fulfilling the Law and the prophets, Jesus validated the Jewish relationship with God, while opening this way up for Gentiles through his own person. For others again, the holocaust has changed their perception, so that until Christian lives bear a truer wit-ness, they feel a divine obligation to affirm the Jews in their worship and sense of God who is, for Christians, the Father of Jesus. In all these approaches, Christians bear witness to God as revealed in Jesus and are being called into a fresh, more fruitful relationship with Judaism. We urge that further thought and prayer, in the light of Scripture and the facts of history, be given to the nature of this relationship.

27   All these approaches, however, share a common concern to be sensitive to *Judaism,* to reject all proselytising, that is, aggressive and manipulative attempts to convert, and, of course, any hint of antisemitism. Further, Jews, Muslims and Chris-tians have a common mission. They share a mission to the world that God's name may be honoured: 'Hallowed be your name'. They share a common obligation to love God with their whole being and their neighbours as themselves. 'Your Kingdom come on earth as it is in heaven'. And in the dialogue there will be mutual witness. Through learning from one another they will enter more deeply into their own inheri-tance. Each will recall the other to God, to trust him more fully and obey him more profoundly. This will be mutual witness between equal partners.

28   Genuine sharing requires of Christians that they correct all distorted images of *Judaism and Islam,* as it requires of Jews and Muslims that they correct distorted images of Christian faith. For Christians this will include careful use and explanation of biblical passages, particularly during Holy Week.

29   In this process it is important to remember also the damage that has been done to *Christian-Muslim* relations by a distorted view of Islam and by outright animosity. Jews, Muslims and Eastern Christians often shared a common fate at the hands of Western Christians in the Middle Ages. The centuries of warfare known collectively as the Crusades were directed primarily against the Muslims, although both Jews and Eastern Christians shared in the suffering inflicted by the Western Christian armies as they advanced to and through the Middle East. Jews and some Eastern Christians had earlier experienced persecution under the rule of Byzantium or Persia and then conquest by Islam. Again, Christians have upon occasion seen Islam as a Christian heresy and at other times as the mere product of human imagination. Scholars have always stressed the influence of Jewish-Christian monotheism on Islam, for it was born in an area where both Judaism and Christianity were practised. We should always be careful about how we characterise another person's faith and try to avoid hurtful language. This is especially the case when, as with both Judaism and Islam, the negative characterisations of the past have resulted in much pain and suffering inflicted by Christians in the name of religion, or where it has left a legacy of bitterness and division, a legacy which continues to cause much suffering to innocent Christian communities today through an undiscriminating attitude on the part of others which unjustly associates them with events for which they bear no responsibility. Many Christians, for example, justly point out that their histories do not overlap the European experience of holocaust and pogrom at all or that they themselves fought against the Crusader armies of Western Europe.

30   There is also much in the way of common action that *Jews, Christians and Muslims* can join in; for example:

the struggle against racism, apartheid and antisemitism

the work for human rights, particularly the right of people to practise and teach their religion.

There is a common witness to God and the dignity of human beings in a world always in danger of becoming godless and dehumanised.

31   Understanding and affirming are already ways of sharing. However, if we are truly to share our faith we must not only affirm what we can but share our own deep convictions, even when these appear irreconcilably opposed to our partner's faith and practice. In the case of *Islam* particularly, Christians must first understand Islam if this witness is to be effective. Islam is a missionary religion that is fast gaining many adherents in many parts of the world. This missionary zeal is not confined to the Middle East but is fervent in Africa and South-East Asia and is apparent in the intellectual centres of the West. Muslims are often confidently superior to Christians in much the same way that Christians have often been towards Jews. Many Muslims would simply dismiss views which diverge from Islamic faith and practice with the conviction that if their partner only *understood* Islam he or she would be a Muslim. Christianity will only get a hearing by informed Muslims when it is clear that the Christian who is speaking understands Islam and yet remains a Christian by choice, not, as it were, by default.

32   Many Muslims feel that *Islam* has superseded Christianity the way many Christians have traditionally felt that Christianity superseded Judaism (a view which the same Muslims would share). Just as Christian polemicists have often seized upon the writings of Jewish scholars to try to undermine the faith of the Jewish community, some Muslim intellectuals and propagandists rejoice when they feel able to use some pronouncement of a Western theologian to undermine Christianity and underscore the truth of Islam. Such pronouncements, designed to witness to and explain the Christian faith in liberal societies, are pounced upon and used to damage pressurised Christian Churches in Islamic societies.

33   One pressing concern that Christians will want to share with *Muslims* is the need for clear, strong safeguards for adherents of minority religions in Muslim societies. Any interpretation of Islamic law that seems to deny basic human rights, including the right of people to practise and teach their own faith, must be challenged. We recognise that here there is positive ground for dialogue because some Muslim thinkers of the Middle Ages and later periods were among the first actually to incorporate ideas of tolerance and safeguards for minorities within their legal systems; sometimes centuries before such ideas were advocated by the European Enlightenment. However limited these ideas may have been in the past, Muslim thinkers of today must be challenged to develop them into even more positive understandings of the role of minorities in Islamic society. In particular, the law of apostasy is undergoing considerable discussion today by Muslim thinkers and jurists and is an area where Christians versed in Islamic law must enter into dialogue with Muslims. In matters such as this the sometimes tiny, struggling Churches set in Islamic societies need the support of the wider church.

34   It is quite clear that there can be no genuine understanding, affirmation or sharing with *Islam* without quite detailed study by at least some experts. In this respect Jewish–Christian dialogue is better served. Most of the important works of traditional and contemporary Jewish thought are available in English, French, Spanish or German translations (if indeed these are not the language of the original). Most of the basic works of traditional Islamic thought have not been translated into these languages and are accessible only to those with a knowledge of Arabic. Even today, although more Muslims are writing in these languages, most of the contemporary intellectual activity within the world of Islam is being conducted in Arabic, Urdu, Persian and Bahasa (Malaysia/Indonesia). Valuable work is being done by Christian institutions, in which Anglicans play a part, such as the Centre for the Study of Islam and Christian-Muslim Relations at the Selly Oak Colleges (Birmingham, UK); the Henry Martyn Institute (Hyderabad, India); the Duncan Black MacDonald Center (Hartford, USA) and the Christian-Muslim Study Centre (Rawalpindi, Pakistan). There is also the new study centre recently established in the Gulf by the Bishop of Cyprus. Such work needs to be extended and supported by the Churches of the Anglican Communion.

Resolution that the Anglican Communion:

Commends the document *Jews, Christians and Muslims: The Way of Dialogue* for study and encourages the Churches of the Anglican Communion to engage in dialogue with Jews and Muslims on the basis of understanding, affirmation and sharing *illustrated* in it.

Recommends that the Anglican Consultative Council gives consideration to the setting up of an Inter-Faith Committee, which Committee, in the interest of cost and in practical pursuance of our commitment to ecumenism, would work in close co-operation with the Inter-Faith Dialogue Committee of the WCC; and that this Committee, amongst its other work, establishes a common approach to people of other faiths on a Communion-wide basis and appoints working parties to draw up more detailed guidelines for relationships with Judaism and Islam and other faiths as appropriate.

Recommends that Provinces initiate talks wherever possible on a tripartite basis, with both Jews and Muslims.

Urges Provinces to support those institutions which are helping Christians towards a more informed understanding of Judaism and Islam.

TRUSTWORTHY AND TRUE

PASTORAL LETTERS
from
THE LAMBETH CONFERENCE 1988

Published separately September 1988

FOREWORD BY THE ARCHBISHOP OF CANTERBURY

Five hundred and twenty-five bishops from the world-wide Anglican Communion gathered for the twelfth Lambeth Conference at Canterbury. They brought with them a wealth of Christian experience. Their preparation was based on wider consultation than ever before.

During our time together we tried in a variety of ways to listen to God and to each other and so discern what the Spirit was saying to the Churches.

I believe we now have a duty to share something of our reflections with the whole of the Anglican Communion, with Christians belonging to other Churches, and with other men and women of good will.

The Pastoral Letters which follow give a first impression of the issues which the bishops identified and tried to reflect on as they emerged during the Conference. A fuller description of these reflections and the resolutions they prompted will be found in the official Report of the Conference which is due for publication on All Saints' Day 1988. I intend that my own considered thoughts on the Lambeth Conference and reactions to it should be the theme of my annual Christmas letter to the Communion.

Meanwhile these Pastoral Letters are composed in a way which allows their use to be adapted to a wide variety of circumstances and languages. I commend them as a means by which the bishops may bring Lambeth '88 back into their dioceses.

It was a time when we were conscious of divine protection and guidance. May we all give thanks to God for such blessings and pray more confidently for the health and integrity of the Anglican Communion.

ROBERT CANTUAR:

Feast of the Blessed Virgin Mary
8th September 1988

A CONFERENCE PRAYER

O God our Father, you are always leading us into fresh understanding of your good providence. We commend our thoughts, words and deeds to you. Bless all that accords with your will, and put away all that hinders our mission to make the world know and see your saving love and patient goodness revealed in Jesus Christ, to whom with you and the Holy Spirit be honour and glory now and for ever.   Amen.

And he who sat upon the throne said, 'Behold, I make all things new.' Also he said, 'Write this, for these words are trustworthy and true.' (Revelation 21.5, RSV)

PREFACE

The work of producing these pastoral letters began on the very first working day of the Conference. Four participants from each Section, usually bishops, but in one case a woman member of the Anglican Consultative Council, were appointed to assist the officers of their Section and the editors in identifying issues which could become the subjects of pastoral letters. Over the next week or so, a number of issues emerged in each of the Sections. Through a process of consultation, these were reduced to two each from the Sections on Mission and Ministry, Dogmatic and Pastoral Concerns, and Christianity and the Social Order. The Ecumenical Section chose to provide one letter which covers all aspects of their work.

Draft outlines of these letters were first approved by the Sections concerned, and then presented to the Conference in plenary session. The pastoral letters which follow are developed from these outlines. The editors, Michael Nazir-Ali and Derek Pattinson, have restricted themselves, in the main, to the tasks of revision, clarification of language and the provision of a theological style. Rubrics have been provided, suggesting possible dates in the Church's year when it might be suitable for a particular letter to be used. End-notes have also been provided, suggesting reading for those interested in pursuing a matter further. The official report of the conference will contain more detailed material on the themes treated in the letters.

In a Communion as diverse as ours, it hardly needs to be said that there will be a variety of uses to which these letters are put. In some places, they may be read aloud in church. In others, the parish priest or some other minister may choose to preach on the theme of a letter and may read out aloud only portions of the letter concerned. In others again, the letters may become suitable material for study groups. (Biblical quotations in the letters are from the Revised Standard Version.)

We believe that the post-Lambeth Video being prepared for the bishops and for use within the Communion will echo some of the themes of the letters. It would be appropriate, therefore, to use the letters in conjunction with this video. The letter on **The Family as a Gift from God** could well be used alongside a video produced by the International Project on Family and Community (IPOFAC), entitled **Communities of Hope.** Their address is: IPOFAC, Mission of St James and St John, 12 Batman St, West Melbourne, 3003, Australia.

The letters on **Showing the Hospitality of God** and on **Our Place in God's World** could be used with audio-visual and printed material from Christian relief and development agencies. The letters on **The Gospel and Transformation** and on **Showing the Hospitality of God** could be used along with material produced by provincial mission boards or missionary societies. Bible Societies would gladly provide material for use with the letter on **The Reading of Scripture** and National Councils of Churches would be able to guide local churches on what materials would be suitable for use with the letter on **Our Lord's Prayer for Unity : 'Even as we are one'.**

Not all letters will have the same urgency and relevance in different situations. It is for the bishop and, under his direction, the parish clergy to decide which letters are of special relevance to the particular situation of the local church.

The Lambeth Conference was a time of renewal for the bishops. It is their hope that these letters will communicate something of that renewal to the wider Church.

1 THE READING OF SCRIPTURE

1   It happened in a small study group during the Lambeth Conference. Twelve bishops from as many different countries sat together around a table. One of our number began to tell us about his diocese. He spoke of a land torn by war, a hundred thousand people dead, the diocesan centre burned to the ground. One by one the others talked of their hopes, their fears, their needs. Then we read from the Gospel of John, where Jesus says to his disciples, 'Abide in me, and I in you' (John 15.4).

2   We write to share our experience with you. During the Lambeth Conference we, your bishops, took counsel together on many issues which face us and some which may seem to divide us. But out of such events as happened that day we came to share something deeper, more lasting, our unity in love and faith and hope. That unity grew out of our shared reading of Holy Scripture.

3   Throughout our meeting we took part in a daily process of listening to God's Word. Our whole conference met each morning in small groups – ten or twelve persons in each group – to study the Scriptures, to pray, to hear one another's testimony. Morning and afternoon we listened to the Scriptures in the context of the Church's daily worship, and one whole night we kept vigil as we meditated on the Word and prayed for peace and justice in our lands.

4   We were especially moved and our faith was strengthened by the witness of the Church in areas of the world where Christian faith is being presented and received for the first time and in those situations where Christians are being persecuted for their faith. We discovered that the bonds of our unity are deeply rooted in a common sharing of the presence of the Risen and Ascended Lord, the one revealed in the New Testament record itself. To every one of his followers Jesus' question is still the one he put to his first disciples, 'Who do you say that I am?' (Mark 8.29).

5   The answer to that question depends in large part on how we understand and express, in word and deed, what we believe Christ through the Scriptures has shown us about God and ourselves.

6   We affirm that the Scriptures are best seen as the Church's books – a body of writing which, for the earliest Christian communities, defined the Word which they had received and by which the Church lives. Through the ages the living and growing 'mind' of the Church has best been formed when the Church has been attentive to the scriptural word within the context of its liturgy, prayer and communal life.[†] [1] Whether as bishops at the Lambeth Conference or as a local congregation, any Christian community is called to be attentive to Scripture and to interpret it in the light of its own situation.

7   Such interpretation takes place in a number of ways:

- in the public and private reading of Scripture
- through preaching and teaching
- in small group study
- through the work of scholars who engage the horizon of the Bible with that of the contemporary world[2]
- by its application in the daily lives of Christian men and women.

† The notes at the end of each letter give suggested reading for those interested in pursuing a matter further.

The meaning of Scripture must be, in fact always is, declared and explained within changing circumstances, cultural settings and languages. Scripture must not be made to serve the ends of a particular culture nor be tied too closely to scholarly trends, nor must it be read apart from the particular experiences of people. Discernment is the process through which a body of believers *receives* the Word of God in its own time and context.[3]

8   The disciplined daily reading and study of Scripture and a searching of the accumulated 'mind' of the Church's tradition enabled us at the Lambeth Conference to address a wide range of issues confronting Christians around the globe. We commend this pattern to you, our sisters and brothers in local communities of faith. The task of declaring, explaining and living God's message belongs to the whole people of God. We invite you to join us in a process such as we have been privileged to share – waiting upon God, studying God's word in a reflective way, taking care to listen to those fellow believers whose life and experiences differ from ours, and making broad use of resources of interpretation.

9   Together, let us wait on the Word of God in prayer and expectation.

SUGGESTION FOR USE

In Provinces where the Second Sunday in Advent is observed as Bible Sunday it would be particularly appropriate to use this letter on that day.

NOTES ON FURTHER READING

1   Robert B. Eno (ed.), **Teaching Authority in the Early Church,** Delaware, 1984. Michael J. Nazir-Ali, 'Church, Culture and Change', in J. Draper (ed.), **Communion and Episcopacy,** Ripon College, Cuddesdon, Oxford, 1988.

2   See further, A. Thiselton, **The Two Horizons,** Paternoster Press, Exeter, 1980.

3   Andrew Kirk, **God's Word for a Complex World,** Marshall Pickering, London, 1987. Leonardo and Clodovis Boff, **Introducing Liberation Theology,** Burns & Oates, London, 1987.

2   DISCIPLESHIP AND MINISTRY

1   Greetings in the name of the Lord from the Lambeth Conference.

2   As bishops we have been called and ordained for a particular service and responsibility within the Body of Christ. We have been conscious while here together of an affirmation of this calling, and give thanks for the richness and wonder of our responsibility.

3   Yet our fundamental unity with each other and with all our fellow Christians is rooted in our baptism in Christ.

SALVATION AND CHRISTIAN BAPTISM

4   In Christian baptism every person enters into Christ's dying for us, and is born again into his resurrection (Romans 6.3-4, Colossians 2.12). This means that we put away and die to that which is doomed in human life. And we put on the new life, inde-

structible, that Christ has given us. Baptism is the primary sacrament: it marks us as Christian. It is the common bond for all Christians across the world.

PERSONAL RESPONSE AND ASSENT

5   Whoever has been baptised, either as an infant or as an adult, has been marked by Christ for salvation. Each individual must at some point, however, personally respond to that salvation, make that grace their own in Jesus Christ. In some this happens at their baptism, or later at Confirmation, and for others at some other definite time and place in their personal history. In yet others it is a slow and growing awareness of their identity as children of God saved by Jesus Christ. In either case this response is the work of the Holy Spirit in our hearts which leads us into giving obedience to our Lord. Sometimes it may be accompanied by signs and wonders such as the gift of tongues or physical healing. It will always be recognised as genuine by the fruit of the Spirit: qualities of Christian discipleship, such as love, joy, peace, gentleness, kindness, humility and long-suffering.[1]

PERSONAL AND CORPORATE RENEWAL

6   Because we are all baptised into Christ we are never Christians in isolation. We are always part of the whole people of God, the Body of Christ. Our new life in Christ must have an effect on the life of the local church where we live and worship. The renewed life of the Christian is for the Church as for the world. It should lead to new life within the local congregation and to a greater commitment to sharing Christ's love with all in the community where the church is set.

THE RENEWED LIFE OF THE LOCAL CONGREGATION

7   Every local congregation lives its Christian life at a point where two lines of service cross. As a church it is called to build up the lives of its members through prayer and worship, Bible study, preaching and teaching, so that they may grow in grace and Christian maturity, with a deeper love and dependence on the Lord.

8   At the same time the Church is also called to serve the world, in particular the people at its very door. Growth in prayer and response to careful preaching and teaching must lead church members to engage in evangelism and service. The Church has to share the life of the local community and offer the power of Christ's love for all the world in all that happens there. To this the laity are particularly called. They need to be trained, equipped and affirmed for it, since they belong to the everyday life of the local community.[2]

9   These two forms of service are thus the common responsibility of lay and ordained, and we wish to affirm most strongly that ministering the love of Christ in the Church and in the world is a task of partnership between laity and clergy.

10   Both forms of service may be found in both large and small congregations. While giving thanks to God for church growth in so many places, we wish to affirm the life and witness of small congregations and to encourage them to continue in faithfulness to the Lord.

WOMEN'S MINISTRY

11 Before and during our Conference much attention has been focused on the ministries of women in the Church. We wish to express our gratitude under God for the many gifts which women have contributed to the life and mission of the Church in a wide variety of roles such as teachers and theologians, spiritual counsellors and guides, as missionaries and members of religious communities. At Lambeth we have also received testimony from those Provinces in which women are ordained as deacons and priests, serving in parishes and sector ministries.

12 In our Conference we believe that God has enabled us to go forward as a communion of Churches in seeking to know his will for the present and future ministry of women. Responsibility lies with each of our Provinces and with the Communion as a whole to explore at every level the implications for the ministry of women.[3]

YOUNG PEOPLE

13 The bishops at Lambeth have received **Love in any Language,** the Report of the First International Conference of Young Anglicans at Belfast in January of this year.[4] We have greatly valued the presence of four young people's consultants from that gathering who have lived and worked alongside us throughout our Conference. We have heard the young people say, 'We want to affirm the bishops and we want to work with you. We want to put our trust in you and you to trust us. Mutual trust brings growth and life.' They have called for a fresh emphasis on the education of the laity and have regretted the lack of teaching of basic doctrines in our Churches. They rightly seek to participate more fully in all facets of church life. We hope that all dioceses will ensure that young people are involved in ministry, liturgy and decision-making. They wish to work with the Church as fully as they can. We owe it to them, as a vital part of today's Church, that they should have every opportunity to do so. We need their freshness, enthusiasm and clear-sightedness. We need to listen to them, to hear their urgent questions and to learn from them.

THE MINISTRY OF THE WHOLE PEOPLE OF GOD

14 In this Lambeth Conference we have as bishops been refreshed and extended by our worship and prayers together and study of the Bible, and in our common work and counsel; and we have learned greatly from one another. We give thanks for the faithful and often visionary service of the clergy and for their leadership of their people. We urge each baptised member of our Communion to take responsibility for working with the clergy in ministering the love of God, and to do so within the local congregation and within the local community. We are to help each other in the Christian faith, to proclaim the Good News of God's love to every person by deed and word in all the daily affairs of living. To this we are all called, ordained and lay alike, and upon our full commitment to this depends the mission of the Church to the world in our time.

SUGGESTION FOR USE

It would be particularly appropriate to use this Letter on the Ember Days in Advent or on the Third Sunday in Advent when prayer is offered for all who serve the Church in its various ministries, both clerical and lay.

NOTES ON FURTHER READING

1 **Baptism, Eucharist and Ministry,** WCC, Geneva, 1982. Also W.H. Lazareth, **Growing Together in Baptism, Eucharist and Ministry,** WCC, Geneva, 1982. This latter is a study guide which aims to be non-technical and is particularly suitable for group study.

2 **All are Called: Towards a Theology of the Laity,** Church House Publishing, London, 1985, a document produced by the Church of England's Board of Education. F. Ross Kinsler (ed.), **Ministry by the People,** WCC, Geneva, 1983. Michael Nazir-Ali, 'Evangelisation: A Profile' in his **Frontiers in Muslim-Christian Encounter,** Paternoster Press, Exeter, 1987.

3 There is a great deal of literature on the subject. The following is only a selection: **The Ordination of Women to The Priesthood. A Second Report by the House of Bishops,** General Synod of the Church of England, London, 1988. **Women Priests: Obstacle to Unity?,** Catholic Truth Society, London, 1986. Mary S. Donovan, **Women Priests in the Episcopal Church,** Forward Movement, Cincinnati, 1988. Carroll Stuhlmueller (ed.), **Women and Priesthood,** Collegeville, Minnesota, 1978.

4 **Love in any Language,** Church of England National Youth Work Office, London, 1988.

3 THE FAMILY AS A GIFT FROM GOD

The beauty of family life is one of God's most precious gifts, and its preservation is a paramount responsibility of the Church.
(Lambeth Conference 1930)

1 The Book of Genesis speaks of God creating human beings as male and female, as a couple. It is important to note that it is as *both* male and female that human beings are spoken of as being in the image of God. The sacred relationship of marriage is thus seen to mirror the divine image.

2 The family is closely related to the institution of marriage and partakes of its sacredness. In the Old Testament the household, or the extended family, is seen as a basic element in the covenant community and there is detailed legislation about its maintenance and nurture as well as its relationship to the land and to the community as a whole.

3 In the New Testament, Jesus upholds the permanence of marriage over and against the concessions which had been made during the course of Jewish history (Mark 10. 2-12).[1] Again, his own understanding of his unique relationship to God is expressed in his intimate address to God as 'Abba' or Father, a term drawn from human family relationships.

4 At the same time, Jesus sets the values and the demands of the Kingdom of God over and above those of human institutions, including the family (Mark 3. 31-35 and parallels, Matthew 19. 27-30, Matthew 22. 23-30).

5 Nevertheless in the New Testament, as in the Old, the household remains the basic unit of the covenant community. It is often here that people come to faith. It is here that faith is nurtured and strengthened. It is to be noted, however, that the biblical 'household' is vastly different from the modern nuclear family. Grandparents, other relatives, servants and slaves would often be included in a household. Also,

traditions of hospitality made the household 'open' to the rest of the community. This is important for our understanding of both how the Gospel came to be preached in households such as those of Cornelius (Acts 10-11) and Lydia (Acts 16. 11-15) and also how such households themselves became centres for evangelisation and nurture (Acts 18. 24-26).

6   It is important to note that faith is nurtured in the context of the nurture of the whole human person. Discipline is essential for nurture but it should be exercised in a context of security and dignity rather than one of anxiety and aggression. Children are persons not products and their rights must be understood and respected by parents and others with responsibility for their nurture.

7   The changing roles of women and men, the breakdown of the extended family and the consequent emergence of nuclear and single-parent families in many parts of the world have all contributed to stress in family life. While continuing to be faithful to its traditional teaching on marriage and the family, the Church must be sensitive to the needs of those who have become the casualties of this stress. Judgemental attitudes need to be replaced by attitudes and processes of pastoral care which lead to healing.

8   While extended families have provided a much needed network of support for marriage, they have sometimes been restrictive and even oppressive. Nuclear families, while providing greater freedom for the individual, can become exclusive and uncaring. The Church must continue to affirm the value of the widest possible network of family relationships. It should, however, also continue to insist on the freedom of the individual within the context of community.

9   Urbanisation, industrialisation and changing work patterns have also contributed significantly towards the present stress within families, while in some situations marriage and family life must be seen in the context of racist policies. Migrant labour systems and state resettlement policies, for example, directly affect the 'wholeness' of the family. In such situations it is not uncommon to see an increase in illegitimacy, bigamy, prostitution, promiscuity (both homosexual and heterosexual) and the breakdown of parental control.

10   These are not just 'family' or 'sexual' problems. Their origin very often lies in unjust and exploitative social, economic and political structures. The recently concluded **International Project on the Family** surveyed the work of Anglican Churches in different parts of the world in relation to the needs of the family.[2] The consultancy reports show that Churches are engaged in different ways in providing support for families in crisis.[3] These include the provision of employment and educational opportunities, seed capital for small businesses, day care centres, counselling and evangelistic work. The reports also identify, however, the structural injustices and the exploitation of the poor and the vulnerable which are at the root of many 'family' problems. While it is entirely right for the Churches to engage **pastorally** with families experiencing stress, the Churches also have a duty to be **prophetic** about structures which are largely responsible for this stress.

11   Finally, in these difficult times we must ask whether each congregation is a 'household of God' where each member feels supported by the others? Is this household given to hospitality, where the lonely are supported and strangers welcomed? Is it a household where the apostolic teaching is treasured and transmitted? For good or ill, in many places the traditional extended family has disappeared for ever. In such situations, the local congregation may well take the place of the extended family in providing a network of support for individuals as well as for nuclear and single-parent families. Such a creation of community would bring together the missionary and pastoral aspects of a congregation's life. It would further the credibility of the Gospel by relating the claims of Christ to contemporary human need in an immediate and tangible way.

12   We pray that 'the Father from whom every family in heaven and on earth is named' (Ephesians 3.15) will strengthen and refresh you as you continue to serve him in his Church, the Body of Christ, and in his creatures, your fellow human beings of all creeds and none.

SUGGESTION FOR USE
It would be particularly appropriate to use this Letter on or before a feast of the Holy Family, of the Blessed Virgin Mary, or of St Joseph of Nazareth.

NOTES ON FURTHER READING
1   On the integrity of the married relationship and the mutual love, respect and care which are involved see Jack Dominian, **Sexual Integrity,** Darton, Longman & Todd, London, 1987.

2   See further the report of the project, ***Transforming Families and Communities,** Anglican Information Office, Sydney, for ACC, 1987.

3   **Families in Transition.** Consultancy Reports.
Available from IFOPAC, Mission of St James and St John, 12 Batman Street, West Melbourne, 3003, Australia.

No. 1 Hong Kong 1986
No. 2 Kenya 1986
No. 3 The Philippines 1986
No. 4 Canada 1987

No. 5 Australia 1987
No. 6 New Zealand 1987
No. 7 Britain 1988

* Indicates a title published through the Inter-Anglican Publishing Network (see p.343).

4   OUR LORD'S PRAYER FOR UNITY: 'EVEN AS WE ARE ONE'

1   We, the bishops of the twelfth Lambeth Conference, send warm greetings in the name of our Lord Jesus Christ to members of the Anglican Communion and to Christians throughout the world.

2   We were asked to bring the hopes and concerns of our dioceses to the Conference. We have shared these with our brother bishops and we have learnt from each other how God is dealing with his people.

3   We are saddened by the deep divisions of our broken world with all its inequalities and injustices. We have seen how the colour, culture, experience and history of peoples and races have been exploited and debased instead of being recognised as part of the rich diversity of God's creation. We acknowledge that the

Church, which is called to proclaim reconciliation and acceptance through union with Christ, has sometimes allowed itself to become an instrument of disunity. As Anglicans we repent for the part we have played in this disunity.

4   We rejoice at the good news we have heard. There has been a real sense of joy about the Conference's welcome for the work of the international ecumenical dialogues with the Roman Catholics (ARCIC), Orthodox, Oriental Orthodox, Lutheran and Reformed Churches. There was also appreciation for the Report of the Faith and Order Commission of the World Council of Churches on Baptism, Eucharist and Ministry (BEM). These dialogues, and the statements resulting from them, represent new ground and new expressions of our faith which we can hold and express together. We give thanks for Anglican – Lutheran dialogue, and we affirm the desire expressed in this dialogue that our two Churches share the eucharist as one of the steps towards our future unity. On the basis of a common belief in the Gospel, its sacraments and its ministry, we look forward to such sharing with other Churches.[1]

5   We are conscious that these international dialogues may seem far removed from the everyday life of congregations and individuals, but we believe that they challenge us all. We therefore encourage clergy and teachers to draw out their importance and help overcome that which divides us. It is especially important that we do not judge others from a distance but look for friendship with people of other traditions. Deep relationships of friendship and Christian love change our understanding. A relationship of love leads us away from bigotry and closed-mindedness. 'Without relationship, difference divides' was the phrase used by the Archbishop of Canterbury in his opening address to the Conference.

6   We are aware of the need for closer links between the international and official dialogues, on the one hand, and spontaneous ecumenism at the local level. All are important; all are movements of the Spirit; and each needs the others. The local initiative needs the worldwide vision, and the international dialogue needs to hear the local experience.

7   We are encouraged by what many bishops have described as a transformation of the ecumenical scene in their dioceses and parishes. We have heard of groups of Christians meeting together to pray and study the Scriptures, of Councils of Churches taking initiatives in evangelism, and of a growing sense of walking in the love of God as friends. We give this our whole-hearted support and encouragement.

8   We have listened to stories from Africa, Asia, Australasia, the Americas and Europe about ways in which many Christian Churches are uniting in social work, health care and educational programmes, and of how they are ministering together to the isolated, the marginalised and the refugees. We have heard of the work of the united Churches in South Asia, where Anglicans have united with Christians of other traditions, and also of the post-denominational Church in China where, again, there is strong Anglican participation. We have been encouraged by reports that Anglicans in different parts of the world are still engaged in discussion on unity at regional and national levels.[2] Christian unity at all levels is necessary for the sake of mission.

9   Having seen how Churches work together on issues of justice and peace, we have once again appreciated the true meaning of the word 'ecumenical' – that is, related to the whole inhabited earth. Our work for Christian unity is linked to our quest for

321

human unity. In overcoming our Christian divisions we shall be a sign to the world which needs to overcome the injustice and division found in everyday life. Christian unity would thus be a foretaste of the transformation of the whole world into God's Kingdom. In the words of St Paul, 'a plan for the fullness of time, to unite all things in him, things in heaven and things on earth' (Ephesians 1.10).

10   We came to Lambeth from the four corners of the world. We prayed together and we were supported by your prayers for us. We read and studied the Bible together with our different cultural understandings and in our different languages. We shared daily in the Eucharist and together found a common purpose and unity in our work. Prayer is the most important of all ecumenical activities. Prayer changes hearts, and it is our hearts most of all that need to be changed. 'We shall only pass through the door of ecumenism on our knees' (Yves Congar). Prayer brings healing and unites us with Christ who 'is before all things, and in him all things hold together' (Colossians 1.17).

11   Out of our sharing as bishops at this Lambeth Conference, and as a result of listening to your ecumenical experience, we are sure that the time is ripe for new ecumenical initiatives. Let us pray that 'he who began a good work in you will bring it to completion at the day of Jesus Christ' (Philippians 1.6).

12   Let us all work for the full and visible unity of the Church.

13   Let us commit ourselves together to a new realisation of the love of God in Christ so that we may become instruments of that love in the world.

SUGGESTION FOR USE
This letter may be used in the preparation for, and the celebration of, the Week of Prayer for Christian Unity.

NOTES ON FURTHER READING
1   The following are the reports of dialogues in which Anglicans have been engaged in recent years:

Anglican-Roman Catholic International Commission (ARCIC I) **The Final Report,** CTS/SPCK, London, 1982.

Anglican-Roman Catholic International Commission (ARCIC II)* **Salvation and the Church,** CTS/CHP, London, 1987.

Anglican-Orthodox Dialogue: The Dublin Agreed Statement 1984, SPCK, 1984.

Anglican-Reformed International Commission, **God's Reign and our Unity,** SPCK/St Andrew Press, London and Edinburgh, 1984.

Anglican-Lutheran Relations: A Report of the Joint Working Group, ACC/LWF, London and Geneva, 1983.

* **The Niagara Report: Anglican-Lutheran Consultation on Episcope,** ACC/LWF, London and Geneva, 1988.

Baptism, Eucharist and Ministry: The Lima Report, WCC, Geneva, 1982. See also * **The Emmaus Report: An Anglican Ecumenical Consultation 1987,** CHP for ACC, London, 1987.

2   An example of such discussions is to be found in a report of the Commission of the Covenanted Churches in Wales called **Ministry in a Uniting Church: From Recognition to Reconciliation,** Swansea, 1986.

* Indicates titles published through the Inter-Anglican Publishing Network (see p.343).

5 SHOWING THE HOSPITALITY OF GOD

1   As we celebrate the Eucharist we are reminded that the Christ who created our fellowship also inaugurated the Kingdom of God into which people from east and west are to be gathered (Matthew 8.11). We pray for all human beings because God has gathered us together in the fellowship of the Church as a sign of his purpose for all.

2   At the Eucharist the table is the Lord's. God shows his hospitality in the gift of his Son Jesus Christ for the sake of the world. It is in Christ that God reconciles us to himself. Christ is the one who holds the door open. As a loving Father, God in Christ welcomes us back into his fellowship.

3   This welcoming God makes available to us what we have to give to others – the Good News of Jesus Christ, 'God with us'.[1] Christ reflects the glory of God perfectly and bears the very stamp of the divine nature (Hebrews 1.3). Our experience of the hospitality of God, therefore, is rooted in the self-giving ministry of Christ.

4   The Scriptures speak of all human beings as made in the image of God, even though that image is distorted and obscured by sin. It is in Jesus Christ that the image of God in humanity is restored to the perfection that God wills for it. Christ's mission and ministry are about the mediation of this restoration to all humankind.

5   Because God wishes that his image be restored in all human beings, we must therefore affirm the intrinsic value of each human culture as a place where God is at work. This is as true of the cultures of the indigenous peoples of North and South America, Australia or New Zealand as it is of the cultures of immigrant peoples in Europe and North America. It is part of our task in showing God's hospitality that we welcome and affirm the cultures of minority groups such as these.[2]

6   Jesus radically identified himself with the poor, the hungry and the stranger (Matthew 25.31-end). Caring for refugees may be a particular way of serving Christ today. Such hospitality to our neighbour is a response to the divine hospitality.[3]

7   God's hospitality in Christ is seen to be costly. Our hospitality, too, must go beyond mere charity. It must be a costly, and at times painful, sharing of our resources with the deprived and the disadvantaged.[4]

8   Part of our hospitality to people from a variety of backgrounds will be the welcoming of those of other faiths. We know that God has not left himself without witness anywhere (Acts 14.17). This enables us to affirm a degree of commonality with people of other faiths. At the same time, Jesus Christ is for us the definitive apprehension of the divine; and we continue to hold firmly to our conviction that in him God has revealed himself uniquely.[5]

9   As part of God's people, who have experience of God's hospitality, we invite you to offer this hospitality to all your neighbours.

SUGGESTION FOR USE
This letter may well be used as part of the preparations for Lent.

NOTES ON FURTHER READING
1   Jean Stromberg (ed.), **Sharing One Bread, Sharing One Mission,** WCC, Geneva, 1983.
2   Roger Hooker and Christopher Lamb, **Love the Stranger : Ministry in Multi-Faith Areas,** SPCK, London, 1986.

3 **Refugees and Migrants: Report of a Meeting of the Anglican Refugee and Migrant Ministry Network,** ACC, London, 1988.

4 Duncan Forrester and Danus Skene (eds.), **Just Sharing,** a report of the Church of Scotland's Church and Nation Committee, Epworth Press, London, 1988.

5 K. Cragg, **The Christ and the Faiths,** SPCK, London, 1986.

K. Cracknell, **Towards a New Relationship,** Epworth Press, London, 1986.

J.N.D. Anderson, **Christianity and World Religions: The Challenge of Pluralism,** Inter-Varsity Press, London, 1984.

Michael Nazir-Ali, 'That which is not to be found but which finds us' in* **Towards a Theology of Inter-Faith Dialogue,** ACC, London, 1986.

Gavin D'Costa, **Theology and Religious Pluralism,** Blackwell, Oxford, 1986.

* Indicates a title published through the Inter-Anglican Publishing Network (see p.343).

6   ON OUR PLACE IN GOD'S WORLD

1   We thank God for the creation of the world in which we live. Our hope and trust is in him. We believe that he has a plan for his world in which all men, women and children are to have adequate care and sustenance for their bodies, and a relationship with him that brings joy to their lives. We yearn for the fulfilment of the purpose of God in the prayer 'Thy Kingdom come, thy will be done'. Our vision is of a world dedicated to the ways of love, the paths of justice and to a more equitable sharing of all the resources which God gives to humankind.[1]

2   In our own lifetime human invention has made possible achievements which previously were inconceivable. We think, for example, of advances in medicine which have improved the expectancy and quality of life, and of advances in technology in innumerable forms. The potential is there to free men, women and children from many of the ills which in the past have limited human life. We are able in principle to understand and manage our environment in ways and to an extent not open to previous generations. Yet there is a gap, which seems to widen, between our increased potential and our ability to care responsibly for our environment and to transform the social and economic order of our day.[2] People and governments need to make better use of the existing processes of planning and production, of new forms of interdependence, and of the sharing of power between the individual and society.

3   We see a dual role here for the Church, locally, regionally and internationally, in seeking the renewal of society by the spiritual renewal of the individual and the renewal of the individual by the spiritual renewal of society. The Church must first be a prophet to itself, seeking the embodiment in its own life of the mutual interdependence of its many parts as a sign of God's Kingdom of power through love. Thus prepared, it will also be the task of the Church to speak prophetically to the world, to call for mutual interdependence in all personal and social relationships, to oppose injustice and all misuse of power whether by individuals, the tribe, the party, the majority, the minority. Mutual interdependence within the Body of Christ is the Church's own ideal of just and loving relationships. Mutual interdependence is God's way for society generally. This is our Christian vision of society. Our hope, we

repeat, is in God whose Kingdom is where the oppressed are set free, where the hungry are fed, and where children inherit a world made whole.

4   If as Christians we have this vision and this hope, then it is our duty to speak and act on the social, moral, political and economic questions of our day. Many of these questions raise issues about the nature of human life and about ultimate values on which the Churches should comment. What particular Churches ought to do – and what they may be able to do – in terms of social witness and action is likely to vary very greatly in relation to their resources and circumstances. Many Churches are minority groups in cultures which may be friendly, hostile or indifferent. Some issues can be more readily raised than others. The kind of action open to Churches will vary.

5   We, bishops gathered in Conference, cannot lay down specific guidelines about what the Churches should be doing in particular places and on particular issues. We recognise that each of us in his own diocese and province has a special prophetic, pastoral and teaching responsibility in consultation and collaboration with clergy and lay people. But there is a responsibility also upon individual Christians, particularly upon lay people, to be directly involved in social and political action in the places where they live and work, or at regional or national level. There will be opportunity for action by Christians, both collectively and individually. But there will be times when the individual has the opportunity and the duty to act alone. Where governments are doing God's will by working for the welfare of all their people in the fight against poverty, ignorance and disease, they should have the support of the Churches and of individual churchpeople. Christians should not hold back from criticism, but its thrust, wherever possible, should be constructive. Christians, for their part, must carefully examine their own motivation. There will generally be some place for self-interest in the struggle for economic improvement. But there must also be a concern for the common good and for an approach by Christians which is disinterested and public-spirited.[3]

6   In our time together at Lambeth we have given special consideration to a number of social issues which we have tested according to the criteria of Scripture, tradition and reason. We will be sharing the results of these detailed studies in the Conference report and in the individual reports which we will offer to our dioceses. We are conscious, in this work, that no part of human life is excluded from God's care and concern. We assert our confidence that the reconciling power of Christ's love and the motivating power of the Holy Spirit are available to heal, restore and renew God's world. Sin shall not have dominion over us. (Romans 6.14).

SUGGESTION FOR USE
It would be particularly appropriate for this letter to be used during Rogationtide, i.e. on the Fifth Sunday after Easter and the Monday, Tuesday and Wednesday following it.

NOTES ON FURTHER READING
1   Duncan Forrester and Danus Skene (ed.), **Just Sharing**, a report of the Church of Scotland's Church and Nation Committee, Epworth Press, London, 1988.

2 **Our Responsibility for the Living Environment,** Board for Social Responsibility of the Church of England, CHP, London, 1986.

3 See further J. Philip Wogaman, **Christian Perspectives in Politics,** SCM Press, London, 1988; also Duncan B. Forrester, **Theology and Politics,** Blackwell, Oxford, 1988.

7 · ON THE GOSPEL AND TRANSFORMATION

1 We greet you in the name of our Lord Jesus Christ from the Lambeth Conference.

2 Together we have enjoyed through prayer and Bible study and discussion an exchange of insights and stories. We have been made freshly aware of the new love flowing from God our Father, through Christ crucified and risen, and released among us in the Holy Spirit. We have experienced a fresh and urgent longing for each and all of us and for our whole Church to be caught up into a new outgoing movement of that love, changing lives and situations, worldwide.

3 Some lay stress on inner personal change, others on social and political change. But increasingly, as we have learned from each other and grown in commitment to each other, we have recognised the real task into which Jesus Christ is sending us all. We must hold these varied emphases together in one gospel and one witness in the one Body.[1]

4 We heard a story about an Anglican priest and a schoolboy in South Africa.

The schoolboy was one of those picked up by the police and detained under the so-called emergency regulations. He and some of his friends were put in a row of solitary confinement cells.

In a neighbouring cell was a strange priest who amused them all by leading everyone in prayer morning and evening in a loud voice that could be heard along the corridor. Gradually a relationship developed between the schoolboys and the priest which led to an enriching exchange.

For the priest, imprisonment proved a new experience which opened up for him a whole new awareness of injustice and a strong commitment to his fellow prisoners. He started by complaining bitterly to the prison authorities that he was being given better food than the others. He refused to eat until he received the same as they did.

For the schoolboys, as they came to know this priest more closely and to talk with him whenever they could, his response was intriguing. He was clearly moved by their passionate freedom songs as he came to understand the depths of bitter hurt and justified anger from which the songs welled up. But he also suggested ways in which that anger could be expressed without hatred.

One of the schoolboys, as he came closer to the source of his new friend's attitudes and actions, arrived at a new-found faith in Jesus Christ as Saviour and Lord. It was a faith which could strengthen and mature his inmost resolve. The conversations which followed meant much to both.

After the boy had been released he visited the priest at his home and found others from the prison there. Through the priest's friendship they found encouragement and help, and teaching for those who had made a commitment to Christ. Through their friendship the priest found an entry into a new world of struggle for change.

5   The story brings out the way in which Jesus discloses himself to us as we are obedient to his sending and leading. We are plunged into four aspects of his call.

6   First, there is the good news of his love, his presence and his power, his entering into our life and death and his bearing of our sin on the Cross. As we enter through faith into his death and risen life, we find forgiveness and a new way of living. We can only communicate this to others if we are made truly open and vulnerable to them, so that we begin to discover the form this gospel will take in each heart and situation. There, as we seek humbly and gently to persuade, Christ is present, and those who will can respond.

7   Secondly, there is the teaching and nurturing. We have seen afresh how vital it is that we should not just evangelise without following through. The Holy Spirit can work through us to reach and shape new Christians, so that all are true to themselves and to their settings and yet reflecting the One whose likeness is formed in them.

8   But, thirdly, this could only come about where there is practical caring. The priest could nurture the faith of the youngsters only as he became involved with them. Today Christians have to become involved with the many who are suffering and hurting in our world. They have to draw alongside them, to receive from them, if they are to bring them God's love. 'God is the ultimate reason why we should love the poor; not because the poor are good, but because God is good' (Gustavo Gutierrez, a pastor and theologian from Peru, who spoke to us at the Lambeth Conference).[2]

9   And then, finally, this activity compels us to tackle the root causes of suffering. We find ourselves compelled to join the struggle against those political, economic and social forces which cause this misery, oppression and hatred.[3]

10   All these four aspects flow together in the same outgoing impulse of the Spirit released in us through Christ.

11   We have all felt ourselves summoned now afresh into this whole transformation of individual lives and of society and so of our world. Personal evangelism, nurturing disciples, practical caring and the struggle for justice are bound up together and belong together, just as we do in the Body. Different ones among us may be more gifted or concerned for the one or the other, but we all need each other. None must undervalue the other's ministry.

12   Our whole Church across the world needs, now more than ever, to be brought into this movement of transformation.

13   In many parts of the world, Anglicans have emphasised the pastoral model for ministry at the expense of mission. We believe that the Holy Spirit is now leading us to become a movement for mission. Christians are now organising themselves in new ways for mutual support and for mission. The emergence of basic communities and house groups requires us to review our traditional structures in parishes and dioceses.[4] In many places new patterns of training are emerging which begin with people where they are and enable them to reflect on their situations in the light of the Bible and of Christian tradition.

14   We are being called to move out into the unknown outside the gates of our secure, familiar Church life. That is why we have called for the Decade of Evangelism for the '90s, already announced in some Churches, to be declared across the whole Anglican Communion.

15   We sense a stirring of the Spirit breaking the Church open, remaking its every member into an agent of transformation, touching the lives and situations of those around them and being touched upon in turn.[5]

16   In Africa, Asia and Latin America especially, the laity are becoming a freshly creative force. The clergy and bishops can then be a new kind of resource to them.

17   Above all, the young are needed to play a growing part in the new movement of prayer, proclamation and love. At this Conference they have challenged us to make our Church open and welcoming to them, to hear them, to encourage them and to be encouraged by them. As we move out together into the world it is the young who will help us as they helped the priest in the story to bring together evangelism, nurture, loving care and working for a just world.

18   So may we all be made into agents of transformation, so that the New Creation breaks through the old in new lives, new communities and new hope until the day comes when the kingdoms of this world are changed into the Kingdom of God and of his Christ.

SUGGESTION FOR USE
It would be most appropriate for this letter to be used during the season of Pentecost.

NOTES ON FURTHER READING

1   J.R.W. Stott (ed.), **Evangelism and Social Responsibility,** Paternoster Press, Exeter, 1982.
2   As an example of Gutierrez's work see **The Power of the Poor in History,** SCM Press, London, 1983.
3   Vinay Samuel and C.M.N. Sugden (eds.), **The Church in Response to Human Need,** Eerdmans, Grand Rapids, and Regnum, Oxford, 1987.
4   Leonardo Boff, **Ecclesio-Genesis,** Collins, London, 1986.
5   Michael Harper, 'These Stones cry out' in *Open to the Spirit (Colin Craston, ed.), ACC, London, 1987; Josephine Bax, **The Good Wine: Spiritual Renewal in the Church of England,** CHP, London, 1986.

* Indicates a title published through the Inter-Anglican Publishing Network (see p.343).

INDEX

General Index

Index of Biblical References

This index is restricted to references within the four Section Reports and is indexed by paragraph numbers

Inter-Anglican Publishing Network

Australia

Anglican Information Office
St Andrew's House
Sydney Square
Sydney 2000

Canada

Anglican Book Centre
600 Jarvis Street
Toronto, Ontario M4Y 2J6

Ghana

Anglican Press Ltd
PO Box 8
Accra

India

ISPCK
PO Box 1585
Kashmere Gate
Delhi 11006

Kenya

Uzima Press Ltd
PO Box 48127
Nairobi

New Zealand

Collins Liturgical Publications
PO Box 1
Auckland

Nigeria

CSS Press
50 Broad Street
PO Box 174
Lagos

Southern and Central Africa

Publications Committee
C P S A
PO BOX 4849
Johannesburg 2000

Tanzania

Central Tanganyika Press
PO Box 1129
Dodoma

Uganda

Centenary Publishing House
PO Box 2776
Kampala

United Kingdom

Church House Publishing
Church House
Great Smith Street
London SW1P 3NZ

United States of America

Forward Movement
  Publications
412 Sycamore Street
Cincinnati, Ohio 45202

RESOLUTION 30 CONSCIENTIOUS OBJECTION

This Conference, recalling Resolution 8 of the Lambeth Conference 1968 to 'uphold and extend the right of conscientious objection', and learning of the jail sentences given to David Bruce and to Dr Ivan Toms, both young South Africans, who on grounds of conscience refuse to serve in the South African Defence Force:

1 sends them greetings and assures them of our prayers;

2 calls on the South African Government

    (a) to repeal the sentences given to these persons;

    (b) to provide a more comprehensive non-military alternative to compulsory military service;

    (c) to review its legislation regarding conscientious objection.